DIRECTIONS FOR THE GARDINER
and Other Horticultural Advice

DIRECTIONS FOR THE GARDINER

and Other Horticultural Advice

JOHN EVELYN

EDITED BY
Maggie Campbell-Culver

OXFORD
UNIVERSITY PRESS

OXFORD

UNIVERSITY PRESS

Great Clarendon Street, Oxford OX2 6DP

Oxford University Press is a department of the University of Oxford.
It furthers the University's objective of excellence in research, scholarship,
and education by publishing worldwide in

Oxford New York

Auckland Cape Town Dar es Salaam Hong Kong Karachi
Kuala Lumpur Madrid Melbourne Mexico City Nairobi
New Delhi Shanghai Taipei Toronto

With offices in

Argentina Austria Brazil Chile Czech Republic France Greece
Guatemala Hungary Italy Japan Poland Portugal Singapore
South Korea Switzerland Thailand Turkey Ukraine Vietnam

Oxford is a registered trade mark of Oxford University Press
in the UK and in certain other countries

Published in the United States
by Oxford University Press Inc., New York

British Library Cataloguing in Publication Data
Data available

Library of Congress Cataloguing in Publication Data
Library of Congress Control Number: 2009925326

Typeset by SPI Publisher Services, Pondicherry, India
Printed in Italy on acid-free paper by Lego S.p.A.

ISBN 978–0–19–923207–9

1 3 5 7 9 10 8 6 4 2

ACKNOWLEDGEMENTS

IT is always interesting to compare the plants that we grow in our gardens today with those of earlier times, and using John Evelyn's horticultural writings has proved a rich and pleasurable source of information; I would like to acknowledge my debt of gratitude to him and his descendants. Likewise I wish to acknowledge, with gratitude, the long friendship and consistently kindly advice and support that I have received from Mavis Batey MBE. Her enthusiasm for all things historically horticultural has been an inspiration over the years.

My association with OUP and in particular with Judith Luna, my editor, has been of the happiest, and I would wish to thank her and all the team who have worked on the book. Colleagues who have supported me so generously with their greater knowledge include Mary Ambler MA (Oxon.), the Classics teacher at Bedford School, and Leofranc Holford-Strevens, who wrestled with the many Greek and Latin quotations and sources. Frances Harris of the British Library was particularly helpful and her enthusiasm for Evelyn matches my own. I am indebted to Professor Richard Keynes CBE, FRS, who graciously gave his permission to use the late Professor Geoffrey Keynes's detailed transcription of *Directions for the Gardiner at Says-court*. The Linnean Society library has, as usual, been most supportive, as have Lewes District Council, and Dr Colin Brent regarding apple identification. Both Nikki Rowan-Kedge and Angela Rawson have provided ample support in the esoteric delights of seventeenth-century recipes. Judith and Derek Tolman of Bernwode Nursery provided much 'fruity' advice, as did Trish Swain who pointed me in the right direction regarding the history of bee-keeping. I would also like to thank Surrey Gardens Trust, especially Lady Jill Leggat and Marion Woodward, for their support and expertise. For help in identifying the plants Evelyn mentions, I must give my most grateful thanks to the Herts. &

Beds. Group of the NCCPG who with efficiency and speed assisted in the early stages. Edna and Mike Squires from Devon, both plantsmen to their fingertips, gave most kindly of their expertise.

Underpinning all this help has been the unstinting support of my family and friends, who without so much as a twitch of boredom appearing on their faces have listened to my endless praise of John Evelyn. To Michael, Claire, Guy, Lorna, and George, Justin and Steph, who have been forcibly fed choice titbits of garden life in the seventeenth century, I can only give them my grateful love.

M.C.-C.
Brittany, June 2009

For Michael with
my love

CONTENTS

INTRODUCTION

WHEN John Evelyn died on 27 February 1706, he left behind an immense legacy of written material. Best known today for his Diary, in his lifetime he was celebrated as the author of *Sylva, or a Discourse of Forest Trees*, a seminal work on trees and woodland commissioned by the Royal Society to promote the planting and preservation of timber for the Navy. He was also the author of translations on subjects ranging across gardening, religion, and architecture. He lived through some of the most turbulent years in English history, including the Civil War and the Restoration of Charles II, the Second Dutch War, the Plague, and the Great Fire of London. Throughout his long life, garden design and maintenance and the desire to pass on his knowledge about gardening inspired him, and it is the detail and practicality of his advice that make his horticultural writings, four centuries later, so fascinating and timeless.

John Evelyn was born on 31 October 1620, the second son of a substantial landowner whose estate was at Wotton, near Dorking in Surrey. The family were supporters of the Royalist cause, and Evelyn absented himself during the Civil War to travel abroad, meeting other Royalists and associating with the court in exile and the future King Charles II. He travelled extensively throughout France, Italy, and the Low Countries, and it is evident from his earliest diary entries that he was interested in the gardens and parks he visited, recording their design and content, a habit he continued throughout his life. In Holland he commented favourably on the outstanding garden of the Prince of Orange when he visited The Hague. During his stay in Paris, as well as seeing all the sights, he recorded with pleasure viewing Pierre Morin's oval garden, planted with cypress 'cutt flat and set as even as a wall'. On a second visit seven years later he notes that there were at least ten thousand flowering tulips. He toured the Tuileries, where he reflected on the hedge of pomegranates he saw, calling it 'a noble hedge'; a few weeks later, this time while viewing the Luxembourg Gardens in Paris, he again noted the 'hedge-worke' of hornbeam. The highlight for Evelyn must have been his time spent touring the vast estate of Fontainebleau; although he thought the house 'nothing so stately and uniforme as Hampton Court', it took two days to be shown the grounds with all their spectacular features, and he wrote that the 'beauty of all are the Gardens'. In Italy, while walking through the Pope's Palace of Monte Cavallo, he could not resist again referring to a hedge, this time 'of myrtle above a man's height'. There were other sights to see, including the grand Ville d'Este with its 'jetting out waters', and the 'elysium' of Villa Borghese. The formal style of the Italian and French gardens was quite different from that of the gardens he had seen in England, and showed a modernity and sophistication that appealed to Evelyn, set as they were against a background of gushing and splashing water, groves, avenues, copses, and vistas, and when he returned to England in 1652 he must have been enthusiastic to begin creating a garden that would reflect all he had seen.

By now married to Mary, the daughter of Sir Richard Browne, the King's Ambassador to the French court, he took up residence at Sayes Court, his wife's ancestral home by the banks of the Thames, in the then village of Deptford, where they would live for the next forty years. The estate contained the three-storied Elizabethan mansion which was Crown property, but had been seized by the Parliamentary Commission following the execution of Charles I. Evelyn purchased the lease for £3,500. He became a trusted courtier during the reign of Charles II, and after the publication of *Sylva* became Councillor for Foreign Plantations, mainly those in North America. Under James II he was made a Commissioner for the Privy Seal in 1685. During all this time his courtly and public life was balanced by his interest in gardening and horticulture. When, in 1658, he translated the best-selling French garden book by Nicolas de Bonnefons entitled *Le Jardinier François*, he announced his intention to publish a work he called *Elysium Britannicum*, his magnum opus on the garden, 'a place of terrestriall enjoyments the most resembling Heaven'. Although he wrote assiduously towards the book's completion, and eventually assembled nearly 900 folio pages, only 300 pages survive, and the work was never finished. All three of the manuscripts printed here were originally intended for inclusion in *Elysium Britannicum*; the *Kalendarium Hortense*, however, was included as an appendix to *Sylva* in 1664, while *Acetaria* was published independently in 1699; *Directions for the Gardiner* was never published in his lifetime.

KALENDARIUM HORTENSE

Kalendarium Hortense: or the Gard'ners Almanac; Directing what he is to do Monethly, throughout the Year; And what Fruits and Flowers are in Prime, to give it its full title, is one of the earliest gardening calendars to be published. Its layout is refreshingly simple. Evelyn divides the year into separate months, each one given its zodiacal sign so that one may 'plant by the signs'. Each month is allotted its number of days, and, helpfully for the gardener, the appropriate hours of sunlight. Instructions are given for what the gardener should be doing each month in the fruit and vegetable garden, and in the flower and decorative garden. Each section is followed by a catalogue of the fruits and flowers that are at their best ('in Prime') this month. In all the practical recommendations and timetables that follow, one crucial adjustment needs to be made: Evelyn was working to the Julian calendar, which was replaced in 1752 by the Gregorian calendar that we follow today, and which is eleven days in advance of Evelyn's dates. So when he recommends, as he does for February, that it is the time to 'sow Beans, Pease, Radish, Parsneps, Carrots, Onions, Garlick', an accommodation of those 'missing' days must be taken into account.

The importance given to the 'Orchard, and the Olitory-Garden' reflects one of the fundamental differences between gardening then and now. 'Olitory', pertaining to the kitchen, was a word introduced by Evelyn into his English edition of Bonnefons's *Le Jardinier François*; whereas today gardening is a leisure activity, for Evelyn and his contemporaries it was primarily a means of sustenance, and essential for providing fruit and vegetables throughout the year. Evelyn suggests the cultivation of a wide selection of vegetables. Most are still familiar, but one or two have become unfashionable. One that is no longer grown or eaten is Alexanders (*Smyrnium olustratum*), whose thick stalks look and taste similar to celery. Some vegetables have changed their names: 'succory' is better known today as chicory, and 'smalladge' usually refers to either parsley or celery.

Advice on winter work includes 'hostility against Vermin', as well as protecting the fountain pipes with 'warm litter out of the stable', and warning the reader that, if left, 'the frost crack them, remember it in time, and the Advice will save you both trouble and charge'. If the weather is 'over-wet, or hard', Evelyn recommends activities that any gardener would do well to follow: 'cleanse, mend, sharpen and prepare Garden-tools.' During March, 'stercoration', or the spreading of dung, in both the orchard and kitchen garden is advised.

In the flower garden, the 'farewell-frosts and the easterly-winds prejudice your choicest tulips…therefore cover with Mats or Canvas to prevent freckles'. In May, Evelyn was pleased to include two tips that he says 'had been kept as considerable Secrets amongst our Gard'ners'. The first is to attend to our house-plants and to apply fresh earth 'in place of some of the old earth, and loosning the rest with a fork without wounding the Roots'; the second is to brush and cleanse plants that have been brought indoors 'from the dust contracted during their enclosure'—both recommendations well worth following today. The composition of the monthly flower lists is exhaustive and shows an eclectic mix of both native and introduced plants: pansies, delphiniums, roses, foxgloves, stock-gilly flower, and the hollyhock. Tucked away in the July list is '*Flos Africanus*', a colourful plant that was brought to Britain from North Africa in the sixteenth century and known as African marigold (*Tagetes erecta*), although it was originally a native of Mexico.

Evelyn also reminds his readers about the necessity of being self-sufficient in the collection, saving, and sowing of seed, at a time when there were few seed merchants or nurseries. The production of honey was of importance too (sugar was rare and expensive), and Evelyn mentions bees and the housekeeping of hives during at least seven separate months. Something else that would be unusual in a modern gardening calendar, but that Evelyn had on the 'to do' list for the three months from August, was the making of cider and perry, putting all the apples and pears grown in the orchard to good use. There are some delightfully descriptive names: December apples include 'Great-belly' and 'Go-no-further'; we are told that the January pears 'Winter-musk' and 'Winter-Norwich' 'both bake well'.

Evelyn finishes the *Kalendarium* with advice on how to keep plants through the winter that are 'lest patient of Cold'. He lists over a hundred that are vulnerable, dividing them into three categories, with about twenty-five exotics that should be 'first into the Conservatory' (a second newly introduced Evelyn word). The middle group include oleanders, myrtles, and oranges, 'Enduring the second degree of Cold' and that also need protection, while the largest number are 'not perishing, but in excessive Colds, are therefore to be last set in or rather protected under Mattrasses, and sleighter coverings'. Even after three hundred years, and despite changes in climate, the challenge of overwintering plants remains the same as it did for Evelyn. Evelyn grew oranges at Sayes Court, where during the autumn of 1679 he was able to offer the fruits to his guests, recording proudly in his Diary that they were 'as good, I think as were ever eaten'. They were housed in an 'orangerie', whose design differed from the conservatory, although the plants they housed were interchangeable.

DIRECTIONS FOR THE GARDINER

Directions for the Gardiner at Says-Court, But which may be of Use for Other Gardens is a unique record of the maintenance and management of a post-Restoration garden. It is inscribed to 'Jonathan Mosse' who, Evelyn notes, 'came to me Apprentice for six yeares 24 June 1686' and is clearly aimed at the professional estate gardener.

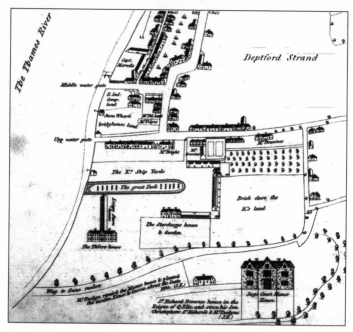

From a map of Deptford, 1623.
Original pen and ink sketch with additional remarks by Evelyn.
The Bodleian Library, University of Oxford (228580. 7, 8, vol 1)

The manuscript was first transcribed and privately published in 1932 by Sir Geoffrey Keynes.

The 40.47 hectares (100 acres) of farmland belonging to Sayes Court were a good size to create a great garden. The soil would have been well worked, there was a stream running along its eastern boundary, debouching into the Thames on its northern edge, to which there was direct access via 'the Stayres'. The site was flat, and as Evelyn noted the 'intire field…without any hedge, except the hither holly hedge'. It was a blank canvas upon which Evelyn could make his mark; he had prepared well, having studied the great Continental gardens, as well as English gardens such as Hatfield House which, with its elaborate waterworks and lavish planting, had a distinctly 'Mediterranean' feel to its design. Nothing remains of the garden at Sayes Court and as there are no paintings or images, it is fortuitous that the 1652 detailed plan with its 126 legends is still extant. It is, as Evelyn remarks, 'the guide of all our designs'. The garden also became the living laboratory of his writing, where he observed the growth and behaviour of the plants. Evelyn had set about learning all he could about stylish garden design and the plants he would grow. He read the most up-to-date books on the subject, including John Parkinson's 'Paradisi in Sole, Paradisus Terrestris' of 1629, as well as an earlier book by Thomas Hill, 'A Most Briefe and Pleasante Treatyse Teachyng how to Dresse, Sowe and Set a Garden'. He also had numerous books by classical authors, many of which he quoted from, some in Latin and Greek and some in translation, including the 1601 translation by Philemon Holland of the thirty-seven volumes of 'Historia Naturalis' by Pliny the Elder, as well as 'De Re Rustica', the works of Columella. Evelyn was a formidable networker, and kept up a huge correspondence with everyone connected with the world of horticulture, from aristocratic friends to gardeners.

Gardening in the early part of the seventeenth century still retained that heady combination from the medieval world of bewitching magic and practicality. It emerged with a clear division between the apothecary and his physic garden and the vegetables and flowers cultivated for eating or admiring in the kitchen or flower garden. Growing vegetables was divided between the production of field crops, and those grown in what was originally named the 'leacgarth', leeks being one of the oldest of vegetables; peas and beans were usually grown in fields. Onions of all descriptions and the lettuce joined leeks in being grown in a more domestic situation. Although seeds were originally broadcast, in both the field and the garden, with the invention of the horse-drawn field seed-drill the idea of growing in rows gradually became the established practice in the garden. By Evelyn's time the drill system had become well established as gardeners came to realize it was more economic to sow seeds in defined rows—trayls or drills as they were known—as young plants were both easier to thin out and to keep weed-free. It was also recognized that faster germinating seeds (such as radish, for example) could be both a swift crop and a help in defining the rows of the slower-growing parsnip or similar root vegetables. The early seventeenth-century garden would have been very formal and orderly, filled with knots and stylized patterns made to look as unnatural as possible; Evelyn was to be influential in introducing more relaxed design. Topiary and mazes of clipped evergreens (usually box) were fashionable. Evelyn created numerous hedges at Sayes Court, and a great holly hedge became his pride and joy.

In *Directions*, Evelyn covers every aspect of running a self-sufficient garden, one that provides both aesthetic enjoyment from the pleasures of the flower garden and practical use from the food harvested from the kitchen garden and orchard, as well as the medical remedies made from the plants grown in the physic garden. He describes gardening terms and their meanings, provides instruction as to what is to be done, and lists the tools that will be needed. Intermixed with the practical advice are catalogues of fruit trees, specified areas of planting, lists of perennials, annuals, root vegetables, salads, potherbs and sweet herbs, shrubs and trees, including a separate section for evergreens.

Evelyn starts with a gardening vocabulary of nearly a hundred words, 'Termes of Art Used by Learned Gardners'. Each word is given a succinct definition, and most words and explanations are still in use today: 'offsets', 'annuals', and 'topiary' are still part of the gardener's vocabulary. Some are no longer used, such as 'vindemiate' meaning to gather grapes, and 'repastinate' meaning to lightly dig or to hoe. One or two of the words have changed their meaning, such as 'drilling', which no longer means 'cutting a narrow trench to convey away water' but (in the garden sense) to 'making a furrow to sow seeds': Evelyn understood that activity by the term 'rilling'. The list of practical work includes grafting, dunging, pruning, watering, and transplanting, as Evelyn sets out his 'Method for the Gardiner of Sayes-Court or any other with little alteration'. Sensibly the very first thing he recommends is that 'The Gardiner should walke aboute the whole Gardens every Monday-morning duely, not omitting the least corner…'. He explains the intricacies of the hotbed where 'you raise all your choicer seedes', and he gives detailed instructions on the planning and running of the nursery, as the horticultural and propagating skills of a good gardener were highly prized.

The practicality of maintaining a garden then is easily transferred to today's gardener, although there are some exceptions. Evelyn's instructions on how to deal with 'Vermine and Diseases' contain some surprising advice. Three hundred years ago worms were considered a pest, and Evelyn's 'best remedy against Garden earthwormes' was to drown them in a mixture of water and potash. He deals equally firmly with the vexatious question of caterpillars, recommending that their cobwebs be destroyed by cutting away the branch or twig to which they are attached, or 'else burne them with a torch & do this early'. Caterpillars can cause a great deal of damage, but we would today be more discriminating in our approach. There is sensible advice about controlling ants, wasps, and flies, the best remedy being a jar of beer sweetened with honey to attract them, although he hastens to add that bees not liking the smell avoid the mixture; but Evelyn warns that if a solution of just sweetened water is put out, bees will be attracted to it and drown. One of his best suggestions, designed to protect fruit in particular from insect attack, is to place hollow sticks known as kexes upright in the ground. These supply a dark refuge during the hottest part of the day for earwigs and other insects to escape to, from which 'the Vermine' are to be shaken out.

Evelyn names nearly 800 plants in the three manuscripts collected here, excluding fruit varieties, of which there are in excess of 400. He lists over 154 pear and 75 apple varieties. Today apple varieties far outstrip pear; one modern specialist nursery, Bernwode Plants, lists nearly 300 apples in its catalogue but only forty varieties of pear. In Evelyn's seventeenth-century catalogue, the largest number of plants under cultivation were either native or from Europe, some 60 per cent of the total. About 22 per cent had originated from Asia, while plants arriving from North America are represented by some 5 per cent or forty-two plants. There are just five plants listed from South America, while South Africa provides a possible four:

the Guernsey Lily, *Nerine sarniensis,* Geranium triste (now *Pelargonium triste*), and what Evelyn then called the 'Indian Lily Narcissus', and the 'Sphaerical Narciss'. Most lilies were at that time classed as narcissus, and innumerable plants had 'Indian' attached to their name (the Geranium was known as the Sweet Indian Cranesbill) to indicate the plant's exotic nature rather than its actual country of origin. Under the name 'Indian narcissus' this lily appears in the garden book of Evelyn's friend Thomas Hanmer as well as on the list drawn up by John Tradescant in 1656, where he refers to it as 'Lilio Narcissus Indicus'. Expert opinion considers this could be an early introduction of *Amaryllis belladona* collected from South Africa, although the accepted date of introduction is half a century later; the 'Sphaerical Narciss' is believed to be a relation of the Amaryllis, *Brunsvigia gigantea,* which again has a much later accepted introduction date. For various reasons, not least the paucity of its native flora, Great Britain, and in particular England, is singularly blessed with the recording of introduced plants, but this uncertainty illustrates some of the problems that can arise.

ACETARIA

Acetaria, A Discourse of Sallets was published in October 1699, a few days after the death of Evelyn's 83-year-old 'worthy brother' George. The manuscript is in a very different style from the previous two, and is in that rare genre of a gardening cookbook as it not only concentrates on the growing of salad plants, but also gives recipes for using and dressing them. For most of his adult life Evelyn was interested in the production of food and how it was, or should be, cooked, and he began collecting recipes soon after he moved to Sayes Court with his young bride.

The book concentrates on salad plants ('acetaria' is the Latin word for salad), and how they should be grown and eaten, and Evelyn is surprisingly adventurous in the wide range of his recommendations. Who today would consider using seedling oranges and lemons, or young wild nettle-tops or the afore-mentioned

Alexanders, whose stalks are like celery but whose leaves, we are assured, taste similar to parsley? Evelyn describes the way to dress the salad once it has been 'exquisitely cull'd and cleans'd', stressing that the 'sallet-oyl' should not have developed 'the least touch of rancid'. The wine-vinegar should be infused with the 'virtues' of flowers: clove-gillyflowers, elder, roses, and rosemary are some of those that Evelyn recommends.

By Evelyn's time there were well-rehearsed arguments regarding the benefits of abstaining from eating red meat. People 'living on herbs and roots, arrive to incredible age in constant health and vigour'; Evelyn quotes both classical writers and distinguished contemporary authors as well as his own Christian views to support or reject both sides of the arguments. He writes of 'the intemperance, luxury and softer education and effeminacy of the age' and wants everyone to have a healthy and long life. Always keen to give a balanced view, Evelyn suggests that 'flesh-eaters...be much wiser and more sagacious', as well as reputedly becoming 'heavy, dull, unactive, and much more stupid'. Although he was prepared to use up-to-date scientific ideas, Evelyn also kept to the long-held belief in the classical doctrine of the Four Elements, Fire, Earth, Air, and Water which, combined with the Four Humours of Choler, Melancholy, Blood, and Phlegm, helped the apothecary to prepare the right physic for the patient. Every plant had both an element and a humour associated with it. Lettuce, for example, was considered cold and moist, fennel and garlic hot and dry. The moon, the sun, and the zodiacal signs could all be efficacious contributors to a remedy.

After over forty years of living at Sayes Court, and creating his garden, at the age of 73 John Evelyn retired to the family estate of Wotton. He sent seeds, plants, and a large number of 'evergreens' from Sayes Court, and he and his wife followed on 4 May 1694. His 'retirement' did not mean that he had lost his love of gardens; a year later he was paying a visit to Marden Park, near Caterham, the home of Sir Robert Clayton, who according to Evelyn had 'so chang'd the natural situation of the hill, valleys and solitary mountains' to create the perfect walks and mazes which 'were preserv'd

with the utmost care'. A few days later he visited nearby Beddington, where he reported on the decay of the garden and estate, and
in particular the state of the 120-year-old orange trees (Seville oranges, *Citrus aurantium*) which he had first seen in their prime in
1658. Evelyn was invited by Henry Wise in 1701 to view the garden
alterations taking place at Kensington Palace to which Wise had
been appointed superintendent soon after the accession of William
III. Into his eighties Evelyn continued attending the lectures of
the Royal Society and met the Duke of Marlborough to congrat-
ulate him on his victory at Blenheim. He survived to the grand age
of 85.

In the three hundred years since his death, John Evelyn's reputation has undergone some changes. Both during his lifetime and
until the mid-nineteenth century it rested on his great book *Sylva*.
With the publication of his Diary in 1818 his record of public events
came to prominence, only to be eclipsed by that other Diary by his
friend Pepys. Throughout his long life he wrote for publication
principally to educate and communicate his horticultural knowledge
to a wider audience. He was responsible for garden design not only
at his own homes of Sayes Court and Wotton, but also at other
estates at Albury, Cornbury, Euston Hall, and Cassiobury Park,
and was a pioneer of more open and attractive gardening in contrast
to the formal Tudor and early Stuart fashions. He has had a
lasting influence on arboriculture and silviculture, and his horticultural prowess can be placed among the most important of the
seventeenth century. It is our good fortune that even after three
hundred years we can still learn from someone Pepys called 'a man
so much above others'.

NOTE ON THE TEXTS

The *Kalendarium Hortense* was first published in 1664 as an appendix to *Sylva*. It was frequently reprinted and expanded, and the text reproduced here is that of 1669.

Directions for the Gardiner was transcribed and privately printed by Sir Geoffrey Keynes in 1932. The text printed here is based on his transcription, corrected against the manuscript.

Acetaria was first published in 1699 and the text in this volume is based on the first edition.

Original spelling, punctuation, and capitalization has been retained, the long 'ſ' modernized, and the use of italics modified in places. Footnote citations of classical sources in *Acetaria* have been omitted.

In the Explanatory Notes, parenthetical dates refer to the first recorded usage of a word or phrase. In the Glossary, dates not otherwise ascribed refer to a plant's recorded introduction.

A CHRONOLOGY OF JOHN EVELYN

1620   September: *Mayflower* sails for New England, with the Pilgrim Fathers aboard.

1620   31 October: John Evelyn born.

1625   27 March: James I and VI dies; is succeeded by Charles I.

1626   John Aubrey, antiquary and biographer, born.

1629   John Parkinson, *Paradisi in Sole Paradisus Terrestris*.

1632   Henry Compton, Bishop of London and plantsman, born.

1635   29 September: Evelyn's mother dies.

1637   9 May: goes up to Balliol College, Oxford, as a Fellow Commoner.

1640   27 April: sent to Middle Temple to study law.

      24 December: father dies.

1641   12 May: execution of Thomas Wentworth, Earl of Strafford, principal adviser to Charles I.

      21 July: first visit to Holland and the Spanish Netherlands.

1642   22 August: outbreak of English Civil War.

      23 October: battle of Edgehill.

      11 November: Evelyn sails for France, where he spends two years travelling.

1644   2 July: battle of Marston Moor.

      13 October: Evelyn travels to Italy.

1645   14 June: battle of Naseby.

1646   May: crosses Simplon into Switzerland.

      October: returns to Paris.

1647   27 June: marries Mary Browne, daughter of Sir Richard Browne, Royalist Ambassador to France.

12 October: returns to England, leaving his wife with her parents in Paris.

1648   Portrait of Evelyn by Robert Walker

1649   30 January: Charles I beheaded.

12 July: Evelyn to France.

1650   November: Evelyn's portrait engraved by Robert Nanteuil.

1651   3 September: battle of Worcester.

1652   6 February: Evelyn returns to England, and takes up residence at Sayes Court, Deptford.

4 June: Mary Evelyn arrives in England.

24 August: son Richard born.

1653   17 January: begins laying out the garden at Sayes Court.

1654   8 June: Evelyn and his wife set out on a tour of relations and friends around England. Return to Sayes Court in October.

12 July: visits Oxford Botanic Garden, and is given a transparent glass apiary for the garden by Dr Wilkins.

September: visits Audley End, Saffron Walden, Essex, built by Howard, Earl of Suffolk.

1655   14 January: son John born.

1656   29 October: Edmond Halley (1656–1742), astronomer and oceanographer, born.

1657   7 June: son George born.

1658   27 January: death of son Richard.

15 February: death of son George.

2 June: Evelyn records a bad storm; the following day a whale is stranded on his land abutting the Thames.

3 September: death of Oliver Cromwell.

1659   Evelyn translates *Le Jardinier François* by Nicolas de Bonnefons and publishes it under the title *The French Gardiner*, in which he announces his planned book *Elysium Britannicum,* of which the *Kalendarium, Directions for the Gardiner,* and *Acetaria* were to form part.

1660 29 May: restoration of Charles II.

17 October: regicides executed at Charing Cross .

1661 January: Evelyn made a Fellow of the 'Philosophic Society', later to become the Royal Society.

23 April: coronation of Charles II.

Thomas Hobbes, *Leviathan*.

1662 15 July: the Royal Society receives its charter.

20 August: admitted to the Council of the Royal Society.

15 October: delivers 'Discourse concerning Forest-trees' to the Royal Society.

1663 30 April: Charles II visits Sayes Court.

1664 16 February: publication of *Sylva, or a Discourse of Forest Trees in His Majestie's Dominions* with the supplement of *Kalendarium Hortense, or the Gard'ners Almanac*.

28 October: nominated a Commissioner for the Wounded and Prisoners of War.

1665 Outbreak of Second Dutch War.

July: the Plague begins to spread.

1 October: daughter Mary born.

John Rea, *Flora* (praised by Evelyn).

1666 2 September: the Great Fire of London.

13 September: Evelyn presents *A Survey of the ruines, and a Plot for a new Citty, with a discourse on it* to the King.

1667 11 June: the Dutch Navy reaches Chatham.

14 September: daughter Elizabeth born.

19 September: persuades Henry Howard to bestow the Arundel Marbles on the University of Oxford.

John Milton, *Paradise Lost*.

1668 20 May: daughter Susanna born.

1669 7 July: attends the Encaenia at the Sheldonian Theatre in Oxford and is given an Honorary Doctorate.

1670 6 March: death of Evelyn's brother Richard.

1671 Discovers Grinling Gibbons at work in a cottage near Sayes Court and introduces his work to Christopher Wren and the king.

May: appointed Standing Councillor on Plantations for Foreign Plantations.

John Milton, *Paradise Regained*.

1672 Outbreak of Third Dutch War. Evelyn on Council for Trade and Commerce, and Secretary of the Royal Society.

1678 1 October: the Popish Plot.

Bunyan, *The Pilgrim's Progress*, Part I.

1679 4 June: dines with Samuel Pepys in the Tower, where Pepys had been committed 'for misdemeanors in the Admiralty'.

1680 24 February: son John marries Martha Spencer.

30 November: Robert Boyle elected President of the Royal Society.

1682 Discusses plans for Chelsea Hospital with Stephen Fox and Christopher Wren.

1 March: John (Jack) born to Evelyn's eldest son John. Died 1763.

Nehemiah Grew, pioneer of plant anatomy, *Anatomy of Plants*.

1685 6 February: death of Charles II.

14 March: daughter Mary dies of smallpox.

23 April: coronation of James II.

June–July: the Monmouth Rebellion.

27 July: daughter Elizabeth elopes.

29 August: daughter Elizabeth dies of smallpox.

3 September: nominated a Commissioner of the Privy Seal by the King.

1686 24 June: Jonathan Mosse begins six-year apprenticeship as gardener to John Evelyn.

1687 Isaac Newton, *Principia Mathematica*.

1688 November: invasion of William of Orange.

24 December: James II flees to France.

1689 Portrait of Evelyn, holding a copy of his book *Sylva*, by Sir Godfrey Kneller.

11 April: coronation of William and Mary.

1690 John Ray, *Synopsis Methodica Stirpium Britannicarum*.

John Locke, *An Essay concerning Human Understanding*.

1691 May: Chelsea Hospital completed.

1692 Death of Robert Boyle.

1693 27 April: daughter Susanna marries William Draper.

1694 4 May: John and Mary Evelyn returned to live at Wotton.

28 December: Queen Mary dies of smallpox.

1698 6 February–21 April: Peter I of Russia and his retinue stay at Sayes Court.

6 August: Evelyn meets William Dampier (1652–1715), the famous buccaneer, explorer, and hydrographer.

Lord Somers elected President of the Royal Society.

1699 24 March: Evelyn's only remaining son, John, dies.

4 October: death of brother George. Evelyn inherits the estate at Wotton.

21 October: Evelyn's *Acetaria* published.

1702 Outbreak of the War of the Spanish Succession.

March: William III dies; is succeeded by Queen Anne.

1703   26 May: Samuel Pepys dies.

1704   2 August: battle of Blenheim.

26–7 November: hurricane and tempest, many lives lost.

1705   18 September: grandson Jack, Evelyn's heir, marries Ann
Boscawen, niece of Lord Godolphin.

1706   27 February: Evelyn dies.

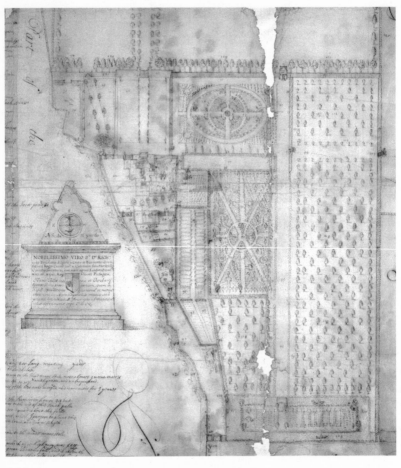

Evelyn's plan of his garden at Sayes Court.

The key facing is reproduced for the reader's interest although the
numbers on the plan are indistinct.

KEY TO THE PLAN

1. Porch, sustein'd with two Doricke Collumnes, paved underneath, over it my wives Closset of Collections.

2. Hall, over it my Chamber.

3. Parlour, over it the great Chamber, the Pallat or Clockhouse, (Chamber by it with a new light & upright seeling.)

4. Parlour Chimney.

6. The Entry, which hath a Large Arch towards the Hall discovering the Staires at full.

7. Kitchin, over it a hansome Chamber, the Chimney removed to the midle, at one side of it a Closset, at the other a passage to the new Buildings.

8. Butterie, heretofore an hovel, now much enlarged and built upright, over it is my Studie; and over my Studie a prettie Lodging Chamber. This I have built from the ground so that my Studie is 23 foot long, & 11 broad besides a litle Studie within it neere halfe as big.

9. A Litle Kitchin or preserving Roome with a Chimney over. Stills etc: this is partlie under my Studie.

10. A Large and faire Stairecase forced up to the Roofe, from whence it receives a great Light by a Cupola.

11. A withdrawing roome to the Parlour, with a new Window, it was heretofore the Clockehouse. An Aviarie before it in the Private Garden.

12. The Storehouse made out of a Part of the Litle Parlour where the Bed Stood. The Presse Chamber now a wardrope, and studie to it hath new lights.

13. The Litle parlour with a new Light: the Chamber over it with an upright seeling & new Light.

14. A with-drawing Roome, formerly a Studie, now enlarged.

15. The entry or passage behind the Kitchin Chimney where the Presses are.

16. The Kitchin Chimney.

17. Passage towards the Backestayres, and Kitchin yard doore.

18. Backestayres much Larger and Lighter.

19. Pastry, formerly the Cheesehouse.

20. The new Cellars, much enlarged, formerly an hovell now an upright building with the fairest Chamber in the house over it, a closset Studie, and Servants Chamber to it, over all which three Convenient garret = Lodgings for servants.

21. The Larder.

22. The Milkhouse.

23. The Sinke in the Kitching elevated and altered.

24. Staires into the Butterie old Cellers much Lighter, and in the passage to the Butterie a Vault for Bottles, and a Cocke of Water.

25. The Court, with faire gravel walkes planted with Cipresse and the walls with fruit.

26. The Bowling Greenes betwixt.

27. The Bricke walles 10 foote high with double Gates.

28. The Milking close planted with eight walnutt trees.

29. Grass plotts where the Cowes are milked.

30. The Carpe pond, new dug, and rail'd, it is likewise the watring Place: note that the…Ditch being made Deeper feeds the Pond at every tyde.

31. The Garden dore out of the Court.

32. …te out of the Court…

33. …feild before the house, which I call the…feild.

34. Double gates and doore out of the Kitchin yard into the Milking Close.

35. The great hollow Elme.

36. The Garden, and walkes of Gravel about the oval Square.

37. The evergreen thicket, for Birds private walkes, shades and Cabinetts.

38. The Grasse plotts sett about with a Border, in which flower Potts.

39. The Round Par = terre of Box with 12 Beds of flowers & passages betwixt each bed.

40. The Mount, Center, and Dial, sett about with Cypresse as Likewise in everie Corner of the Parterres and Grasse plotts.

41. The Pale, 8 foot high, with a thicke Planke at Bottome All Planted with alliternes, as is likewise the Ovall, and Square to it, which are Palisadoed.

42. Two Cantons, with a strait and very private passage out of the oval neich into the walke 43. This planted with dwarfe fruit. Raspberris, Strawberries, Currants & Cherries, and 2 Cabinetts of Ivie, and Aliternes.

43. The Long Pourmenade from the Banquetting house to the Island being 526 foot long, 21. broad.

44. The Banquetting House.

45. A Lower Pale planted with aliternies, heretofore a Row of Ashes, and a narrow private walke behind them. This Pale reacheth to the breadth of the mount or Terras walke.

46. The Great Orchard dore.

47. The Terras walke or mount.

48. That TRACT of Pricks shew where formerlie the row of great Elmes grew towards the Pingle, which I feld filling the hollow to accomodate the orchard.

49. A Palisadoed hedg'd of Codlins and peare maines, reaching from the Mount 47 and discontinuance of the Pale 45 on both hands to the Island, and about the mote.

50. The Grove with the severall walkes, meanders and thickets &c: The entrances into it, are where the Codlin hedge does open.

51. The mount or Center planted with Bayes, but the Circle walke with Laurel.

52. 14 Cabinetts of Aliternies, and a great french walnutt at every one, whereof I have planted 24 in all, and above 500 standard trees of oake, ash elme, Cervise, beech, chesnutt, besides the thicketts with Birch, hazel, Thorne, wild fruites, greenes &c: the close walkes, and Spiders Clawes Leading to the Cabinetts, you may perceive by the designe &c.

53. The Thicketts.

54. My Private Garden of choice flowers, and Simples.

55. The Fountaine.

56. The walkes or alleyes; at the end of one is an arbour under 2 tall elmes in the Corner. This Garden is walled about.

57. My Elaboratorie, with a Portico of 20 foot long upon Pillars open towards the Private Garden.

58. The Elaboratorie, over it is a Pigeon house for wilde pigeons.

59. The Gardeners toolehouse, and for fruits.

60. The Pump and Cisterne which I remooved to the Nursery for infusion of Dungs, and watering the Garden.

61. The Passage toward the old back of office, through the Nurserie.

62. The doore out of the great garden into the private garden.

63. The doore out of the Private Garden into the Nurserie.

64. The Beehive in the Private Garden.

65. The Nursery where is a doore into the Kitchin garden Leading to the new house of office.

66. The Doore out of the Kitching Court into the Kitching garden.

67. The Pale, and doore to the Dunghil.

68. The new house of office over the Dunghill.

69. The Kitching Backe yard, new paved and palled.

70. The Passage of the Kitching Sinke.

71. The Pale gate, and Dore into the woodyard, wash = house and Brew-house.

72. A Row of tall Elmes.

73. The Coachhouse, contiguous to the Stable with a Chamber and Chimney over it, a Coale Seller under it.

74. The Stables built with Bricke with six Dorique Columnes to the 5 stalls, upright racks, and a large h(ay) loft.

75. The hole to throw the Dung into the Dungpitt.

76. The Dungpitt, lying to the Stable, Kitching garden, privy and hog = pen.

77. The hog = sties, and court divided.

78. The washouse, made of the old Stable, that stood by the Barne, at num^r 109. over it a fish house & chamber.

79. Brewhouse, made of Part of the same Stable.

80. The malt mill.

81. The 2 Caldrons for brewing & washing.

82. The Chimney serving Both.

83. The Hogg = pen.

84. The henhouse, and Court.

85. The Calfe and Cowhouse.

Key to the Plan

86. The Close common for the Cowes & hens.

87. The Woodyard.

88. The Doore of the Coale Seller under the Coach house.

89. The woodhouse, Carthouse and Woodstacke.

90. The servants Privies.

91. The farther gate of the woodyard.

92. The Hollye hedge, at the side of the mount or Terras.

93. The Berbery hedge.

94. The Kitchin Garden made into 38 bedds of Pottherbs besides borders &c.

95. A Plott for melons.

96. An hedge of Lelacke reaching from the mount to the Island.

97. Plotts for pease and beanes &c.

98. The Saw Pitt and magazine of old tymber left of the building.

99. The way into the 10 Acres.

100. The Sewer which from the Thames feeds the horse pond. 30.

101. The Gate of the 10 Acres.

102. The way Leading to the Stayres on the Thames.

103. The moate about the Island stored with Carpe, Swannes, Duckes &c and a boate.

104. The Lower dore of the Orchard.

105. The Drawbridge of the Island.

106. The Island just as it is planted with an hedge of severall fruits twixt 8 bedds of Asperge &c: At the two ends are raspberries, and a Summer house at the marke * the mulberrie tree at the mark X.

107. The Gate of the Orchard Leading towards the Blindmans Stile. note that the Pale. 41. westward is placed upon the Foundation of the old Stalls which were burnt.

108. The Raile encloseing the Fothering yard.

109. The foundation or marke of the Place where the Stables stood, now Removed, and made a Brewhouse. numb 79.

110. The Barne.

111. An extravagant place mangled by digging Gravell.

112. The old watring Pond.

113. The Ditch of the 10 Acres.

114. The feild before the house which I call the hither Broomefeild, being 100 yards broad and 200 long wanting…yards.

115. An extravagant part of the feild joyning to Brickclose.

116. The Tracke of the old footway from the Lower towne to the blindmans Stile now almost growne over with grasse, and unfrequented.

117. Two Rowes of Dwarfe Cherries leading from 46–107.

118. The Great Orchard planted with 300 fruit trees of the best sorts mingled, and warranted for 3 yeares upon a bond of 20 pound.

119. The Ash trees, which are yet no farther then the Summer house 44 but intended to be this yeare continued with elmes to the end of this south pale.

120. The elmes which I intend to Continue, as you see, round about this feild.

121. Two Rowes of Lime trees at 4 yards ½ distant, which I purpose to plant this yeare Leading to the Gate, the walke is 21 foot broad and 300 in length.

122. The Gates leading into the Present footway.

123. The foote way leading from the Lower Towne to the blindmans stile. this way heretofore was in 116.

124. The Coachway towards the new highway, which new highway was sett out by Consent, at the first dividing of the great Broomefeild, and is at the South part of it, leads to New Crosse, I am thinking to plant that also with Elmes, but yet not fully resolved.

125. The Quick which I have planted upon a very high Banke which is turfed and hath a very deep fosse. This Qucke I purpose to keep Cutt & Square. note that this Quick runneth about also all the Pales both South and west. This feild, I caused to be taken out of the great feild, and turn'd the way without the least opposition, to the estreame Beautie, and privacy of the Villa.

126. Divers Elmes growing irregularly which I have placed here as if they were on the farther side of the Ditch 100. but indeed they are next the Pale of the severall Closes but the Errour is not great.

FINIS

KALENDARIUM HORTENSE:

OR, THE

Gard'ners Almanac;

Directing what he is to do

MONETHLY,

THROUGHOUT THE

YEAR;

And what

FRUITS and FLOWERS

are in

PRIME

Invigilate viri, tacito nam tempora gressu
Diffugiunt, nulloque sono convertitur annus.

Columella *de cult. Hort.* Lib. 10.

(Be wakeful, men, for the seasons flee with silent tread,
And the year turns without a sound.)

INTRODUCTION
TO THE
KALENDAR

A S Paradise (*though* of Gods *own* Planting) was *no longer* Paradise, than the Man was put into it, to dress it and to keep it; so nor will our Gardens (as near as we can contrive them to the resemblance of that blessed Abode) remain long in their perfection, unless they are also continually cultivated. But when we have so much celebrated the life and felicity of *an excellent* Gard'ner, as to think it preferable to all other diversions whatsoever; it is not because of the leisure which he enjoys above other men; ease and opportunity which ministers to vain and insignificant delights; such as Fools derive from sensual objects: we dare boldly pronounce it, there is not amongst Men a more laborious life than is that *of a good* Gard'ners; but because a labour full of tranquillity and satisfaction; Natural and Instructive, and such as (if any) contributes to Piety and Contemplation, Experience, Health and Longevity, *munera nondum intellecta Deum.** In sum a condition it is, furnished with the most innocent, laudable, and purest of earthly felicities, and such as does certainly make the nearest approaches to that Blessed state, where only they enjoy all things without pains; so as those who were led only by the light of Nature, because they could fancy none more glorious thought it worthy of entertaining the Souls of their departed Heroes and most illustrious of Mortals.

3

But to return to the Labour, because there is nothing excellent which is to be attained without it: A Gard'ners work is never at an end; *it begins with the* Year, and continues to the next: He *prepares the Ground*, and then he Sows it, *after that he* Plants, and then he gathers the Fruits, but in all the intermedial spaces* he is careful to dress it, so as Columella,* speaking of this *continual assiduity*, tells us, A Gard'ner *is not only to reckon upon the loss* of bare twelve hours but of an whole Year, unless he perform what is at the present requisite in *its due period* and therefore is such a Monethly Notice of his Task as depends upon the Signs and Seasons, highly necessary.

> *Gardners had need each Star as well to know*
> *The Kid, the Dragon*, and Arcturus too,*
> *As Sea-men, who through dismal storms are wont*
> *To pass the oyster-breeding Hellespont*
>
> Georgic I*

All which duly weigh'd how precious the time is, how precipitous the Occasion, how many things to be done in their just Season, and how intolerable a confusion will succeed the smallest neglect, after once a Ground is in order, we thought we should not attempt an unacceptable Work, if here we endeavour to present our Gard'ners with a complete Cycle of what is requisite *to be done throughout every* Moneth of the year: We say each Moneth; because by dividing it *into Parts so distinct*, the Order in which they shall find each particular to be dispos'd, may not only render the work more facile and delightful; but redeem it from that extreme perplexity, which for want of *a constant and uniform Method*, we find does so universally distract the vulgar sort of Them: They know not (*for the most part*) the Seasons when things *are to be done*, and when at any time they come to know, there often falls out so many things to be done on the sudden, that some of them

4

must of necessity be neglected for that whole Year, which is the greatest detriment to this Mystery, and *frequently irrecoverable.*

We are yet *far from imposing* (by any thing we have here alledg'd concerning these Menstrual Periods)* those nice and hypercritical Puntillos* which some Astrologers, and such as pursue their Rules, seem to oblige our Gard'ners to; as if forsooth, all were lost, and our pains to no purpose, unless the Sowing and the Planting, the Cutting and the Pruning, *were perform'd in such and such an exact minute* of the Moon:* *In hac autem Ruris disciplina non desideratur ejusmodi scrupulositas.** There are indeed some certain Seasons, and *suspecta tempora** which the prudent Gard'ner ought carefully (as much as in him lies) to prevent: But as to the rest, let it suffice, that *he diligently follow the* Observations which (by great Industry) we have collected together, and here present him as so many Synoptical Tables,* calculated for his Monethly use, to the end he may pretermit* nothing which is under his Inspection, and is necessary, or distract his Thoughts and Employment *before* the Seasons require it.

And now, however This *may seem but a* Trifle to some who esteem Books by the bulk, not the benefit; let them forbear yet to despise these few ensuing Pages; For never was any thing of this pretence more fully and ingenuously imparted; I shall not say to the regret of all our Mercenary Gard'ners, because I have much obligation to some above that Epithete; *M. Rose, Gard'ner to His Majesty,* and lately at Essex-house to *Her Grace the Duchess of Somerset;** and *M Turner,* formerly of *Wimbleton in Surrey;** who being certainly amongst the most expert of their Profession in England, are no less to be celebrated for their free communications to the Publick, by divers Observations of theirs, which have *furnished to this* Design. And it is from the Result of very much Experience, and an extraordinary inclination to cherish so innocent and laudable a Diversion, and to incite an Affection in the Nobless of this Nation towards it that I begin to open to them *so many of the interior* Secrets, and most precious Rules of this Mysterious Art, without Imposture, *or invidious* Reserve. The very Catalogue of Fruits and Flowers, for the Orchard and the Parterre,* will gratifie the most innocent of the Senses, and whoever else shall be to *seek a rare and universal choice for his* Plantation.

Touching the Method, it is so obvious, that there needs no further direction; and the Consequent will prove so certain, that a Work of the busiest pains is by this little Instrument rendered the most facile and agreeable, as by which you shall continually preserve your Garden in that perfection of beauty and lustre, without confusion or prejudice; Nor indeed could we think of a *more comprehensive* Expedient, whereby to a assist the frail and torpent* Memory through so multifarious and numerous an Employment (*the daily subject* of a Gard'ners care) than by the Oeconomy and Discipline which we have here consigned it to, and which our industrious Gard'ner may himself be continually Improving from his own Observations and Experience. In the meantime we have at the instance of very many Persons, who have been pleased to acknowledge the effects of a former less perfect Impression, thought good to publish this third Edition in a smaller Volume, that as an Enchiridion* it may be the more ready and useful; but the Kalendar might be considerably augmented, and recommend it self to more Universal use, by taking in the Monethly Employments of *all the parts of* Agriculture, as they have been begun to us in *Columella, Palladius, de Serres, Augustino Gallo, Vincenzo Tanara, Herrera,* our *Tusser, Markham,** and others especially if well and judiciously applied to the Climate and several Countries: *but it were here besides* our Institution, nor would the Pages contain them; what is yet found vacant, has been purposely left, that our Gard'ner may supply as he finds cause; for which reason likewise we have ranged both the Fruits and Flowers in Prime after *somewhat a promiscuous* Order, and not after the Letters of the Alphabet, that the Method might be pursued with the least disorder.

Lastly

The Fruits *and* Flowers in Prime are to be as well considered in relation to their lasting and continuance, as to their maturity and beauty.

J.E.

Kalendarium Hortense

Sun	rises-08-00 sets-04-00	JANUARY	Hath Days xxxi	long-8-00

Note, that for the Rising *and* Setting *of the Sun and* Length *Of the* days, *I compute from the first of every* Moneth. London Lat.

To be done

In the *Orchard,* and *Olitory-Garden**

TRENCH the Ground, and make it ready for the Spring: prepare also Soil, and use it where you have occasion: Dig *Borders*, &c. uncover as yet *Roots* of *Trees*, where Ablaqueation* is requisite.

Plant *Quick-Sets* and Transplant *Fruit-trees*, if not finished Set *Vines* and begin to prune the old: Prune the branches of *Orchard fruit-trees*; especially the long planted, and that towards the decrease; but for such as are newly planted, they need not be disbranched till the sap begins to stir, that so the wound may be healed with the Scar, and Stub, which our frosts do frequently leave: In this work cut off all the shoot of *August* unless the nakedness of the place incline you to spare it: Consult my *French Gard'ner,** part 1 sect. 3 for this is a most material Address. You may now begin to *Naile*, and trim your *Wall-fruit*, and *Espaliers*.

Cleanse Trees of Moss &c. the Weather moist.

Gather *Cyons* for *Graffs** before the buds sprout; and about the latter end, *Graff* them in the *Stock, Pears, Cherries* and *Plums*, and remove your *Kernel-stocks* to more commodious distances in your *Nursery,* cutting off the *top-root*: Set *Beans, Pease,* &c.

Sow also (if you please) for *early Caully-flowers*.

Sow *Chervil, Lettuce, Radish*, and other (more delicate) *Salletings*, if you will raise in the *Hot-bed*.*

In over-wet, or hard weather, *cleanse, mend sharpen* and prepare *Garden-tools*. Turn up your *Bee-hives*,* and sprinkle them with a little warm and sweet Wort,* do it dextrously.

Fruits in *Prime*, and yet *lasting*

APPLES

K ENTISH-PEPIN, Russet-pepin, Golden-pepin, French-pepin, Kirton-pepin, Holland-pepin, John-apple, Winter-Queening, Mari-gold, Harvey-apple, Pome-water, Pome-roy, Golden-Doucet, Reineting, Lones-Pearmain, Winter-Pearmain, &c.

PEARS

Winter-Musk (bakes well) Winter-Norwich (excellently baked) Winter-Bergamot, Winter-Bon-crestien, both Mural: the great surrein, &c.

✵

Sun $\left\{\begin{array}{l}\text{rises-08-00}\\\text{sets-04-00}\end{array}\right\}$ JANUARY $\left\{\begin{array}{c}\text{Hath Days}\\\text{xxxi}\end{array}\right\}$long-8-00

To be done

In the *Parterre,* and *Flower-Garden*

S ET up your *Traps* for *Vermine*; especially in your *Nurseries* of *Kernels* and *Stones,* and amongst your *Bulbous-Roots*: About the middle of this Moneth, plant your *Anemony-roots*, and *Ranunculus's*, which you will be secure of, without covering, or farther trouble: Preserve from too great, and continuing Rains (if they happen) Snow and Frost, your choicest

Anemonies, and *Ranunculus's* sow'd in September or October
for earlier Flowers: Also your *Carnations*, and such *Seeds* as
are in peril of being washed out, or *over-chill'd* and *frozen*;
covering them under shelter, and striking off the Snow where
it lies too weighty; for it certainly rots, and bursts your early-
set *Anemonies* and Ranunculus's &c. unless planted now in
the *Hot-bed*; for now is the Season, and they will flower even
in London. Towards the end, earth-up, with fresh and light
mould,* the *Roots* of those Auriculas which the frosts may
have uncover'd; filling up the chinks about the sides of the
Pots where your choicest are set; but they need not be house'd;
it is a hardy Plant.

Flowers in *Prime,* or yet *lasting*

WINTER-ACONITE, some Anemonies, Winter-Cycla-
men, Black Hellebor, Brumal-Hyacinth, Oriental-
Jacinth, Levantine-Narcissus, Hepatica, Prim-roses,
Laurus-tinus, Mezereon, Praecose Tulips, &c. especially if
raised in the Hot-bed. Note, That both these Fruits, and
Flowers, are more early, or tardy both as to their prime Sea-
sons for eating, and perfection of blowing,* according as the
Soil and Situation are qualified by Nature, or Accident.

Note also, That in this Recension* of *Monethly Flowers*, it
is to be understood for the whole period that any Flower continues, from its first appearing to its final *withering*.

♓

Sun $\left\{\begin{array}{l}\text{rises-07-13}\\\text{sets-04-45}\end{array}\right\}$ FEBRUARY $\left\{\begin{array}{l}\text{Hath Days}\\\text{xxviii}\end{array}\right\}$ long-9-24

To be done

In the *Orchard*, and *Olitory-Garden*

PRUNE *Fruit-trees*, and *Vines* as yet; For now is your Season to bind, plash,* nail, and dress, without danger of Frost; This to be understood of the most tender and delicate *Wall-fruit*, not finished before; do this before the buds and bearers grow turgid; and yet in the *Nectarine* and like delicate *Mural-fruit*,* the later your Pruning, the better, whatever has been, and still is the contrary custom. Remove *Graffs* of former years Graffing. Cut, and lay *Quick-sets*; and trim up your *Palisade Hedges*,* and *Espaliers*. Plant *Vines* as yet, other *Shrubs, Hops* &c.

Set all sorts of *Kernels* and *Stony-seeds*. Also sow *Beans, Pease, Rounsevals, Corn-sallet, Marygold, Aniseed, Radish, Parsneps, Carrots, Onions, Garlick* &c. and plant *Potatoes* in your worst ground.

Now is your Season for Circumposition* by Tubs or *Baskets of Earth*, and for laying of Branches to take root. You may plant forth your *Cabbage-plants*.

Rub *Moss* off your *Trees* after a soaking Rain, and scrape and cleanse them of Cankers, &c. draining away the wet (if need require) from the too much moistned Roots, and earth up those *Roots* of *your Fruit-trees*, if any were uncovered. Cut off the *Webbs of Caterpillars* &c. (from the Tops of Twigs and Trees) to burn. Gather *Worms* in the Evenings after Rain.

Kitchen-Garden *herbs* may now be planted, as *Parsly, Spinage*, and other *hardy Pot-herbs*. Towards the middle, or latter end of this Moneth, till the Sap rises briskly, *Graff* in the

Cleft,* and so continue till the last of March; they will hold, *Apples, Pears, Cherries, Plums*, &c. the *New-Moon*,* and the *Old Wood* is best. Now also plant out your *Caully-flowers* to have early; and begin to make your *Hot-bed* for the first *Melons* and *Cucumbers* to be sowed in the Full; but trust not altogether to them. Sow *Asparagus*.

Lastly, half open your passages for the *Bees*, or a little before (if weather invite;) but continue to feed weak Stocks, &c.

Fruits in *Prime* or *yet lasting*

APPLES

KENTISH, Kirton, Russet, Holland Pepins; Deux-ans, Winter Queening, Harvey sometimes, Pome-water, Pome-roy, Golden Doucet, Reineting, Lones Pearmain, Winter Pearmain &c.

PEARS

Bon-Chrestien of Winter, Winter Poppering, Little Dagobert, &c.

♓

Sun $\begin{cases} \text{rises-07-13} \\ \text{sets-04-45} \end{cases}$ FEBRUARY $\begin{cases} \text{Hath Days} \\ \text{xxviii} \end{cases}$ long-9-24

To be done

In the *Parterre*, and *Flower-Garden*

CONTINUE *Vermine Traps* &c.
Sow *Alaternus* seeds in *Cases,* or open Beds, cover them with thorns, that the *Poultry* scratch them not out. Sow also Larks-spurs, &c.

Now and then air your house'd *Carnations,* in warm days

especially, and mild showers, but if like to prove cold, set them in again at night.

Furnish (now towards the end) your *Aviaries* with *Birds* before they couple &c.

Flowers in *Prime*, or yet *Lasting*

WINTER Aconite, single Anemonies, and some double, Tulips praecoce, Hyacinthus stellatus, Vernal Crocus, Black Hellebore, single Hepatica, Persian Iris, Leuconium bulbosum, Dens Caninus three-leav'd, Vernal Cyclamen white and red, Mezereon, Ornithogal: max: alb: Yellow Violets with large leaves, early Daffodils &c.

♈

Sun $\begin{Bmatrix} \text{rises-06-19} \\ \text{sets-05-41} \end{Bmatrix}$ MARCH $\begin{Bmatrix} \text{Hath Days} \\ \text{xxxi} \end{Bmatrix}$ long-11-22

To be done

In the *Orchard*, and *Olitory-Garden*

YET Stercoration* is seasonable, and you may plant what *Trees* are left, though it be something of the latest, unless in very backward, or moist places.

Now is your chiefest and best time for raising on *the Hot-bed Melons, Cucumbers, Gourds*, &c. which about the sixth, eight or tenth day will be ready for the Seeds. And eight days after prick them forth at distances, according to the Method &c.

If you will have them later, begin again in ten or twelve days after the first; and so a third time to make Experiments. Remember to preserve the *Hot-bed* as much as possible from

Rain; for cool him you may easily if too violent, but not give it a competent heat if it be spent, without new-making.

Graff all this Moneth, beginning with *Pears*, and ending with *Apples*, unless the Spring prove extraordinary forwards.

Now also plant *Peaches* and Nectarines, but cut not off the top-roots, as you do of other *Trees*; for 'twill much prejudice them: Prune last years *Graffs* and cut off the heads of your budded-stocks. Take off the Littier from your *Kirnel-beds*; see Octob. or you may forbear till April.

You may as yet cut *Quick-sets*, and cover such Tree-roots as you laid bare in Autumn.

It were profitable now also to top your Rose-trees a little with your Knife, near a leaf-bud, and to prune off the dead and withered branches, keeping them lower than the custom is and to a single Stem.

Slip, and set *Sage, Rosemary, Lavender, Thyme* &c.

Sow in the beginning *Endive, Succory, Leeks, Radish, Beets, Chard-Beet, Scorzonera, Parsnips, Skirrets, Parsley, Sorrel, Bugloss, Borrage, Chervil, Sellery, Smalladge, Alisanders*, &c. Several of which continue many years without renewing, and are most of them to be blanch'd by laying them under littier and earthing up.

Sow *also Lettuce, Onions, Garlick, Orach, Purslan, Turneps* (to have early) monethly *Pease* &c. these annually.

Transplant the *Beet-chard* which you sowed in August, to have most ample *Chards*.

Sow also *Carrots, Cabbages, Cresses, Fennel, Majoran, Basil, Tobacco* &c. and transplant any sort of *Medicinal Herbs*.

Mid-March dress up, and string your *Strawberry-beds*, and uncover your *Asparagus*, spreading and loosning the Mould about them for their more easie penetrating: Also may you now transplant *Asparagus* roots to make new Beds.

By this time your *Bees* sit; keep them close Night and Morning, if the weather prove ill.

Turn your *Fruit* in the Room where it lies, but open not yet the windows.

Fruits in Prime or yet lasting

APPLES

GOLDEN Ducket [Doucet] Pepins, Reineting, Lones Pearmain, Winter Pearmain, John Apple &c.

PEARS

Later Bon-Chrestien, Double Blossom Pear, &c.

♈

Sun $\left\{\begin{array}{l}\text{rises-06-19}\\\text{sets-05-41}\end{array}\right\}$ MARCH $\left\{\begin{array}{c}\text{Hath Days}\\\text{xxxi}\end{array}\right\}$long-11-22

To be done

In the *Parterre*, and *Flower-Garden*

STAKE and bind up your weakest *Plants* and *Flowers* against the Winds, before they come too fiercely and in a moment prostrate a whole years labour.

Plant *Box* &c. in Parterres: Sow *Pinks, Sweet-williams*, and *Carnations*, from the middle to the end of this Month. Sow *Pine-kernels, Firr-seeds, Bays Alaternus, Philyrea*, and most perennial Greens* &c. or you may stay till somewhat later in the Month. Sow *Auricula-seeds* in pots or cases, in fine willow earth,* a little loamy; and place what you sow'd in September (which is the more proper Season) now in the shade, and water it.

Plant some *Anemony roots* to bear late, and successively; especially in and about London, where the Smoak is anything tolerable; and if the Season be very dry, water them well once in two or three days as likewise *Ranunculus's*. Fibrous roots may be transplanted about the middle of this Month; such as *Hepatica's, Primroses, Auricula's, Cammomile Hyacinth Tuberose, Matricaria, Gentianella, Hellebore* and other *Summer Flowers*; Set *Leucoium*; Slip* the *Keris* or *Wall-flower*, and towards the end, *Lupines, Convolvulus's, Spanish* or ordinary *Jasmine*. You may now a little after the *Æquinox*, prune *Pine* and *Fir-trees*: See Septemb.

Towards the middle, or latter end of March sow on the *Hot-bed* such Plants as are late bearing Flowers or Fruit in our Climate; as Balsamine, and *Balsamun mas, Pomum Amoris, Datura, Æthiopic Apples*, some choice *Amaranthus, Dactyls, Geraniums, Hedysarum Clypeatum, Humble,* and *Sensitive Plants, Lentiscus, Myrtle-berries* (steep;d a while), *Capsicum Indicum, Canna Indica, Flos Africanus, Mirabile Peruian: Nasturtum Ind: Indian Phaseoli, Volubilis, Myrrh, Carrobs, Marococ,* five *Flos Passionis*, and the like rare, and exotic Plants which are brought us from hot Countries. Note, that the *Nasturtium Ind. African Marygolds Voubilis*, and some others, will come (though not altogether so forwards) in the *Cold-bed* without Art: but the rest require much, and constant heat, and therefore several *Hot-beds* 'till the common earth be very warm by the advance of the Sun, to bring them to a due stature, and perfect their Seeds; Therefore your choicest *Amaranthus* being risen pretty high, remove them into another temperate *Hot-bed*; the same you may do with your *African*, and *Sensitive Plants*, especially, which always keep under *Glasses*.

About the expiration of this Month carry into the shade such *Auriculas*, Seedlings, or Plants as are for their choiceness reserved in Pots.

Transplant also *Carnation* seedlings, giving your Layers fresh earth, and setting them in the shade for a week; then likewise cut off all the sick and infected leaves; for now you may set your choice ones out of *Covert*, as directed in February.

Now do the *farewel-frosts*, and Easterly-winds prejudice your choicest *Tulips*, and spot them; therefore cover such with *Mats* or *Canvas* to prevent freckles, and sometimes destruction. The same care have of your most precious *Anemonies, Auricula's, Chame-iris, Brumal Jacynths,** early *Cyclamen*, &c. Wrap your shorn *Cypress tops* with straw *wisps*, if the Eastern blasts prove very tedious; and forget not to cover with dry straw, or *Pease-hame*, your young exposed *Ever-greens* as yet Seedlings; such as *Firr, Pine, Phillyrea, Bays, Cypress*, &c. 'till they have pass'd two or three years in the *Nursery*, and are fit to be transplanted; for the sharp Easterly and Northerly winds transpierce, and dry them up. Let this also caution you upon all such extremities of weather, during the whole Winter; but be mindful to uncover them in all benigne and tolerable seasons and intermissions; it being these acute *Winds* and seldom or never the *hardest Frosts*, or Snows which do the mischief. About the end uncover even your choicer Plants, but with Caution; for the tail of the Frosts yet continuing, and sharp Winds, with the sudden darting heat of the *Sun*, scorch and destroy them in a moment; and in such weather neither sow nor transplant.

Sow *Stock gilly-flower* seeds in the Full, to produce double flowers.

Now may you set your *Oranges, Lemmons, Myrtles, Oleanders, Lentises, Dates, Aloes, Amomums*, and like tender *Trees* and *Plants* in the *Portico*, or with the windows, and doors of the *Green-houses* and *Conservatories* open for eight or ten days before April or earlier, if the Season invite (that is, if the sharp winds be past) to acquaint them gradually with the Air; I say gradually, and carefully; for this change is the *most*

Critical of the whole year; trust not therefore the Nights too confidently, unless the weather be thorowly setled. Now is also your *Season* to raise Stocks to bud *Oranges* and *Lemmons* on, by sowing the Seeds; and some of the hardiest Evergreens may be transplanted, especially, if the weather be moist and temperate.

Lastly, Bring in materials for the *Birds* in the *Aviary* to build their *Nests* withal.

Flowers in *Prime*, and yet *Lasting*

Anemonies, Spring Cyclamen, Winter Aconite, Crocus, Bellis, white and black Hellebor, single and double Hepatica, Leuconion, Chama-iris of all colours, Dens Caninus, Violets, Fritillaria, Chelidonium small with double Flowers, Hermodactyls, Tuberous Iris, Hyacinth Zeboin, Brumal, Oriental, &c. Junquills, great Chalic'd, Dutch Mezereon, Persian Iris, Auricula's, Narcissus with large tufts, common, double and single. Primroses, Praecoce Tulips, Spanish Trumpets or Junquilles; Violets, yellow Dutch Violets, Ornithogalum max: alb: Crown Imperial, Grape Flowers, Almonds and Peach blossoms, Rubus odaratus, Arbor Jude, &c.

♉

| Sun | Hath Days sets-05-42 | **APRIL** | rises-05-18 xxx | long-13-23 |

To be done

In the *Orchard*, and *Olitory-Garden*

Sow sweet *Majoran, Hyssop, Basil, Thyme, Winter-Savoury, Scurvey-grass*, and all the fine and tender Seeds that require the *Hot-bed*.

Sow also *Lettuce, Purslan, Caully-flower, Radish*, &c.

Plant *Artichock-slips* &c.

Set *French-beans*, &c. and sow *Turneps* to have them early.

You may yet slip *Lavander, Thyme, Peneroyal, Sage, Rose-mary*, &c.

Towards the middle of this Moneth begin to plant forth your *Melons* and *Cucumbers*, and so to the later end; your Ridges well prepar'd.

Gather up *Worms,* and *snails*, after evening showers; continue this also after all Summer-rains.

Open now your *Bee-hives*, for now they hatch; look carefully to them, and prepare your Hives, &c.

Fruits in *Prime* or *yet laſting*

APPLES

Pepins, Deuxans, West-berry-apple, Russeting, Gilly-flowers, flat Reinet, &c.

PEARS

Later Bon-crestien, Oak-pear, &c. double Blossom, &c.

♉

Sun $\left\{\begin{array}{l}\text{rises-05-18}\\\text{sets-05-42}\end{array}\right\}$ **APRIL** $\left\{\begin{array}{c}\text{Hath Days}\\\text{xxx}\end{array}\right\}$long-13-23

To be done

In the *Parterre*, and *Flower-Garden*

Sow divers *Annuals* to have Flowers all *Summer,* as double *Marigolds, Digitalis, Delphinium, Cyanus* of all sorts, *Candy-tufts, Garden Pansy, Muscipula, Scabious, Scorpoides, Medica, Holy-hocks; Columbines*, which renew every five or six years, else they will degenerate &c.

Continue new, and fresh *Hot-beds* to entertain such exotic Plants as arrive not to their perfection without them, till the *Air* and common earth be qualified with sufficient warmth to preserve them abroad; *A Catalogue* of these you have in the former Moneth.

Transplant such *Fibrous-roots* as you had not finish'd in March; as *Violets, Hepatica, Primroses, Hellebor, Matricaria,* &c. Place *Auricula* Seedlings in the shade.

Sow *Pinks, Carnations*, which you may continue to trim up, and cleanse from dead and rotten leaves, viz. your old roots: Sow *Sweet-Williams*, &c. to flower next year: this after rain.

Set *Lupines* &c.

Sow *Lucoium* in *Full-Moon*,* sprinkle it thin, frequently remove them, and replant in moist weather the following Spring.

Sow also yet *Pine-kernels, Fir-seeds, Phillyrea, Alaternus*, and most perennial *Greens*. Vide Sept.

Now take out your *Indian Tuberoses*, parting the Off-sets (but with care, lest you break their fangs) then pot them in *natural* (not forc'd) Earth; a layer of rich mould beneath, and about this, natural earth to nourish the fibres,* but not so as to touch the Bulbs: then plunge your pots in a *Hot-bed* temperately warm, and give them no water till they spring, and then set them under a South-wall: In dry weather water them freely, and expect an incomparable flower in August.

Thus likewise treat the *Narcissus* of *Japan*, or *Garnsey-Lilly*, for a later flower; although that nice curiosity, set only in a warm corner, expos'd to the South, without any removal at all for many years, has sometimes prospered better: the protuberant fangs of the *Yuca* are to be treated like the *Tuberoses*. Make much of this precious Direction.

Set out and *expose Flos Cardinalis: Slip, and set Marums:*

Water Anemonies, Ranunculus's, and Plants in Pots and Cases once in two or three days, if drouth* require it. But carefully protect from *violent storms* of Rain, Hail, and to the too parching darts of the Sun, your Pennach'd* *Tulips, Ranunculus's, Anemonies, Auricula's*, covering them with *Matrasses* supported on cradles of hoops,* which have now in readiness. Now is the *Season* for you to bring the choice and tender *Shrubs*, &c. out of the *Conservatory*;* such as you durst not adventure forth in March: let it be in a fair day; only your *Orange-trees* may remain in the house till May, to prevent all danger. You may now *graff* these tender shrubs, &c. by Aproach, viz. *Oranges, Lemmons, Pomegranads, Jasmines*, &c.

Now, towards the end of April, you may *Transplant*, and Remove your tender shrubs, &c, as *Spanish Jasmins, Myrtles, Oleanders*, young *Oranges, Cyclamen, Pomegranads*, &c. But first let them begin to sprout; placing them a fort-night in the shade: but about London it may be better to defer this work till *mid-August*: Vide also May, from whence take Directions how to refresh and trim them: Prune now your Spanish Jasmine within an inch or two of the stock: but first see it begin to shoot. Mow *Carpet-walks*, and ply Weeding, &c.

Towards the end (if the cold winds are past) and especially after showers, clip *Phillyrea, Alaternus, Cypress, Box, Myrtls, Barba Jovis*, and other tonsile* shrubs, &c.

Flowers in *Prime*, or yet *Lasting*

ANEMONIES, Ranunculus's, Auricula Ursi Chame-iris, Crown Imperial, Caprifolium, Cyclamen, Bell-flower, Dens Caninus, Fritillaria, Gentianella, Hypericum frutex, double Hepatic's, Jacynth starry, double Daisies, Florence-Iris, tufted Narcissus, white, double and common, English double: Primrose, Cowslips, Pulsatillla, Ladies-Smock, Tulips medias, Ranunculus's of Tipoly, white Violets, Musk-Grape-

flower, Geranium, Radix Cava, Caltha palustris, Parietaria
Lutea, Leucoium, Persian Lillies, Paeonies, double Jonquils,
Muscara revers'd, Cochlearia, Persian Jasmine, Acanthus,
Lilac, Rosemary, Cherries, Wall-pears, Almonds, Abricots,
Peaches, White-thorn, Arbor Jude blossoming &c.

II

Sun $\begin{cases} \text{rises-04-25} \\ \text{sets-07-35} \end{cases}$ MAY $\begin{cases} \text{Hath Days} \\ \text{xxxi} \end{cases}$ long-15-09

To be done

In the *Orchard*, and *Olitory-Garden*

Sow Sweet *Majoran, Basil, Thyme*, hot and *Aromatic Herbs* and Plants which are the most tender.

Sow *Purslan*, to have young: Lettuce, large-sided *Cabbage*, painted *Beans* &c.

Look carefully to your *Mellons*; and towards the end of this Moneth, forbear to cover them any longer on the Ridges either with *Straw*, or *Matrasses*, &c.

Ply the *Laboratory*,* and distill Plants for Waters, Spirits, &c.

Continue *Weeding* before they run to Seeds.

Now set your *Bees* at full Liberty, look out often, and expect *Swarms*, &c.

Fruits in *Prime* or *yet laſting*

APPLES

Pepins, Deuxans or John-apples, West-berry-apples, Russeting, Gilly-flower-apples, the Maligar, &c. Codling.

PEARS

Great Kairville, Winter-Bon-Cretienne, Black-pear of Worcester Surrein, Double-Blossom-pear, &c.

CHERRIES &C.

The May-Cherry. Strawberries, &c.

II

Sun $\begin{Bmatrix} \text{rises-04-25} \\ \text{sets-07-35} \end{Bmatrix}$ MAY $\begin{Bmatrix} \text{Hath Days} \\ \text{xxxi} \end{Bmatrix}$ long-15-09

To be done

In the *Parterre*, and *Flower-Garden*

Now bring your *Oranges*, &c. boldly out of the *Conservatory*; 'tis your only *Season* to *Transplant* and *Remove* them: let the Cases be fill'd with natural earth (such as is taken the first half spit, from just under the *Turf* of the best *Pasture* ground, in a place that has been well fother'd on)* mixing it with one part of rotten *Cow-dung*, or very mellow Soil screen'd* and prepar'd some time before; if this be too stiff, sift a little *Lime* discreetly with it, with the rotten sticks of *Willows*: Then cutting the too thick, and extravagant *Roots* a little, especially at bottom, set your Plant; but not too deep; rather let some of the Roots appear: Lastly settle it with temperately enrich'd water (such as is impregnated with Neat* and *Sheep-dung* especially, set, and stirr'd in the Sun some few days before; but be careful, not to drench them too much at first; but giving it by degrees day after day, without touching with it the Stem) having before put some rubbish of *Lime-stones*, pebbles, shells, *Faggot-spray* or the like at the bottom of the Cases, to make the moisture passage, and keep the earth loose for fear of rotting the fibres:* See Novemb.

Then set them in the shade for a fort-night, and afterwards expose them to the *Sun*.

Give now also all your *hous'd plants* (such as you do not think requisite to take out) fresh *Earth* at the surface, in place of some of the old Earth (a hand-depth or so) and loosning the rest with a fork, without wounding the *Roots*: let this be of excellent rich soil, such as is thoroughly consumed, and will first, that it may *wash* in the *vertue*,* and comfort the *Plant*: Brush and cleanse them likewise from the dust contracted during their Enclosure. *These two last directions* have till now been kept as considerable Secrets amongst our Gard'ners: vide *August* and *September*.

Shade your *Carnations*, and *Gilly-flowers* after mid-day about this Season: Plant also your *Stock-gilly-flowers* in beds, full *Moon*.

Continue watering *Ranunculus's*: Transplant forth your *Amaranthus's*, where you would have them stand: Sow *Antirrhinum*; or you may set it.

Gather what *Anemony-seed* you find ripe, and that is worth saving, preserving it very dry.

Cut likewise the Stalks of such *Bulbous-flowers* as you find dry.

Towards the end take up those *Tulips* which are dri'd in the stalk; covering what you find to lie bare from the Sun and showers.

Flowers in *Prime*, or yet *Lasting*

LATE set Anemonies and Ranunculus omn. gen. Anapodophylon, Blattaria, Chame-iris, Augusti-sol. Cyanus, Cytisus Maranthe, Cyclamen, Heleborine, Columbines, Caltha palustris, double Cotyledon, Digitatis, Fraxinella, Gladiolus, Geranium, Horminum Creticum, yellow Hemerocallis, strip'ed Jacynth, early Bulbous Iris, Asphodel, yellow

Lillies, Lychnis, Jacea, Bellis, double, white and red, Mille-folium luteum, Phalangium, Orchis, Lilium Convallium, Span. Pinkes, Deptford Pinkes, Rosa common, Cinnamon, Guelder & Centifol. &c. Oleaster, Chery-bay, Trachelium, Cowslips, Hesperis, Antirrhinum, Syringa's Sedums, Tulips Serotin, &c. Valerian, Veronica double and single, Musk Violets, Ladies Slipper, Stock-gilly-flowers, Spanish Nut, Star-flower, Chalcedons, ordinary Crow-foot, red Martagon, Bee-flowers, Campanula's white and blew, Persian Lilly, Hony-suckles, Bugloss, Homers Moly, and the white of Dioscorides, Pansys, Prunella, purple Thalictrum, Sisymbrium double and simple, Leucoium bulbosum serotinum, Peonies, Sambucus, Rosemary, Stoechas, Sea-Narcissus, Barba Jovis, Laurus, Satyrion, Oxyacanthus, Tamariscus, Apple-blossoms, &c.

℮

Sun $\left\{\begin{array}{l}\text{rises-03-51}\\\text{sets-08-09}\end{array}\right\}$ JUNE $\left\{\begin{array}{l}\text{Hath Days}\\\text{xxx}\end{array}\right\}$long-16-17

To be done

In the *Orchard*, and *Olitory-Garden*

Sow *Lettuce, Chervil, Radish*, &c. to have young, and tender *Salleting*.

About the midst of June you may Inoculate* *Peaches, Abri-cots, Cherries, Plums, Apples, Pears*, &c.

You may now also (or in *May* before) cleanse *Vines* of ex-uberant branches and tendrels,) and stopping the second joint immediately before the *Fruit*, and some of the under branches which bear no fruit; especially in young *Vineyards* when they first begin to bear, and thence forwards; binding up the rest to props.

Gather *Herbs* in the *Full* to keep dry; they keep and retain their *virtue* and *sweet smell*, better dry'd in the shade than Sun, whatever some pretend.

Now is your Season to distill *Aromatick Plants*, &c.

Water lately planted *Trees*, and put moist, and half rotten *Fearn*, &c. about the foot of their Stems, having first clear'd them of weeds, and a little stirred the earth.

Look to your *Bees* for *Swarm*s, and Casts; and begin to destroy *Insect*s with *Hoofs*,* *Canes*, and tempting baits, &c. gather *Snails* after Rain &c.

Fruits in *Prime* or *yet lasting*

APPLES

JUNITING (first ripe) Pepins, John-apples, Robillard, Red Fennouil, &c. French.

PEARS

The Maudlin (first ripe) Madera, Green-Royal, St Laurence-pear &c.

CHERRIES &C.

Duke, Flanders, Heart { Black / Red / White.

Luke-ward, early Flanders, the Common-Cherry, Spanish-black, Naples Cherries, &c.

Rasberries, Corinths, Straw-berries, Melons, &c.

～

Sun $\begin{Bmatrix} \text{rises-03-51} \\ \text{sets-08-09} \end{Bmatrix}$ JUNE $\begin{Bmatrix} \text{Hath Days} \\ \text{xxx} \end{Bmatrix}$ long-16-17

To be done

In the *Parterre*, and *Flower-Garden*

T RANSPLANT *Autumnal Cyclamens* now if you would change their place, otherwise let them stand. Take up *Iris Chalcedon*.

Gather the ripe seeds of *Flowers* worth the saving, as of choicest *Oriental Jacynth*, *Narcissus* (the two lesser, pale spurious *Daffodils* of a whitish green, often produce varieties) *Auricula's*, *Ranunculus's*, &c. and preserve them dry: Shade your *Carnations* from the afternoon *Sun*.

You may now begin to lay your *Gilly-flowers*.

Take up your rarest *Anemonies*, and *Ranunculus's* after rain (if it come seasonable) the stalk wither'd, and dry the roots well: This, about the end of the *Moneth*: In mid-June inoculate *Jasmine, Roses*, and some other rare *Shrubs*.

Sow now also some *Anemony-seeds*. Take up your *Tulip-bulbs*, burying such immediately as you find naked upon your beds; or else plant them in some cooler place; and refresh over-parch'd beds with water. Water your Pots of *Narcissus* of Japan (that *rare Flower*) &c. Stop some of your *Scabious* from running to seed the first year, by now removing them, and next year they will produce excellent flowers. Also may you now take up all such *Plants* and *Flower-roots* as endure not well out of the ground, and replant them again immediately; such as the early *Cyclamen, Jacynth-Oriental,* and other bulbous *Jacynths, Iris, Fritillaria, Crown-Imperial, Martagon, Muscaris, Dens Caninus,* &c. The slips of *Myrtil* set in some cool and moist place do now frequently take root: Also *Cytisus* *lunatus* will be multiplied by slips in a moist place, such as are an handful long of that *Spring*, but neither by Seeds or Layers. Look now to your *Aviary*; for now the birds grow sick of their *Feathers*; therefore assist them with Emulsions of the cooler seeds* bruis'd in their water, as *Melons, Cucumbers*, &c. Also give them *Succory, Beets, Groundsell, Chick-weed*, fresh-*Gravel*, and *Earth* &c.

Flowers in *Prime*, or yet *Lasting*

AMARANTHUS, Antirrhinum, Asphodel, Campanula, Convolvulus, Cyclamen, Clematis Pannonica, Cyanus, Blattaria, Digitalis, Gladiolus, Hedysarum, Geranium, Horminum Creticum, Hieracium, Hesperis, bulbous Iris, and divers others, Lychnis var. generum, Martagon white and red, Millefolium white and yellow, Nasturtium Indicum, Nigella, Aster Atticus, Hellebor Alb. Gentiana, Trachelium, Ficus Indica, Fraxinella, shrub Night-shade, Jasmines, Honey-suckles, Genista Hisp. Carnations, Pinks, Armerius, Ornithogalum, Pansy, Phalangium Virginianum, Larks-heel early, Philosella, Roses, Thlaspi Creticum, &c. Veronica, Viola pentaphyl. Campions or Sultans, Mountain Lillies white, red: double Poppies, Palma-Christi, Stock-gillyflowers, Corn-flag, Hollyhoc, Muscaria, Serpillum Citratum, Phalangium Allobrogicum, Oranges, Rosemary, Lentiscus, Pomegranade, the Lime-tree, &c.

♉

Sun $\begin{Bmatrix} \text{rises-04-00} \\ \text{sets-08-00} \end{Bmatrix}$ J U L Y $\begin{Bmatrix} \text{Hath Days} \\ \text{xxxi} \end{Bmatrix}$ long-15-59

To be done

In the *Orchard,* and *Olitory-Garden*

Sow *Lettuce, Radish,* &c. to have tender *Salletting.*
Sow later *Pease* to be ripe six weeks after *Michaelmas.**

Water young planted *Trees,* and Layers, &c. and reprune now *Abricots,* and *Peaches,* saving as many of the young like-liest shoots as are well placed; for the now Bearers commonly perish, the new ones succeeding: Cut close and even, purging your *Wall-fruit* of superfluous leaves which hinder from the *Sun,* but do it discreetly.

You may now also begin to Inoculate.

Let such *Olitory-herbs* run to seed as you would save.

Towards the later end, visit your *Vineyards* again, &c. and stop the exuberant shoots at the second joint above the *fruit* (if not finish'd before); but not so as to expose it to the Sun, without some umbrage.*

Remove long-sided *Cabages* planted in May, to head in Autumne; 'tis the best *Cabage* in the World.

Now begin to straighten the entrance of your *Bees* a little; and help them to kill their *Drones* if you observe too many; setting the new-invented *Cucurbit-Glasses** of Beer mingled with *Honey,* to entice the *Wasps, Flies,* &c. which waste your store; Also hang Bottles of the same Mixture neer your *Red-Roman-Nectarines,* and other tempting *fruits,* for their de-struction; else they many times invade your best *Fruit.*

Look now also diligently under the leaves of *Mural-trees* for the *Snails;* they stick commonly somewhat above the *fruit;* pull not off what is bitten; for then they will certainly begin afresh.

Fruits in *Prime* or yet *lasting*

APPLES

Deux-ans, Pepins, Winter Russetting, Andrew-apples, Cinnamon-apple, red and white Juneting, the Margaret-apple, &c.

PEARS

The Primat, Ruset pears, Summer-pears, green Chesil-pears, Pearl-pear, &c.

CHERRIES

Carnations, Morella, Great-bearer, Morocca-Cherry, the Egriot, Bigarreaux &c.

PEACHES

Nutmeg, Isabella, Persian, Newington, Violet-muscat, Rambouillet.

PLUMS, &C.

Primordial, Myrobalan, the red, blew, and amber Violet, Damasc, Denny Damasc. Pear-plum, Damasc. Violet, or Cheson-plum, Abricot plum, Cinnamon-plum, the Kings-plum, Spanish, Morocco-plum, Lady Eliz. plum, Tawny, Damascene, &c. Rasberries, Goose-berries, Corinths, Strawberries, Melons, &c.

♋

Sun $\begin{cases} \text{rises-04-00} \\ \text{sets-08-00} \end{cases}$ JULY $\begin{cases} \text{Hath Days} \\ \text{xxxi} \end{cases}$ long-15-59

To be done

In the *Parterre*, and *Flower-Garden*

Slip *Stocks*, and other lignous Plants* and Flowers; From henceforth to *Michaelmas* you may also lay *Gillyflowers*, and *Carnations* for Increase, leaving not above two, or three spindles* for flowers, and nipping off superfluous buds, with supports, cradles, canes or hoofs, to establish them against winds, and destroy *Earwigs*.

The Layers will (in a *month* or six weeks) strike root, being planted in a light loamy earth, mix'd with excellent rotten soil and sifted: plant six, or eight in a pot to save room in the *Winter*: keep them well from too much Rains; yet water them in drouth, sparing the leaves: If it prove too wet, lay your pots side-long; but shade those which blow from the afternoon *Sun*, as in the former *Month*.

Yet also you may lay *Myrtils, Laurels*, and other curious *Greens*.

Water young planted *Shrubs* and Layers, &c. as *Orange-Trees, Myrtles, Granads, Amomum* especially, which *shrub* you can hardly refresh too often and he requires abundant compost; as do likewise both the *Myrtle*, and *Granad-Trees*; therefore whenever you trim their *Roots*, or change their *Earth*, apply the richest soil (so it be sweet, and well consum'd) you can to them, &c. Clip *Box*, &c, in Parterres, Knots, and *Compartiments*, if need be, and that it grow out of order; do it after Rain.

Graff by Approach, Inarch,* or Inoculate *Jasmines, Oranges*, and other your choicest *Shrubs*.

Take up your early *autumnal Cyclamen, Tulips*, and Bulbs (if you will Remove them, &c.) before mention'd; Transplanting them immediately, or a *Month* after if you please, and then cutting off, and trimming the fibres, spread them to Air in some dry place.

Gather *Tulip-seed*, if you please: but let it lie in the *pods*.

Gather now also your early *Cyclamen-seed*, and sow it presently in Pots.

Remove seedling *Crocus*'s sow'd in September constantly at this *Season*, placing them at wider intervals, till they begin to bear.

Likewise you may take up some *Anemonies, Ranunculus's, Crocus, Crown Imperial, Persian Iris, Fritillaria,* and *Colchicums*; but plant the three last as soon as you have taken them up, as you did the *Cyclamens*; or you may stay till *August* or September 'ere you take them up, and replant *Colchicums.*

Remove now *Dens Caninus* &c.

Take up your *Gladiolus* now yearly, the blades being dry, or else their Off-sets will poison the ground.*

Latter end of July, sieft your *Beds,* for Off-sets of *Tulips,* and all *Bulbous Roots*; also for *Anemonies, Ranunculus's,* &c. which will prepare it for re-planting with such things as you have ready in Pots to plunge, or set in the naked earth till the next season; as *Amaranths, Canna Ind. Mirabile Peruv. Capsicum Ind. Nasturtium Ind.* &c. that they may not lie empty, and disfurnish'd.

You may sow some *Anemonies,* keeping them temperately moist.

Continue to *cut off* the withered stalks of your lower *flowers,* &c. and all others, covering with earth the *bared* roots, &c.

Now (in the driest Season) with *Brine, Pot-ashes,* and *Water,* or a decoction of *Tobacco refuse,** water your gravel-walks, &c. to destroy both *Worms* and *Weeds,* of which it will cure them for some *years.*

Flowers in *Prime*, or yet *Lasting*

AMARANTHUS, Asphodel, Antirrhinum, Campanula, Clematis, Cyanus, Convolvulus, Sultana, Veronica purple and odoriferous; Digitalis, Eryngium Planum, Ind. Phaseolus, Geranium triste, and Creticum, Gladiolus, Gentiana, Hesperis, Nigella, Hedysarum, Fraxinella, Lynchnis Chalcedon, Jace white and double, Nasturt. Ind. Millefolium, Musk-rose, Flos Africanus, Thlaspi Creticum, Veronica mag. & parva,

Volubilis, Balsam-apple, Holy-hoc, Cornflower, Alkekengi, Lupines, Scorpion-grass, Caryophyllata emn. gen. Stock-gillyflower, Scabiosa, Mirab. Peru: Spartum Hispan. Monthly-rose, Jasmine, Indian Tuberous Jacynth, Limonium, Linaria Cretica, Pansies, Prunella, Delphinium, Phalangium, Periploca Virgin. Flos Passionis, Flos Cardinalis, Yucca, Oranges, Amomum Plinii, Oleanders red and white, Agnus Castus, Arbutus, Olive, Ligustrum, Tilia, &c.

♍

Sun $\begin{Bmatrix} \text{rises-04-43} \\ \text{sets-07-17} \end{Bmatrix}$ A U G U S T $\begin{Bmatrix} \text{Hath Days} \\ \text{xxxi} \end{Bmatrix}$ long-14-33

To be done

In the *Orchard*, and *Olitory-Garden*

INOCULATE now *early*, if before you began not, and gather your *bud* of that year: Let this work be done before you remove the *Stocks*.

Prune off yet also superfluous *branches*, and shoots of this second spring; but be careful not to expose the *fruit*, without leaves sufficient to skreen it from the *Sun*; furnishing, and nailing up what you will spare to cover the defects of your Walls. Continue yet to cleanse your *Vines* from exuberant branches that too much hinder the *Sun*.

Pull up the *Suckers*.

Clip *Roses* now done bearing.

Sow *Raddish*, especially the *Black*, to prevent running up to seed, pale tender-*Cabbages, Caully-flowers* for Winter Plants, *Corn-sallet, Marygolds, Lettuce, Carrots, Parsneps, Turneps, Spinage, Onions*; also curl'd *Endive, Angelica, Scurvy-grass*, &c.

Likewise now pull up ripe *Onions* and *Garlic*, &c.

Towards the end sow *Purslan, Chard-beet, Chervile,* &c.

Transplant such *Lettuce* as you will have abide all *Winter*.

Gather your *Olitory-seeds*, and clip, and cut all such *Herbs* and *Plants* within one handful of the ground before the full.

Lastly, *Unbind*, and release the *Buds* you inoculated if taken, &c. likewise stop, and prune them.

Now vindemiate,* and take your *Bees* towards the expiration of this *Month*; unless you see cause (by reason of the *Weather* and *Season*) to defer it till mid-September: But if your *Stocks* be very light and weak, begin the earlier.

Make your Summer *Perry*, and *Cider*.

Fruits in *Prime* or *yet laſting*

APPLES

THE Ladies Longing, the Kirkham Apple, John Apple; the Seaming Apple, Cushion Apple, Spicing, Mayflower, Sheeps Snout.

PEARS

Windsor, Sovereign, Orange, Bergamot, Slipper Pear, Red Catherine, King Catherine, Denny Pear, Prusia Pear, Summer Poppering, Sugar Pear, Lording Pear, &c.

PEACHES

Roman Peach, Man Peach, Quince Peach, Rambouillet, Musk-Peach, Grand Carnation, Portugal Peach, Crown Peach, Bourdeaux Peach, Lavar Peach, the Peach Des pot, Savoy Malacoten, which last till Michaelmas.

NECTARINES

The Muroy Nectarine, Tawny, Red-Roman, little Green Nectarine, Cluster Nectarine, Yellow Nectarine.

PLUMS

Imperial, Blew, White Dates, Yellow Pear-plum, Black Pear-plum, White Nutmeg, late Pear-plum, Great Anthony, Turkey Plum, the Jane Plum.

OTHER FRUIT

Cluster-grape, Muscadine, Corinths, Cornelians, Mulberries, Figs, Filberts, Melons, &c.

♍

Sun $\left\{\begin{array}{l}\text{rises-04-43}\\\text{sets-07-17}\end{array}\right\}$ AUGUST $\left\{\begin{array}{l}\text{Hath Days}\\\text{xxxi}\end{array}\right\}$long-14-33

To be done

In the *Parterre*, and *Flower-Garden*

Now (and not till *now*, if you expect success) is the just *Season* for the *budding* of the *Orange Tree*: Inoculate therefore at the commencement of this *Month*.

Now likewise take up your bulbous *Iris's*; or you may sow their seeds, as also those of *Larks-heel, Candy-tufts, Columbines, Iron-colour'd Fox-gloves, Holly-hocks*, and such Plants as endure *Winter*, and the approaching *Seasons*.

Plant some *Anemony roots* to have Flowers all *Winter*, if the roots escape; and take up your seedlings of last year, which now transplant for bearing: also plant *Dens Caninus, Autumnal Crocus*, and *Colchicums*: Note, that *English Saffron* may be suffered to stand for increase to the third or fourth year without *removing*.

You may now sow *Narcissus*, and *Oriental Jacynths*, and re-plant such as will not do well out of the *Earth*, as *Fritillaria, Hyacinths, Martagon, Dens Caninus, Lillies*.

Gilly-flowers may yet be slipp'd.

Continue your taking up of *Bulbs*, dry them and lay them up; *Lillies*, &c. of which before.

Gather from day to day your *Alaternus* seed as it grows black and ripe, and spread it to sweat, and *dry* before you put it up; therefore move it sometimes with a broom, that the seeds clog not together, unless you will separate it from the *Mucilage*,* for then you must a little bruise it wet; wash and dry them in a cloth.

Water well your *Balsamine fœm*.

Most other *Seeds* may now likewise be gathered from *Shrubs*, which you find ripe.

About mid-August, transplant *Auricula's*, dividing old, and lusty roots; also prick out your *Seedlings*: They best like a loamy sand, or light moist *Earth*; yet rich, and shaded: You may likewise sow *Auricula*.

Now, towards the latter end, you may sow *Anemony* seeds, *Ranunculus's*, &c. lightly cover'd with fit mould in *Cases*, shaded and frequently refresh'd: Also *Cyclamen, Jacynths, Iris, Hepatica, Primroses, Fritillaria, Martagon, Fraxinella, Tulips*, &c. but with *patience*, for some of them; because they *flower* not till three, four, five, six, and seven years after, especially the *Tulips*; therefore disturb not their beds, and let them be under some *warm place*, shaded yet, till the heats are past, lest the seeds dry; only the *Hepatica's*, and *Primroses* may be sow'd in some less expos'd Beds.

Now about *Bartholomew-tide*,* is the only secure-season for removing, and laying your perennial *Greens; Oranges, Lemmons, Myrtils, Phillyreas, Oleanders, Jasmines, Arbutus*, and other rare *Shrubs* as *Pomegranads, Monthly Roses*, and whatever is most obnoxious to frosts; taking the shoots, and branches of the past *Spring*, and pegging them down in very *rich earth* and soil perfectly consum'd, watering them upon all occasions

during the *Summer*, and by this time *twelve month* they will
be ready to remove, *Transplanted* in fit earth, set in the shade,
and kept moderately moist, not over wet, lest the young *fibres*
rot; after three weeks set them in some more airy place, but
not in the *Sun*, till fifteen days more; Vide our *Observations*
in April, and May for the rest of these choice *Directions*.

Flowers in *Prime*, or yet *Lasting*

AMARANTHUS, Anagallis Lusitanica, Aster Atticus,
Blattaria, Spanish Bells, Belvedere, Carnations, Cam-
panula, Clematis, Cyclamen Vernum, Datura Turica, Elio-
chryson, Eryngium planum & Amethystinum, Geranium
Creticum, and Triste, Yellow Stocks, Hieracion minus
Alpesire, Tuberose Hyacinth, Limonium, Linaria Cretica,
Lychnis, Mirabile Peruvian. Yellow Millefol. Nasturt. Ind.
Yellow mountain Hearts-ease, Maracoc, Africanus flos,
Convolvulus's, Scabious, Asphodils, Delphinium, Lupines,
Colchicum, Leucoion, Autumnal Hyacinth, Holly-hoc, Star
wort, Heliotrop, French Mary-gold, Daisies, Geranium nocte
olens, Common Pansies, Larks-heels of all colours, Nigella,
Helleborus, Balsamin: fœm: Lobells Catch-fly, Thlaspi
Creticum, Rosemary, Musk-Rose, Monthly Rose, Oleanders,
Spanish Jasmine, Yellow Indian Jasmine, Myrtyls, Oranges,
Pomegranads double, and single flowers, Shrub Spirae Agnus
Castum, the Virginian Martagon, Malva arborescens, &c.

♎

Sun $\begin{Bmatrix} \text{rises-05-41} \\ \text{sets-06-19} \end{Bmatrix}$ SEPTEMBER $\begin{Bmatrix} \text{Hath Days} \\ \text{xxx} \end{Bmatrix}$ long-12-37

To be done

In the *Orchard*, and *Olitory-Garden*

GATHER now (if ripe) your *Winter Fruits*, as *Apples, Pears, Plums,* &c. to prevent their falling by the great Winds: Also gather your Wind-falls from day to day: do this work in dry weather.

Release Inoculated *Buds*: or sooner, if they pinch.

Sow *Lettuce, Radish, Spinage, Parsneps, Skirrets,* & *Caully-flowers, Cabbages, Onions,* and *Scurvy-grass, Anniseeds,* &c.

Now may you Transplant most sorts of *Esculent,* or *Physical* Plants,* &c.

Also *Artichocks,* and *Asparagus-roots.*

Sow also *Winter-Herbs* and Roots, and plant *Straw-berries* out of the Woods.

Towards the end, Earth up your Winter-plants, and *Sallad herbs*; and plant forth your *Caully-flowers,* and *Cabbages* which were sown in August.

No longer now defer the taking of your *Bees,* streightning the entrances of such Hives as you leave to a small passage, and continue still your hostility against *Wasps,* and other robbing Insects.

*Cider-making** continues.

Fruits in *Prime* or *yet lasting*

APPLES

THE Belle-bonne, the William, Summer Pearmain, Lording apple, Pear-apple, Quince-apple, Red-greening ribb'd, Bloody-Pepin, Harvey, Violet-apple, &c.

PEARS

Hamdens Bergamot (first ripe) Summer Bon Chrestien, Norwich, Black Worcester, (baking) Green-field, Orange, Bergamot, the Queen hedg-pear, Lewes-pear (to dry excellent) Frith-pear, Arundel-pear, (also to bake) Brunswick-pear, Winter Poppering, Bings-pear, Bishops-pear (baking) Diego, Emperours-pear, Bluster-pear, Melsire Jean, Rowling-pear, Balsam-pear, Bezy d'Hery, &c.

PEACHES, &C.

Malacoton, and some others, if the year prove backwards, Almonds, &c.

Quinces.

Little Blew-grape, Muscadine-grape, Frontiniac, Parsley, great Blew-grape, the Verjuice-grape excellent for sauce, &c.

Berberries, &c.

Ω

Sun $\begin{Bmatrix} \text{rises-05-41} \\ \text{sets-06-19} \end{Bmatrix}$ SEPTEMBER $\begin{Bmatrix} \text{Hath Days} \\ \text{xxx} \end{Bmatrix}$ long-12-37

To be done

In the *Parterre*, and *Flower-Garden*

PLANT some of all the sorts of *Anemonies* in good, rich natural earth, especially the Latifol* after the first Rains, if you will have flowers very forwards; but it is surer to attend till October, or the *Month* after, lest the over moisture of the *Autumnal* seasons, give you cause to repent.

Now is the most proper season to sow *Auricula* seeds, setting the Cases in the *Sun* till *April*: See April.

Begin now also to plant some *Tulips*, unless you will stay

till the later end of *October*, to prevent all hazard of rotting the *Bulbs;* Plant *Daffodils*, and *Colchicum*.

All Fibrous Plants, such as Hepatica, Hellebor, Cam-momile, &c. Also the *Capillaries;** *Matricaria, Violets, Prim-roses*, &c. may now be transplanted; as likewise *Iris-Chalcedon, Cyclamen*, &c.

Now you may also continue to sow *Alaternus, Phillyrea*, (or you may forbear till the Spring), *Iris, Crown Imperial, Marta-gon, Tulips, Delphinium, Nigella, Candy-tufts, Poppy*; and gen-erally all the *Annuals* which are not impair'd by the Frosts.

Sow *Primroses* likewise: Remove seedling *Digitalis*, and plant the slips of *Lychnis* at the beginning.

Your *Tuberoses* will not endure the wet of this Season, therefore set the Pots into your *Conserve*,* and keep them very dry; It is best to take them out of the Pots, about the begin-ning of this *Month*, and either to preserve them in dry sand, or to wrap them up in Papers, and so put them in a box near the *Chimny*.

Bind now up your *Autumnal Flowers*, and Plants to stakes, to prevent sudden Gusts which will else prostate all you have so industriously rais'd.

Now you may take off *Gillyflower-layers* with earth and all, and plant them in pots, or borders shaded.

Crocus will be now rais'd of Seeds.

Prune *Pines*, and *Firrs* a little after this *Æquinox*, if you omitted it in March. Vide March.

About *Michaelmas* (sooner, or later, as the *Season* directs) the weather fair, and by no means foggy, retire your choice *Greens*, and rarest Plants (being dry) as *Oranges, Lemmons, In-dian*, and *Span. Jasmine, Oleanders, Barba-Jovis, Amomum Plin. Citysus Lunatus, Chamelea tricoceos, Citrus Ledon Clusii, Dates, Aloes, Sedum's* &c. into your *Conservatory*; ordering them with fresh mould, as you were taught in May and July,

viz. taking away some of the upmost exhausted earth, and
stirring up the rest, fill the Cases with rich, and well consumed soil, to wash in and nourish the *Roots* during *Winter*;
but as yet leaving the doors and windows open, and giving
them much Air, so the Winds be not sharp and high, nor
weather foggy; do thus till the cold being more intense, ad-
vertise you to enclose them altogether: *Myrtils* will endure
abroad near a *Month longer*.

The cold now advancing, set such *Plants* as will not endure
the *House*, into the earth; the Pots two or three inches lower
than the surface of some bed under a *Southern exposure*: Then
cover them with glasses, having cloath'd them first with sweet,
and dry Moss; but upon all warm, and benigne emissions of
the Sun, and sweet showers, giving them air, by taking off all
that covers them: Thus you shall preserve your costly, and precious *Marum-Syriacum, Cistus's Geranium nocte olens, Flos
Cardinalis, Maracoes*, seedling *Arbutus's* (a very hardy Plant
when greater) choicest *Ranunculus's* and *Anemonies, Acacia
Egpyt* [*sic*] &c. Thus governing them till *April*. Secrets not till
now divulg'd.

Note, That Cats will eat, and destroy your *Marum-
Syriacum* if they can come at it, therefore guard it with a *Furs*,
or *Holy-branch*.

Flowers in *Prime*, or yet *Lasting*

AMARANTHUS tricolor, and others; Anagallis of Portugal, Antirrhinum, African flo. Amomum Plinii, Aster
Atticus; Belvedere, Bellis, Campanula's Colchium, Autumnal Cyclamen, Clematis, Chrysanthemum angustifol. Expatorium of Canada, Sun-flower, Stock-gil.flo. Geranium
Creticum, and nocte olens, Gentianella annual, Hieracion
minus Alpestre, Tuberous Indian Jacynth, Linaria Cretica,
Lychnis Constant. single and double; Limonium, Indian

Lilly, Narciss. Pomum Aureum, and Amoris, & Spinosum Ind. Marvel of Peru, Millefolium yellow, Moly Monspeliens. Nasturtium Indicum, Persian autumnal Narcissus, Virginian Phalangium, Indian Phaseolus, Scarlet Beans, Convolvulus, divers. gen. Candy-tufts, Veronica, purple Volubilis, Asphodel, Crocus, or English Saffron, Garnsey Lilly or Narcissus of Japan, Poppy of all colours, single, and double, Malva arborescens, Indian Pinks, Æthiopic Apples, Capsicum Ind. Gilly-flowers, Passion-flower, Dature double and sing. Portugal Ranunculus's, Spanish Jasmine, yellow Virginian Jasmine, Rhododendron white and red, Oranges, Myrtils, Balaustia, Musk-rose, and Monthly-Rose, Malva arborescens, &c.

♏

| Sun | $\begin{cases} \text{rises-06-26} \\ \text{sets-05-24} \end{cases}$ | OCTOBER | $\begin{cases} \text{Hath Days} \\ \text{xxxi} \end{cases}$ long-10-47 |

To be done

In the *Orchard*, and *Olitory-Garden*

TRENCH Grounds for *Orcharding*,* and the Kitchen-Garden, to lie for a *Winter* mellowing.

Plant dry *Trees*Fruit* of all sorts, *Standard, Mural*, or *Shrubs* which lose their leaf; and that so soon as it falls: but be sure you chuse no *Trees* for the *Wall* of above two years *Grafting* at the most, sound and smooth.

Now is the time for *Ablaqueation*,* and laying bare the *Roots* of old un-thriving, or over hasty-blooming trees.

Moon now decreasing, gather *Winter-fruit* that remains, weather dry; take heed of bruising, lay them up clean lest they taint; Cut and prune *Roses* yearly, reducing them to a *Standard* not over tall.

Plant, and Plash Quick-sets.

Remove *Graffs* after the second year, unless *Dwarfs*, which you may let stand till the third.

Save, and sow all stony, and hard *kernels* and *seeds;* such as black *Cherry, Morellos, black Heart,* all good; *Pear-plum, Peach, Almond-stones,* &c. Also *Nuts, Haws, Ashen, Sycomor,* and *Maple keys; Acorns, Beech-mast, Apple, Pear,* and *Crab kernels,* for *Stocks;* or you may defer it till the next *Month* towards the latter end, keeping them dry, and free from mustiness; remembering to cover the beds with littier.

You may yet sow *Genoa Lettuce* which will last all the *Winter, Reddish* &c.

Make *Winter Cider,* and *Perry.*

Towards the latter end, plant Abricots, Cherries, Plums, Vines, Winter-pears &c.

Fruits in *Prime* or *yet laſting*

APPLES

Belle-et-bonne, William, Costard, Lording, Parsley-apples, Pearmain, Pear-apple, Honey-meal, Apis, &c.

PEARS

The Caw-pear, (baking) Green-butter-pear, Thorn-pear, Clove-pear, Roussel-pear, Lombart-pear, Russet-pear, Saffron-pear, and some of the former Moneth, Violet-pear, Petworth-pear, otherwise call'd the Winter-Windsor.

Bullis, and divers of the September Plums and Grapes, Pines, Arbutus, &c.

♏

Sun $\left\{\begin{array}{l}\text{rises-06-26}\\\text{sets-05-24}\end{array}\right\}$ OCTOBER $\left\{\begin{array}{c}\text{Hath Days}\\\text{xxxi}\end{array}\right\}$ long-10-47

To be done

In the *Parterre*, and *Flower-Garden*

Now your *Hyacinthus Tuberose* not enduring the wet, must be set into the house, and preserved very dry till *April*.

Continue sowing what you did in *September* if you please: Likewise *Cypress* may be sown, but take heed of the Frost: vide *March*.

Also, You may plant some *Anemonies*, especially the *Tenuifolia's* and *Ranunculus's* in fresh sandish earth, taken from under the turf, but lay richer mould at the bottom of the bed, which the *fibres* may reach, but not touch the *main roots*, which are to be covered with the natural earth two inches deep: and so soon as they appear, secure them with *Mats*, or dry *Straw*, from the winds, and frosts, giving them air in all benigne intervals, if possible once a day.

Plant also *Ranunculus's* of *Tripoly, Vernal Crocus's* &c. Remove seedling *Holy-hocs*, or others.

Plant now your choice *Tulips*, &c. which you feared to interre at the beginning of *September*; they will be more secure, and forward enough: but plant them in natural earth somewhat impoverished with very *fine sand*; else they will soon lose their variegations; some more rich earth may lie at the bottom, within reach of the *fibres* (as above:) Now have a care your *Carnations* catch not too much wet; therefore retire them to covert where they may be kept from the *rain*, not the air, or lay them on the sides; trimming them with fresh *mould*.

All sorts of *Bulbous roots* may now also be safely buried; likewise *Iris's* &c.

You may yet sow *Alaternus,* and *Phillyrea seeds*: It will now be good to Beat, Roll, and Mow *Carpet-walks,** and *Cammomile;* for now the ground is supple, and it will even all inequalities: Finish your last *Weeding* &c.

Sweep, and cleanse your *Walks*, and all other places from *Autumnal leaves* fallen, lest the *Worms* draw them into their holes, and foul your *Gardens* &c.

Flowers in *Prime*, or yet *Lasting*

Amaranthus tricolor, &c. Aster Atticus, Amomum, Antirrhinum, Colchicum, Saffron, Cyclamen, Clematis, Heliotrops, Stock-gilly-flo. Geranium triste, Ind. Tuberose Jacynth, Limonium, Lychnis, white and double, Pomum Amoris and Æthiop. Marvel of Peru, Millefol. luteum, Autumnal Narciss. Pansies, Aleppo Narciss. Sphærical Narciss. Nasturt. Persicum, Gilly-flo. Virgin. Phalangium, Pilosella, Violets, Veronica, Arbutus, Span. Jasmine, and yellow Ind. Jasmine, Monethly Rose, Oranges, Myrtils, Balaust.

Sun $\begin{cases} \text{rises-07-34} \\ \text{sets-04-26} \end{cases}$ NOVEMBER $\begin{cases} \text{Hath Days} \\ \text{xxx} \end{cases}$ long-08-52

To be done

In the *Orchard*, and *Olitory-Garden*

Carry *Compost* out of your *Melon-ground*, or turn, and mingle it with the earth, and lay it in *Ridges* ready for the *Spring:* Also trench, and fit ground for *Artichocks*, &c.

Continue your *Setting*, and *Transplanting* of *Trees*; lose no time, hard Frosts come on apace: Yet you may lay bare *old roots*.

Plant young *Trees, Standards*, or *Mural*. Furnish your *Nursery* with Stocks to *graft* on the following year.

Sow, and set *early Beans*, and *Pease* till *Shrove-tide*; and now lay up in your *Cellars* for spending,* and for *Seed* to be transplanted at *Spring, Carrots, Parsneps, Turneps, Cabbages, Caully-flower,* &c.

Cut off the tops of *Asparagus*, and cover it with *long-dung*,* or make *Beds* to plant in spring, &c.

Now, in a dry day, gather your last *Orchard-fruits*.

Take up your *Potatos* for *Winter* spending, there will enough remain for *Stock*, though never so exactly gather'd.

Fruits in *Prime* or *yet lasting*

APPLES

THE Belle-bonne, the William, Summer Pearmain, Lording-apple, Pear-apple, Cardinal, Winter Chess-nut, Short-start, &c. and some others of the former two last Moneths, &c.

PEARS

Messire Jean, Lord-pear, long Bergamot, Warden (to bake) Burnt-Cat, Sugar-pear, Lady-pear, Ice-pear, Dove-pear, Deadmans-pear, Winter Bergamot, Bell-pear, &c. Arbutus, Bullis, Medlars, Services.

Sun $\begin{cases} \text{rises-07-34} \\ \text{sets-04-26} \end{cases}$ NOVEMBER $\begin{cases} \text{Hath Days} \\ \text{xxx} \end{cases}$ long-08-52

To be done

In the *Parterre*, and *Flower-Garden*

Sow *Auricula* seeds thus; prepare very rich *earth*, more than half dung, upon that sieft some very light sandy mould, and the earth gotten out of old hollow *Willow-trees*; and then sow: set your *Cases* or *Pans* in the Sun till March or April.

Cover your peeping *Ranunculus's* &c. and see the *Advice* in March, for *Ever-green* Seedlings; especially, if long *Snows*, and bitter winds be feared.

Now is your best *Season* (the weather open) to plant your fairest *Tulips* in places of *Shelter*, and under *Espaliers*; but let not your earth be too rich; vide *October*. Transplant ordinary *Jasmine*, &c.

About the middle of this *Moneth* (or sooner, if weather require) quite *enclose* your tender *Plants*, and perennial *Greens*, *Shrubs*, &c. in your *Conservatory*, secluding all entrance of cold, and especially sharp winds; and if the *Plants* become exceeding dry, and that it do not actually freeze, refresh them sparingly with qualified water,* (i) mingled with a little *Sheeps*, or *Cow-dung*: If the *Season* prove exceeding piercing (which you may know by the freezing of a dish of water, or moistned *Cloth*, set for that purpose in your *Greenhouse*)* kindle some *Charcoals*, and when they have done smoaking, put them in a hole sunk a little into the floor about the middle of it: This is the safest *Stove*: At all other times, when the air is *warm'd* by the beams of a fine day, and that the *Sun* darts full upon the house, without the least wind stirring, shew them the light;

but enclose them again before the *Sun* be gone off: Note, That you must never give your *Aloes*, or *Sedums* one drop of water during the whole Winter: And indeed, you can hardly be too sparing of *Water* to your *hous'd plants*; the not observing of this, destroys more Plants than all the rudenesses of the *Season*: To know when they want refreshing consider the leaves; if they *shrivel* and fold up, give them drink; if *pale* and whitish, they have already too much; and the defect is at the roots, which are in peril of rotting. If your *Aloes* grow manifestly too dry, expose it a while to the air, when clear, 'twill immediately recover them; but give them not a drop of water how dry soever their pots be.

House your choicest *Carnations*, or rather set them under a *Pent-house** against a South-wall, so as a *Covering* being thrown over them to preserve them in extremity of weather, they may yet enjoy the freer air at all other times.

Prepare also *Mattrasses, Boxes, Cases, Pots* &c. for *Shelter* to your tender Plants and Seedlings newly sown, if the weather prove very bitter.

Plant Roses, Althæa frutex, Lilac, Syringas, Cytisus, Peonies, &c.

Plant also *Fibrous roots*, specified in the precedent *Moneth*.

Sow also *Stony-seeds*, mentioned in *October*.

Plant all *Forest-trees* for *Walks, Avenues* and *Groves*.

Sweep, and cleanse your *Garden-walks*, and all other places, from *Autumnal* leaves, the last time.

Flowers in *Prime*, or yet *Lasting*

A NEMONIES, Meadow Saffron, Antirrhinum, Stock-gilly-flo. Bellis, Clematis, Pansies, some Carnations, double Violets, Veronica, Spanish and Indian Jasmine, Myrtils, Musk Rose &c.

♉

Sun $\left\{\begin{array}{l}\text{rises-08-10}\\\text{sets-03-50}\end{array}\right\}$ DECEMBER $\left\{\begin{array}{l}\text{Hath Days}\\\text{xxxi}\end{array}\right\}$ long-07-40

To be done

In the *Orchard*, and *Olitory-Garden*

PRUNE, and Nail *Wall-fruit*, (which yet you may defer a *Moneth* or two longer) and *Standard-trees*.

You may now plant *Vines*, &c.

Also *Stocks* for *Grafting*, &c.

Sow as yet, *Pomace* of *Cider-pressings** to rais: *Nurseries*; and set all sorts of *Kernels, Stones*, &c.

Sow for *early Beans*, and *Pease*, but take heed of the *Frosts; therefore surest to defer it till after *Christmas,* unless the *Winter* promise very moderate.

All this *Moneth* you may continue to *Trench Ground*, and dung it, to be ready for *Bordures,* or the planting of *Fruit-trees*, &c.

Either late in this month, or in *January*, prune, and cut off all your *Vine-shoots* to the very root, save one, or two of the stoutest, to be left with three, or four eyes of young wood: This for the *Vineyard.*

Now feed your weak *Stocks.*

Turn, and refresh your *Autumnal Fruit*, lest it taint, and open the *Windows* where it lies, in a clear and *Serene day.*

Fruits in *Prime* or *yet lasting*

APPLES

ROUSSETING, Leather-coat, Winter Reed, Chess-nut-Apple, Great-belly, the Go-no-further, or Cats-head, with some of the precedent Moneth.

PEARS

The Squib-pear, Spindle-pear, Doyoniere, Virgin, Gascogne-Bergomot, Scarlet-pear, Stopple-pear, White, red and French Wardens (to bake or rost) &c. the Dead-mans pear, excellent, &c.

♉

Sun $\left\{\begin{array}{l}\text{rises-08-10}\\\text{sets-03-50}\end{array}\right\}$ DECEMBER $\left\{\begin{array}{c}\text{Hath Days}\\\text{xxxi}\end{array}\right\}$long-07-40

To be done

In the *Parterre*, and *Flower-Garden*

As in *January*, continue your hostility against *Vermine*. Preserve from too much *Rain* and *Frost*, your choicest *Anemonies, Ranunculus's, Carnations*, &c.

Be careful now to keep the *Doors* and *Windows* of your *Conservatories* well matted, and guarded from the piercing Air: for your *Oranges*, &c. are now put to the test: *Temper* the cold with a few *Charcoal* govern'd as directed in *November*; but never accustom your *Plants* to it, unless the utmost severity of the *Season* require; therefore, if the place be exquisitely close, they will even then hardly require it, &c.

Set *Bay-berries*, &c. dropping ripe.

Look to your *Fountain-pipes*, and cover them with fresh, and warm *Littier* out of the *Stable*, a good *thickness*, lest the frosts crack them; remember it in time, and the *Advice* will save you both trouble and charge.

Flowers in *Prime*, and yet *lasting*

Anemonies some, Persian, and Common winter Cyclamen, Antirrhinum, Black Hellebor, Laurus tinus, single

Primroses, Stock-gilly-flo. Iris Clusii, Snow flowers, or drops, Yucca, &c.

For by such a *Kalendar* it is that a *Royal Garden* or *Plantation* may be contrived, according to my *Lord Verulam's* design,* *pro singullis Anni Mensibus*, for every *Moneth* of the *Year*.

But, because it is in this cold *Season*, that our *Gard'ner* is chiefly diligent about preserving his more tender, rare, exotic, and costly *Shrubs*, *Plants*, and *Flowers*; We have thought fit to add the *Catalogue*, as it is (much after this sort) collected to our hands, by the *Learned and Industrious Doctor Sharrock** (though with some reformation and improvement) of all such, as according to their different *Natures*, do require *more*, or less indulgence: And these we have distributed likewise, into the three following *Classes*.

I CLASSE

Being least *patient* of *Cold*, and therefore to be *first* set into the *Conservatory*, or other ways defended.

Acacia Ægyptaca, Aloe American, Amaranthus tricolor, Aspalathus Cret. Balsamum, Helichryson, Chamelæa tricoccos, Nasturtium Indicum, Indian Narcissus, Ornithogalon Arab. Ind. Phaseol. Capsicum Ind. Pomum Æthiop. Aureum, Spinosum, Summer Sweet Majoran, the two Marums Syriac. &c. Dactyls, Pistacio's, the great Indian Fig, Lilac flo. alb. Lavendula Multif. Clus. Cistus Ragusæus flo. alb. Colutea Odorata Cretica, Narcissus Tuberosus, Styrax Arbor, &c.

II CLASSE

Enduring the second degree of *Cold*, and accordingly to
be *secur'd* in the *Conservatory*

Amomum Plinii, Carob, Chamelæa Alpestris; Cistus Ledon
Clus. Citron Vernal Cyclamen, Summer Purple Cyclamen,
Digitalis Hispan. Geranium triste, Hedysarum Clypeatum,
Aspalathus Creticus, Span. Jasmine, Virgin. Jasmine, Suza
Iris, Jacobæa Marina, Alexandrian Laurel, Oleanders Limo-
nium elegans, Myrtils, Oranges, Lentiscus, Levantine tufted
Narcissus, Gill. flo. and choicest Carnations, Phalangium
Creticum, Asiatic double and single Ranunculus's Narcissus
of Japan, Cytisus rubra, Canna Indica, Thymus Capitatus,
Verbena nodi flo. Cretica, &c.

III CLASSE

Which not *perishing* but in excessive *Colds*, are therefore to
be *last* set in; or rather *protected* under *Mattrasses*, and
sleighter *Coverings*, abroad in the *Earth, Cases, Boxes*,
or *Pots*, &c.

Abrotonum mas. fæm. Winter Aconite, Adiantum Verum,
Bellis Hispan. Calceolus Mariæ, Capparis, Cineraria, Cneorum Matthioli, Cytisus Maranthe, rub. Lunatus, Eryngium
planum totum Cæruleum, Fritillaria mont. Genista Hispan.
flo alb. Pomegranads, Oriental Jacynth, Bulbous Iris, Laurels,
Cherry Laurel, Lychnis double white, Matricaria double flo.
Olives, Pancration, Papaver Spinociss. Maracoc, Rosemary,
Sisynrichium, Turpentine-tree, Teuchrium mas, Tithymal.
Myrtifol. Vetonica doub. flo. single Violets, Lavender, Ser-
pentaria trifol. &c. Ornithogalon Arab. white and doub. Nar-
cissus of Constantinople, late Pine-apples, Moly, Persian
Jasmine, Opuntia or the smaller Indian fig, Jucca, Seseli
Æthiop. Agnus Castus, Malva Arborescens, Cistus mas.

Althea Frutex, Sarsaparilla, Cupressus, Crithmum marinum, &c.

And to *these* might some others be *added*; but we conceive them *sufficient,* and more than (we fear) some envious, and *mercinary Gard'ners* will thank us for; but they deserve not the name of that *Communicative,* and noble *Profession*: However, this, as a specimen of our *Affection to the Publick*; and in *Commiseration* of divers *honourable,* and Industrious *Persons,* whose Inclination to this innocent *Toil,* has made them spare no *Treasure,* or *Pains* for the furniture of their *Parterres* with variety, the *miscarriage* whereof being some-times universal to the *Curious,* has made us the more freely to impart both what we have *experimentally* learn'd by our own *Observations,* and from others of undoubted *Candor* and *Ingenuity*: But of this, we promise a more ample *Illustration,* as it concerns the entire *Art,* together with all its *Ornaments* of *Use,* and Magnificence, as these *endeavours* of ours shall find entertainment, and opportunity contribute to the *Design.*

FINIS.

DIRECTIONS
FOR
THE GARDINER
AT
SAYS-COURT

But which may be of Use for

OTHER GARDENS

Jonathan Mosse came to me
Apprentice for six yeares,
24 June 1686

*Venio nunc ad voluptates Agricolarum**
Cic: in Cat: Ma:

Quis non Epicurum
*Suspicit, exigui lætum plantaribus Horti?**
Juv: 13, 123

The Table

※??蒸

Terms of Art used
by Learned Gardners
※※

Aspect, the quarter of the heaven East, West, North & South

Region, place or Country

Clime, diferrence of place or Country

Botanist, One who has knowledge in plants

Viscous, clammy, like bird-lime

Digest, to rott and consume like dung

Classes, Ranks & Order

Vernal, such as come to perfection in the Spring

Estival, such as in Summer

Autumnal, such as in Autumn ⎫

Hyemal, such as in Winter, the same as *Brumal* ⎭ flourish:

Insects, smaller vermine, as Errucas, Wasps, Ants, &c.

Medical, belonging to physick

Mucilage, clammy stuff, such as is in yew-berries &c.

Vindemiate, Time to Gather grapes, or grape-gathering

Interr, to bury

Percolate, to straine

Cucurbits, Glasses made like smaller bells, or Gourds

Tonsile, that which may be shorn with sheares

Topiary, the art of making hedges in divers shapes

S.S.S. Stratum super stratum, the laying a row or layer of seedes, &
a layer of Earth, one upon another, til the pot, or pit, be full, that
they may be ready to sprout, & fitted for sowing, as *Haws*, *Yew-
seedes*, *Holly-berries*, & other hard seedes

Impregnat, made fruitfull, & ready to bring forth

Præcoce, are the flowers that blow most early, & so of fruits rip'ning

Medias, that come next, applied to *Tulips* chiefly

Serotine, which blow late, or beare late

Menstrual, monthly

Diurnal, daily

Horti-Culture, Dressing & keeping a Garden

Carpet, is grasse turfe, as in walks & bowling-greenes

To *plush*, is to cut a branch neere halfe thro', the easier to bend & lay it

Layers, as branches bent-downe & a little slit, & peg'd downe the better to cover them with earth, to take roote

Avenues, long walkes leading to the House

Oriental, Eastward: *Occidental*, Westward

Arrable, that may be plowd. *Arenous*, Sandy

Repent, when a plant is a creeper

Scandent
Climaxes } when Climbing

Repastination, is a slight digging

Extirpation
Erradication } pulling-up by the rootes

Lætation, Dunging

Legumens, all sort of pulse, as *peas*, *beanes*, &c.

Stolon, is a sucker

Infusion, is the steeping in water: the same wth *Maceration*

Insolation, is the setting that water, or thing in the hot sun

Hyemation, is the setting a plant to winter in the Green-house

Pedament, is the prop set to a Vine

Semination, is sowing

Seminarie, is the Nursery, or Imp-Garden

Blanching, is the burying in the ground to make white & tender

Pampination, is the taking off superfluous vine-leaves, &c.

Trenching, is the diging two-spades depth deepe, & making a Trench, laying the first spade-depth of earth formost, the second & worst behind it, so as when the trenches are finish'd, the first earth be thrown in, the next above it

Irrigation, is watering

Esculent plants are such as are wholesome to be eaten, *Culinary*

Mould, is natural Earth without dung

Virgin-Earth, is the first mould taken under the turfe in pasture ground

Fosse, is any pitt

Aquatic plants, such as grow in the water, or neere it

Exotic-plants, such as are sent from beyond the seas

Ferment, is to boile, or woorke

Resinous, such trees as are gummi, & extill clammy juice, as pines &c.

Cones, or *Cloggs*, the fruite of the Firr, & pine Apples

Cultivate, is to Dresse & labour the ground

Species, of the same, or another sort

Influence, the vertue or power of the sun, aire, & heavens, upon plants

Drilling, is the cutting a narrow trench to convey away water

Rilling, is the same, & also to make a shallow furrow to sow any-thing in

Vegetable, whatever grows & increases

Verdure, Greene

Meridian, Noone-day

Æquinox, when day & night are of equal length, as in *March* & *September*

Fiberous plants, are such whose Rootes are stringy

Capillaries, such whose Rootes are like haire

Bulbous, such whose Rootes are round like Onions

Tuberous, almost the same, but of a longer shape

Lignous, such whose Rootes are woody

Inoculate, is to Bud, or Graffe wth the Bud: *Emplastration* ye same

March, is to Graffe by Approch, bending the branch to ye stock

Ablaqueation, is to lay the Roote quite bare all winter

Amputation, to cut a branch quite off

Graff in the *Crowne*, is to graffe severall cions 'twixt ye bark & the wood of an old Tree

Splicing, or *Whipstock*, is fitting the Cyon & stock by a slant cutting

Emuscation, is to rub off the Mosse from trees

Offsetts, are the small increase of bulbous rootes

Parterr, is a flower-bed, or flower-garden

Olitorie-garden, is a Kitchin or potherb Garden

Mural Fruite is Wall-fruite

Espallieres, are pole-hedges

Conservatorie, is the Greene-house for tender plants

Annuals, such plants as dye in the winter

Perennial plants, such as continue all the yeare

Tendrells, are the strings of vines by which they take hold of ye props

Compost, is all sort of Dung: *stercoration*, dunging

ABBREVIATIONS

A. *Annualy* to be sown

C. *Continuing* many yeares

D. *Dwarfs*

G. *Greene-house*, to be wintered-in

P. signifies *Plants*

S. *Seede*, to be rais'd of Seede

Sl. *Slips*, to be rais'd of Slips

St. *Standard Fruit*-trees

W. *Wall-Fruit*

Sayes-Court-Gardine, 1687

❦

Fruit–Trees planted upon the Wall by the Stables, 1669

DWARFS

White-peare-plum	— peare
Black-peare-plum	Abricot
Black-peare-plum	Peach
White-peare-plum	Abricot
Bonne-Chrestienne—Winter	Abricot
— Peare	Abricot
Abricot	Abricot
Abricot	Abricot
Peach le Chancelière	Peach Brignon Musquè
Peach Narbonne	Cherry-Morello
Abricot	Cherry-Black-heart
Abricot	Cherry

Bonne-Chrestienne Summer ⎤   At the End of ⎤
Bonne-Chrestienne Winter ⎦   the Coach-house ⎦

Every peere is planted with a *vine*

Fruit–Trees in the Great–Court Planted at Severall times

Peach	Peach—*Magdalene*
Peach—*Mignon*	Peach—*Brignon*
Abricot	Peach—*persique*
Peach	Peach
Peach	Peach—*Alberge*
Fig	Nectarine—*Newington*
Peare—*Bezy-d'Herie*	Peach—*Le bonne Clerke*

Peare—*Martinsec* Abricot
Peach—*la belle Chevreuse* Vine
Peare Vine
Peach—*Montaban*—& Abricot Plumm: *White Nutmeg*
Peach—*Admirable*: late, but Peare
   good Plumm: *White Holland*

Vines at every peere

Fruit-Trees planted in the Fountaine-Garden

Vine—*parsley* Vine—*White Frontiniac*
Peach—*Vergoleuze* Grape—*Black Frontiniaque*
Peach—*Newington* Bonne *Chrestienne sans pepin*
Peach—*Syon* Cherry—*Morella*
Peach—*Newington* [*Spaces left for 9 more*]

Fruit-Trees planted in the Greene-house Garden

Vine Vine
Peach Vine
Abricot Peach—*Violet*
Peach—*Brignon*: violet-Nectarine Peach—*Royall*
Vine Pavie—*Magdalene*
Vine Nectarine—*Red Roman*

White & Black Frontiniaque vines at the peeres

Fruit-Trees planted in the Iland

Artichocks { *flatheaded* Cucumbers
        — Cabbages
Melons Beetes

Fruit-Trees planted in Other Places

Quinces *Nutts*
  Portugal quince   Greate haisell
Wall-nuts Filbert { Red
  The great Whinnsheld   White

Medlars without stones

Cornelians	*white*	Services:
	red	Pines:

Fruit-Trees planted in the Bowling-Greene 1684, 85, 86

ON THE WALL

Peach *Magdalene*—white &
   red
Nectarin *Red Roman* &
   Vergoleuze
Peare *Amidot*, & *peach de peau*
Plumm *Peascod*
Abricot

Abricot
Peach
Fig
Plumm *White perdrigon*
Plumm *Blew perdrigon*
Two *Abricots* left-hand of
   ye court doore

CHERRIES ABOUT THE CIRCLE

Duke [Cherry]
Duke Cherry
Duke Cherry
Morroco Cherry
Croone Cherry
Morocco Cherry
Petworth Amber Cherry
True *Black-heart* Cherry
Carnation Cherry
Luke-Ward Cherry
Prince-Royall Cherry
Flanders Cherry
Carnation Cherry

Luke-Ward Cherry
Red-heart Cherry
Prince Royall Cherry
Luke-Ward Cherry
Carnation Cherry
True Black-heart Cherry
Petworth Amber Cherry
Morocco Cherry
Flanders Cherry
Croone Cherry
Duke Cherry
Black-Orleans Cherry
   [*Space left for 1 more*]

IN THE EAST QUARTER
PEARES DWARFES

Messier Jean
Petit Rousslet
Cassolett

Vermillion
Lansaque, or *Dauphin* or
Frangepan d'Autune

French King	*Elias Rose*
Beurie du Roy	*Calliot Rosat, Caillo,* or [*Prester*
Brute bonne	*July-Flowre*
Grosse Rousslet	*Swan's Egg*
Jargonell	*Musque Robin*
St. Andrew	*Golden peare of Xaintonge*
Orange Bergamot	*Poire sans pepin*
Ambrosia	*Espine d'Yver*

STANDARD APPLES IN THE EAST QUARTER

Five Golden pepins	*Pome d'Apis*

STANDARDS IN THE WEST QUAR^TR

Nine Damson trees	The Cherrys are *Flanders*

Vines at every *peere* of ye wall. *White Muscadine* at the corner peere next the doore into the East quarter.

Corrinth & *Gooseberrys* betweene the Trees in both quarters: *Strawberries* in the Bordures. *Violets* about the halfe-circle.

Fruit-Trees planted in the foure Ortyard quarters

IN THE SPRING-QUARTER:
S. EAST
John Apple
Peare-*maine*:
Kentish-pepin
[*Space left for thirty-three others*]

IN THE AUTUMNE-QUARTER:
S. WEST
Holland pepin:
[*this name twice: space left for sixty-four others*]

IN THE SUMMER-QUARTER
N. EAST
Golden-Rousset pepin
[*Space left for thirty-two others*]

IN THE WINTER-QUARTER
N. WEST
Golden mundi apple
Kentish pepin
Mullberry:
[*Space left for fifty-two others*]

Total number: 189

Notes for
FRUITE-TREES

❧ 1. Plant strawberries (especially the large sort) in tufts at a foote distance, so as you may stirr & strew rich earth about them, and water them well. Thus will one tuft produce more & better fruite than where planted so thick together.

❧ 2. Strawberries will grow & beare well even amongst pible stones & pavements, so you string them dilligently: & the water wherein strawberries are washed, being full of the seede (which sticks about the fruite) if cast upon the ground will produce the plant.

Notes for the
KITCHIN-GARDEN

🌿 1. Beds of *Sweete-herbs** should be stirrd up, and new moulded,* every second yeare in the Spring, to make them strike fresh rootes.

🌿 2. Bell glasses* will preserve Lettuce, & many other salading all the winter long:

🌿 3. One may sow Reddish, & Carrots together on the same bed: so as the first may be drawn, whilst the other is ready: or sow Lettuce, purselan, parsneps, carrots, Reddis on the same beds, & gather each kind in their season, leaving the parsneps to Winter:

🌿 4. It is good to change the ground for *Carrots* & *parsneps* now and then: when they are two Inches high weede them: and a little after, thinn them with a small *Haw*:* The old beds should be well trenched:

🌿 5. Chervill is handsom and proper for the edging of Kitchin Garden beds:

🌿 6. When *Mary-Golds* are tender, collect as many as you can well compasse within your hand & fingers, and sinke them into the Earth-bed by thrusting them down strongly into it as they grow, having before a little stirred the mould. Then cutt off their tops so as but very little appeare, and they will produce goodly flowers.

🌿 7. *Skirrits* should be sown in rich mellow fresh earth & moist, and when removed set deepe, let them be a finger long before removed. To prevent their seeding, sow in March, planting but a single slip in a hole at a foote distance.

🌿 8. If plants hasten to run to seede (as *cabbage* and the like will, if sown early) pull the rootes a little out of the earth, and lay them along in it slanting, & clap some mould about them.*

🌿 9. When Cauley-flowers hasten to pome & head* (as apt to do in hot weather) before they have quite gotten a full head: pluck them quite up. Lay them in the Cellar, burying the whole roote & stalke to the very head, and so they will finish a goody head without sun or exposure to the aire:

❧ 10. Sow *Turneps* from mid-June to July: but in Aprill & May to have early rootes.

For gathering and dressing Salads for the Table see p. 115 &c: and my *Acetaria*.

Plants for the Kitchin-Gardens: *

ROOTES

P	*Artichocks*	P	Rampions
	Chardon	R	Potatos
	Lady Thistle		Melons
	Cabbages		Cucumiers
	Cauly-flowres	P	Horse-reddish
P	Aspargus		Beetes
	Carrots		peas
	parsneps		Beanes
	Turneps		*Harricos*
	Navets		*Onions*
	Skirrets		Eschalots
	Salsifex		Leekes
	Scorzonera		Scives
	Reddish	R	Garlick

Roccombo

SALADS & POT-HERBS

P Lettuce
Sorell
P Wood-Sorrell
Allelujah
Spinach
Porselan
Orrach
P Trip-madame
Sampier
Sellerie
Smalledye
Alesanders

Chervill
Spanish Myrrh
Fenell—Sweete
Tarragon
Cressus
Nasturtium *Indicum*
Corne-Sallad
Rochett
Orang-Seedlings
P Tansy
Clary
Nep

Harts-horn

POT-HERBS

parsley
Burnet
Borrage

Buglosse
Spinach
Endive

SWEETE-HERBS

sl Sweete-Majoran
Pot-Majoran
sl Time—*severall sorts*
Hyssop
sl Sommer ⎫
Winter ⎭ savory
Mary-gold
P.sl Pene-royall

s Basile
sl Sage *of all kinds*
P.sl Balme
P Mint
Annis
Fennell
Dill
P.sl Lavender

Notes for the
PHYSIC-GARDEN

PHYSICAL plants,* should be set in Alphabetical order, for the better retaining them in memorie:

*Garden and Physical Plants necessary
to be known and had*

A
sl Abrotanum
p Aconite
   Angelica
p Adders tongue
   Alkikengi
   Alcanet
   Apocynum
   Arch-Angel
sl Aristolochia
p Arum
   Ars-Smart
   Assara-bassa
   Assarum

B
sl Balsame
   Barren-wort
   Basil
   Beares-breech
p Betonie
sl Bistort
   Blite
p Blood-wort
sl Brook-lime

sl Brionia
   Burdoch
   Broome

C
   Calamint
   Camomile
   Caltha palustris
   Catmint
   Caraway
   Carduus benedictus
p Centaurie
   Celedon
p Cinq-foile
p Consolidum regale
p Coltsfoot
   Comfery
   Coriander
   Costmary
s Cummin

D
   Daucus
   Dan-delion
sl Dames-violet

s Dill
p Dittander
p Devils-bit
p Dog-bane
p Dragons
p Dulcamara

E
p Ægrimonie
p Elicampane
Eupatorium

F
Febrefeu
Flag
Flea-bane
Fluellen
p Fern
Fumary
Fraxinella
Fœnugreeke

G
p Galingale
sl Germander
Goates-Rue
p Golden rod

H
p Harts-tongue
Hauk-Weede
p Hellebore
p Helleborine
Hemloc
p Hercules-All-heale
p Herba-paris

Hen-bane
Hounds-tongue
p Horse-Mint
p Hore-hound
p House-Leeke
p Horse-taile
Hypericon

I
Iron-wort
Ground Ivy

K
p Knap-weede

L
sl Lavender Cotton
Lady-Smock
Langue de Bœuf
p Licoris
p Liverwort
p Lilly-Convalle
p Lovage
p Lunaria

M
Madder
p Maudlin
p Marsh-Mallows
p Master-wort
p Mandrake
p Mercurie
Melilote
Motherwort
p Moly
p Monks-hood

p Mug-wort
p Mullein
s Mustard
s Myrrhis

N
s Nasturtium
Dead Nettle
Night-shade
Noli-me-tangere

O
p Orchis
Origanon
p Orpin
Occulus christi

P
p Pellitarie
R Peonie
p Philipendula
p Peper-wort
p Pile-wort
p Peny-wort
p Plantanes
Polypode
Poppy-white
Garden-poppy
p Pulsatella
sl Prunella

Q

R
Rag-wort
p Radix-Cava

p Rib-wort
p Ros-Solis
p Rhubarb
p Rue

S
R Saffran
p Satyrion

p.R Sabine
p Sanicle
p Saponaria
Sedum
s Scurvy-grasse
Shepherds-purse
sl Scordium
p Serpillum
smallage
Sneeze-wort
p Spurge
p Solomons-Seales
p Stitch-wort
Stramonium

T
s Tabacco
Teasel
Thoro-wax
Toad-flax
p Tout-saine
Tre-foile

V
p Valerian
sl Veronica

W	*p* Wolfe-bane
Water-Lilly	
Water-Cresses	X
Willow-Weede	
Woad	Y
p Wood-Sorell	*p* Yarrow
s Worme-wood	

Notes for
RARER SIMPLES & EXOTICS*

Calamus Aromaticus must be planted in the water, it being a Flag onely.

Plants and rarer Simples

Exotic

G Stoecas	G Cistus *of all kinds*
G Vermicularis	Gnaphalium Americanum
Calamus aromaticus	Absynthium Latifolium
G Marum Syriacum	arborescens
Marum. *Mastic–thyme*	Chrysanthemum
Sedum *of all sorts*	frutiferum
Tragacantha	Androsænum maximum
Lotus—*several sorts*	Hispanicum
Dorichnium congener Clusii	Senetio Arborescens
Polium Montanum	G Capsicum Indicum
Abrotanum Unguentarium	

Notes for the
CORONARY GARDEN*

❧ 1. You are not to separate off setts from y^r *Tulips*, 'til the are quite dry.

❧ 2. If you stirr the earth of such seedlings Annuals as escape the frosts they must be new-sown, else they may sometimes continue.

❧ 3. Lavender Cotton kept clip'd makes a pretty hedge or bordure for a Flower garden, and may be maintained a foote high.

❧ 4. A layer of short stable Littiers a foote under the mould, planted with Tulips, Anemonies, Ranunculus &c will cause them to thrive without being removed, or so often changing their beds.

❧ 5. To have *Stock Gillyflowers* very faire, choose a plant which beares excellent double flowers, suffering it to beare but only one branch of flowers: Save and sow the seedes of those flowers in February on the Hot-bed, and plant them forth in Michaelmas: This is a precious seacret.

Coronarie Flowres for the parterr & Bordures

Tulips
Narcissus
Anemonie
Crocus
Croun-Imperial
Ranunculus
Jacynths
Fritillaria
Carnations
Stock-Gilly-flowres
Junquills
Iris
Asphodill
Martagon
Campanula
Gladiolus
—Lillies { white
{ red
Persian Lilly
Auricula

All which neede not often removing {
Polyanthies
Prime-roses
Peonie
Violets: Bulbous violets
Pansies
Day-Eies
Phalangium
Pinks
Sweete-Williams
Pride of London
Hepatica
Cyclamen
Gentianella
Muscaris
Geranium
Ornithogallum
Yellow-Moly
—Keri
Sultans
Lychnis

Holy-hoch
Snow-drops
Scabious
Snap-dragon
Hellibore
Colombine
Everlasting-pease
Dens-Caninus
Cyanus
Veronica
Colchicum

ANNUALS

Popies
Convolvulus
Bell-vedere
Nasturtium Indicum
Marvell of Peru
Flos Africanus
Flos-Solis
Lupines
Candy-Tufts
Larks-spurr
Nigella Romana

To be yearely-sown {
Fraxinella
French-Mary-gold
Venus looking-glasse
Rose-Campion
Valerian
Flos Adonis
Prime-rose Tree
Lobels Catchfly
Globe-thistle
Scarlet-beane
Caterpillars
Hedg-hogs &c
Foxtaile & Glove
Monks-hood
Fraxinella

78

Notes for

CORONARY FLOWERS RARER

🌿 1. Generaly all *exotics* and outlandish plants are to be raised in the Hot-bed.

🌿 2. The *Japon Lillie* will not thrive without some sea-sand be mixed with the mould, which may be of the under turfe.

🌿 3. You cannot keepe the Narcissus Tuberosus too dry in Winter & after you take the rootes out of the Earth.

Coronary Flowres Rarer Exotics

G Flos Cardinalis	Narcissus of Constantinople
Japon or Garnzy Lillie	G Marcoc or Passion flowre
Narcissus Tuberosus	G Geranium Nocte olens

Flowres to be raised in yᵉ Hot-bed

Amaranthus	Tuberose
Sensitive ⎫ plants	Nasturtium Indicum
Humble ⎭	Flos Africanus
Bellvedere	Heliotrop
G Capsicum Indicum	G Oranges
G Flos Cardinalis	G Limons
G Geranium Nocte olens	Gourds
Marcoc	

Notes for
EVER-GREENES

❧ 1. Never expose your *Oranges*, *Limons*, & like tender Trees, what-ever season flatter; 'til the Mulbery puts-forth its leafe, then bring them boldly out of the Greene-house; but for a fortnight, let them stand in the shade of an hedge, where the sun may glimmer onely upon them.

❧ 2. Give Oranges &c no water during all the winter: but if exces-sively dry, which you'l perceive by the shrivling leafe; let the water be rich, and warmed moderately.

❧ 3. Give plentifull & frequent water to *Myrtils*, and often fresh & rich-mould.

Myrtils	will be variegated by
Philyrea	being inoculated with
Holly	cions of variegated
Alaternus	plants but not by their
Oranges	seeds.*

Rosemary thrives better by cutt plants, than by ragged slips: not for the growing of the slip, but for that the old plant whenc you slip it, never recovers the scarr: wherefore cut it some distance from the stem, when it flowers & not in Aprill, as is usual.

Where Rosemary will not thrive by reason of the soile, clay, or bogg; mingle it with Brick dust exceedingly.

Ever-greenes

TREES

Abies *Firrs*

Pinus

Pinaster

Picea

Cypresse:

Cedrus
1 Libani
2 Bermudas
3 Goa
4 Virginia

Laurus—*common bay tree*

Laurus—*Cerasus, Cherry-bay*

Taxus yew

Holy
1 *gilded white*
2 *gilded yellow*
3 *Hirsutus*

Lignum vitæ or *Arbor Thyrea*

Ilix—*Scarlet Oake*

Suber—*Cork-tree*

Olive

Sabina *baccifera*

Lotus hersutus Creticus

SHRUBS

Arbutus

Alaternus prima Clusii

Alaternus variegatus—ex { Albo fusco

Philyrea { folio serrato angusti folio

G Cytisus Lunatus

G Myrtus angusti folius *florens*

G Myrtus *upright birds-nest*

G Myrtus flo: amplo, *florens*

G Limons

Lentiscus

G Barba Jovis: silver-bush

G Cistus *of all kinds*

Juniperus

G Laurus verus *Græcorum*

Laurus tinus: *the strip'd*

Rosemarie [*Laurell*

Sesele *Æthiopicum*

G Myrtus angustifol: *non florens*
broad-leav'd of Portugal

G Myrtus Orange-leav'd Tip'd wth white

G Jasminum Americanum flo: luteo

G Oleander *white*

G Oleander *red*

G Oranges

Buxus *Box-tree*

Hedera *Ivy*

Genista *Hispanica*

Erica *Fuzz*

Ruscus *Butchers broome*

Ligustrum *privet*

Clematis

Halimus Latifolius

Notes for
SHRUBS & EVER-GREENES

You must give *Aloës* no water in winter, if it shrinke, set it a while in open aire. In Summer you cannot water it too much: be sure to set it in dry in the winter.

Shrubs & Plants

EVER-GREENES

G Azedarack: *Bead-tree*
  Opuntia
  Ficus-Indicus
  Sarsaparilla or *Smilax aspera*
  Malva arborescens
G Camilea Tricoccos
G Yucca

G Aloës
G Jacobœa marina
G Tragacantha
G Sedum arborescens
  Lavender-Cotton
  Rue

ROSES

Damasque
Red
Province
Cinamon
Eglantine or dog-rose
Yello-rose { double / single

Monethlie
White-rose: *single: Double*
Rosa *Mundi*
Plush or Velvet-rose
Guelder-rose
Centifol-rose

Notes for
SHRUBS NOT EVER-GREENE

YOU can not water *Amomum Plinii* too much in summer: nor in-rich the mould too often, for it exhausts the mould exceedingly: best planted all in Dung almost.

Trees, shrubs &c. rare not Ever-greenes

Larix	Syringa { flo: *purple* / flo: *white*
G Amomum plinii	
Agnus, *Castus*	Caprifolium *Americanum*
Carob Tree	Caprifol: *Honisuckle vulgar*
Althæa Frutex	The white-*hony-suckle*
Persian Jasmine { *Spanish* / *Vulgar*	The yallow-*hony-suckle*
	Spixia *Theophrasti*
Acacia { flo: albo / Ægyptiaca: G.	Canna piscatoria
	Oleaster
Terebinthus	Senna
Arbor *Judæ*	Ruta Caprina
Mezerion	G Pome *Granade*
Laburnum { majus / minus	Clematis *verginiana*
	Virgin bowre
Tamariscus	Paliurus
Sambucus	Rhus, myrtil & *virginian sumach*
Rhamnus - *Buck-horne*	

Notes for
FOREST TREES

🙺 1. The ELME will be grafted on an Elme-stock and much improve the stem, & leafe.

🙺 2. The *Constantinople*, or *Horse-Chess-nut*, is beautifull for greate walks & *Avenues*, but should be planted where the winds come not fiercely, which is apt to take off whole branches.

🙺 3. The *Acacia* is also apt to split by high winds.

🙺 4. *Horn-beame*, *Elme*, *Beech*, make excellent, tall, and thick strong hedges, planted in single row onely & kept clip'd.

🙺 5. You cannot plant the *Oriental platanus* in too moist & feeding a ground; it loves the water & watering exceedingly.

🙺 6. The *Larch-Tree* is like the *pine*, but looses its leafe in Winter.

Forest, & Grove Trees

VULGAR*

Oake	Service
Ash	Quick-beame or *Whichen*
Elme	Withy
Chessnut	Willow { Salow
Beech	Ozier
Poplar { white / black	White-*thorne*
Abele: or	Black-*thorne*
Aspen	Spindle *tree*
Maple	Dog-wood
Lime { male / female	Alder
Horn-beame	Elder
Haysel { *Filberd* / —	Sycomore or Maple
	Black-cherry
	Birds-cherry

84

NOT-VULGAR*

Horse-Chessnutt	Spanish-Oake
Platanus { Oriental, or Zinar / Occidental	White-Mulberie
	Virginian Wallnutt
Larinx	Lentiscus
Tulip-tree, or *Virgin Maple*	*Acacia*
Cork-tree	

A Catalogue of the best & choicest
FRUIT-TREES
standards, Dwarfe, or for y^e
Walls & Espalliere

APPLES

Pepin—Kentish
Pepin—Russet
Pepin—Holland
Pepin { Golden / Russet
Pear-maine { Lones / —
Harvy-Apple
Queene Apple
Mary-gold
Winter queening
Kerkham *Apple*

Reinet
John-Apple, or *Deux Anns*
Standards Passe-pome
Pome-Apis
Courpendus *of all sorts*
Calvils *omn: generum*
Golden mundi: *excellent*
Julyfloore
st Leathern Coate
st Chessnut
Catts-head

PEARES

Bonne Chrestienne:
    Winter: Summer
W Bergamot *ordinary*
W Bergamot *de Busy*
W Vergoleuse: *Octob.: ex^t:*
    winter
W Poire a double fleur
W Windsore-peare
Greenefield
Beurie du Roy
Ambret: *Decemb^r.*
Espine d'Yver. *Dec^r*
Chessom: *Jan:*

Cassolet: oct: ex^t
Rousslet-champagne
    Octo:
Petit Tupin: *Novemb*
Messire Jean
Amadot
French—King
Jargonell
St. Andrew
Ambrosia
Vermillion
Lansac
Elias Rose

86

st Petit Muscat: *Jan:*
st Petit Blanquet: *July*
st Blanquet Musque, *July*
st Orange Bergamot: *Sept:*
W Petit Rousslet: *excellent*
   St.V.W
St Cuisse Madame *Aug:*
st Boudin Musque *Aug:*
st Mouille bouch: *Aug:*
st Brute v. bonne: *Oct:*
st King-peare: *Sep:*
st Lewes-peare: *to dry excellent*
st Bezy d'Herie
   Rousslet de Rheyms: *Octob:*
   Vert longue: *Octob:*
   Bishops peare, *baking*
   Bing-peare: st [standard
   Caw-peare, baking
   Lewes red *warden*
   the best of all for baking

Standards (vertical label)

Calliot Rosat
Swans-egg
Musque Robin
Golden *de Xaintonge*
Poire sans pepin
st Popering
Hamden's *Bergamot*
Norwich, *Baking: excellent*
Black Worcester: *for baking*
Arundell: *to Bake*
Rolling peare
Juniting: first ⎰ *Red*
   ripe ⎱ White
Codling
st *Dove peare*
st Squib
st Stopple-peare
st Deadman's peare to
   bake excell^t

Catalogue of Fruite-Trees

PEARES

Winter musque *baking*
Chesil *peare*

Catherine *red: & King*
   Saygar   [*Catherine*
Lording

CHERRIES

Hartlib
D Carnation
   Duke *Flanders*
   Black-Cher: s^r W; Temple*
   Black-heart: true
   Greate-bearer
   Black-Orleans

Duke
Luke-Ward
Morocco
Prince Royal
Petworth *Amber*
Flanders
Red heart

Kentish
May-*cherrie*

Croone
Bigarreaux

ABRICOTS

Musque Abricot
Ordinary great bearer

Orange Abricot
Bish: of Lond:* Abricot, *Fullham*

PEACHES

Magdalen { white / red

Bourdin
Mignon
Admirable
Montaban
Rambullion
Morello
Musque Violet
Newington
Syon-peach

Orleans
Alberge, s^r: H: Capel, Sheens*
Alberge, y^e *Small yellow*
Elruge Nectarine: *excell^t*
Belle Chervreuse
Persique
Murry Nectarine: & *yellow*
Red Roman Nectarine
White Nutmeg
Almond Violet
Savoy Malacotan: *very lasting*

VINES

Frontinaque { white / blew

Early-*blew*
Muscat-*black*
Morillon
Muscat *white*

Shasellas
Cluster *grape*
Parsley *grape*
Greate Verjuice
Corinth Grape

PLUMS

Perdrigon { *white* / *Blew*

Primordial
Reyne *Claud*
Mirabel
White-*Nutmeg*

Damasque violet
Date *plum*
Damazcene
Damson { *white* / *black*
Chesson

peare-plum ⎰ *white*
⎱ *Black*
Pescod
Prune *de L Isle vert*

Imperial *plum*
Bullas ⎰ *white*
⎱ *Black*
June *plum*

FIGGS

The White *Scio*   purple   Blew

GOOSE-BERRIES

The greate Amber
Chrystal

Red
Black ⎱ Gooseberry
Transparent

CORINTHS

White   Red

BERBERIES

without-stones: & others

RASPRIS

White   Red

STRAWBERRIES

Verginian   Wood strawberies
Great-White

Now of all these Fruite-trees which I have named for pomp and
variety; the very best are those undernamed, almost all the others
hardly worth the Curiosity: so as to be well stored with these few
may suffice for a most usefull plantation, preferrable to any other:

viz:

APPLES

Golden pepin   Hervey   John
Kentish   Russet

PEARES

Blanquet		Bueree	
Robin		Verte longue	Autum
Rousslet	Summer	Bergamot	
Rosati		Vergolat	
Sans-pepin		Chasseraque	
Jargonel		St. Michael	Winter
		St. Germain	
		Ambret	

PEACHES

Maudlin	White / red	Chevreuse
		Ramboullet
Sion		Musque
Minion		Admirable: late

OF Yᴱ PAVIES OR HARD PEACHES &c

Newington

Nutmeg	white & brown	forward	Persian / Violet Musqe	forward

OF NECTARINES

The Murry   The Elruge
French: of which 2 sorts,
   one round, whilst the other
   longish.

PLUMS

St. Julian		Q. Mother
Catharin		Sheen-plum
White & Blew	Perdrigon	Chestom

ABRICOTS

Lang^{dque} Masculin   Bi. of London
Brussels—standard

VINES

Chasselas (1) the best sort of
    ye white muscadin; tis cal'd
    here ye pearle-Grape
The Currand or Common
    black
Parsley
White Frontiniac, when it
    ripens excell^t

Arboyse, a small white grape
(i) divers small grapes
    amongst them: excellent:
Burgundy of pale red juice,
    ripens well
Black Muscat or *Dowager*
Grizlin Frontiniac the noblest
    & most ex^t of all the rest

FIGGS

Blew two sorts
That which swells most is
    best

White 2 sorts
one ripe early in July.
The other in September
    ex^t: but rare to be gotten

The Compleate Culture of the
ORANGE &c.
After the Holland Way

Earthing them wth 3 parts of Cow-dung when 2 y^rs old to one p^t of Tanners' stuff taken out of the botome of the Tan-pit,* mixed for all sorts of Greenes, w^thout the addition of any other Earth. Cow-dung well rotted or good under-pasture earth is to me better than dug. Planting w^thout any stones,[1] sticks or dung at ye bottome of their Cases, never cutting the rootes, but when too big for the boxes remove them into larger by a size, which should be don every 3 yeares if the tree grow prosperously. If weake, upon removing, set them under glasse Covers 1 foote in length & 4 over, let downe 4 foote into ye ground.

Sometimes also in the hot-bed is good to make trees that are weake, strike roote & some have given them a milk diet, diluted wth a portion of water discreetely applied, not too long but as the plant is affected, & you perceive it to amend. House y^r Oranges about Mich: & take them not out 'til mid Aprill,*[2] water them if they shoote wth warme water, putting 4 Gallons to 20 to render it blood-warme: If the leaves flag, give them a little water, but at no time *wet* either leaves or stem: Never water in Summer, but wth water inso-lated:* Spring & pump-water, most pernicious, as also shaded pond water: All cold & noysomeness hurts them.*

Pruning & cutting of the tops, when the shoote above 5 Inches at the beginning of Aprill is good.

Inoculat about the end of March, as you do peaches about Mid-somer: The stock should be of 3 years age budded with 2 buds on each side opposite, within 3 inches of the ground.

Never house y^r Trees in misty or rainy weather.

---

[1] this I think not so well, & therefore something should be layd for ye passage of the water.

[2] The most secure season for the exposing *Orang-Trees* &c is not before the Mulbery-Tree buds & begins to sprout.

Take off y^r Earth in Mid-May from the cases to the sides of them for an Inche deepe, and put cow-dung of a yeare old in the place, covering it over with the same mould: Do this also about later end of July to refresh & nourish, as well as to keepe them coole, never cover them wth Mosse or any other thing.

Sow the seeds of Sevial Oranges about the beginning of March in the same Earth as above mentioned, in small pots, put 6 seedes in a pot & plunge them in the hot-bed, as you do Tuberose: this for 2 moneths & then put them into a fresh hot-bed about beginn^g of May for these orange-potts: Thus order'd they will shoote above a foote from the seed before ye Winter.

Cases & Tubbs should be of 3 sizes, the first of 16 Inch. The 2^d of 2 foote, the 3^d 2 foote & 8 Inches from outside to outside, & of a square forme, unlesse Tubbs: let their feete support them 4 Inches from the ground.

Draw y^r Trees out of the old case when you at any time change (by first loosning the Earth from the sides) with a pully, tying a broad horse girth at the end of the rope, to prevent galling the trees.

Shut not ye Orangerie unlesse in moist & rainy or foggy weather or East or North wind untill it actually freezes a Cloath in the house; & unlesse it freezes, let the house be open all night even in Winter, as well as Autumn or Spring. If it freezes a little, shut onely the glasse windows. If hard, shut the wooden shutts also: But when by continuance of frost, the shutters being close, the Trees grow musty: make fire in the stove, & open all the windows for 3 or four houres in midd day. Then shut up all close againe, continuing y^r fire, but without renewing it; onely make one fire at night, wh. will hold for the whole 24 houres.

The Conservatories in Holland are of Timber, boarded both within & without, a foote in thicknesse, or rather distance fill'd be-tweene wth sawdust, ramm'd in when dry, & so also all the Tops & Cover, a foote thick on ye Ceiling. The Roofe shelves back-ward, at w^t distance you think convenient: Glasse windows without, wooden-shutters within.

Generall & Use-full Observations
for the well-keeping
of a
GARDEN NURSERIE

T H E very first thing a *Gardner* is to provide, is a *Nursery*, both for *Trees*, *plants* & *Flowers* &c, for which end, let there be an Aker of good Ground divided into five parts, and well defended by pale or Wall: that is 1. for Fruite Trees: 2. Evergreenes, 3. Flowers & rare plants & shrubs, 4. Forest Trees, 5. Hot-bed, & to make trials.

Of these, let the largest part be for Fruit-trees, which should be divided into Beds for seedling stocks, and to remove the stocks into at farther distances in order to Graffing, and untill they be transplanted. Reserve the shady moist part of the Nursery for Layers: Whatever you sow or plant, observe to do it in even Lines.

❧ 1. In the Fruite-tree Nursery These stocks are proper for the Severall kinds

Apples	Sow a bed of Apple-Kirnels, such as are to be had from those who presse Apples for Cyder: dry them, or wash off the pulp, & then clense & dry them with a warme coarse cloth, and so they will be fit for sowing.
Peare	Sow another Bed of peare kirnells.
Cheries	Sow another Bed of Black-Cherry-stones, Morello, or Black-heart, or small bitter early cherry stones.
Peaches	Sett a Bed of peach-stones.
Plums	A Bed of peare-plum-stones, the white plum is best: also the black Damson-stone: and blak-peare-plum.
quinces	One range of the succkers of the Portugal Quince, which you may raise in aboundance from an old tree cut neere the ground, nipping the branches.
Figs	One rang for Figgs.
Medlars	One range of the white-thorne for Medlars.

94

Mulberies	One Range trunchions* of Mulberies, and Layers.
Vines	One or two Ranges for Vines.
Corinths	Others for Corinths & Gooseberries: Berberies.
Goosberies	

Some Ranges for Woodbynds, Jassmines & a bed for Sweete-bryer, sewed of berrys, ripe & clensed, a bed for Hawes &c: the berrys clensed.

Notes for

THE NURSERIES

THE Ground for the Nurseries should first be Trenched, well picked & clensed from weedes, stones and trash: and note that without a Nursery of your owne, you shall never have good fruite from the Gardiners: Graff therefore of onely such fruit as you have either tasted, or received from skillfull friends.

Your Nursery must be kept exactly cleane from Weedes, also somewhat moist in hot weather by laing fearn or the like stuff upon the earth, but so as often to stir it least it contract mustinesse.
Also give the ground an halfe digging or stirring once every 4 moneths.

Make it not over rich.

After two yeares from the Seede, remove and plant them in lines, at two foote distance, where they are to be Grafted when fit, & to remaine til they be transplanted.

Trim, and prune seedlings, as you see occasion, that they may prove smooth & even, & shoote upright: choose all seedes from the lustiest plants, & best bearers. Sow no sort of seedes too-deepe, 'tis sufficient if they be covered, and secur'd from birds & poultrie, Mice &c.

Defend early sown-seedes from cold, the later from heate. Sow not too thick, but with an even & discreete hand, kept allways in a direct motion.

Sow ever in dry-weather, and water not 'til a day or two after.

Remember to clense the chery-stones from their pulp before you sow them.

Figs will be rais'd of layers & cuttings, as also Mulberies.

Plums, peares &c: stocks, may be taken from the suckers of plum & peare trees, & planted in the Nursery.

Nurserie Ever-greens

Cypresse	A Bed for Cypresse seede, or in wooden Cases to be removed into the Beds, when halfe a foote high.
Savine	A Bed layd with Savine slips supplys for Cypresse, & resist all frosts whatever.
Alaternus	A Bed for Alaternus seede.
Phillyrea	A Bed for each sort of *Phillyreas* seedes.
Firr	A Bed for Firrs Seedes.
Pine	A Bed for pine-kirnells, which should be set like beanes: Also Ilix, Cork, Cedar &c.
Yew	A Bed for Yew berries; clensed & washed, dried.
Holly	A Bed for Holly-berries, washed, clensed & dried.
Bayes	A bed of Bay-berries, and so for all other Greenes to be raised of seede.
Juniper	A Bed for Juniper-berries: &c.
Pyracanth	A Bed for pyracanth: Laurell &c.
Laurell	

And beds reserved to plant all these into at farther distances, as they become fit to remove.

Layers	In this Nurserie are to be disposed, all your Layers,
Cuttings	and Cuttings of Laurell, Yews, Firrs and all other Evergreenes produc'd of Layers, and Cuttings.

Note that slips & cuttings layd in moist ground & water'd often will take roote of almost all sorts of ever-greens.

Notes for

THE EVERGREENE NURSERIES

D RY-SEEDES, as Myrtils &c, may be steeped in warme-milk, or
water, a little dunged, or without; but let them not remaine 'til
they become sower.

All sorts of seedlings, whether Ever-greens, or others, are
carefully to be defended from Winds, scorching sun, and hard
frosts, and have some fine-mould seifted among them to refresh &
establish their rootes as they spring up, 'til they are able to be drawn
& removed into the second beds.

Cleane dry & sweete straw, is best to cover seedlings: but it
should be now and then stirred-up, & refreshed to preserve them
from mustinesse & vermine.

Ever-greenes should not be removed & transplanted till the bud
begins to shew & put out; as about *Aprill:* but they may be success-
fully transplanted also towards the later-end of July, if the season be
anything moist.

The Illix & ever-greene Oake (otherwise hardy enough) will
not well endure transplanting; unless planted of acorns & not removed or else grafted upon an Oake-stock, & so may be removed,
and makes rare hedges, & ex^t in Groves of ever-greens.

Nursery Flowers, and rarer shrubs

I N this quarter of the Nurserie, you should raise in their distinct
beds; all sorts of Flowers, which spring & are increased from
Seedes, Bulbs or other Rootes, that continue, as

Tulips	Narcissus	Peonie
Polyanthos	Iris	Martagon
Anemonies	Crocus	Crown-Imperial
Carnations	Hepatica	Sancianella
Ranunculus's	Junquills	Auricula
Jacynths	Stock-Gilly-flo:	

And whatsoever are not Annuals, that they may be ready to supply the flower Gardens & bordures, and be gathered for Bough-pots,* & adorning the house.

Let also a part of this ground be for the raising and laying the choicer shrubs &c: as

Jasmine
Hony-suckle, severall kinds
Syringa
Althea Frutex
Sweete-brier

Carobe
Roses, the severall sorts
Arbor-Judae, Mezerion:
Spirea, Paliurus & the like

Notes for
THE FLOWER NURSERIE

L ET Carnation-seedes, abide in their pods 'til ye Frosts.

Nursery of Forest-Trees

IN this quarter, which may be as large as the Fruite Nursery, should be sowed, and planted in distinct Beds, all sort of Trees fit for Groves, Walkes and Avenues: such as Oakes, best Akorns sowed in lines at small distance like Beanes; or if you have very large ground, at 3 foote, for their better clensing, dressing and removall.

Elmes are raised by succkers.
Ashes by sowing their Keys, so also Sycomore.
Maple
Beech, by sowing the Mast.
Whitchin Elme, sowing the Berries.
Service-Tree, Berries.
Lime-Tree-Berries, or layers & Cuttings.

| Wall-nut Chess-nutt | Virginian Wall-nut setting the Nutts: by Nutts & Layers as well. |

Poplar Trunchions* & Succkers.

Horn-beame Suckers.

Black-cherry-stones.

Platanus, succkers, in moist ground { Tzina^r

Haisell-nutts: Filberts [white { Occidental

[red

A larg-bed sown with *Haws* &c

Of all which you should have beds & Ranges furnished for Transplanting, as they are in stature upon all occasions.

Nursery for The Hot-Bed

THE Hot-Bed should be in the warmest corner of the Nurserie,
well secured from the weather by wall, pale, or reede-pannells
of five-foote high or more.

Herein you raise all your choicer seedes, both for fruite, flower,
and many exotiq plants & Trees, under covers of Glasse frames, or
Bells, Matresses &c. 'til they are fit to be transplanted such as

Melons	Nasturtium Ind
Gourds	Marvell of Peru &c
Cucumers	Oranges } Seedes
Amaranths	Limons }
Tuberoses	Myrtle-berries

Notes for
THE HOT-BED NURSERIE

THE seedes of Oranges & Lemmons should be sown in potts, or
cases, that they may be carried into the Greene house to winter:
so also *Myrtils*, and all others, which indure not the frost.

Stocks Proper for
GRAFTING
each sort of Fruite-Trees

Apples	*Apples* for *standards* are best graffed on the Apple-Kernel, or Crab stock.
	Apples for *Dwarfs*, on the paradise Kernell-stock,* which are best raised from the sweete Apple, or of the pearemaine Kernell graffed on the Quince-stock: or by Layers from the Swede-Apple.
Peares	*Peares* for standards, graffe on the peare-kirnell stock.
	Peares for *Dwarfs*, upon the succker of the Portugall-quince.
Cherries	*Cherries* for *standards* on the Common black Cherry-stone-stock.
	Cherries for *Dwarfes*, & the wall, on the stock of the Morella Cherry, the Black-heart, or small bitter early cherry.
Peaches	*Peaches* Inoculate on the peach, or plum stock.
	If you graff upon the Almond, the Almond stone should be set in the place where you will have your peach to remaine, for the Almond stock dos not thrive if removed.
Nectarine	*Nectarine*, bud upon the peach or peare plum stock.
Abricots	*Abricotts*,[3] best on the white-peare-plum stock, also on the Almond. These do not so well upon the Abricot stock from the stone.
Plum	*Plums*, upon the plum-stock.
Medlar	*Medlar* Graft on the White-thorne, or Quince stock neere the ground: It beares the second yeare.
Oranges	Oranges and Lemons bud on the wild stock of the Sevil
Lemons	orange seede at fouer-yeares groth.

---

[3] Sr Wm Temple says Abricot does best on a peach-stock.

Notes concerning
STOCKS

L ET peach-stones be crack't with an Hammer, easily don without prejudice to the *kernel*, setting them sideways on a stone, the shell will divide in two & let out the *Kernel*, which place at side-long or set in good mould, they will in one yeare be fit to *bud*, & advance two or three, above other stocks: This is a greate, but profitable seacret: & known by few.

Some kinds of peaches produce excellent Fruit from the stone without Graffing; as *peach de pau*.

Grafting

Apples	*Apples*, *peares*, & *Cherries*, are best grafted in the Cleft,
Peares	or by Whipstock* beginning in January 'til the end of
Cherries	February.
Peach	*Peaches*, *Abricots*, *Nectarines*, and all delicate Wall-fruit,
Abricot	Inoculate in August, or July, as you find the stock proud
Nectarine	with sap.
Oranges	*Oranges* are securely budded in *August*, as well as March
	upon stocks of 3 or 4 yeares growth.

Notes for
GRAFFING &c

E VER take your *Cyon* from a goodly & plentifully bearing Tree, for if the Tree have not borne, or but poorely, it will be long 'ere your Cyon come to produce any Fruit.

M. de la *Quintine** affirmes, that the very best season to graff *Aples* in the *Cleft*, is any time before *Aprill*, so it be a little before they *blossom* & shoote.

TRANSPLANTING

FIRST dig the pitts, some weekes (or were it a whole yeare the better) before you transplant, that the ground may be well aired and mellow'd, and in doing this, fling out the first spade bit deepe upon one side of the pit (because it is ever the sweetest mould) and the second spit, on the contrary side: and when you have trimmd your tree, place its roote upon a small heape of mould, just at the center thereof: & then spreading the tender rootes equaly, cast in the first, & best mould you flung out, & then the other to fill the pit, shaking and gently pressing it with your foote, to fix the tree and lastly, with your hand, leaving a little heape or ridge of Earth just to the stemm, forme a small Trench at convenient distance, to containe the waterings, so as to carry the vertue thereoff to the rootes, and not wash the mould from it, as watering at the bare stem dos certainely do. Be carefull to set the Tree upright, and to plant it to the same point of the wind it first grew, which you may distinguish by chalking that part of the stem, before it was removed out of the Nursery.

Be sure to stake and establish your Tree against winds, & fence it from Cattell, yet so as not to gall it.

If the season prove dry, lay some halfe rotted littier upon the Earth, so as not to touch the stem, which stuff must frequently be stirred, or renewed to prevent mustinesse: It may be quite removed in moist weather, & applied againe in winter frosts, according to discretion.

Plant when the wind is south or west.

Plant very little deeper than it grew before.

You cannot plant too early in the Autumn, all such trees as loose their leaves in Winter.

But plant not Ever-greenes 'til the beginning of Aprill, when you perceive them begin to shoote, or at St. James' tide* towards the later end of July, especialy if the season be somewhat moist. For the scorching sunn in March is worse than Winter-frost, especialy for newly Transplanted Ever-greenes (Oranges &c.) by reason also of the piercing easter & northern continual blasts. Wherefore it is good to place your tender shrubs under the protection of some hedge, thro' which the warmth of the sunn may dart comfortably, and so let them remaine a fortnight or more not exposing them to the wide aire but by degrees from the time they are brought out of the Greene-house.

Greate growne Trees (Forest, or other) which one would Transplant, may almost at any time & season of the yeare be removed with successe, by plunging the rootes in the mould made papp, like well wrought mortar, and so kept steady and continualy moist.

Rosemary slip'd never recovers the scar: It is best therefore to cut it some distance from the stemm, about flowring time, & not in Aprill.

When Oranges have their leaves cru[m]pl'd up, it shewes the rootes are matted: therefore you must search it, and trim the rootes, or inlarge the case, and give fresh mould.

In Transplanting the Orange, Lemmon & all other case & Tubb Trees, place them in rich mould taken from under the first Turfe of a pasture field a little loamy: & carefully lay store of lime stone, shards of earthen ware, shells, pibbles* & brush wood so as to make passage for the waterings, that it corrupt not the Rootes.

Plant *Amomum Plinii* almost all in dung, for it else exceedingly impoverishes the mould.

Notes for

TRANSPLANTING

B E curious not to suffer any greate stones, grasse rootes or weedes to be mingled with the mould; least the rootes lying too hollow, corrupt & rott the Tree.

The greater the distance the better.

Many trees wth but a competent burden of fruit better than to be over laden.

Vines do best in a sharp gravell on a South exposure & far from shade, in airy & expos'd places.

WATERING

T H E best water is from Rivers, and running streames, so it be not too leane and cold: That which is allways standing or shaded corrupts & is not good: But the water of ponds, and wherein cattel soile is excellent; but *Raine water* has no fellow: If Water be too thin & poore, inrich it with the dung of sheepe or pidgeons; but hanging a Basket full of it into the water, & letting it steepe: Cow-dung is also profitable: Water over dunged brings a black smutt on orange leaves &c.

If you be necessitated to use cold raw spring water, let it stand a while in the sunn; and therefore keepe allways ready an Infusing Tub or Vessell: 4 gallons of heated water, qualifies 20 gallons to milkwarm.

In the Spring time water in the mornings, in Summer, the evenings: In Winter be sparing of watering; & ever let it be a little warmed.

Water gently, not hastily, or in a greate streame, for it onely hardens the ground, & not penetrate: therefore imitate the natural showers.

Never cast the water upon plants newly planted, nor on flowers, as Auricula, Hepatica, primeroses, or other fibrous plants, but at some convenient distance; so as to moisten the earth about the Roots, and not wett the leaves; for it makes them apt to scorch.

In Winter waterings, the water somewhat warmed, poure it on by gentle degrees, not all at once.

Signes of want of water, are the extreame crumpling, & fall of the leafe.

Oranges are not to be watred, after removing into fresh-mould, but by little & little at a time & so as the earth may never remaine quite dry.

Oranges & *Lemmons* &c: require rather frequent than much watring, as every third, or fourth day in Summer: Let the water be pretty rich not quite raw.

Myrtils and *Amomum plinii* require continual watring, and inriching with dung.

Pome-Granade care not for so rich water nor so much but to make it flower.

Orange & the like plants, & indeede all other trees, grow pale & white when they are too much waterd. Shrivell & crumple when they are in want of it.

Fruit-Trees, which are planted by Walles, as *peaches*, *Abricots*, &c: are best watred by pouring it in at holes, made halfe a foote, or more from the stem (but not so deepe as to wound the rootes) with a wooden stake pointed. Make up of good rich watre, especially during the time the Fruite is forming: and at other dry seasons: You may leave the short stakes in the holes, & take them out when you have watred, or else fill the holes againe with mould.

Thus may you feede *Vines* with blood,* so it be sweete, & mingle it with a little water.

Strawberrys should be Watered aboundantly or not at all.

Aloës, cannot be watered too much in summer nor too little in winter: And when it dos then require it, expose it rather in the aire, so as no Raine fall upon it; this will fill and plump the plant without watering; which in that season will kill it: then house it againe.

Layers of all sorts & cuttings, whether in plaine earth, or in potts & Cases should continualy be kept moist and shaded. This is best don by narrow longish piece of flannell, or other clowt,* so placed in a vessell, that a corner of it hanging over, may continualy be dropping upon the mould, not the plants.

Notes for

WATERING

Oranges &
Lemons

Oranges, Lemmons &c to be but moderatly watred when first brought out of the Greene-house, & after new earthing but by degrees, & so kept rather moist, than in mudd: this may be don every second evening also in the heate of Summ:
Seldome watring, & not save in extreame want, in winter, and then let the water be made tepid over the fire.

PRUNING

THE principal Art of a Gardner, consists in pruning: for which observe these Rules:

Learn first to know the bearing buds from the leafe buds,* & those which will be fruite-buds next yeare; sparing all the fruite budds of standard Apples, Peares & wall-fruite with discretion.

Cut allwayes above the bud slanting that the water may passe off, & let the kniffe be very sharp, that you leave no raggs.

If you take off an whole Branch, cutt it close to the stemm, that the wound may heale the sooner & a new bark succeede.

Those budds, which either put forth just between the stemm and the wall, or immediately before, and opposite to the wall (in wall fruite) rubb off, sparing onely the side branches: This is onely to be observed in wall-fruit, that the branches may be spread the better.

Orange-Trees may be aboundantly cleansed to forme their heads, but be more sparing in *Lemon-Trees* yet take off the stragling weake shootes which deforme the head, & impaire the whole.

The *Pome-Granade* delights to be often purged.*

Cut away the principal top-bows of fruite-trees that they may spread, & make beautifull heads, and not run-up too hastily, which is no good signe.

Take quite away the Water-bows, which are those that grow low-est, are shaded, and are commonly smooth without budds: Cutt them close.

Where you would have no more to sprout, or put forth againe, rub, or cutt the budds off at *Midsumer*.

To make the *peach* or *Abricot* spread & garnish & produce fruit, cutt smooth-off the next unbearing branches.

Clense your Fruite-Trees of all succkers carefully; for they rob the Trees: most of them (if don in Winter) may be planted for stocks in the Nursery, as *plums, peares, Quinces* &c.

The oftner you cutt, and clip off the old-wood of *Vines, Raspris, Roses* (which allwayes beare on the fresh-sprouts of the same spring) the better: Yet this work neede not be don above once in two-yeares.

Cut away some branches of the *Monethly Rose*, close after the first bearing.

The oftner you cutt & clip sweete-herbs (as *Thyme, Lavender, Sage* &c) the more they will thrive.

Sage being clipp'd spring & Autumn, will make it continue long, & faire.

Clip-away all strings of *strawberries* 'til they blossome.

Prune *Spanish Jasmine* within an Inch of the stem, but never before it beginns to put forth:

Spare the top branches and buds of *Wall-nuts*, *Figs* and like pithy trees: & when you do prune them, let it be before they grow too woody & hard, and not til after the greate frosts are past.

No choice greenes should be pruned or cutt, till the begin of themselves to bud.

Clip not the greene hedges of *Cypresse, Box, Yew*, and the like 'til the first raines in Aprill or Spring.

Anemonies, and some other like flowers, should also be prund, where they matt too thick, (& so Gilly-flowers & Carnations) to have faire flowers.

The best season for pruning generaly, are the hard woody-trees before Christmas, & as long as the cold continues; the tender Fruite, such as *Abricots, peaches* &c, not 'til *February*.

Vines should be pruned all the Winter, before any sap rises, least the bleede too death.

Clense all Fruite Trees from what too much hinders the sunn & aire, especialy, within the bodies of standards and dwarfe trees, which keepe hollow like a Bell.

In summer pruning vines & wall fruite, expose it not naked to the sunn, but discreetely thin the leaves where there is occasion; for too much baring, shrivells and exhausts the fruite.

Notes for

PRUNING

IN pruning vines, cut so close as to resemble a ragged-staff onely not above 2 or 3 eyes or buds, upon the bearing-branches is enough, & the lower the vine, & fewer the branches, the better the Grapes.

Suffer the Vines w^h you plant twixt peaches & wall fruit, not to spread above 3 or 4 foote in widness, but keep them like pilasters.*

| *Soile* | DUNGING | *Composts* |
| *Mould* | | *Dressing* |

HAVE allways ready prepar'd severall Composts, mixed with natural pasture earth, a little loamy: skreene the mould, and mingle it discreetely with rotten Cow-dung; not suffering it to abide in heapes too long, but be frequently turning & stirring it, nor let weedes grow on it; & that it may be moist & sweete, & not wash away the salts, it were best kept & prepared in some large pit, or hollow place which has a hard bottom and in the shade.

Horse-dung is commonly too hot, unlesse in very cold grounds; & if it be not exceedingly rotted, it produces couch grasse, mallows, bean bind & other weedes, the seedes where of horses swallow downe without chewing, and cast them out whole againe.

It is starke naught for *Aspargus* & *strawberries*, unlesse to cover in winter, & it be very cleane raked off at spring.

The best use of *Horse dung* (fresh made) is to raise the Hot-bed.

Cows-Dung well rotted, not too dry, is best for hot, dry, leane & sandy grounds; It should be gathred in the *Autumn*, and saved in heapes, to be broken and mingled afterwards.

Pidgeons & dung of poultry is excellent when cold, and well tempered & rotted with mould: Use it at the beginning of Winter: especialy for *Aspargus* & strawberries: but being applied to anything, being hot and newly made, it burnes, and kills all it touches.

Pidgens and sheepes dung infused in Water is excellent for Oranges, choice greenes, & indeed any Fruite.

The Scouring of muddy-ponds, & where cattell drinke & stand, is good for all plants.

The scowring of privies & sinkes so well dried and made sweete, well mixed with fresh earth so as to retaine no heady scent, is above all other excellent for *Oranges* & the like choice fruits.

The bottomes of wood-stacks, & where fagotts have been placed, well rotted & mixed with some loame and pasture-earth, is good for all choice plants, and most fit to sow *Auricula, stocks* & the like seedes in.

Abricots & *peaches* &c require rather rich mould than over dunged.

Figs, more delight in dry ground, than much dung; the best for them is pidgeons, & poultries.

The Beds of Sweete-herbs should be new moulded every second yeare at least, & that with rich, rather than over much dunged earth.

Poverty, & leanesse of Ground, causes plants to run hastily to seede.

Sweepings of the house, and buck-ashes,* excellent for purselan.

Prepare all Dung & Composts before winter, that it may be frosted, & become short, sweete & mellow.

The worme-casts scraped from the Rolling of Carpet grasses & sweepings, is excellent mould, and so is the fresh raisings of Moll-hills.

Mould made of the rottings of weedes, being put to any garden use, is apt to produce the same weedes againe.

Notes for
DUNGING
Mould & Soile

L ET the Nursery be leaner than the soile into which you trans-plant, else yʳ Tree will not thrive nor beare so soone by much.

For peaches & Grapes the best is a sandy sharp gravel, nor is it material the mould should be very deepe, yet it must be harty & inriched.

The richer soile is for Abricots, plums, peares, Figs; yet the more sandy the better: yet a little eye of loame is good in all: especially for flowers.

Wet & moist quite naught for Fruit.

The size of Fruite may be faired on rich ground, but not the goodnesse.

Lay bare all winter, such trees as do not beare well.

WEEDING,
HOWING, ROLLING, &c

Above all, be carefull not to suffer weedes (especially *Nettles, Dendelion, Groundsill,* & all downy-plants) to run up to seede; for they will in a moment infect the whole ground: wherefore, whatever work you neglect, ply weeding at the first peeping of ye Spring. Malows, Thistles, Beane-bind, Couch, must be grubb'd up and the ground forked & dilligently pick'd.

Whatever you How-up, rake-soone away off the ground, for most weedes will run to seede, and some rootes fasten againe in the ground:

The halfe-spit digging among Fruite-Trees, and bordures, & rough stirring, is much better than weeding.

Suffer no weedes, nor strawbery plants, violets, or whatever is to continue, to be set within two foote of your fruite-trees: unlesse for young lettuce &c.

Ground, walkes & Carpet grasse is best Rolled after soaking raines: the worme-casts pared off becomes good mould: These Carpet grasse walkes & Greenes, should also be sometimes beaten in moist seasons with a broad Rammer* where the grasse rises in Tufts, & the ground uneven.

Mould made of rotted weedes, infects the ground againe where it is used.

VERMINE & DISEASES

THE best remedy against Garden earth-wormes, is well to water the places infected with water wherein {pot soape}-ashes* have been dissolved, & well stirred. This is excellent for Carpet, & Bowling-greenes, and produces a thick & verdant grasse: lime newly from the Kiln* dos rather better; put it into a tub of water & stirr it, a bushell or two, watring carpets or walkes wth a watring pot; it need not be too thick.

Gather wormes at night, in Spring, & Summer, after gentle raines; also snailes, which commonly lurke under the leafe, a little above the fruite, they have begun; but take not that fruite away, for they will then begin afresh.

Soote Ashes strawed about Tree rootes, so as not to touch the stemm; prevents the crawling up of snailes, and so dos the sweepings of refuse *Tabacco*.*

Place bottles of Beare, or wide mouth'd glasses folded in, and sweetened with a little hony or suggar, for Flies, Wasps, Ants &c: Bees will not indure the smell of Beere; but in sweetned water they will drowne themselves.

Set up hoofes for Eare-wiggs, & place Canes and Kexes* cut about a foote length, amongst the branches of your choice wall fruite: shaking the Vermine out (which come there for shadow) at noone; ply this whilst the Fruite is ripning.

Cutt quite off the branch or twig, on which *Caterpillars* make their webbs, or else burne them with a torch, & do this early, before disclosure.

Molles should be kill'd & Water Ratts, in March, when they breede, & September.

Take *Mice* about Christmas, & before, with Trapps, and Sampsons-posts:* Or lay baites of greene glasse powdered with as much beaten coprus* mixed with coarse hony, 'til it become a past, & lay it about their haunts.

Birds are frighted away, with feathers stuck in the ground, or made to play in the wind on a line.

Poultrie & Catts are to be hinder'd from scraping & basking by laying brambles, & holy-bushes on the beds.

Notes for
VIRMINE & DISEASES

R EMEMBER to cut away all rotten leaves from Cabbages, least they infect the earth and aire.

A *Tulip* or other roote being cankered is cured by putting the bulb immediately into the earth againe, before it become dry.*

Tulips & other flowers that peepe early, may be secur'd from the frosts by strewing sawdust thinly over the bed, or laying on sweete mosse.

Unslack'd lime* put into Water as is directed [for] pot-ashes, dos the same effect ag^t wormes: A bushell to a greate Tubfull, stirred till white &c.

Slugs & black un-shelled snailes, are destroy'd, by strewing lime dry upon the plants: The most of all infest olitory & kitchin gardens.

A plaster of *Diachylon** is good to unite any bark, which having been flaw'd off from the wood, be adapted to it againe.

TRYALS, IMPROVEMENTS & ORNAMENTS

Medlar:	Graft a Medlar on the white-thorn or quince neere ye Earth it will beare the 2^d or 3^d yeare.
Laureoli:	Inoculate the Laurall on a Black-cherry-stock for a standard.
Roses:	Inoculate all sorts of Roses early in Spring, upon the same stock.
	Try if the Rose will take upon the Almond, to produce early Flowers, or being budded on the Holly, phillyrea, or Yew, bring a greene flower.
Apples Peares:	Graffe severall sorts of Apples, & peares on the same stock, for Curiosity.
Orange:	Graffe an *Orange* seedling on the Quince-stock.
Fig:	Graffe a Fig into a peare stock; as the Bergamot.

Melon:	Set a Melon plant into a pumkin or Gourd, being brought up in the hot bed at the Spring.
Coliflowre	Plant a Coliflowre in the stemm of an old Cabbage, the head cutt off & kept down.
Fig:	Before Winter bend downe the twiggs of the fig-tree which have small greene fruite on them, & cover them quite over with earth, & release them in the spring & they will ripen before any others: Mr. Berckley.*
Tulip:	Sow Tulip-seede shallow, & under the bed lay a slate, broad stone or board under the Earth about 2 Inches, & the second yeare plant the young seedelings, do the same the 3ᵈ yeare, sinking the slat or board about an inch lower, & they will beare the 3ᵈ yeare this keepes the bulbe from sinking, which else they will yearely do, which hinders their bearing for many yeares: Ch: Howard.*

Graffe the Ilex on a oaken stock.

Barrenesse Recovering witherd fruit	As where a Chery-tree or other fruit withers, by being too much shaded, or scorched &c. About a fortnight before the Cherrys begin to redden considerably, or so soone as they do change colour: Bare the Rootes, by making an hole or trench aboute them, & give them a Gallon of Water morning & evening during a fortnight before they come to rednesse, or make an hole onely about the tree, & treat it as the other: the successe was that the fruit which was apt to be wither'd & not come to perfection filled very plump & was exᵗ: Another such Tree let alone had none of its fruite ripe. This was practis'd on a May-Cherry, which was shaded 4 months 'til the beginning of March. *Dr Merret.**
Uniting Barke	A plaster of *Diachylon* is good to lay over the bark which may accidentaly be stripp'd from a Tree, the same (or perhaps any fresh bark of the same species) being adapted to the excorticated place.

Wall-Fruite planted at Wotton in the Flower gardens, 1700*

Morello-chery
Duke-cherry
Blew-perdrigon plumm
Dutch Abricot
White Magdalen-peach
Winter Bergamot peach
White-Figg
Montauban peach

Duke Chery
Bonn-Chrestien Winter
La Marquaise peare
Brigniole round Nectarine
Peach Admirable
St Germaines peare
Newington peach
White Figg

Directions for the
Gathering, Ordering, & Dressing of
SALADS for the TABLE:
according to their Seasons

A SALADE *is a Composition of Olitory Herbs Blanched or Greene, of several species: Thus prepared & Selected:*

BLANCH'D HERBS

Tyed-up to blanch	1 Endive
Earthed up	2 Succory
Earthed up	3 Sellerie
Earthed-up	4 Fennel Sweete
Earthed-up	5 Rampions
Tyed-up to blanch	6 Roman lettuce
Ty'd up	7 Cosse lettuce
Close together	8 Silesian lettuce
so Blanch of themselves	9 Cabbage lettuce

GREENE HERBS UNBLANCH'D

The leaves all of a fine midling size	1 Lop Lettuce
	2 Corne salad
	3 Purselan
Leaves next the seede-leaves and the next to them	4 Cresses broad & curl'd
	5 Spinach
Gather only the fine young leaves wth the first shooting	6 Sorrell—Greene-land
Seede leaves only	7 Radish
Seede leaves & next them only	8 Cresses
Onely the seede leaves	9 Turneps
	10 Mustard
	11 Scurvy-grasse

The young leaves after the seede-lings	12	Chervill-sweete
	13	Burnet
	14	Rocket Spanish
	15	Parsley
The young shoots & Topps	16	Tarragon
	17	Minths
The young tender leaves & Shoots	18	Sampier
	19	Balame
	20	Red-sage topps
The young tender leaves	21	Shalott & young-onions
	22	Chives
Flowers & bud flower	23	Indian Cresses or *Nasturtium*
Seede leaves & young topps	24	Rampion
	25	Trip-Madame

To Gather them according to their Seasons

JANUARY

Rootes

Of the Blanch'd herbs cultivated as before	10	Rampions
	2	Endive
	5	Succory
	10	Sweete Fenell
	4	Sellarie

FEBRUARY & MARCH

Green herbs

pugil or small handfull of each	Lop-Lettuce
	Lambs Lettuce
Three parts each	Reddish
	Cresses
One part each	Turneps
	Mustard
	Scurvy Grasse
Two parts	Spinach

One part each	Sorell—Greenland
	Sorell—French
One part each	Sweete Chervill
	Burnet
	Rochell
20 large tops	Tarragon
	Balme
One very small part of each	Menth
	Sampier
Very few	Shallots
	Cives

APRILL

Blanched Herbs

2 pugils or small handfulls	Winter cabbage lettuce
	Lop Lettuce
One pugil	Winter Silesian Lettuce
One pugil	Winter Roman Lettuce

MAY & JUNE

Green-Herbs

3 parts of	Radishes
2 parts of	Cresses
A small handfull	Purselan
2 parts of Sorell	Sorell French
One part of	Sampier
Six of	Young Onions
2 parts of	Red-sage tops
One part of each	Parsley
	Indian Cresses
	Crumpen Belgand
	Trip-Madam
	Sweete Chervil
2 parts of	Burnet

Note: That Orange & Lemmon leaves produc'd of seedes, when first come up & very young, are also excellent to mingle with the rest.

JULY & AUGUST

Blanched, Which may	1 part of	Silesian Lettuce
be Eaten by themselves onely	2 part of	Roman Lettuce
Adding some *Nasturtium*	2 parts of	Cosse Lettuce
flowers as before	4 parts of	Cabidge Lettuce

SEPTEMBER

Greene-Herbs by themselves	3 parts of	Cresses
or Mingl'd with the Blanch'd	3 p^ts	of Nasturtium
	Pugil	of Purselan
	Pugil	of Lop Lettuce
	1 pt	of Tarragon
	2 pts	of French Sorell
	2 pts	of Burnet
	1 pt	of Trip-Madame
	2 pts	of Cru[m]pen belgrade

OCTOBER

Blanched	2 rootes if large	Endive	} must be slic'd
	4 if not large	Sellery	

NOVEMBER & DECEMBER

Greene	1 Pugil	Lop Lettuce	
	1 Pugil	Lambs Lettuce	
	3 parts of	Radish	Pick'd
	2 pts of	Cresses	wash'd &
	1 part of	Turneps	clens'd
	1 pt of	Mustard	swung
	2 parts of	Cresses broade	dry
	2 pts of	Spinnach	

Note: That all these sorts are not to be had at ye same season & therefore are they dispos'd into 4 quarters, 3 moneths each.

Note: That *pugil* is as much as one can take up with 3 fingers & the thumb, or 2 or one & the thumb. the same is to be understood by *Part* or Handfull.

Dressing

IN *Octob, Endive* & *Sellery* must be slic'd taking out all the outside hollow green stem, taking off all the out-leaves, & slice in the white, cutting ye Roote & middle into 4 quarters.

Nov: Dec: *Lettuce, Raddish, Cresses,* &c: must be pick'd, wash'd, put into a thin strainer, & swong dry: then shaken together, the Blanch'd & Greene together if you please, or separtely. Because some persons like not so well the blanch'd herbs, as too strong or bitter if eaten severally: others mix *Endive, Succory* & *Rampions* together and the *Sellery* by itselfe, as also the sweete *Fennell.*

Note: That these proportions are sufficient for a table of six or 8 persons lovers of salads. The dishes are garnished wth slices of black-spanish radish & thus have you a salad secundum Artem.*

Dressing & Sauce

FROM *Aprill* to *September,* leave out Horse-Radish & Ginny-pepper. From *October* to *March* Take of cleare unsmelling salade oyle 3 parts, of *Vinegar* or *Orange* juice one part, letting some horse radish steepe in it, straine it in another part of vinegar & bruse a pod of Ginny pepper in it, straine it off also, and add as much of grated Tewksberry mustard* as will cover halfe a crown; then add the juice of a lemmon, a little salt, beate all well together: But put not in the Oyle & Vinegar 'til the salad is to be eaten, & then beate them all together with 2 yolkes of an Egg, boyled somewhat hard, knap'd with a spoon. Cutt all wth a silver knife.

It is best to beate the liquide in an Earthen glaz'd or China-dish, than either silver or pewter, which leaves its tincture in the accid juices of ye limmon & vinegar which must be more or lesse sharp, as the Company please: In a word, The old Recipe is that

A Wise man should gather the Herbs
An Avaricious man fling in ye salt & vinegar:
A prodigal the Oyle.

In the Spring, & Summer months, sow orange & limon seedes, for the young leaves are excellent, to mingle with the rest of ye salade.

The tender tops of Vine-Tendrills, Hopps, & of almost any wholesome plant, compose an excellent salad.

Furnitures* are all hot & spicy herbs; mixed with the more cold & mild, discreetely to temper & give them relish, such as rocket, basil, tarragon, sage tops, &c.

At Wotton has been sowne & planted as follows

Anno 1694. Was plotted & lay'd out an *evergreene Grove* on the west side of the Garden: upon the high wall these fruites, viz: [*not filled in*]

1695/6 March: In the Nursery were sow'd in the North-end Triangular piece, [*diagram omitted*]

Black chery-stone	firr, Norway
Alaternus	silver firr
Giniper	silver firr
Yew	Laburnum
Lawrall	Spanish Broome

METHOD
for the Gardiner of Sayes-Court
or any other with little
alteration

THE Gardiner should walke aboute the whole Gardens every Monday-morning duely, not omitting the least corner, and so observe what Flowers or Trees & plants want staking, binding and redressing, watering, or are in danger; especialy after greate stormes, & high winds and then immediately to reforme, establish, shade, water &c what he finds amisse, before he go about any other work.

Monday	☾ *Walkes—1. Weekes Mowing* ☾
	Early, before the deaw be off in Mowing season, and as his grasse is growne too high (that is, if any daiysie or like appeare) he is to cut the grasse of the greate Court, & roll all the gravell: having rolled also the carpet, the *Saturday* night before, and this Monday evening the upper Terrace & lower.
Tuesday ♂	Mow the upper & Lower Terrace grasse walkes: rolling the grasse of the Fountaine & Greene-house garden grasse with the grasse walkes of both Groves that evening: and Gravell walkes.
Wednesday ☿	Mow the Fountaine & Greene-house Garden, with both the Groves, & Roll in the evening the long middle grasse walk to the Iland.
Thursday ♃	Mow the Middle grasse walk to the Iland: Roll the Broad Gravell-walke, The Holy-hedge, and grove gravell-walkes: & this evening roll the three crosse walkes from the Ortyarde to the Iland moate.
Friday ♀	Mow the three former crosse grasse walkes.

Saturday ♄	Evening, Roll the Bowling Greene: & Court.

The 2d: weekes Mowing

Monday ☽	Begin to Mow the Bowling-greene.
Tuesday ♂	Finish the mowing of the bowling greene.
Wednesday ☿	Roll all the gravell walkes.
Thursday ♃	
Friday ♀	
Saturday ♄	

And thus alternatively may all the Grasse & Walkes be rolled, & cut once a fortnight, with ease: that is the grasse every 15 dayes, & the gravell rolled twice every six dayes.

Weeder: Note that whilst the Gardener rolls or Mowes, the Weder is to sweepe & clense in the same method, and never to be taken from that work 'til she have finished: first the gravell walkes & flower-bordures; then the Kitchin-Gardens; to go over all this she is allowed One moneth every three-moneths, with the Gardiners assistance of the haw, & rough digging; where curious hand-weeding is lesse necessary.

Every fortnight looke on Saturday to your seede and roote boxes, to aire & preserve them from mouldinesse & vermine.

Looke every moneth (the last day of it) & see in what state the Bee-hives are: and every day, about noone if the weather be warme, and the Bees hang out for swarmes; having y^r hives prepar'd & ready dressed.

The Tooles are to be carried into the Toole-house, and all other instruments set in their places, every night when you leave work: & in wett weather you are to clense, sharpen, & repaire them.

The heapes of Dung, & Magazines* of Mould &c: are to be stirred once every quarter, the first weeke.

In Aprill, Mid-August, clip Cypresse, Box, & generally most ever-greene hedges: & closes, as quick-setts.

Prune standard-fruit & Mural Trees the later end of July, & beginning of August for the second spring: Vines in January & exuberant branches that hinder the fruite ripning in June.

1. The Gardner, is every night to aske what Rootes, sallading, garnishing, &c will be used the next day, which he is accordingly to bring to the Cook in the morning; and therefore from time to time to informe her what garden provision & fruite is ripe and in season to be spent.

2. He is also to Gather, & bring in to the House-Keeper all such Fruit of Apples, peares, quinces, Cherrys, Grapes, peaches, Abricots, Mulberies, strawberry, Rasberies, Corinths, Cornelians, Nutts, Plums, & generally all sort of Fruite, as the seasone ripens them, gathering all the windfalls by themselves: That they may be immediately spent, or reserved in the Fruite & store-house.

3. He may not dispose of any the above said Fruite nor sell any Artichock, Cabbages, Aspargus, Melons, strawberries, Rasberies, Wall, or standard & dwarfe fruite, Roses, Violets, Cloves, or any Greenes, or other flowers or plants, without first asking, and having leave of his Master or Mistress; nor till there be sufficient of all garden furniture for the Grounds stock and families use.

4. He is to give his Mistris notice when any Fruites, Rootes, Flowers, or plants under his care are fit to be spent, reserved, cutt, dried, & to be gathered for the still house and like uses, & to receive her directions.

5. He is, when any Tooles are broaken or worn out, to bring the Instrument so unserviceable to his Master and shew it before another be bought.

Let him for all these observations, continualy reade and consult my Gardiners Almanac & Discourse of Earth.*

THE GARDINERS SEASONS

Jan: *January:*
In this moneth Graff in the cleft,* decrease of the Moone;* &
towards the end thereof prune wall fruit, 'til the sap rises briskly,
especialy finish cutting your Vines.

Feb: *February:*
Naile yet & prune: sow all sorts of Kernels, towards yᵉ later end
Melons & rare seedes on the Hot-bed.

Mar: *March:*
Sow Endive, Succory, Chervil, Sellerie, purselan (which you may
also continue sowing all the summer to have tender) leeks,
Beetes, parsneps, salsifix, skirrits, Turneps, &c. and now Cherish
and Earth-up your flowers, and set stakes to the tallest: sow also
lettuce.

Apr: *Aprill:*
Set Artichock-slips, transplant cabages, sow Lettuce, clip hedges, &
greenes; & sow the seedes of all hot sweete-herbs & plants.

May: *May:*
Bring forth of the Greene-house the Oranges, Lemons and most
tender Ever-greenes, trim and refresh them, placing them in shade
a fortnight, by degrees accostuming them to the sunn: sow also
cabbage-seedes, Lettuce, French-beanes, Harricos &c.

June: *June:*
Sow Lettuce, Raddish—

July: *July:*
Sow Lettuce, remove Cabbage-plants, Lay ever-greens, and transplant such as are rooted, do this about St. Jamestide.

Aug: *August:*
Sow Cabbages, Carrots, Turneps, purselan—Innoculate oranges and
other rare plants: Begin to prune over shady shootes of the Spring,
yet so as not to expose the Fruit.

Sept: *September:*

Sow Lettuce, Spinach—plant primroses, violets & such fibrous rootes.

Octob: *October:*

Sow Lettuce, Alaternus, phillyrea seedes, Kirnels &c. and now begin to secure & by little & little, as the season proves, withdraw your choicer & tender Greenes & prepare them for the Greene house.

Nov: *November:*

Trench & prepare ground with compost—sow as yet all sorts of greenes.

Decm: *December:*

Carry, & spread dung & compost.

MEASURES

Which a Gardiner ought to Understand

3 *Barly-Corns* make an *Inch*: 12 *Inches* a *Foote*: 3 *Foote* a *Yard*: 3 foote 9 Inches an *Ell*: 6 Foote a *Fathom*: 16 foote & ½ a *Pearch*: one perch in bredth, & foure in length is a *Roode*: 4 Rood an *Aker*: 40 Roodes in Length is a *Furlong*: 8 *Furlongs* is a *Mile*. 60 Miles is a *Degree*.

or thus:

A Mile containes		An *Aker* containes	
8	furlongs	4	Roodes
88	stords	40	Days-work
320	perch	160	Square paces
1058	paces	4840	yards
1760	yards	14520	Foote
5280	foote		

Measures of Seedes & Graine

A	*Gallon* is 2 *pottles*	*Liquid & Moist things*
	Bushell 4 pecks	A *pint* of any Liquid is a *pound*
	A peck—2 Gallons	A *quart* is 2 *pints*
	Comb: 4 Bushells	Two *Quarts* is a *pottle*
	2 Combs a Quarter	
	Last is 10 quarters	
	20 Combs 40 strikes, 80 Bushells	

Weights & their Notes

Notes:

Gr:—	A *Graine* & weighs a *Barly-Corne*
Э	A *Scrupull* is 20 *Graines*
Эs	*Obolus* is 10 *Graines*
ʒ	A *Dram* is 13 *Oboluis*
ʒ	An *Ounce*
℔	A *pound* 12 *Ounces* of physical ingredients: 16 of other things
2000 lb	Is a *Tunn*
M	A *Manuple* is a good hand-full
p.	A *pugill* is a small hand-full, or as much as you can take up with the tops of your fingers: 3, wth ye thumb
Ana:	Is of each thing, a like quantity
Q.s.	As much as suffices
qr.	A quarter part of anything
ʃs	The halfe of a thing
℞	Stands for Recipe, or Take &c.

TOOLES

& Instruments Necessary
for a Gardiner &c.

Three spades of severall sizes
A shovell. 1 Matocck. 1 Pick-Axe
Spade Staff: 3 Hawes of different size
3 Rakes of several sizes & finenesse
A plow-rill for seedes
An Infusing tub hoop'd wth yron
A Water-barrow & Tub: A Cooke-staff
2 Couch forks: 1 Iron crow & spoone
3 Water pots of severall siz'd holes
A Tree-pump
3 sythes, 12 Rubstones, 1 whetstone
1 Grinding stone
An Iron Reele & pin fitted wth whipcord
2 Hand-bills, 1 Hoock-bill & Cycle
2 flower Googes: 3 extracting cases
2 Trowells: 2 paire of shares
1 Water paile: 2 Wooden dibbers
1 yron setting stick
1 paire of wooden compasses
A Measure of 10 foote divided
A Tracing staff shod
2 wheele-barrows
A large levell & one for Uprights
1 Hand-barrow: 3 weeding baskets
1 Sallad-basket
Fruite & Flower baskets of severall sizes
2 Weeding knives
1 Wyre seive, one Wyre skreene
1 Fine haire seive
1 Iron roller: 1 stone-Roller
1 Wooden-Roller

2 ladders, a long & shorter

1 Tree stage & ladder to gather fruite on

2 Tressells & a board to remove and clip hedges on: or a Forme to
raise

1 steele vermine trap

3 Mouse Traps, Moule Traps, grained to strike the heaving moule

1 Bird clapper: 1 Trap-cage

A Net to preserve seedes from Birds

1 Tray to clense & van seedes

Saile-cloths to dry seedes on and hang before blossoming wall
fruit

12 Mattrasses to cover Beds with

A case of drawers for seedes

A Tin-box with divisions for seedes: and flower rootes

Bags & paper hoods for seedes

Flower Shades, & for newly set plants

Wooden Squares, & one well glaz'd for the Hott-beds

50 Melon glasses

1 Turfe beater: 1 Rammer

1 Measuring chaine

1 Halfe-rod-pole

1 Water-levell

2 pruning knives

2 Graffing knives & Iron Wedge

1 Inoculating Gouge

2 Graffing saws: 1 Hatchett

1 Broad strong chezell

1 Mallet: 1 Augur: 2 Gimletts

1 Shaving-knife

2 Hammers

1 Naile box divided in 4

1 paire of pincers

1 paire of pliers for Wyre

2 files: 1 Betell

1 Chopping block

A set of Letters, & Figures

A Bushell, Gallon, pint measure
A parcell of Wyres
A basket of shreads & felt cuttings: to tack up wall fruite
Bundle of ash-poles
Stakes
Tubs, cases & Boxes, Flower pots
Layer pots, shading potts, of severall sizes
Canes, Hoops, Insect Glasses
Pack threid & Basse to bind with
Saw-dust, sand, Mosse
A Ruler, Black lead pen: paper
Behives of all sizes
Tallies of Lead
Finer threid to bind up Nose-gays w^{th}
A paper-book to note what when & where he sows & plants, &
    register the successe of Tryalls
The Bee Calendar

Tooles bought since I came into Surrey
for my Garden Grove at Wotton
1695

A New wheele-barrow	Ladder
A New Rake	Reele
A new How	Mattoc
A New Spade	A Quadrant level for Banks & Allys
A — Sythe	A foote Measure
Hatchet	Large Wooden Compasse
Wood-bill	
Hammer	

THE BEE CALENDAR

1687

10 May: Swarme

> [*This calendar was not taken any further*]

The Castrating hooke, to use when one would cut out a portion of the combs, & drive the *Bees* leaving sufficient for their winter foode, as in some countries they practise.

ACETARIA:
A DISCOURSE
OF
SALLETS.

By J. E. S.R.S. Author of
the *Kalendarium*.

To the Right Honourable
JOHN
Lord Somers
*of Evesham**
Lord *High-Chancellor* of England,
and *President of the Royal-Society.*

My Lord,

THE *Idea* and *Plan* of the *Royal-Society* having been first conceiv'd and delineated by a *Great* and *Learned Chancellor*,* which High Office your Lordship deservedly bears; not as an Acquisition of Fortune, but your Intellectual Endowments; Conspicuous (among other Excellencies) by the Inclination Your Lordship discovers to promote *Natural Knowledge*: As it justifies the Discernment of that *Assembly*, to pitch upon Your Lordship for their *President*, so does it no less discover the Candor, yea, I presume to say, the Sublimity of your Mind, in so generously honoring them with your *Acceptance* of the *Choice* they have made.

A *Chancellor*, and a very Learned Lord,* was the *First* who honoured the *Chair*; and a no less Honorable and Learned *Chancellor*,* resigns it to Your Lordship: So as after all the Difficulties and Hardships the *Society* has hitherto gone through; it has thro' the Favour and Protection of its *Presidents*, not only preserv'd its Reputation from the Malevolence of Enemies and Detracters, but gone on *Culminating*, and now *Triumphantly* in Your Lordship: Under whose propitious Influence, I am perswaded, it may promise it self *That*, which indeed has hitherto been wanting, to justifie the Glorious *Title* it bears of a ROYAL SOCIETY. The *Emancipating* it from some Remaining and Discouraging Circumstances, which it as yet labours under; among which, that of a *Precarious* and unsteady Abode, is not the least.

This *Honor* was reserv'd for Your Lordship; and an *Honor*, permit me to call it, not at all unworthy the Owning of the Greatest Person living: Namely, the Establishing and Promoting *Real Knowledge*; and (next to what is *Divine*) truly so called; as far, at least, as Humane Nature extends towards the Knowledge of Nature, by enlarging her Empire beyond the Land of *Spectres, Forms, Intentional Species, Vacuum, Occult Qualities*, and other *Inadequate Notions*; which, by their Obstreperous and Noisy Disputes, affrighting, and (till of late) deterring Men from adventuring on further Discoveries, confin'd them in a lazy Acquiescence, and to be fed with *Fantasms* and fruitless Speculations, which signifie nothing to the *specifick* Nature of Things, solid and useful knowledge; by the *Investigation of Causes, Principles, Energies, Powers*, and *Effects* of *Bodies*, and *Things Visible*; and to improve them for the Good and Benefit of Mankind.

My Lord, That which the *Royal Society* needs to accomplish an entire Freedom, and (by rendring their Circumstances more easie) capable to subsist with Honor, and to reach indeed the Glorious Ends of its *Institution*, is an Establishment in a more Settl'd, *Appropriate*, and *Commodious Place*; having hitherto (like the *Tabernacle* in the *Wilderness*) been only *Ambulatory* for almost *Forty Years*: But *Solomon* built the First *Temple*; and what forbids us to hope, that as Great a *Prince* may build *Solomon's House*, as that Great *Chancellor* (one of Your Lordship's Learned *Predecessors*)* had design'd the *Plan*; there being nothing in that *August* and *Noble Model* impossible, or beyond the *Power* of *Nature* and Learned Industry.

Thus, whilst King *Solomon's* Temple was *Consecrated* to the *God* of *Nature*, and his true Worship; *This* may be *Dedicated*, and set apart for the *Works* of *Nature*; deliver'd from those Illusions and Impostors, that are still endeavouring to cloud and depress the True, and *Substantial Philosophy*: A *shallow* and *Superficial Insight*, wherein (as that Incomparable Person rightly observes) having made so many *Atheists*: whilst a *profound* and thorow *Penetration* into her *Recesses* (which is the *Business* of the *Royal Society*) would lead Men to the *Knowledge*, and *Admiration* of the *Glorious Author*.

And now, *My Lord*, I expect some will wonder what my Meaning is, to usher in a *Trifle*, with so much Magnificence, and end at last in a fine *Receipt* for the *Dressing* of a *Sallet* with an Handful of *Pot-Herbs*! But yet, *My Lord*, this *Subject*, as low and despicable as it appears, challenges a Part of *Natural History*, and the Greatest Princes have thought it no Disgrace, not only to make it their *Diversion*, but their *Care*, and to promote and encourage it in the midst of their weightiest Affairs: He who wrote of the *Cedar* of *Libanus*, wrote also of the *Hysop which grows upon the Wall*.

To verifie this, how much might I say of *Gardens* and *Rural Employments*, preferrable to the Pomp and Grandeur of other Secular Business, and that in the Estimate of as Great Men as any Age has produc'd! And it is of such *Great Souls* we have it recorded; That after they had perform'd the Noblest Exploits for the Publick, they sometimes chang'd their *Scepters* for the *Spade*, and their *Purple* for the Gardiner's *Apron*. And of these, some, My *Lord*, were *Emperors, Kings, Consuls, Dictators*, and Wise *Statesmen*; who amidst the most important Affairs, both in Peace and War, have quitted all their Pomp and Dignity in Exchange of this Learned Pleasure: Nor that of the most *refin'd* Part of *Agriculture* (the *Philosophy* of the *Garden* and *Parterre* only) but of *Herbs*, and wholesom *Sallets*, and other plain and useful Parts of *Geoponicks*,* and Wrote *Books* of *Tillage* and *Husbandry*; and took the *Plough-Tackle* for their *Banner*, and their *Names* from the *Grain* and *Pulse* they sow'd, as the Marks and Characters of the highest Honor.

But I proceed no farther on a *Topic* so well known to Your Lordship: Nor urge I Examples of such Illustrious Persons laying aside their Grandeur, and even of deserting their Stations; (which would infinitely prejudice the Publick, when worthy Men are in Place, and at the Helm) But to shew how consistent the Diversions of the *Garden* and *Villa* were, with the highest and busiest Employment of the *Commonwealth*, and never thought a Reproch, or the least Diminution to the Gravity and Veneration due to their Persons, and the Noble Rank they held.

Will Your Lordship give me Leave to repeat what is said of the Younger *Pliny*,* (Nephew to the *Naturalist*)* and whom I think we may parallel with the Greatest of his time (and perhaps of any since) under the Worthiest *Emperor* the *Roman* world ever had?* A Person of vast Abilities, Rich, and High in his Master's Favour; that so Husbanded his time, as in the Midst of the weightiest Affairs, to have Answer'd, and by his *Example*, made good what I have said on this Occasion. The Ancient and best Magistrates of *Rome* allow'd but the *Ninth* Day* for the *City* and *Publick Business*; the rest for the *Country* and the *Sallet Garden*: There were then fewer *Causes* indeed at the *Bar*; but never greater *Justice*, nor *better Judges* and *Advocates*. And 'tis hence observed, that we hardly find a Great and Wise Man among the Ancients, *qui nullos habuit hortos*,* excepting only *Pomponius Atticus*;* wilst his Dear *Cicero** professes, that he never laid out his Money more readily, than in the purchasing of *Gardens*, and those sweet Retirements, for which he so often left the *Rostra** (and Court of the Greatest and most flourishing State of the World) to visit, prune, and water them with his own Hands.

But, *My Lord*, I forget with whom I am talking thus; and a *Gardiner* ought not to be so bold. The present I humbly make your Lordship, is indeed but a *Sallet* of *Crude Herbs*: But there is among them that which was a *Prize* at the *Isthmian Games*;* and Your Lordship knows who it was both accepted, and rewarded as despicable an Oblation of this kind. The Favor I humbly beg, is Your Lordship's Pardon for this Presumption. The Subject is *mean*, and requires it, and my *Reputation* in danger; should Your Lordship hence suspect that one could never write so much of *dressing Sallets*, who minded anything serious, besides the gratifying a Sensual Appetite with a Voluptuary *Apician* Art.*

Truly, *My Lord*, I am so far from designing to promote those *Supplicia Luxuriæ*,* (as *Seneca** calls them) by what I have here written; that were it in my Power, I would recall the World, if not altogether to their Pristine *Diet*, yet to a much more *wholsome* and *temperate* than is now in Fashion: And what if they find me like to some who are eager after *Hunting* and other Field-Sports, which are *Laborious* Exercises? and *Fishing*, which is indeed a *Lazy* one? who, after all their Pains and Fatigue, never eat what they take and catch in either: For some such I have known: And tho' I cannot affirm so of my self, (when a well drest and excellent *Sallet* is before me) I am yet a very moderate Eater of them. So as to this *Book-Luxury*, I can affirm, and that truly what the *Poet* says of himself (on a less innocent Occasion) *Lasciva pagina, vita proba** God forbid, that after all I have advanc'd in Praise of *Sallets*, I should be thought to plead for the Vice I censure, and chuse that of *Epicurus* for my *Lemma*;* *In hac arte consenui*;* or to have spent my time in nothing else. The *Plan* annext to these Papers,* and the *Apparatus* made to superstruct upon it, would acquit me of having bent all my Contemplations on *Sallets* only. What I humbly offer Your Lordship, is (as I said) Part of *Natural History*, the Product of *Horticulture*, and the *Field*, dignified by the most illustrious, and sometimes tilled *Laureato Vomere*;* which, as it concerns a Part of *Philosophy*, I may (without Vanity) be allow'd to have taken some Pains in Cultivating, as an inferior Member of the *Royal Society*.

But, *My Lord*, wilst You read on (if at least You vouchsafe me that Honor to read at all) I am conscious I rob the Publick of its most Precious Moments.

I therefore Humbly again Implore Your Lordship's Pardon: Nor indeed needed I to have said half this, to kindle in Your Breast, that which is already shining there (Your Lordship's Esteem of the *Royal Society*) after what You were pleas'd to Express in such an Obliging manner, when it was lately to wait upon Your Lordship; among whom I had the Honor to be a Witness of Your Generous, and Favourable Acceptance of their Addresses, who am,

> *My Lord,*
> *Your Lordship's Most Humble*
> *and Most Obedient Servant,*
> *JOHN EVELYN.*

THE PREFACE

THE Favourable Entertainment which the *Kalendar* has found, encouraging the *Bookseller* to adventure upon a *Ninth Impression*, I could not refuse his Request of my Revising, and Giving it the best Improvement I was capable, to an *Inexhaustible Subject*, as it regards a Part of *Horticulture*; and offer some little Aid to such as love a Diversion so Innocent and Laudable. There are those of late, who have arrogated, and given the Glorious Title *of Compleat* and *Accomplish'd Gardiners*, to what they have Publish'd; as if there were nothing wanting, nothing more remaining, or farther to be expected from the Field; and that *Nature* had been quite emptied of all her fertile Store: Whilst those who thus magnifie their Discoveries, have after all, penetrated but a very little Way into this Vast, Ample, and as yet, Unknown Territory; Who see not, that it would still require the Revolution of many Ages; deep, and long *Experience*, for any Man to Emerge that Perfect, and Accomplish'd Artist *Gardiner* they boast themselves to be: Nor do I think, Men will ever reach the End, and far extended Limits of the *Vegetable Kingdom*, so incomprehensible is the Variety it every Day produces, of the most Useful, and Admirable of all the Aspectable Works of God; since almost all we *see*, and *touch*, and *taste*, and *smell*, eat and *drink*, *are clad* with, and *defended* (from the Greatest *Prince* to the Meanest *Peasant*) is furnished from that Great and Universal Plantation, *Epitomiz'd* in our *Gardens*, highly worth the Contemplation of the most Profound Divine, and Deepest *Philosopher*.

I should be asham'd to acknowledge how little I have advanced, could I find that ever any Mortal Man from *Adam, Noah, Solomon, Aristotle,* * *Theophrastus,* * *Dioscorides,* * and the rest of Nature's Interpreters, had ever arriv'd to the perfect Knowledge of any one *Plant*, or *Vulgar Weed* whatsoever: But this perhaps may yet possibly be reserv'd for another State of Things, and a longer Day; that is, *When Time shall be no more, but Knowledge shall be encreas'd.*

We have heard of one who studied and contemplated the Nature of *Bees* only, for *Sixty Years*: After which, you will not wonder, that a Person of my Acquaintance, should have spent almost *Forty*, in Gathering and Amassing Materials for an *Hortulan* Design, to so enormous an Heap, as to fill some *Thousand Pages*; and yet be comprehended within two, or three Acres of Ground; nay, within the Square of less than *One* (skilfully Planted and Cultivated) sufficient to furnish, and entertain his Time and Thoughts all his Life long, with a most Innocent, Agreeable, and Useful Employment. But you may justly wonder, and Condemn the Vanity of it too, with that Reproach, *This Man began to build, but was not able to finish!* This has been the Fate of that Undertaking; and I dare promise, will be of whosoever imagines (without the Circumstances of extraordinary Assistance, and no ordinary Expence) to pursue the *Plan*, erect, and finish the *Fabrick* as it ought to be.

But this is that which *Abortives* the Perfection of the most Glorious and Useful Undertakings; the Unsatiable Coveting to Exhaust all that should, or can be said upon every Head: If such a one have any thing else to mind, or do in the World, let me tell him, he thinks of Building too late; and rarely find we any, who care to superstruct upon the Foundation of another, and whose *Ideas* are alike. There ought therefore to be as many *Hands*, and *Subsidiaries* to such a Design (and those *Matters* too) as there are distinct Parts of the Whole (according to the subsequent Table) that those who have the Means and Courage, may (tho' they do not undertake the *Whole*) finish a *Part* at least, and in time Unite their Labours into one Intire, Compleat, and Consummate Work indeed.

Of *One* or *Two* of these, *I* attempted only a *Specimen* in my SILVA and the KALENDAR; *Imperfect*, I say, because they are both capable of Great Improvements: It is not therefore to be expected (Let me use the Words of an Old, and Experienced *Gardiner*) *Cuncta me dicturum, quae vastitas ejus scientiæ contineret, sed plurima; nam illud in unius hominis prudentiam cadere non poterit, neque est ulla Disciplina aut Ars, quae singulari consummata sit ingenio.**

May it then suffice *aliquam partem tradidisse*,* and that I have done my Endeavour.

> ... *Inutilis olim*
> *Ne Videar vixisse.**

Much more might I add upon this Charming, and Fruitful Subject (I mean, concerning *Gardening*:) But this is not a Place to Expatiate, deterr'd, as I have long since been, from so bold an Enterprize, as the Fabrick I mentioned. I content my self then with an *Humble Cottage*, and a Simple *Potagere*, Appendant to the *Calendar*; which, Treating only (and that briefly) of the *Culture of Moderate Gardens*; Nothing seems to me, shou'd be more *Welcome* and *Agreeable*, than whilst the Product of them is come into more *Request* and *Use* amongst us, than heretofore (beside what we call, and distinguish by the Name of *Fruit*) I did annex some particular Directions concerning SALLETS.

ACETARIA:
A Discourse of Sallets

SALLETS in general consist of certain *Esculent* Plants and Herbs, improv'd by Culture, Industry, and Art of the *Gard'ner*: Or, as others say, they are a Composition of *Edule* Plants and Roots of several kinds, to be eaten *Raw* or *Green, Blanch'd* or *Candied*: simple—and *per'se*, or intermingl'd with others according to the Season. The Boil'd, Bak'd, Pickl'd, or otherwise disguis'd, variously accommodated by the skilful Cooks, to render them grateful to the more feminine Palat, or Herbs rather for the Pot, &c. challenge not the name of *Sallet* so properly here, tho' sometimes mention'd; And therefore,

Those who *Criticize* not so nicely upon the Word, seem to distinguish the *Olera* (which were never eaten *Raw*) from *Acetaria*, which were never *Boil'd;* and so they derive the Etymology of *Olus*, from *Olla, the Pot.* But others deduce it from Ὅλος,* comprehending the *Universal Genus* of the Vegetable Kingdom; as from Πᾶν* *Panis;* esteeming that he who had *Bread* and *Herbs*, was sufficiently bless'd with all a frugal Man cou'd need or desire: Others again will have it, *ab Olendo,* i.e. *Crescendo,** from its continual *growth and springing up*: So the younger *Scaliger* on *Varro*: But his Father *Julius,** extends it not so generally to all Plants, as to all the *Esculents*, according to the Text: *We call those* Olera (says *Theophrastus*)* *which are commonly eaten*, in which sense it may be taken, to include both *Boil'd* and *Raw*: Last of all, *ab Alendo,** as having been the Original, and genuine Food of all Mankind from the Creation.

A great deal more of this Learned Stuff were to be pick'd up from the *Cumini Sectores,** and impertinently Curious; whilst as it concerns the business in hand, we are by *Sallet* to understand a particular Composition of certain *Crude* and fresh Herbs, such as usually are, or may safely be eaten with some *Acetous* Juice, *Oyl, Salt*, &c. to give them a grateful Gust and *Vehicle*; exclusive of the ψυχραὶ τράπεζαι,* eaten without their due Correctives, which the Learned *Salmasius** and, indeed generally, the old *Physicians* affirm (and that truly) all *Crude* and raw λάχανα* require to render them wholsome; so as probably they were from hence, as *Pliny** thinks, call'd *Acetaria*: and not (as *Hermolaus** and some others) *Acceptaria ab Accipiendo*; nor from Accedere, though so ready at hand, and easily dress'd; requiring neither *Fire, Cost,* or *Attendance,* to boil, roast, and prepare them as did Flesh, and other Provisions; from which, and other Prerogatives, they were always in use, &c. And hence indeed the more frugal *Italians* and *French,* to this Day, gather *Ogni Verdura,* any thing almost that's *Green* and Tender, to the very Tops of *Nettles*; so as every Hedge affords a *Sallet* (not unagreeable) season'd with its proper *Oxybaphon** of *Vinegar, Salt, Oyl,* &c. which doubtless gives it both the Relish and Name of *Salad, Emsalada,* as with us of *Sallet*; from the *Sapidity,** which renders not *Plants* and *Herbs* alone, but *Men* themselves, and their Conversations, pleasant and agreeable: But of this enough, and perhaps too much; least whilst I write of *Salt* and *Sallet,* I appear my self *Insipid*: I pass therefore to the Ingredients, which we will call

Furniture *and* Materials

THE *Materials* of *Sallets,* which together with the grosser *Olera,* consist of *Roots, Stalks, Leaves, Buds, Flowers,* &c. *Fruits* (belonging to another Class) would require a much ampler Volume, than would suit our Kalendar, (of which this pretends to be an *Appendix* only) should we extend the following *Catalogue* further than to a brief enumeration only of such *Herbaceous* Plants, *Oluscula** and smaller *Esculents,* as are chiefly us'd in *Cold Sallets,* of whose Culture we have treated there; and as we gather them from the *Mother* and *Genial Bed,* with a touch only of their *Qualities,* for Reasons hereafter given.

❧ 1. Alexanders, *Hipposelinum; S. Smyrnium vulgare* (much of the nature of *Persly*) is moderately hot, and of a cleansing Faculty, De-obstructing, nourishing, and comforting the Stomach. The gentle fresh Sprouts, Buds, and Tops are to be chosen, and the Stalks eaten in the Spring; and when *Blanch'd*, in Winter likewise, with *Oyl, Pepper, Salt,* &c. by themselves, or in Composition: They make also an excellent *Vernal* Pottage.

❧ 2. Artichaux, *Cinara,* (*Carduus Sativus*) hot and dry. The Heads being slit in quarters first eaten raw, with *Oyl,* a little *Vinegar, Salt,* and *Pepper,* gratefully recommend a Glass of *Wine*; Dr. *Muffet** says, at the end of Meals.

They are likewise, whilst tender and small, fried in fresh *Butter* crisp with *Persley.* But then become a most delicate and excellent Restorative, when full grown, they are boil'd the common way. The *Bottoms* are also bak'd in *Pies,* with *Marrow, Dates,* and other rich Ingredients: In *Italy* they sometimes broil them, and as the Scaly Leaves open, baste them with fresh and sweet *Oyl*; but with Care extraordinary, for if a drop fall upon the Coals, all is marr'd; that hazard escap'd, they eat them with the Juice of *Orange* and *Sugar.*

The Stalk is *Blanch'd* in Autumn, and the *Pith* eaten raw or boil'd. The way of preserving them fresh all Winter, is by separating the *Bottoms* from the *Leaves,* and after Parboiling, allowing to every *Bottom,* a small earthen glaz'd Pot; burying it all over in fresh melted *Butter,* as they do Wild-Fowl, &c. Or if more than one, in a larger Pot, in the same Bed and Covering, *Layer* upon *Layer.*

They are also preserv'd by stringing them on Pack-thread, a clean Paper being put between every *Bottom,* to hinder them from touching one another, and so hung up in a dry place. They are like-wise *Pickl'd.*

'Tis not very long since this noble *Thistle* came first into *Italy,* Improv'd to this Magnitude by Culture; and so rare in *England,* that they were commonly sold for *Crowns* a piece: But what *Carthage* yearly spent in them (as *Pliny** computes the Sum) amounted to *Sestertia Sena Millia,** 30000 *l.* Sterling.

Note, That the *Spanish Cardon,* a wild and smaller *Artichoak,* with sharp pointed Leaves, and lesser Head; the Stalks being *Blanch'd* and tender, are serv'd-up *a la Poiverade* (that is with *Oyl, Pepper*, &c.) as the *French* term is.

❧ 3. Basil, *Ocimum* (as *Baulm*) imparts a grateful Flavour, if not too strong, somewhat offensive to the Eyes; and therefore the tender Tops to be very sparingly us'd in our *Sallet*.

❧ 4. Baulm, *Melissa, Baum*, hot and dry, Cordial and exhilarating, sovereign for the Brain, strengthning the Memory, and powerfully chasing away *Melancholy*. The tender Leaves are us'd in Composition with other Herbs; and the Sprigs fresh gather'd, put into *Wine* or other Drinks, during the heat of Summer, give it a marvellous quickness: This noble Plant yields an incomparable *Wine*, made as is that of *Cowslip*-Flowers.

❧ 5. Beet, *Beta*; of which there is both *Red, Black*, and *White*: The *Costa*, or Rib of the *White Beet* (by the *French* call'd the *Chard*) being boil'd, melts, and eats like Marrow. And the *Roots* (especially of the *Red*) cut into thin slices, boil'd, when cold, is of it self a grateful winter *Sallet*; or being mingl'd with other *Oluscula, Oyl, Vinegar, Salt*, &c. 'Tis of quality Cold and Moist, and naturally somewhat *Laxative*: But however by the *Epigrammatist* stil'd *Foolish* and *Insipid, as Innocentior quam Olus** (for so the Learned *Harduin** reads the place) 'tis by *Diphilus** of old, and others since, preferr'd before *Cabbage* as of better Nourishment: *Martial** (not unlearn'd in the Art of *Sallet*) commends it with *Wine* and *Pepper*: He names it indeed— *Fabrorum prandia,** for its being so vulgar. But eaten with *Oyl* and *Vinegar*, as usually, it is no despicable *Sallet*. There is a *Beet* growing near the Sea, which is the most delicate of all. The Roots of the *Red Beet*, pared into thin Slices and Circles, are by the *French* and *Italians* contriv'd into curious Figures to adorn their *Sallets*.

❧ 6. Blite, *Blitum*; English *Mercury*, or (as our Country House wives call it) *All-good*, the gentle *Turiones,** and Tops may be eaten as *Sparagus*, or sodden in Pottage: There is both a white and red, much us'd in *Spain* and *Italy*; but besides its humidity and detersive Nature, 'tis *Insipid* enough.

❦ 7. Borrage, *Borrago* (*Gaudia semper ago*)* hot and kindly moist, purifying the Blood, is an exhilarating Cordial, of a pleasant Flavour: The tender Leaves, and Flowers especially, may be eaten in Composition; but above all, the Sprigs in *Wine*, like those of *Baum*, are of known Vertue to revive the *Hypochondriac*, and chear the hard Student. See *Bugloss*.

❦ 8. Brooklime, *Anagallis aquatica*; moderately hot and moist, prevalent in the *Scorbute*, and *Stone*.

❦ 9. Bugloss, *Buglossum*; in mature much like *Borrage*, yet something more astringent. The Flowers of both, with the intire Plant, greatly restorative, being Conserv'd: And for the rest, so much commended by *Averroes*;* that for its effects, cherishing the Spirits, justly call'd *Euphrosynum*;* Nay, some will have it the *Nepenthes** of *Homer.** But indeed, what we now call *Bugloss*, was not that of the Ancients, but rather *Borrage*, for the like Virtue named *Corrago*.*

Burnet, See *Pimpinella*.

❦ 10. Buds, *Gemmæ, Turiones*; the first Rudiments and Tops of most *Sallet*-Plants, preferrable to all other less tender Parts; such as *Ashen-Keys, Broom-buds*, hot and dry, retaining the vertue of *Capers*, esteem'd to be very opening, and prevalent against the *Spleen* and *Scurvy*; and being *Pickl'd*, are sprinkl'd among the *Sallets*, or eaten by themselves.

❦ 11. Cabbage, *Brassica* (and its several kinds) *Pompey's** beloved Dish, so highly celebrated by old *Cato*,* *Pythagoras*,* and *Chrysippus* the Physician* (as the only *Panacea*) is not so generally magnify'd by the rest of Doctors, as affording but a crass and melancholy Juice; yet *Loosening* if but moderately boil'd, if over-much, *Astringent*, according to *C. Celsus*;* and therefore seldom eaten raw, excepting by the *Dutch*. The *Cymæ*, or Sprouts rather of the *Cole* are very delicate, so boil'd as to retain their Verdure and green Colour. In raising this *Plant* great care is to be had of the Seed. The best comes from *Denmark* and *Russia*, especially the *Cauly-flower*, (anciently unknown) or from *Aleppo*. Of the *French*, the *Pancaliere a la large Costé*, the white, large and ponderous are to be chosen; and so the *Cauly-flower*. After boiling some steep them in Milk, and seethe them again in Beef-Broth: Of old they added a little *Nitre*.* The *Broccoli* from *Naples*, perhaps the *Halmyridia** of *Pliny** (or *Athenæus** rather) *apiata marina* & *florida*,* our *Sea-keele** (the ancient *Crambe**) and growing on our Coast, are very delicate, as are the *Savoys*, commended for being not so rank, but agreeable to most *Palates*, and of better Nourishment: In general, *Cabbages* are thought to allay Fumes, and prevent Intoxication: But some will have them noxious to the Sight; others impute it to the *Cauly-flower* rather: But whilst the Learned are not agreed about it, *Theophrastus** affirms the contrary, and* *Pliny* commends the Juice raw, with a little *Honey*, for the moist and weeping Eye, not the dry or dull. But after all, *Cabbage* ('tis confess'd) is greatly accus'd for lying undigested in the Stomach, and provoking Eructations;* which makes me wonder at the Veneration we read the Ancients had for them, calling them *Divine*, and Swearing, *per Brassicam*. 'Tis scarce an hundred Years since we first had *Cabbages* out of *Holland*. Sir *Anth. Ashley** of *Wiburg St. Giles* in *Dorsetshire*, being (as I am told) the first who planted them in *England*.

❧ 12. Cardon, See *Artichaux*.

❧ 13. Carrots, *Dauci*, or *Pastinaca Sativa*; temperately warm and dry, Spicy; the best are yellow, very nourishing; let them be rais'd in Ground naturally rich, but not too heavy.

❧ 14. Chervile, *Chærophyllum, Myrrhis*; The sweet aromatick *Spanish Chervile*, moderately hot and dry: The tender *Cimæ*, and Tops, with other Herbs, are never to be wanting in our *Sallets*, (as long as they may be had) being exceedingly wholsome and chearing the Spirits: The *Roots* are also boil'd and eaten Cold; much commended for Aged Persons: This (as likewise *Spinach*) is us'd in *Tarts*, and serves alone for divers Sauces.

Cibbols. ⎤ Vide Onions,
Cives. ⎦ *Schænopræsson*.

❧ 15. Clary, *Horminum*, when tender not to be rejected, and in *Omlets*, made up with *Cream*, fried in sweet *Butter*,* are eaten with *Sugar*, Juice of *Orange*, or *Limon*.

✻ 16. Clavers, *Aparine*; the tender Winders, with young *Nettle-Tops*, are us'd in *Lenten* Pottages.

✻ 17. Corn-sallet, *Valerianella*; loos'ning and refreshing: The Tops and Leaves are a *Sallet* of themselves, seasonably eaten with other Salleting, the whole Winter long, and early Spring: The *French* call them *Salad de Preter*, for their being generally eaten in *Lent*.

✻ 18. Cowslips, *Paralysis*: See *Flowers*.

✻ 19. Cresses, *Nasturtium*, Garden *Cresses*; to be monthly sown: But above all the *Indian*, moderately hot, and aromatick, quicken the torpent Spirits, and purge the Brain, and are of singular effect against the *Scorbute*. Both the tender Leaves, *Calices*,* *Cappuchin Capers*, and *Flowers*, are laudably mixed with the colder Plants. The *Buds* being Candy'd, are likewise us'd in Strewings all Winter. There is the *Nastur. Hybernicum* commended also, and the vulgar *Water-Cress*, proper in the Spring, all of the same Nature, tho' of different Degrees, and best for raw and cold Stomachs, but nourish little.

✻ 20. Cucumber, *Cucumis*; tho' very cold and moist, the most approved *Sallet* alone, or in Composition, of all the *Vinaigrets*, to sharpen the Appetite, and cool the Liver, &c. if rightly prepar'd; that is, by rectifying the vulgar Mistake of altogether extracting the Juice, in which it should rather be soak'd: Nor ought it to be over *Oyl'd*, too much abating of its grateful *Acidity*, and *palling* the Taste from a contrariety of Particles: Let them therefore be pared, and cut in thin Slices, with a *Clove* or two of *Onion* to correct the Crudity, macerated in the Juice, often turn'd and moderately drain'd. Others prepare them, by shaking the Slices between two Dishes, and dress them with very little *Oyl*, well beaten, and mingled with the Juice of *Limon, Orange*, or *Vinegar, Salt* and *Pepper*. Some again, (and indeed the most approv'd) eat them as soon as they are cut, retaining their Liquor, which being exhausted (by the former Method) have nothing remaining in them to help the Concoction. Of old they boil'd the *Cucumber*, and paring off the Rind, eat them with *Oyl, Vinegar*, and *Honey*; *Sugar* not being so well known. Lastly, the *Pulp* in Broth is greatly refreshing, and may be mingl'd in most

Sallets, without the least damage, contrary to the common Opinion; it not being long, since *Cucumber*, however dress'd, was thought fit to be thrown away, being accounted little better than Poyson. *Tavernier** tells us, that in the *Levant*, if a Child cry for something to Eat, they give it a raw *Cucumber* instead of *Bread*. The young ones may be boil'd in White-Wine. The smaller sort (known by the name of *Gerckems*) muriated with the Seeds of *Dill*, and the *Mango* Pickle are for the Winter.

❦ 21. Daisy, *Buphthalmum*, Ox-Eye, or *Bellis-major*: The young *Roots* are frequently eaten by the *Spaniards* and *Italians* all the Spring till *June*.

❦ 22. Dandelion, *Dens Leonis, Condrilla*: Macerated in several Waters, to extract the bitterness; tho' somewhat opening, is very wholsome, and little inferior to *Succory, Endive*, &c. The *French* Country-People eat the Roots; and 'twas with this homely *Sallet*, the Good-Wife *Hecale** entertain'd *Theseus.** See *Sowthistle*.

❦ 23. Dock, *Oxylapathum*, or sharp-pointed Dock: Emollient, and tho' otherwise not for our *Sallet*, the *Roots* brewed in *Ale* or *Beer*, are excellent for the *Scorbute*.

Earth-Nuts, *Bulbo-Castanum*; (found in divers places of *Surry*, near *Kingston*, and other parts) the Rind par'd off, are eaten crude by Rustics, with a little *Pepper*; but are best boil'd like other Roots, or in Pottage rather, and are sweet and nourishing.

❦ 24. Elder, *Sambucus*; The Flowers infus'd in *Vinegar*, grateful both to the Stomach and Taste; attenuate thick and viscid Humours; and tho' the Leaves are somewhat rank of Smell, and so not commendable in *Sallet*; they are otherwise (as indeed is the intire Shrub) of the most sovereign Vertue; and the spring Buds and tender Leaves, excellently wholsome in Pottage at that Season of the Year. See *Flowers*.

❦ 25. Endive, *Endivium, Intubum Sativum*; the largest, whitest, and tenderest Leaves best boil'd, and less crude. It is naturally Cold, profitable for hot Stomachs; *Incisive* and opening Obstructions of the Liver: The curled is more delicate, being eaten alone, or in

Composition, with the usual *Intinctus*: It is also excellent being boil'd; the middle part of the Blanch'd-Stalk separated, eats firm, and the ampler Leaves by many perferr'd before *Lettuce*. See *Succory*. Eschalot. See *Onions*.

❧ 26. Fennel, *Fœniculum*: The sweetest of *Bolognia*: Aromatick, hot, and dry; expels Wind, sharpens the Sight, and recreates the Brain; especially the tender *Umbella* and Seed-Pods. The Stalks are to be peel'd when young, and then dress'd like *Sellery*. The tender Tufts and Leaves emerging, being minc'd, are eaten alone with *Vinegar*, or *Oyl*, and *Pepper*, and to correct the colder Materials, enter properly into Composition. The *Italians* eat the blanch'd Stalk (which they call *Cartucci*) all Winter long. There is a very small *Green-Worm*, which sometimes lodges in the Stemm of this Plant, which is to be taken out, as the *Red* one in that of *Sellery*.

❧ 27. Flowers, *Flores*; chiefly of the *Aromatick Esculents* and Plants are preferrable, as generally endow'd with the Vertues of their *Simples*, in a more intense degree; and may therefore be eaten alone in their proper *Vehicles*, or Composition with other *Salleting*, sprinkl'd among them; But give a more palatable Relish, being Infus'd in *Vinegar*; Especially those of the *Clove-Gillyflower, Elder, Orange, Cowslip, Rosemary, Arch-Angel, Sage, Nasturtium Indicum*, &c. Some of them are Pickl'd, and divers of them make also very pleasant and wholsome *Theas*,* as do likewise the Wild *Time, Bugloss, Mint*, &c.

❧ 28. Garlick, *Allium*; dry towards Excess; and tho' both by *Spaniards* and *Italians*, and the more Southern People, familiarly eaten, with almost every thing, and esteem'd of such singular Vertue to help Conception, and thought a Charm against all Infection and Poyson (by which it has obtain'd the Name of the *Country-man's Theriacle*)* we yet think it more proper for our Northern Rustics, especially living in *Uliginous** and moist places, or such as use the *Sea*: Whilst we absolutely forbid it entrance into our *Salleting*, by reason of its intolerable Rankness, and which made it so detested of old; that the eating of it was (as we read) part of the Punishment for such as had committed the horrid'st Crimes. To be sure, 'tis not for

Ladies Palats, nor those who court them, farther than to permit a light touch on the Dish, with a *Clove* thereof, much better supply'd by the gentler *Roccombo*.

Note, That in *Spain* they sometimes eat it boil'd, which taming its fierceness, turns it into Nourishment, or rather *Medicine*.

Ginny-Pepper, *Capsicum*. See *Pepper*.

❧ 29. Goats-beard, *Trago-pogon:* The *Root* is excellent even in *Sallet*, and very Nutritive, exceeding profitable for the Breast, and may be stew'd and dress'd as *Scorzonera*.

❧ 30. Hops, *Lupulus*: Hot and moist, rather *Medicinal*, than fit for *Sallet*; the *Buds* and young *Tendrels* excepted, which may be eaten raw; but more conveniently being boil'd, and cold like *Asparagus*: They are *Diuretic*; depurate the Blood, and open Obstructions.

❧ 31. Hyssop, *Hyssopus; Thymus Capitatus Creticus; Majoran, Mary-gold*, &c. as all hot, spicy *Aromatics*, (commonly growing in *Kitchin-Gardens*) are of Faculty to Comfort, and strengthen; prevalent against Melancoly and Phlegm; Plants, like these, going under the Names of *Pot Herbs*, are much more proper for *Broths* and *Decoctions*, than the tender *Sallet*: Yet the *Tops* and *Flowers* reduc'd to Powder, are by some reserv'd for Strewings, upon the colder Ingredients; communicating no ungrateful Fragrancy.

❧ 32. Jack-by-the-Hedge, *Alliaria*, or *Sauce-alone*; has many Medicinal Properties, and is eaten as other *Sallets*, especially by Country People, growing wild under their Banks and Hedges.

❧ 33. Leeks, and *Cibbols, Porrum*; hot, and of Vertue Prolifick, since *Latona*,* the Mother of *Apollo* long'd after them: The *Welch*, who eat them much, are observ'd to be very fruitful: They are also friendly to the Lungs and Stomach, being sod in Milk; a few therefore of the slender and green Summities, a little shred, do not amiss in Composition. See *Onion*.

❧ 34. Lettuce, *Lactuca*: Tho' by *Metaphor* call'd *Mortuorum Cibi*,* (to say nothing of *Adonis* and his sad *Mistriss*)* by reason of its *Soporiferous* quality, ever was, and still continues the principal Foundation of the universal *Tribe* of *Sallets*; which is to Cool and Refresh, besides its other Properties: And therefore in such high esteem with the Ancients; that divers of the *Valerian* Family, dignify'd and enobled their Name with that of *Lactucinii*.

It is indeed of Nature more cold and moist than any of the rest; yet less astringent, and so harmless that it may safely be eaten raw in Fevers; for it allays Heat, bridles Choler, extinguishes Thirst, excites Appetite, kindly Nourishes, and above all represses Vapours, conciliates Sleep, mitigates Pain; besides the effect it has upon the Morals, *Temperance* and *Chastity*. Galen* (whose beloved *Sallet* it was) from its *pinguid,* *subdulcid......** and agreeable Nature, says it breeds the most laudable Blood. No marvel then that they were by the Ancients called *Sana,** by way of eminency, and so highly valu'd by the great *Augustus,** that attributing his Recovery of a dangerous Sickness to them, 'tis reported, he erected a *Statue*, and built an *Altar* to this noble Plant. And that the most abstemious and excellent Emperor *Tacitus** (spending almost nothing at his frugal Table in other Dainties) was yet so great a Friend to *Lettuce*, that he was us'd to say of his Prodigality, *Somnum se mercari illa sumptus effusione.** How it was celebrated by *Galen* we have heard; how he us'd it he tells himself; namely, beginning with *Lettuce* in his younger Days, and concluding with it when he grew old, and that to his great advantage. In a word, we meet with nothing among all our crude Materials and *Sallet* store, so proper to mingle with any of the rest, nor so wholsome to be eaten alone, or in Composition, moderately, and with the usual *Oxelæum* of *Vinegar*, *Pepper*, and *Oyl*, &c. which last does not so perfectly agree with the *Alphange*, to which the Juice of *Orange*, or *Limon* and *Sugar* is more desirable: *Aristoxenus** is reported to have irrigated his *Lettuce*-Beds with an *Oinomelite*, or mixture of *Wine* and *Honey*: And certainly 'tis not for nothing that our Garden-Lovers, and *Brothers of the Sallet*, have been so exceedingly Industrious to cultivate this Noble Plant, and multiply its *Species*; for to name a few in present use: We have the *Alphange* of *Montpelier*, crisp and delicate; the *Arabic; Ambervelleres; Belgrade, Cabbage, Capuchin, Coss-Lettuce, Curl'd*; the *Genoa* (lasting all the Winter) the *Imperial, Lambs*, or *Agnine*, and *Lobbs* or *Lop-Lettuces*. The *French Minion* a dwarf kind: The *Oak-Leaf, Passion,*

Roman, Shell, and *Silesian,* hard and crimp (esteemed of the best and rarest) with divers more: And here let it be noted, that besides three or four sorts of this Plant, and some few of the rest, there was within our remembrance, rarely any other *Salleting* serv'd up to the best Tables; with unblanch'd *Endive, Succory, Purselan,* (and indeed little other variety) *Sugar* and *Vinegar* being the constant *Vehicles* (without *Oyl*......) but now *Sugar* is almost wholly banish'd from all, except the more effeminate Palates, as too much palling, and taking from the grateful *Acid* now in use, tho' otherwise not totally to be reproved: *Lettuce* boil'd and *Condited* is sometimes spoken of.

35. Limon, *Limonia, citrea mala;* exceedingly refreshing, *Cordial,* &c. The Pulp being blended with the Juice, secluding the over-sweet or bitter. See *Orange.*

36. Mallow, *Malva;* the curl'd, emollient, and friendly to the *Ventricle,* and so rather Medicinal; yet may the Tops, well boil'd, be admitted, and the rest (tho' out of use at present) was taken by the Poets for all *Sallets* in general. *Pythagoras** held *Malvæ folium Sanctisimum;* and we find *Epimenides** in Plato* at his *Mallows* and *Asphodel;* and indeed it was of old the first Dish at Table: The *Romans* had it also *in deliciis, Malvæ salubres corpori,* approved by *Galen** and *Dioscorides;** namely the *Garden-Mallow,* by others the *Wild;* but I think both proper rather for the *Pot,* than *Sallet. Nonius** supposes the tall *Rosea, Arborescent Holi-hocks,* that bears the broad Flower, for the best, and very *Laxative;* but by reason of their clamminess and *Lentor,** banished from our *Sallet,* tho' by some commended and eaten with *Oyl* and *Vinegar,* and some with *Butter.*

Mercury, *Bonus Henricus,* English Mercury, or *Lapathum Unctuosum.* See *Blitum.*

37. Melon, *Melo;* to have been reckon'd rather among *Fruits;* and tho' an usual Ingredient in our *Sallet;* yet for its transcendent delicacy and flavor, cooling and exhilarating Nature (if sweet, dry, weighty, and well-fed) not only superior to all the *Gourd*-kind, but Paragon with the noblest Productions of the Garden. *Jos. Scaliger* and *Casaubon,** think our *Melon* unknown to the Ancients, (which others contradict) as yet under the name of *Cucumers:* But he who

reads how artificially they were Cultivated, rais'd under Glasses, and expos'd to the hot Sun, (for *Tiberius*)* cannot well doubt of their being the same with ours.

There is also a *Winter-Melon*, large and with black Seeds, exceedingly Cooling, brought us from abroad, and the hotter Climates, where they drink *Water* after eating *Melons*; but in the colder (after all dispute) *Wine* is judg'd the better: That it has indeed by some been accus'd as apt to corrupt in the Stomach (as do all things else eaten in excess) is not deny'd: But a perfect good *Melon* is certainly as harmless a Fruit as any whatsoever; and may safely be mingl'd with *Sallet*, in Pulp or Slices, or more properly eaten by it self, with a little *Salt* and *Pepper*; for a *Melon* which requires *Sugar* to commend it, wants of Perfection. *Note*, That this Fruit was very rarely cultivated in *England*, so as to bring it to Maturity, till Sir *Geo. Gardner* came out of *Spain*. I my self remembring, when an ordinary *Melon* would have been sold for five or six Shillings. The small unripe Fruit, when the others are past, may be Pickl'd with *Mango*, and are very delicate.

❧ 38. Mint, *Mentha*; the *Angustifolia Spicata*, Spear-Mint; dry and warm, very fragrant, a little press'd, is friendly to the weak Stomach, and powerful against all *Nervous* Crudities: The gentler Tops of the *Orange-Mint*, enter well into our Composition, or are grateful alone (as are also the other sorts) with the Juice of *Orange*, and a little *Sugar*.

❧ 39. Mushroms, *Fungi*; By the Orator call'd *Terræ*, by *Porphyry Deorum filii*,* without Seed (as produc'd by the Midwifry of *Autumnal* Thunder-Storms, portending the Mischief they cause) by the *French*, *Champignons*, with all the Species of the *Boletus*, &c. for being, as some hold, neither *Root, Herb, Flower*, nor *Fruit*, nor to be eaten crude; should be therefore banish'd entry into our *Sallet*, were I to order the Composition; however so highly contended for by many, as the very principal and top of all the rest; whilst I think them tolerable only (at least in this *Climate*) if being fresh and skilfully chosen, they are accommodated with the nicest Care and Circumspection; generally reported to have something malignant and noxious in them: Nor without cause; from the many sad Examples, frequent Mischiefs, and funest Accidents they have produc'd, not only to particular Persons, but whole Families: Exalted indeed they were to the second Course of the *Cæsarian Tables*, with the noble Title Βρῶμα θεῶν,* a Dainty fit for the *Gods* alone; to whom they sent the Emperor *Claudius*,* as they have many since, to the other World. But he that reads how *Seneca* deplores his lost Friend, that brave Commander *Annæus Serenus*,* and several other gallant Persons with him, who all of them perish'd at the same Repast; would be apt to ask with the *Naturalist** (speaking of this suspicious Dainty) *Quæ voluptas tanta ancipitis cibi?** and who indeed would hazard it? So true is that of the Poet; He that eats *Mushroms*, many time *Nil amplius edit*,* eats no more perhaps all his Life after. What other deterring *Epithets* are given for our Caution, Βάρη πνιγόεντα-μυκήτων,* *heavy* and *choaking*. (*Athenæus** reporting of the Poet *Euripides's*,* finding a Woman and her three Children strangl'd by eating of them) one would think sufficient warning.

Among these comes in the *Fungus Reticularis*, to be found about *London*, as at *Fulham* and other places; whilst at no small charge we send for them into *France*; as we also do for *Trufles*, *Pig-nuts*, and other subterraneous *Tubera*, which in *Italy* they fry in Oyl, and eat with *Pepper*. They are commonly discovered by a *Nasute Swine** purposely brought up; being of a Chessnut Colour, and heady Smell, and not seldom found in *England*, particularly in a Park of my Lord *Cotton's** at *Rushton* or *Rushery* in *Northampton*-shire, and doubtless in other places too were they sought after. How these rank and provocative Excrescences are to be treated (of themselves insipid enough, and only famous for their kindly taking any Pickle or *Conditure*) that they may do the less Mischief we might here set down. But since there be so many ways of Dressing them, that I can incourage none to use them, for Reasons given (besides that they do not at all concern our safer and innocent *Sallet* Furniture) I forbear it; and referr those who long after this beloved *Ragout*, and other *Voluptuaria Venena** (as *Seneca* calls them) to what our Learned Dr. *Lyster** says of the many Venomous *Insects* harbouring and corrupting in a new found-out Species of *Mushroms* had lately in deliciis. Those, in the mean time, which are esteemed best, and less pernicious, (of which see the *Appendix*) are such as rise in rich, airy, and dry Pasture-Grounds; growing on the Staff or *Pedicule** of about an Inch thick and high; moderately Swelling (*Target*-like) round and firm, being underneath of a pale saffronish hue, curiously radiated in parallel Lines and Edges, which becoming either Yellow, Orange, or Black, are to be rejected: But besides what the Harvest-Months produce, they are likewise rais'd Artificially; as at *Naples* in their Wine-Cellars, upon an heap of rank Earth, heaped upon a certain supposed *Stone*, but in truth, (as the curious and noble *Peiresky** tells us, he found to be) nothing but an heap of old *Fungus*'s, reduc'd and compacted to a stony hardness, upon which they lay Earth, and sprinkle it with warm Water, in which *Mushroms* have been steeped. And in *France*, by making an hot Bed of *Asses*-Dung, and when the heat is in Temper, watering it (as above) well impregnated with the Parings and Offals of refuse *Fungus*'s; and such a Bed will last two or three Years, and sometimes our common *Melon*-Beds afford them, besides other Experiments.

40. Mustard, *Sinapi*; exceeding hot and *mordicant*,* not only in the Seed but Leaf also; especially in *Seedling* young Plants, like those of *Radishes* (newly peeping out of the Bed) is of incomparable effect to quicken and revive the Spirits; strengthening the Memory, expelling heaviness, preventing the Vertiginous Palsie, and is a laudable *Cephalick*.* Besides it is an approv'd *Antiscorbutick*;* aids Concoction, cuts and dissipates Phlegmatick Humours.* In short, 'tis the most noble *Embamma*,* and so necessary an Ingredient to all cold and raw *Salleting*, that it is very rarely, if at all, to be left out. In *Italy* in making *Mustard*, they mingle *Limon* and *Orange-Peel*, with the Seeds. How the best is made, see hereafter.

Nasturtium Indicum. See *Cresses*.

41. Nettles, *Urtica*; Hot, dry, *Diuretic, Solvent*; purifies the Blood: The Buds, and very tender *Cimae*, a little bruised, are by some eaten raw, by others boil'd, especially in *Spring-Pottage*, with other Herbs.

🥄 42. Onion, *Cepa*, *Porrum*; the best are such as are brought us out of *Spain*, whence they of St. *Omers* had them, and some that have weigh'd eight Pounds. Choose therefore the large, round, white, and thin Skin'd. Being eaten crude and alone with *Oyl*, *Vinegar*, and *Pepper*, we own them in *Sallet*, not so hot as *Garlick*, nor at all so rank: Boil'd, they give a kindly relish; raise Appetite, corroborate the Stomach, cut Phlegm, and profit the *Asthmatical*: But eaten in excess, are said to offend the Head and Eyes, unless *Edulcorated*...* with a gentle maceration. In the mean time, as to their being noxious to the Sight, is imputable only to the Vapour rising from the raw Onion, when peeled, which some commend for its purging and quickning that Sense. How they are us'd in Pottage, boil'd in Milk, stew'd, &c. concerns the Kitchin. In our cold *Sallet* we supply them with the *Porrum Sectile*, Tops of *Leeks*, and *Eschalots* (*Ascalonia*) of gust more exalted, yet not to the degree of *Garlick*. Or (by what of later use is much preferr'd) with a *Seed* or two of *Raccombo*, of a yet milder and delicate nature, which by rubbing the Dish only, imparts its Vertue agreeably enough. In *Italy* they frequently make a *Sallet* of *Scalions*, *Cives*, and *Chibbols* only season'd with *Oyl* and *Pepper*; and an honest laborious Country-man, with good *Bread*, *Salt*, and a little *Parsley*, will make a contented Meal with a roasted *Onion*. How this noble *Bulb* was deified in *Egypt* we are told, and that whilst they were building the *Pyramids*, there was spent in this Root *Ninety Tun* of *Gold* among the Workmen. So lushious and tempting it seems they were, that as whole Nations have subsisted on them alone; so the *Israelites* were ready to return to *Slavery* and *Brick-making* for the love of them. Indeed *Hecamedes** we find presents them to *Patroclus*,* in *Homer*,* as a *Regalo*;* But certainly we are either mistaken in the *Species* (which some will have to be *Melons*) or use *Poetick* Licence, when we so highly magnify them.

🥄 43. Orach, *Atriplex*: Is cooling, allays the *Pituit* Humor:* Being set over the Fire, neither *this*, nor *Lettuce*, needs any other Water than their own moisture to boil them in, without Expression: The tender Leaves are mingl'd with other cold *Salleting*; but 'tis better in Pottage. See *Blitum*.

❧ 44. Orange, *Arantiæ* (*Malum aureum*) Moderately dry, cooling, and incisive; sharpens Appetite, exceedingly refreshes and resists Putrefaction: We speak of the *Sub acid*; the sweet and bitter *Orange* being of no use in our *Sallet*. The *Limon* is somewhat more acute, cooling and extinguishing Thirst; of all the 'Οξύβαφα* the best *succedaneum** to *Vinegar*. The very Spoils and Rinds of *Orange* and *Limon* being shred and sprinkl'd among the other Herbs, correct the Acrimony. But they are the tender *Seedlings* from the *Hot-Bed*, which impart an *Aromatic* exceedingly grateful to the Stomach. *Vide* Limon.

❧ 45. Parsnep, *Pastinaca*, Carrot: first boil'd, being cold, is of it self a Winter-*Sallet*, eaten with *Oyl*, *Vinegar*, &c. and having something of Spicy, is by some, thought more nourishing than the *Turnep*.

❧ 46. Pease, *Pisum*: the Pod of the *Sugar-Pease*, when first beginning to appear, with the *Husk* and *Tendrels*, affording a pretty *Acid*, enter into the Composition, as do those of *Hops* and the *Vine*.

❧ 47. Peper, *Piper*, hot and dry in a high degree; of approv'd Vertue against all flatulency proceeding from cold and phlegmatic Constitutions, and generally all Crudities whatsoever; and therefore for being of universal use to correct and temper the cooler Herbs, and such as abound in moisture; It is a never to be omitted Ingredient of our *Sallets*; provided it be not too minutely beaten (as oft we find it) to an almost impalpable Dust, which is very pernicious and frequently adheres and sticks in the folds of the Stomach, where, instead of promoting Concoction, it often causes a *Cardialgium*,* and fires the Blood: It should therefore be grosly contus'd only.

Indian Capsicum, superlatively hot and burning, is yet by the *Africans* eaten with *Salt* and *Vinegar* by it self, as an usual Condiment; but wou'd be of dangerous consequence with us; being so much more of an acrimonious and terribly biting quality, which by Art and Mixture is notwithstanding render'd not only safe, but very agreeable in our *Sallet*.

Take the *Pods*, and dry them well in a Pan; and when they are become sufficiently hard, cut them into small pieces, and stamp 'em in a Mortar to dust: To each Ounce of which add a Pound of *Wheat-*

flour, fermented with a little *Levain*:* Kneed and make them into Cakes or Loaves cut long-wise, in shape of *Naples-Biscuit*.* These Re-bake a second time, till they are Stone-hard: Pound them again as before, and ferce it through a fine Sieve, for a very proper Seasoning, instead of vulgar *Peper*. The Mordicancy* thus allay'd, be sure to make the Mortar very clean, after having beaten *Indian Capsicum*, before you stamp any thing in it else. The green Husks, or first peeping Buds of the *Walnut-Tree*, dry'd to Powder, serve for *Peper* in some places, and so do *Myrtle-berries*.

48. Persley, *Petroselinum*, or *Apium hortense*; being hot and dry, opens Obstructions, is very *Diuretic*, yet nourishing, *edulcorated…** in shifted warm Water (the Roots especially) but of less Vertue than *Alexanders*; nor so convenient in our crude *Sallet*, as when decocted on a Medicinal Account. Some few tops of the tender Leaves may yet be admitted; tho' it was of old, we read, never brought to the Table at all, as sacred to *Oblivium* and the *Defunct*. In the mean time, there being nothing more proper for Stuffing, (*Farces*) and other *Sauces*, we consign it to the *Olitories*.* *Note*, that Persley is not so hurtful to the Eyes as is reported. See *Sellery*.

49. Pimpernel, *Pimpinella*; eaten by the *French* and *Italians*, is our common *Burnet*; of so chearing and exhilarating a quality, and so generally commended, as (giving it admittance into all *Sallets*) 'tis pass'd into a Proverb:

> *L'Insalata non è buona, ne bella*
> *Ove non è la Pimpinella.**

But a fresh sprig in *Wine*, recommends it to us as its most genuine Element.

50. Purslain, *Portulaca*; especially the *Golden* whilst tender, next the Seed-leaves, with the young Stalks, being eminently moist and cooling, quickens Appetite, asswages Thirst, and is very profitable for hot and *Bilious* Tempers, as well as *Sanguine*, and generally entertain'd in all our *Sallets*, mingled with the hotter Herbs: 'Tis likewise familiarly eaten alone with *Oyl* and *Vinegar*; but with moderation, as having been sometimes found to corrupt in the

Stomach, which being *Pickl'd* 'tis not so apt to do. Some eat it cold, after it has been boil'd, which Dr. *Muffet* * would have in *Wine*, for Nourishment.

The Shrub *Halimus*, is a sort of *Sea-Purslain*: The newly peeping Leaves (tho' rarely us'd) afford a no unpleasant *Acidule*, even during winter, if it prove not too severe.

Purslain is accus'd for being hurtful to the *Teeth*, if too much eaten.

※ 51. Radish, *Raphanus*. Albeit rather Medicinal, than so commendably accompanying our *Sallets* (wherein they often slice the larger Roots) are much inferior to the young Seedling Leaves and Roots; raised on the Monthly *Hot-Bed*, almost the whole Year round, affording a very grateful mordacity, and sufficiently attempers the cooler Ingredients: The bigger Roots (so much desir'd) should be such as being transparent, eat short and quick, without stringiness, and not too biting. These are eaten alone with *Salt* only, as carrying their *Peper* in them; and were indeed by *Dioscorides* and *Pliny** celebrated above all Roots whatsoever; insomuch as in the *Delphic* Temple, there was *Raphanus ex auro dicatus*,* a Radish of solid Gold; and 'tis said of *Moschius*,* that he wrote a whole Volume in their praise. Notwithstanding all which, I am sure, the great *Hippocrates** utterly condemns them, as *Vitiosae, innantantes ac aegre concoctiles*.* And the *Naturalist* calls it *Cibus Illiberalis*,* fitter for *Rustics* than *Gentlemens* Tables. And indeed (besides that they decay the Teeth) experience tells us, that as the Prince of *Physicians* writes, It is hard of Digestion, *Inimicous** to the Stomach, causing nauseous Eructations, and sometimes Vomiting, tho' otherwise *Diuretic*, and thought to repel the Vapours of *Wine*, when the *Wits* were at their genial *Club. Dioscorides** and *Galen** differ about their Eating; One prescribes it before Meals, the latter for after. Some macerate the young Roots in warm milk, to render them more *Nourishing*.

There is a *Raphanus rusticanus*, the *Spanish* black *Horse Radish*, of a hotter quality, and not so friendly to the Head; but a notable *Antiscorbutic*, which may be eaten all the Winter, and on that account an excellent Ingredient in the Composition of *Mustard*; as are also the thin Shavings, mingled with our cold Herbs. And now before I have done with this Root, for an excellent and universal *Condiment*. Take *Horse-Radish*, whilst newly drawn out of the Earth, otherwise laid to steep in Water a competent time; then *grate* it on a *Grater* which has no bottom, that so it may pass thro', like a Mucilage, into a Dish of Earthen Ware: This temper'd with *Vinegar*, in which a little *Sugar* has been dissolv'd, you have a *Sauce* supplying *Mustard* to the *Sallet*, and serving likewise for any Dish besides.

52. Rampion, *Rapunculus*, or the *Esculent Campanula*: The tender Roots eaten in the Spring, like those of *Radishes*, but much more Nourishing.

53. Rocket, *Erucā Spanish*; hot and dry, to be qualified with *Lettuce*, *Purcelain*, and the rest, &c. See *Tarragon*.

Roccombo. See *Onions*.

54. Rosemary, *Rosmarinus*; Soverainly *Cephalic*, and for the *Memory*, *Sight*, and *Nerves*, incomparable: And tho' not us'd in the Leaf with our *Sallet* furniture, yet the *Flowers*, a little bitter, are always welcome in *Vinegar*; but above all, a fresh Sprig or two in a Glass of *Wine*. See *Flowers*.

55. Sage, *Salvia*; hot and dry. The tops of the *Red*, well pick'd and wash'd (being often defil'd with Venomous Slime, and almost imperceptible *Insects*) with the *Flowers*, retain all the noble Proper-ties of the other hot Plants; more especially for the *Head*, *Memory*, *Eyes*, and all *Paralytical* Affections. In short, 'tis a Plant endu'd with so many and wonderful Properties, as that the assiduous use of it is said to render Men *Immortal*: We cannot therefore but allow the tender *Summities** of the young Leaves; but principally the *Flowers* in our cold *Sallet*; yet so as not to domineer.

Salsifax, *Scorzonera*. See *Vipergrass*.

56. Sampier, *Crithmum*: That growing on the Sea-Cliffs (as about *Dover*, &c.) not only *Pickl'd*, but crude and cold, when young and tender (and such as we may Cultivate, and have in our *Kitchin-Gardens*, almost the Year round) is in my Opinion, for its *Aromatic*,

and other excellent Vertues and Effects against the *Spleen*, Cleansing the Passages, sharpning Appetite, &c. so far preferrable to most of our hotter Herbs, and *Sallet*-Ingredients, that I have long wonder'd, it has not been long since propagated in the *Potagere*, as it is in *France*; from whence I have often receiv'd the Seeds, which have prosper'd better, and more kindly with me, than what comes from our own Coasts: It does not indeed *Pickle* so well, as being of a more tender Stalk and Leaf: But in all other respects for composing *Sallets*, it has nothing like it.

❦ 57. Scalions, *Ascalonia, Cepæ*; The *French* call them *Appetites*, which it notably quickens and stirs up: Corrects Crudities, and promotes Concoction. The *Italians* steep them in Water, mince, and eat them cold with *Oyl, Vinegar, Salt*, &c.

❦ 58. Scurvy-grass, *Cochlearia*, of the Garden, but especially that of the Sea, is sharp, biting, and hot; of Nature like *Nasturtium*, prevalent in the *Scorbute*. A few of the tender Leaves may be admitted in our Composition. See *Nasturtium Indicum*.

❦ 59. Sellery, *Apium Italicum*, (and of the *Petroseline* Family) was formerly a stranger with us (nor very long since in *Italy*) is an hot and more generous sort of *Macedonian Persley*, or *Smallage*. The tender Leaves of the *Blancht* Stalk do well in our *Sallet*, as likewise the slices of the whiten'd Stems, which being crimp and short, first peel'd and slit long wise, are eaten with *Oyl, Vinegar, Salt*, and *Peper*; and for its high and grateful Taste, is ever plac'd in the middle of the *Grand Sallet*, at our Great Mens Tables, and *Prætors* Feasts,* as the Grace of the whole Board. *Caution* is to be given of a small red *Worm*, often lurking in these Stalks, as does the green in *Fennil*.

Shallots. See *Onion*.

❦ 60. Skirrets, *Sisarum*; hot and moist, corroborating, and good for the Stomach, exceedingly nourishing, wholsome and delicate; of all the *Root-kind*, not subject to be Windy, and so valued by the Emperor *Tiberius*, that he accepted them for Tribute.

This excellent Root is seldom eaten raw; but being boil'd, stew'd, roasted under the Embers, bak'd in Pies, whole, sliced, or in pulp, is very acceptable to all Palates. 'Tis reported they were heretofore something bitter; See what Culture and Education effects!

※ 61. Sorrel, *Acetosa*: of which there are divers kinds. The *French Acetocella*, with the round Leaf, growing plentifully in the *North* of *England*; *Roman Oxalis*; the broad *German*, &c. but the best is of *Green-Land*: by nature cold, Abstersive, Acid, sharpning Appetite, asswages Heat, cools the Liver, strengthens the Heart; is an *Anti-scorbutic*, resisting Putrefaction, and imparting so grateful a quickness to the rest, as supplies the want of *Orange, Limon*, and other *Omphacia*,* and therefore never to be excluded. Vide *Wood-Sorrel*.

※ 62. Sow-thistle, *Sonchus*; of the *Intybus*-kind. *Galen** was us'd to eat it as *Lettuce*; exceedingly welcome to the late *Morocco*. Ambassador and his Retinue.

※ 63. Sparagus, *Asparagus (ab Asperitate)* temperately hot, and moist; *Cordial, Diuretic*, easie of Digestion, and next to *Flesh*, nothing more nourishing, as *Sim. Sethius*, an excellent Physician holds. They are sometimes, but very seldom, eaten raw with *Oyl*, and *Vinegar*; but with more delicacy (the bitterness first exhausted) being so speedily boil'd, as not to lose the *verdure* and agreeable tenderness; which is done by letting the Water boil, before you put them in. I do not esteem the *Dutch* great and larger sort (especially rais'd by the rankness of the Beds) so sweet and agreeable, as those of a moderate size.

※ 64. Spinach, *Spinachia*: of old not us'd in *Sallets*, and the oftner kept out the better; I speak of the *crude*: But being boil'd to a *Pult*, and without other Water than its own moisture, is a most excellent Condiment with *Butter, Vinegar*, or *Limon*, for almost all sorts of boil'd Flesh, and may accompany a Sick Man's Diet. 'Tis *Laxative* and *Emollient*, and therefore profitable for the Aged, and (tho' by original a *Spaniard*…) may be had at almost any Season, and in all places.

Stone-Crop, *Sedum Minus*. See *Trick-Madame*.

※ 65. Succory, *Cichorium*, an *Intube*; erratic and wild, with a narrow dark Leaf, different from the *Sative*, tho' probably by culture only; and for being very bitter, a little *edulcorated** with *Sugar* and *Vinegar*, is by some eaten in the Summer, and more grateful to the Stomach than the Palate. See *Endive*.

❧ 66. Tansy, *Tanacetum*; hot and cleansing; but in regard of its domineering relish, sparingly mixt with our cold *Sallet*, and much fitter (tho' in very small quantity) for the Pan, being qualified with the Juices of other fresh Herbs, *Spinach*, *Green Corn*, *Violet*, *Primrose-Leaves*, &c. at entrance of the Spring, and then fried brownish, is eaten hot with the Juice of *Orange* and *Sugar*, as one of the most agreeable of all the boil'd *Herbaceous* Dishes.

❧ 67. Tarragon, *Draco Herba*, of *Spanish* Extraction; hot and spicy: The Tops and young Shoots, like those of *Rochet*, never to be secluded from our Composition, especially where there is much *Lettuce*. 'Tis highly cordial and friendly to the Head, Heart, Liver, correcting the weakness of the Ventricle, &c.

❧ 68. Thistle, *Carduus Mariæ*; our Lady's milky or dappl'd Thistle, disarm'd of its Prickles, is worth esteem: The young Stalk about *May*, being peel'd and soak'd in Water, to extract the bitterness, boil'd or raw, is a very wholsome *Sallet*, eaten with *Oyl*, *Salt*, and *Peper*; some eat them sodden in proper Broath, or bak'd in Pies, like the *Artichoak*; but the tender Stalk boil'd or fry'd, some preferr; both Nourishing and Restorative.

❧ 69. Trick-Madame, *Sedum minus*, Stone-Crop; is cooling and moist, grateful to the Stomach. The *Cimata** and Tops, when young and tender, dress'd as *Purselane*, is a frequent Ingredient in our cold *Sallet*.

❧ 70. Turnep, *Rapum*; moderately hot and moist: *Napus*; the long *Navet* is certainly the most delicate of them, and best Nourishing. *Pliny** speaks of no fewer than six sorts, and of several Colours; some of which were suspected to be artificially tinged. But with us, the yellow is preferr'd; by others the red *Bohemian*. But of whatever kind, being sown upon the *Hot-bed*, and no bigger than seedling *Radish*, they do excellently in Composition; as do also the Stalks of the common *Turnep*, when first beginning to Bud.

And here should not be forgotten, that wholsome, as well as agreeable sort of *Bread*, we are taught to make; and of which we have eaten at the greatest Persons Tables, hardly to be distinguish'd from the best of *Wheat*.

Let the *Turneps* first be peel'd, and boil'd in Water till soft and tender; then strongly pressing out the Juice, mix them together, and when dry (beaten or pounded very fine) with their weight of Wheat-Meal, season it as you do other *Bread*, and knead it up; then letting the Dough remain a little to *ferment*, fashion the Paste into Loaves, and bake it like common Bread.

Some roast *Turneps* in a Paper under the Embers, and eat them with *Sugar* and *Butter*.

⅋ 71. Vine, *Vitis*, the *Capreols*,* *Tendrels*, and *Claspers* (like those of the *Hop*, &c.) whilst very young, have an agreeable *Acid*, which may be eaten alone, or with other *Sallet*.

⅋ 72. Viper-grass, *Tragopogon*, *Scorzonera*, *Salsifex*, &c. tho' Medicinal, and excellent against the *Palpitation of the Heart*, *Faintings*, *Obstruction of the Bowels*, &c. are besides a very sweet and pleasant *Sallet*; being laid to soak out the bitterness, then peel'd, may be eaten raw, or *Condited*; but best of all stew'd with *Marrow*, *Spice*, *Wine*, &c. as *Artichoak*, *Skirrets*, &c. sliced or whole. They likewise may bake, fry, or boil them; a more excellent Root there is hardly growing.

⅋ 73. Wood-Sorrel, *Trifolium acetosum*, or *Alleluja*, of the nature of other *Sorrels*.

To all which might we add sundry more, formerly had in *deliciis*, since grown *obsolete* or quite neglected with us: As among the noblest *Bulbs*, that of the *Tulip*; a Root of which has been valued not to eat, but for the *Flower* (and yet eaten by mistake) at more than an hundred Pounds. The young fresh *Bulbs* are sweet and high of taste. The *Asphodil* or *Daffodil*; a *Sallet* so rare in *Hesiod's** Days, that *Lobel*...* thinks it the *Parsnep*, tho' not at all like it; however it was (with the *Mallow*) taken anciently for any *Edule*-Root.

The *Ornithogalons* roasted, as they do *Chestnuts*, are eaten by the *Italians*, the wild yellow especially, with *Oyl*, *Vinegar*, and *Peper*. And

Sallet-Eaters (who yet bestow as odious an Epithet on the vulgar *Garlick*) would cry out upon it as intolerable, and perhaps hardly believe it: But as *Aristophanes** has brought it in, and sufficiently describ'd it; so the *Scholiast** upon the place, puts it out of Controversy: And that they made use both of the *Leaves, Stalk,* (and *Extract* especially) as we now do *Garlick,* and other *Hautgouts** as nauseous altogether. In the mean time, *Garcius,** *Bontius,** and others, assure us, that the *Indians* at this day universally sauce their Viands with it; and the *Bramins** (who eat no Flesh at all) inrich their *Sallets,* by constantly rubbing the Dishes with it. Nor are some of our own skilful *Cooks* Ignorant, how to condite and use it, with the Applause of those, who, ignorant of the Secret, have admir'd the richness of the Gust it has imparted, when it has been substituted instead of all our *Cipollati,* and other seasonings of that Nature.

And thus have we done with the various *Species* of all such *Esculents* as may properly enter the Composition of our *Acetaria,* and cold *Sallet.* And if I have briefly touch'd upon their Natures, Degrees, and *primary Qualities,* which *Intend* or *Remit,* as to the Scale of *Heat, Cold, Driness, Moisture,* &c. (which is to be understood according to the different Texture of their *component Particles*) it has not been without what I thought necessary for the Instruction of the *Gatherer,* and *Sallet-Dresser;* how he ought to choose, sort, and mingle his Materials and Ingredients together.

What Care and Circumspection should attend the choice and collection of *Sallet* Herbs, has been partly shew'd. I can therefore, by no means, approve of that extravagant Fancy of some, who tell us, that a *Fool* is as fit to be the *Gatherer* of a *Sallet* as a *Wiser* Man. Because, say they, one can hardly choose amiss, provided the Plants be green, young, and tender, where-ever they meet with them: But sad experience shews, how many fatal Mistakes have been committed by those who took the deadly *Cicutæ, Hemlocks, Aconits,* &c. for Garden *Persley,* and *Parsneps;* the *Myrrhis Sylvestris,* or *Cow-Weed,* for *Chaerophilum,* (*Chervil*) *Thapsia* for *Fennel;* the wild *Chondrilla* for *Succory; Dogs-Mercury* instead of *Spinach: Papaver Corniculatum Luteum,* and horn'd *Poppy* for *Eringo; Oenanthe aquatica* for the *Palustral Apium,* and a world more, whose dire effects have been many times sudden Death, and the cause of Mortal Accidents to those who have eaten of them unwittingly: But supposing some of those wild and unknown Plants should not prove so *deleterious* and unwholsome; yet may others of them annoy the *Head*, *Brain*, and *Genus Nervosum*, weaken the *Eyes*, offend the *Stomach*, affect the *Liver*, torment the *Bowels*, and discover their malignity in dangerous and dreadful *Symptoms*. And therefore such *Plants* as are rather *Medicinal* than *Nourishing* and *Refreshing*, are studiously to be rejected. So highly necessary it is, that what we sometimes find in *old Books* concerning *Edules* of other Countries and Climates (frequently call'd by the Names of such as are wholsome in ours, and among us) mislead not the unskilful Gatherer; to prevent which we read of divers *Popes* and *Emperors*, that had sometimes Learned *Physicians* for their *Master-Cooks*. I cannot therefore but exceedingly approve of that charitable Advice of Mr. *Ray** (*Transact. Num.* 238.) who thinks it the Interest of Mankind, that all Persons should be caution'd of advent'ring upon unknown Herbs and Plants to their Prejudice: Of such, I say, with our excellent *Poet** (a little chang'd)

> *Happy from such conceal'd, if still do lie,*
> *Of Roots and Herbs the* unwholsome *Luxury.*

The Illustrious and Learned *Columna** has, by observing what *Insects* did usually feed on, make Conjectures of the Nature of the Plants. But I should not so readily adventure upon it on that account, as to its wholsomness: For tho' indeed one may safely eat of a *Peach* or *Abricot*, after a *Snail* has been Taster, I question whether it might be so of all other Fruits and Herbs attack'd by other *Insects*: Nor would one conclude, the *Hyoscyamus* harmless, because the *Cimex** feeds upon it, as the Learned Dr. *Lyster** has discover'd. Notice should therefore be taken what *Eggs* of *Insects* are found adhering to the Leaves of *Sallet-Herbs*, and frequently cleave so firmly to them, as not easily to be wash'd off, and so not being taken notice of, passing for accidental and harmless Spots only, may yet produce very ill effects.

*Grillus,** who according to the Doctrine of *Transmigration* (as

*Plutarch** tells us) had, in his turn, been a *Beast*; discourses how much better he fed, and liv'd, than when he was turn'd to *Man* again, as knowing then, what Plants were best and most proper for him: Whilst Men, *Sarcophagists** (Flesh-Eaters) in all this time were yet to seek. And 'tis indeed very evident, that Cattel, and other πάνφαγα,* and *herbaceous* Animals which feed on Plants, are directed by their Smell, and accordingly make election of their Food: But Men (bessides the *Smell* and *Taste*) have, or should have, *Reason, Experience*, and the Aids of *Natural Philosophy* to be their Guides in this Matter. We have heard *of Plants*, that (like the *Basilisk*)* kill and infect by looking on them only; and some by the touch. The truth is, there's need of all the Senses to determine *Analogically** concerning the Vertues and Properties, even of the *Leaves* alone of many *Edule Plants*: The most eminent Principles of near the whole Tribe of *Sallet* Vegetables, inclining rather to *Acid* and *Sowre* than to any other quality, especially, Salt, Sweet, or Luscious. There is therefore Skill and Judgment requir'd, how to suit and mingle our *Sallet*-Ingredients, so as may best agree with the Constitution of the (vulgarly reputed) *Humors* of those who either stand in need of, or affect these Refreshments, and by so adjusting them, that as nothing should be suffer'd to domineer, so should none of them lose their genuine Gust, Savour, or Vertue. To this end,

The Cooler, and moderately refreshing, should be chosen to extinguish Thirst, attemper the Blood, repress Vapours, &c.

The Hot, Dry, Aromatic, Cordial and friendly to the Brain, may be qualify'd by the Cold and Moist: The Bitter and Stomachical, with the *Sub-acid* and gentler Herbs: The *Mordicant* and pungent, and such as repress or discuss Flatulency (revive the Spirits, and aid Concoction;) with such as abate, and take off the keenness, mollify and reconcile the more harsh and churlish: The mild and insipid, animated with *piquant* and brisk: The Astringent and Binders, with such as are Laxative and Deobstruct: The over-sluggish, raw, and unactive, with those that are Eupeptic, and promote Concoction: There are *Pectorals** for the Breast and Bowels. Those of middle Nature, according as they appear to be more or less *Specific*; and as their

169

Characters (tho' briefly) are describ'd in our foregoing *Catalogue*:
For notwithstanding it seem in general, that raw *Sallets* and *Herbs*
have experimentally been found to be the most soveraign Diet in
that *Endemial* (and indeed with us, *Epidemical*...* and almost universal) Contagion the *Scorbute*, to which we of this Nation, and
most other *Ilanders* are obnoxious; yet, since the *Nasturtia* are singly,
and alone as it were, the most effectual, and powerful Agents in
conquering and expugning that cruel Enemy; it were enough to give
the *Sallet-Dresser* direction how to choose, mingle, and proportion
his Ingredients; as well as to shew what Remedies there are contain'd in our Magazine of *Sallet-Plants* upon all Occasions, rightly
marshal'd and skilfully apply'd. So as (with our sweet *Cowley*)*

> If thro' the strong and beauteous Fence
> Of Temperance and Innocence,
> And wholsome Labours, and a quiet Mind,
> Diseases passage find;
> They must not think here to assail
> A Land unarm'd, or without Guard,
> They must fight for it, and dispute it hard,
> Before they can prevail;
> Scarce any Plant is used here,
> Which 'gainst some Aile a Weapon does not bear.

We have said how necessary it is, that in the Composure of a
Sallet, every Plant should come in to bear its part, without being
over-power'd by some Herb of a stronger Taste, so as to endanger
the native *Sapor** and vertue of the rest; but fall into their places,
like the *Notes* in *Music*, in which there should be nothing harsh or
grating: And tho' admitting some *Discords* (to distinguish and
illustrate the rest) striking in the more sprightly, and sometimes
gentler Notes, reconcile all Dissonancies, and melt them into an
agreeable Composition. Thus the Comical *Master-Cook*, introduc'd
by *Damoxenus*,* when asked πῶς ἐστιν αὐτοῖς συμφωνία;* *What
Harmony there was in Meats?* The very same (says he) that a *Diatessaron*,* *Diapente*,* and *Diapason** have one to another in a Consort
of Music: And that there was as great care requir'd, not to mingle

Sapores minime consentientes,* jarring and repugnant Tastes; looking upon him as a lamentable Ignorant, who should be no better vers'd in *Democritus.** The whole Scene is very diverting, as *Athenæus* presents it; and to the same sense *Macrobius,** *Saturn. lib.* I. *cap.* I. In short, the main Skill of the Artist lies in this:

> *What choice to choose, for delicacy best;*
> *What Order so contriv'd, as not to mix*
>
> *Tastes not well join'd, inelegant, but bring*
> *Taste after Taste, upheld by kindliest change.*

As our *Paradisian Bard*......* introduces Eve, dressing of a *Sallet* for her *Angelical* Guest.

Thus, by the discreet choice and mixture of the *Oxoleon* (*Oyl*, *Vinegar*, *Salt*, &c.) the Composition is perfect; so as neither the *Prodigal, Niggard*, nor *Insipid*, should (according to the *Italian* Rule) prescribe in my Opinion; since *One* may be too profuse, the *Other* over-saving, and the *Third* (like himself......) give it no Relish at all: It may be too *sharp*, if it exceed a grateful *Acid*; too *Insulse* and flat, if the Profusion be extream. From all which it appears, that a Wise-Man is the proper Composer of an excellent *Sallet*, and how many *Transcendences* belong to an accomplish'd *Sallet-Dresser*, so as to emerge an exact *Critic* indeed, He should be skill'd in the Degrees, Terms, and various *Species* of Tastes, according to the *Scheme* set us down in the *Tables* of the Learned Dr. *Grew*,* to which I refer the Curious.

'Tis moreover to be consider'd, that *Edule* Plants are not in all their Tastes and Vertues alike: For as Providence has made us to consist of different Parts and Members, both Internal and External; so require they different Juices to nourish and supply them: Wherefore the force and activity of some Plants lie in the *Root*; and even the *Leaves* of some *Bitter-Roots* are sweet, and *è contra*. Of others, in the *Stem, Leaves, Buds, Flowers*, &c. Some exert their Vigour without *Decoction*; others being a little press'd or contus'd; others again *Raw*, and best in Consort; some alone, and *per'se* without any σχευασία,* Preparation, or Mixture at all. Care therefore must be taken by the *Collector*, that what he gathers answer to these Qualities; and that as near as he can, they consist (I speak of the *cruder Salleting*) of the *Oluscula*, and *ex foliis pubescentibus*,* or (as *Martial*......* calls them) *Prototomi rudes*,* and very tenderest Parts *Gems*, young *Buds*, and even first Rudiments of their several Plants; such as we sometimes find in the *Craws* of the *Wood-Culver*, *Stock-Dove*,* *Partridge*, *Pheasants*, and other Upland Fowl, where we have a natural *Sallet*, pick'd, and almost dress'd to our hands.

❧ I. Preparatory to the Dressing therefore, let your Herby Ingredients be exquisitely cull'd, and cleans'd of all worm-eaten, slimy, canker'd, dry, spotted, or any ways vitiated Leaves. And then that they be rather discreetly sprinkl'd, than over-much sob'd with Spring-Water, especially *Lettuce*, which Dr. *Muffet* thinks impairs their Vertue; but this, I suppose he means of the *Cabbage*-kind, whose heads are sufficiently protected by the outer Leaves which cover it. After washing, let them remain a while in the *Cullender*, to drain the superfluous moisture: And lastly, swing them altogether gently in a clean course Napkin; and so they will be in perfect condition to receive the *Intinctus** following.

❧ II. That the *Oyl*, an Ingredient so indispensibly and highly necessary, as to have obtain'd the name of *Cibarium** (and with us of *Sallet-Oyl*) be very clean, not high-colour'd, nor yellow; but with an Eye rather of a pallid *Olive* green, without Smell, or the least touch of *rancid*, or indeed of any other sensible Taste or Scent at all; but smooth, light, and pleasant upon the Tongue; such as the genuine *Omphacine*,* and native *Luca Olives** afford, fit to allay the tartness of *Vinegar*, and other *Acids*, yet gently to warm and humectate* where it passes. Some who have an aversion to *Oyl*, substitute fresh *Butter* in its stead; but 'tis so exceedingly clogging to the Stomach, as by no means to be allow'd.

❧ III. *Thirdly*, That the *Vinegar* and other liquid *Acids*, perfectly clear, neither sowre, *Vapid* or spent; be of the best Wine Vinegar, whether Distill'd, or otherwise *Aromatiz'd*, and impregnated with the Infusion of *Clove-gillyflowers*, *Elder*, *Roses*, *Rosemary*, *Nasturtium*, &c. inrich'd with the Vertues of the Plant.

A *Verjuice* not unfit for *Sallet*, is made by a *Grape* of that Name, or the green immature Clusters of most other Grapes, press'd and put into a small Vessel to ferment.

𝕾 IV. *Fourthly,* That the *Salt (aliorum Condimentorum Condimentum,*[*] as *Plutarch* calls it) detersive,[*] penetrating, quickning (and so great a resister of Putrefaction, and universal use, as to have sometimes merited Divine Epithets) be of the brightest *Bay grey-Salt;*[*] moderately dried, and *contus'd,* as being the least Corrosive: But of this, as of *Sugar* also, which some mingle with the *Salt* (as warming without heating) if perfectly refin'd, there would be no great difficulty; provided none, save Ladies, were of the Mess; whilst the perfection of *Sallets,* and that which gives them the name, consists in the grateful *Saline Acid*-point, temper'd as is directed, and which we find to be most esteem'd by judicious Palates: Some, in the mean time, have been so nice, and luxuriously curious as for the heightning, and (as they affect to speak) giving the utmost *poinant* and *Relevèe*[*] in lieu of our vulgar *Salt,* to recommend and cry-up the *Essential-Salts* and *Spirits* of the most Sanative Vegetables; or such of the *Alcalizate*[*] and *Fixt,* extracted from the *Calcination* of *Baulm,*[*] *Rosemary, Wormwood, Scurvy-grass,* &c. Affirming that without the gross Plant, we might have healing, cooling, generous, and refreshing *Cordials,* and all the *Materia Medica* out of the *Salt-Cellar* only: But to say no more of this Impertinence, as to *Salts* of *Vegetables;* many indeed there be, who reckon them not much unlike in Operation, however different in *Taste, Crystals,* and *Figure:* It being a question, whether they at all retain the Vertues and Faculties of their *Simples,* unless they could be made without *Colcination. Franciscus Redi,*[*] gives us his Opinion of this, in a *Process* how they are to be prepar'd; and so does our Learned Doctor[*] (whom we lately nam'd) whether *Lixivial,*[*] *Essential, Marine,* or other factitious *Salts* of Plants, with their Qualities, and how they differ: But since 'tis thought all *Fixed Salts* made the *common way,* are little better than our *common Salt,* let it suffice, that our *Sallet-Salt* be of the best ordinary *Bay-Salt,* clean, bright, dry, and without claminess.

Of *Sugar* (by some call'd *Indian-Salt*)[*] as it is rarely us'd in *Sallet,* it should be of the best refined, white, hard, close, yet light and sweet as the *Madera's:* Nourishing, preserving, cleansing, delighting the Taste, and preferrable to *Honey* for most uses. *Note,* That both *this, Salt,* and *Vinegar,* are to be proportion'd to the Constitution, as well as what is said of the Plants themselves. The one for cold, the other for hot stomachs.

V. That the *Mustard* (another noble Ingredient) be of the best *Tewksberry;* or else compos'd of the soundest and weightiest *York-shire Seed,** exquisitely sifted, winnow'd, and freed from the Husks, a little (not over-much) dry'd by the Fire, temper'd to the consistence of a Pap with *Vinegar,* in which shavings of the *Horse-Radish* have been steep'd: Then cutting an *Onion,* and putting it into a small Earthen *Gally-Pot,** or some thick *Glass* of that shape; pour the *Mustard* over it, and close it very well with a *Cork.* There be, who preserve the Flower and Dust of the bruised Seed in a well-stopp'd Glass, to temper, and have it fresh when they please. But what is yet by some esteem'd beyond all these, is compos'd of the dried Seeds of the *Indian Nasturtium,* reduc'd to Powder, finely bolted, and mixt with a little *Levain,* and so from time to time made fresh, as indeed all other *Mustard* should be.

Note, That the Seeds are pounded in a Mortar; or bruis'd with a polish'd *Cannon-Bullet,* in a large wooden Bowl-Dish, or which is most preferr'd, ground in a *Quern* contriv'd for this purpose only.

VI. *Sixthly,* That the *Pepper* (white or black) be not bruis'd to too small a Dust; which, as we caution'd, is very prejudicial. And here let me mention the *Root* of the *Minor Pimpinella,* or small *Burnet Saxifrage;* which being dried, is by some extoll'd beyond all other *Peppers,* and more wholsom.

Of other *Strewings* and *Aromatizers,* which may likewise be admitted to inrich our *Sallet,* we have already spoken, where we mention *Orange* and *Limon-peel;* to which may also be added, *Jamaica-Pepper,** *Juniper-berries,* &c. as of singular Vertue.

Nor here should I omit (the mentioning at least of......) *Saffron,* which the *German* Housewives have a *way* of forming into Balls, by mingling it with a little *Honey;* which throughly dried, they reduce to Powder, and sprinkle it over their *Sallets* for a noble *Cordial.* Those of *Spain* and *Italy,* we know, generally make use of this Flower, mingling its golden Tincture with almost every thing they eat; But its being so apt to prevail above every thing with which 'tis blended, we little incourage its admittance into our *Sallet*.

❧ VII. Seventhly, That there be the Yolks of fresh and new-laid *Eggs*, boil'd moderately hard, to be mingl'd and mash'd with the *Mustard*, *Oyl*, and *Vinegar*; and part to cut into quarters, and eat with the Herbs.

❧ VIII. *Eighthly*, (according to the *super*-curious) that the *Knife*, with which the *Sallet Herbs* are cut (especially *Oranges*, *Limons*, &c.) be of *Silver*, and by no means of *Steel*, which all *Acids* are apt to corrode, and retain a Metalic relish of.

❧ IX. *Ninthly* and *Lastly*, That the *Saladiere*, (Sallet-Dishes) be of *Porcelane*, or of the *Holland-Delft-Ware*; neither too deep nor shallow, according to the quantity of the *Sallet* Ingredients; *Pewter*, or even *Silver*, not at all so well agreeing with *Oyl* and *Vinegar*, which leave their several Tinctures. And note, That there ought to be one of the Dishes, in which to beat and mingle the Liquid *Vehicles*; and a second to receive the crude Herbs in, upon which they are to be pour'd; and then with a Fork and a Spoon kept continually stirr'd, 'till all the Furniture be equally moisten'd: Some, who are husbands of their *Oyl*, pour at first the *Oyl* alone, as more apt to communicate and diffuse its Slipperiness, than when it is mingled and beaten with the *Acids*; which they pour on last of all; and 'tis incredible how small a quantity of *Oyl* (in this quality, like the gilding of *Wyer*) is sufficient, to imbue a very plentiful assembly of *Sallet-Herbs*.

The *Sallet-Gatherer* likewise should be provided with a light, and neatly made *Withy-Dutch-Basket*, divided into several Partitions. Thus instructed and knowing in the *Apparatus*; the *Species*, *Proportions*, and manner of *Dressing*, according to the several Seasons you have in the following Table.

It being one of the Inquiries of the Noble Mr. *Boyle*,* what *Herbs* were proper and fit to make *Sallets* with, and how best to order them? we have here (by the Assistance of Mr. *London*,* His Majesty's Principal Gard'ner) reduc'd them to a competent Number, not exceeding *Thirty Five*; but which may be vary'd and inlarg'd, by taking in, or leaving out, any other *Sallet*-Plant, mention'd in the foregoing List, under these three or four Heads.

But all these sorts are not to be had at the very same time, and therefore we have divided them into the *Quarterly Seasons*, each containing and lasting Three Months.

Note, That by *Parts* is to be understood a *Pugil*,* which is no more than one does usually take up between the Thumb and the two next Fingers. By *Fascicule** a reasonable full Grip, or Handful.

Species.	Ordering and Culture
1. *Endive,*	Tied-up to Blanch.
2. *Cichory,*	
3. *Sellery,*	Earth'd-up
4. *Sweet-Fennel,*	
5. *Rampions,*	
6. *Roman*	Tied-up to Blanch.
7. *Cosse*	*Lettuce,*
8. *Silesian*	Tied close up.
9. *Cabbage*	Pome and Blanch of themselves.

IX. Blanch'd *(bracket spanning items 1–9)*

10. *Lob-Lettuce,*	Leaves, all of a midling size.
11. *Corn-Sallet,*	
12. *Purslane,*	
13. *Cresses* broad,	Seed-Leaves, and the next to them.
14. *Spinach,* curled,	
15. *Sorrel* French,	The fine young Leaves only, with the
16. *Sorrel,* Greenland,	first Shoots.
17. *Radish,*	Only the tender young Leaves.
18. *Cresses,*	The Seed-Leaves, and those only next them.
19. *Turnep,*	The Seed-Leaves only.
20. *Mustard,*	
21. *Scurvy-grass,*	
22. *Chervil,*	The young Leaves immediately after
23. *Burnet,*	the Seedlings.
24. *Rocket,* Spanish	
25. *Persley,*	
26. *Tarragon,*	The tender Shoots and Tops.
27. *Mints,*	
28. *Sampier,*	The young tender Leaves and Shoots.
29. *Balm,*	
30. *Sage,* Red	
31. *Shalots,*	The tender young Leaves.
32. *Cives* and *Onion,*	
33. *Nasturtium,* Indian	The Flowers and Bud-Flowers.
34. *Rampion,* Belgrade	The Seed-Leaves and young Tops.
35. *Trip-Madame,*	

XXVI. Green Unblanch'd *(bracket spanning items 10–35)*

177

Month. *January*, *February*, and *March*.

Order. and Cult.	Species.	Proportion.
Blanch'd as before	*Rampions*, 10 *Endive*, 2 *Succory*, 5 *Fennel*, sweet, 10 *Sellery*, 4	} Roots in Number.
Green and Unblanch'd	*Lamb-Lettuce*, *Lob-Lettuce*,	} A pugil of each.
	Radish, *Cresses*,	} Three parts each.
	Turneps, *Mustard* Seedlings, *Scurvy-grass*,	} Of each One part.
	Spinach,	Two parts.
	Sorrel, Greenland, *Sorrel*, French, *Chervel*, sweet, *Burnet*, *Rocket*,	} One part of each.
	Tarragon,	Twenty large Leaves.
	Balm, *Mint*, *Sampier*,	} One small part of each.
	Shalots, *Cives*,	} Very few.
	Cabbage-Winter,	Two pugils or small handfuls.

Month. *April*, *May*, and *June*.

Order. and Cult.	Species.	Proportion.
Blanch'd	*Lop*, *Silesian* Winter } *Lettuce*. *Roman* Winter	Of each a pugil.
Green Herbs Unblanch'd.	*Radishes*,	Three parts.
	Cresses,	Two parts.
	Purselan,	1 Fasciat, or pretty full gripe.
	Sorrel, French	Two parts.
	Sampier,	One part.

Order.
and
Cult.   **Species.**   **Proportion.**

Month. *April*, *May*, and *June*. (continued)

Note, *That*	*Onions*, young	Six parts.
the young	*Sage*-tops, the Red,	Two parts.
Seedling Leaves	*Persley*,	
of Orange *and*	*Cresses*, the Indian,	
Limon *may all*	*Lettuce*, Belgrade,	Of each One part.
these Months be	*Trip-Madame*,	
mingled with	*Chervil*, sweet,	
the Sallet.	*Burnet*,	Two parts.

Month. *July*, *August*, and *September*.

Blanch'd, *and*	Silesian *Lettuce*,	One whole *Lettuce*.
may be eaten	Roman *Lettuce*,	Two parts.
by themselves	*Cress*,	
with some		
Nasturtium-	*Cabbage*,	Four parts.
Flowers		
	Cresses,	Two parts.
	Nasturtium,	
Green Herbs	*Purslane*,	One part.
by themselves,	*Lop-Lettuce*,	
or mingl'd	*Belgrade*, or Crumpen-	Two parts.
with the	*Lettuce*,	
Blanch'd.	*Tarragon*,	One part.
	Sorrel, French	Two parts of each.
	Burnet,	
	Trip-Madame,	One part.

Month. *October*, *November*, and *December*.

	Endive,	Two if large, four if small,
	Sellery,	Stalk and part of the Root and tenderest Leaves.
Blanch'd	*Lop-Lettuce*,	An handful of each.
	Lambs-Lettuce,	
	Radish,	Three parts.
	Cresses,	Two parts.
	Turneps,	One part of each.
Green	*Mustard* Seedlings,	
	Cresses, broad	Two parts of each.
	Spinach,	

Farther Directions concerning the proper Seasons *for the* Gathering, Composing, *and* Dressing *of a* Sallet.

AND *First*, as to the *Season* both *Plants* and *Roots* are then prop-erly to be *Gather'd*, and in prime, when most they abound with Juice and in Vigour: Some in the *Spring*, or a little anticipating it be-fore they Blossom, or are in full Flower: Some in the *Autumnal* Months; which later Season many prefer, the Sap of the Herb, tho' not in such exuberance, yet as being then better concocted, and so render'd fit for *Salleting*, 'till the Spring begins a fresh to put forth new, and tender Shoots and Leaves.

This, indeed, as to the *Root*, newly taken out of the Ground is true; and therefore should such have their *Germination* stopt the sooner: The approaching and prevailing Cold, both Maturing and Impregnating them; as does Heat the contrary, which now would but exhaust them: But for those other *Esculents* and Herbs imploy'd in our *Composition* of *Sallets*, the early *Spring*, and ensuing Months (till they begin to mount, and prepare to *Seed*) is certainly the most natural, and kindly Season to collect and accommodate them for the Table. Let none then consult *Culpeper*,* or the *Figure-flingers*,* to inform them when the governing *Planet* is in its *Exaltation*; but look upon the *Plants* themselves, and judge of their Vertues by their own Complexions.

Moreover, in *Gathering*, Respect is to be had to their Propor-tions, as provided for in the *Table* under that Head, be the Quality whatsoever: For tho' there is indeed nothing more wholsome than *Lettuce* and *Mustard* for the *Head* and *Eyes*; yet either of them eaten in excess, were highly prejudicial to them both: Too much of the *first* extreamly debilitating and weakning the *Ventricle*, and hastning the further decay of sickly *Teeth*; and of the *second* the *Optic Nerves*, and *Sight* it self; the like may be said of all the rest. I conceive there-fore, a Prudent Person, well acquainted with the Nature and Properties of *Sallet-Herbs*, &c. to be both the fittest *Gatherer* and *Composer* too; which yet will require no great Cunning, after once he is acquainted with our *Table* and *Catalogue*.

We purposely, and *in transitu* only, take notice here of the Pickl'd, *Muriated,** or otherwise prepared Herbs; excepting some such Plants, and Proportions of them, as are of hard digestion, and not fit to be eaten altogether *Crude*, (of which in the *Appendix*) and among which I reckon *Ash-keys*, *Broom-buds* and *Pods*, *Haricos*, *Gurkems*, *Olives*, *Capers*, the Buds and Seeds of *Nasturtia*, *Young Wall-nuts*, *Pineapples*, *Eringo*, *Cherries*, *Cornelians*, *Berberries*, *&c.* together with several Stalks, Roots, and Fruits; Ordinary Pot-herbs, *Anis*, *Cistus Hortorum*, *Horminum*, *Pulegium*, *Satureia*, *Thyme*; the intire Family of Pulse and *Legumena*; or other *Sauces*, *Pies*, *Tarts*, *Omlets*, *Tansie*,* *Farces*, &c. *Condites** and Preserves with *Sugar* by the Hand of Ladies; tho' they are all of them the genuine Production of the *Garden*, and mention'd in our *Kalendar*, together with their Culture; whilst we confine our selves to such Plants and *Esculenta* as we find at hand; delight our selves to gather, and are easily prepar'd for an *Extemporary Collation*, or to Usher in, and Accompany other (more Solid, tho' haply not more Agreeable) Dishes, as the Custom is.

But there now starts up a Question, Whether it were better, or more proper, to *Begin* with *Sallets*, or End and Conclude with them? Some think the harder Meats should first be eaten for better Concoction; others, those of easiest Digestion, to make way, and prevent Obstruction; and this makes for our *Sallets*, *Horarii*,* and *Fugaces Fructus** (as they call 'em) to be eaten first of all, as agreeable to the general Opinion of the great *Hippocrates*, and *Galen*, and of *Celsus** before him. And therefore the *French* do well, to begin with their *Herbaceous Pottage*, and for the *Cruder*, a Reason is given:

> *Prima tibi dabitur Ventri* Lactuca *movendo*
> *Utilis, & Porris fila refecta suis.**

And tho' this Custom came in about Domitian's* time, οἱ μέντοι ἀρχαῖοι,* they anciently did quite the contrary,

> *Gratáque nobilium Lactuca ciborum.**

But of later Times, they were constant at the *Ante-cœnia*,* eating plentifully of *Sallet*, especially of *Lettuce*, and more refrigerating Herbs. Nor without Cause: For drinking liberally they were found to expell, and allay the Fumes and Vapors of the *genial Compotation*, the spirituous Liquor gently conciliating Sleep: Besides, that being of a crude nature, more dispos'd, and apt to fluctuate, corrupt, and disturb a surcharg'd Stomach; they thought convenient to begin with *Sallets*, and innovate the ancient Usage.

> ——*Nam Lactuca innatat acri*
> *Post Vinum Stomacho*——

> For if on drinking Wine you Lettuce eat,
> It floats upon the Stomach——

The *Spaniards*, notwithstanding, eat but sparingly of Herbs at Dinner, especially *Lettuce*, beginning with *Fruit*, even before the *Olio*＊ and Hot-Meats come to the Table; drinking their Wine pure, and eating the best Bread in the World; so as it seems the Question still remains undecided with them,

> *Claudere quae cœnas* Lactuca *solebat avorum*
> *Dic mihi cur nostras inchoat illa dapes?*

> The *Sallet*, which of old came in at last,
> Why now with it begin we our Repast?

And now since we mention'd *Fruit*, there rises another Scruple: Whether *Apples*, *Pears*, *Abricots*, *Cherries*, *Plums*, and other Tree, and *Ort-yard-Fruit*, are to be reckon'd among *Salleting*; and when likewise most seasonably to be eaten? But as none of these do properly belong to our *Catalogue* of *Herbs* and *Plants*, to which this Discourse is confin'd (bessides what we may occasionally speak of hereafter) there is a very useful Treatise on that Subject already publish'd. We hasten then in the next place to the *Dressing*, and *Composing* of our Sallet: For by this time, our Scholar may long to see the *Rules* reduc'd to *Practice*, and Refresh himself with what he finds growing among his own *Lactuceta* and other Beds of the *Kitchin-Garden*.

Dressing

I AM not ambitious of being thought an excellent *Cook*, or of those who set up, and value themselves, for their skill in *Sauces*; such as was *Mithacus** a *Culinary Philosopher*, and other *Eruditæ Gulæ;** who read Lectures of *Hautgouts,** like the *Archestratus** in *Athenæus*: Tho' after what we find the *Heroes* did of old, and see them chining out the slaughter'd *Ox*, dressing the Meat, and do the Offices of both *Cook* and *Butcher*, (for so *Homer* represents *Achilles* himself, and the rest of those Illustrious *Greeks*) I say, after this, let none reproach our *Sallet-Dresser*, or disdain so clean, innocent, sweet, and Natural a Quality; compar'd with the Shambles* Filth and *Nidor,** Blood and Cruelty; whilst all the World were *Eaters*, and *Composers* of *Sallets* in its best and brightest Age.

The Ingredients therefore gather'd and proportion'd, as above; Let the *Endive* have all its out-side Leaves stripped off, slicing *in* the White: In like manner the *Sellery* is also to have the hollow green Stem or Stalk trimm'd and divided; slicing-in the blanched Part, and cutting the Root into four equal Parts.

Lettuce, *Cresses*, *Radish*, &c. (as was directed) must be exquisitely pick'd, cleans'd, wash'd, and put into the Strainer; swing'd, and shaken gently, and, if you please, separately, or all together; Because some like not so well the *Blanch'd* and Bitter Herbs, if eaten with the rest: Others mingle *Endive*, *Succory*, and *Rampions*, without distinction, and generally eat *Sellery* by it self, as also Sweet *Fennel*.

From *April* till *September* (and during all the Hot *Months*) may *Guinny-Pepper,** and *Horse-Radish* be left out; and therefore we only mention them in the Dressing, which should be in this manner.

Your *Herbs* being handsomely parcell'd, and spread on a clean Napkin before you, are to be mingl'd together in one of the Earthen glaz'd Dishes: Then, for the *Oxoleon*; Take of clear, and perfectly good *Oyl-Olive*, three Parts; of sharpest *Vinegar* (sweetest of all *Condiments*) *Limon*, or Juice of *Orange*, one Part; and therein let steep some Slices of *Horse-Radish*, with a little *Salt*; Some in a separate *Vinegar*, gently bruise a *Pod* of *Guinny-Pepper*, straining both the *Vinegars* apart, to make Use of Either, or One alone, or of both, as they best like; then add as much *Tewkesbury*, or other dry *Mustard* grated, as will lie upon an Half-Crown Piece:* Beat, and mingle all these very well together; but pour not on the *Oyl* and *Vinegar*, 'till immediately before the *Sallet* is ready to be eaten: And then with the *Yolk* of two new-laid *Eggs* (boyl'd and prepar'd, as before is taught) squash, and bruise them all into mash with a Spoon; and lastly, pour it all upon the *Herbs*, stirring, and mingling them 'till they are well and throughly imbib'd; not forgetting the Sprinklings of *Aromaticks*, and such Flowers, as we have already mentioned, if you think fit, and garnishing the Dish with the thin Slices of *Horse-Radish*, *Red Beet*, *Berberries*, &c.

Note, That the *Liquids* may be made more, or less *Acid*, as is most agreeable to your Taste.

These *Rules*, and *Prescriptions* duly *Observ'd*; you have a *Sallet* (for a Table of Six or Eight Persons) *Dress'd*, and Accommodated *secundum Artem*: For, as the Proverb has it,

Οὐ παντὸς ἀνδρός ἐστιν ἀρτῦσαι καλῶς.*

*Non est cujusvis rectè condire.**

AND now after all we have advanc'd in favour of the *Herbaceous* Diet, there still emerges a third Inquiry; namely, Whether the Use of *Crude Herbs* and *Plants* are so wholesom as is pretended?

What Opinion the Prince of Physicians had of them, we shall see hereafter; as also what the Sacred Records of elder Times seem to infer, before there were any Flesh-Shambles* in the World; together with the Reports of such as are often conversant among many Nations and People, who to this Day, living on *Herbs* and *Roots*, arrive to incredible Age, in constant Health and Vigour: Which, whether attributable to the *Air* and *Climate*, *Custom*, *Constitution*, &c. should be inquir'd into; especially, when we compare the *Antediluvians* mention'd *Gen.* 1. 29*—the whole *Fifth* and *Ninth* Chapters, *ver.* 3. confining them to *Fruit* and wholesom Sallets: I deny not that both the *Air* and *Earth* might then be less humid and clammy, and consequently Plants, and Herbs better fermented, concocted, and less Rheumatick, than since, and presently after; to say nothing of the infinite Numbers of putrid Carcasses of Dead Animals, perishing in the Flood, (of which I find few, if any, have taken notice) which needs must have corrupted the Air: Those who live in Marshes, and Uliginous Places (like the Hundreds of *Essex*)* being more obnoxious to *Fevers*, *Agues*, *Pleurisies*, and generally unhealthful: The Earth also then a very Bog, compar'd with what it likely was before that destructive *Cataclysm*, when Men breath'd the pure *Paradisian* Air, sucking in a more *æthereal*, nourishing, and baulmy *Pabulum*,* so foully vitiated now, thro' the Intemperance, Luxury, and softer Education and Effeminacy of the Ages since.

Custom, and *Constitution* come next to be examin'd, together with the Qualities, and *Vertue* of the Food; and I confess, the two first, especially that of *Constitution*, seems to me the more likely Cause of Health, and consequently of Long-life; which induc'd me to consider of what Quality the usual *Sallet* Furniture did more eminently consist, that so it might become more safely applicable to the Temper, Humour, and Disposition of our Bodies; according to which, the various Mixtures might be regulated and proportion'd: There's no doubt, but those whose Constitutions are Cold and Moist, are naturally affected with Things which are Hot and Dry; as on the contrary, Hot, and Dry Complexions, with such as cool and refrigerate; which perhaps made the *Junior Gordian** (and others like him) prefer the *frigidæ Mensæ* (as of old they call'd *Sallets*) which, according to *Cornelius Celsus*, is the fittest Diet for *Obese* and Corpulent Persons, as not so Nutritive, and apt to Pamper: And consequently, that for the Cold, Lean, and Emaciated; such Herby Ingredients should be made choice of, as warm, and cherish the Natural Heat, depure the Blood, breed a laudable Juice, and revive the Spirits: And therefore my *Lord Bacon** shews what are best Raw, what Boil'd, and what Parts of Plants fittest to nourish. *Galen* indeed seems to exclude them all, unless well accompanied with their due Correctives, of which we have taken care: Notwithstanding yet, that even the most *Crude* and *Herby*, actually Cold and Weak, may potentially be Hot, and Strengthning, as we find in the most vigorous Animals, whose Food is only Grass. 'Tis true indeed, Nature has providentially mingl'd, and dress'd a *Sallet* for them in every field, besides what they distinguish by Smell; nor question I, but Man at first knew what Plants and Fruits were good, before the Fall, by his Natural Sagacity, and not Experience; which since by Art, and Trial, and long Observation of their Properties and Effects, they hardly recover: But in all Events, supposing with *Cardan,** that Plants nourish little, they hurt as little. Nay, Experience tells us, that they not only hurt not at all, but exceedingly benefit those who use them; indu'd as they are with such admirable Properties as they every day discover: For some Plants not only nourish laudably, but induce a manifest and wholesom Change; as *Onions, Garlick, Rochet,* &c. which are both nutritive and warm; *Lettuce, Purselan,* the *Intybs,* &c. and indeed most of the *Olera,* refresh and cool: And as their respective Juices being converted into the Substances of our Bodies, they become *Aliment;* so in regard of their Change and Alteration, we may allow them *Medicinal;* especially the greater Numbers, among which we all this while have skill but of very few (not only in the Vegetable Kingdom, but in the whole *Materia Medica*) which may be justly call'd *Infallible Specifics,* and upon whose Performance we may as safely depend, as we may on such as familiarly we use for a Crude *Herb-Sallet;* discreetly chosen, mingl'd, and dress'd accordingly: Not but that many of them may be improv'd, and render'd better in Broths, and Decoctions, than in *Oyl, Vinegar,* and other Liquids and Ingredients: But as this holds not in all, nay, perhaps in few comparatively, (provided, as I said, the Choice, Mixture, Constitution, and *Season* rightly be understood) we stand up in Defence and Vindication of our *Sallet,* against all Attacks and Opposers whoever.

We have mentioned *Season* and with the great *Hippocrates,* pronounce them more proper for the Summer, than the Winter; and when those Parts of Plants us'd in *Sallet* are yet tender, delicate, and impregnated with the Vertue of the Spring, to cool, refresh, and allay the Heat and Drought of the Hot and *Bilious,* Young and over-*Sanguine,* Cold, *Pituit,** and Melancholy; in a word, for Persons of all Ages, Humours, and Constitutions whatsoever.

To this of the *Annual Seasons,* we add that of *Culture* also, as of very great Importance: And this is often discover'd in the taste and consequently in the Goodness of such Plants and *Salleting*, as are Rais'd and brought us fresh out of the Country, compar'd with those which the Avarice of the *Gardiner*, or Luxury rather of the Age, tempts them to force and *Resuscitate* of the most desirable and delicious Plants.

It is certain, says a Learned Person,* that about populous Cities, where Grounds are over-forc'd for Fruit and early *Salleting*, nothing is more unwholsom: Men in the Country look so much more healthy and fresh; and commonly are longer liv'd than those who dwell in the Middle and Skirts of vast and crowded Cities, inviron'd with rotten Dung, loathsome and common Lay Stalls; whose noisome Steams, wafted by the Wind, poison and infect the ambient Air and vital Spirits, with those pernicious Exhalations, and Materials of which they make the *Hot Beds* for the raising those *Præcoces** indeed, and forward Plants and Roots for the wanton Palate; but which being corrupt in the Original, cannot but produce malignant and ill Effects to those who feed upon them. And the same was well observ'd by the *Editor* of our famous *Roger Bacon's** Treatise concerning the *Cure of Old Age*, and *Preservation of Youth*: There being nothing so proper for *Sallet Herbs* and other *Edule Plants*, as the Genial and Natural Mould, impregnate, and enrich'd with well-digested Compost (when requisite) without any Mixture of Garbage, odious Carrion, and other filthy Ordure, not half consum'd and ventilated and indeed reduc'd to the next Disposition of Earth it self, as it should be; and that in Sweet, Rising, Aery and moderately Perflatile* Grounds; where not only *Plants* but *Men* do last, and live much longer. Nor doubt I, but that every body would prefer Corn, and other Grain rais'd from *Marle, Chalk, Lime,** and other sweet Soil and Amendments, before that which is produc'd from the *Dunghil* only. Beside, Experience shews, that the Rankness of *Dung* is frequently the Cause of Blasts and Smuttiness; as if the *Lord* of the *Universe*, by an Act of visible Providence would check us, to take heed of all unnatural Sordidness and Mixtures. We sensibly find this Difference in Cattle and their Pasture; but most powerfully in *Fowl*, from such as are nourish'd with Corn, sweet and

dry Food: And as of Vegetable *Meats*, so of *Drinks*, 'tis observ'd, that
the same Vine, according to the Soil, produces a *Wine* twice as
heady as in the same, and a less forc'd Ground; and the like I believe
of all other Fruit, not to determine any thing of the *Peach* said to be
Poison in *Persia*; because 'tis a *Vulgar Error*.

Now, because among other things, nothing more betrays its un-
clean and spurious Birth than what is so impatiently longed after as
Early Asparagus, &c. Dr. *Lister*, (according to his communicative
and obliging Nature) has taught us how to raise such as our *Gardiners* cover with nasty Litter, during the Winter; by rather laying
of Clean and Sweet *Wheat-Straw* upon the Beds, *super-seminating**
and over-strowing them thick with the Powder of bruised *Oyster-
Shells*, &c. to produce that most tender and delicious *Sallet*. In the
mean while, if nothing will satisfie save what is rais'd *Ex tempore*,
and by Miracles of Art so long before the time; let them study (like
the *Adepti**) as did a very ingenious Gentleman whom I knew; That
having some Friends of his accidentally come to Dine with him,
and wanting an early Sallet, Before they sate down to Table, sowed
Lettuce and some other Seeds in a certain Composition of Mould
he had prepared; which within the space of two Hours, being risen
near two Inches high, presented them with a delicate and tender
Sallet; and this, without making use of any nauseous or fulsome
Mixture; but of Ingredients not altogether so cheap perhaps. *Honoratus Faber** (no mean *Philosopher*) shews us another Method by
sowing the Seeds steep'd in *Vinegar*, casting on it a good quantity of
Bean-Shell Ashes, irrigating them with *Spirit of Wine*, and keeping
the Beds well cover'd under dry Matts. Such another Process for
the raising early *Peas* and *Beans*, &c. we have the like Accounts of:
But were they practicable and certain, I confess I should not be
fonder of them, than of such as the honest industrious Country-
man's Field, and Good Wife's Garden seasonably produce; where
they are legitimately born in just time, and without forcing Nature.

But to return again to *Health* and *Long Life*, and the Whole-
somness of the Herby-Diet, *John Beverovicius*, a Learn'd Physician
(out of *Peter Moxa*,* a *Spaniard*) treating of the extream Age, which
those of *America* usually arrive to, asserts in behalf of Crude and

Natural Herbs: *Diphilus** of old, as *Athenæus** tells us, was on the other side, against all the Tribe of *Olera* in general; and *Cardan** of late (as already noted) no great Friend to them; Affirming Flesh-Eaters to be much wiser and more sagacious. But this his Learned Antagonist* utterly denies; Whole Nations, Flesh-Devourers (such as the farthest *Northern*) becoming Heavy, Dull, Unactive, and much more Stupid than the *Southern*; and such as feed much on Plants, are more Acute, Subtil, and of deeper Penetration: Witness the *Chaldæans*, *Assyrians*, *Ægyptians*, &c. And further argues from the short Lives of most *Carnivorous* Animals, compared with Grass Feeders, and the Ruminating kind; as the *Hart*, *Camel*, and the longævous *Elephant*, and other Feeders on Roots and Vegetables.

I know what is pretended of our Bodies being composed of *Dissimilar* Parts, and so requiring Variety of Food: Nor do I reject the Opinion, keeping to the same *Species*; of which there is infinitely more Variety in the *Herby* Family, than in all Nature bessides: But the Danger is in the *Generical* Difference of *Flesh*, *Fish*, *Fruit*, &c. with other made Dishes and exotic Sauces; which a wanton and expensive Luxury has introduc'd; debauching the Stomach, and sharpening it to devour things of such difficult Concoction, with those of more easie Digestion, and of contrary Substances, more than it can well dispose of: Otherwise Food of the same kind would do us little hurt: So true is that of *Celsus*,* *Eduntur facilius; ad concoctionem autem materiæ, genus, & modus pertinent*.* They are (says he) easily eaten and taken in: But regard should be had to their Digestion, Nature, Quantity and Quality of the Matter. As to that of *Dissimilar* Parts, requiring this contended for Variety: If we may judge by other Animals (as I know not why we may not) there is (after all the late Contests about *Comparative Anatomy*) so little Difference in the Structure, as to the Use of those Parts and Vessels destin'd to serve the Offices of Concoction, Nutrition, and other Separations for Supply of Life, &c. That it does not appear why there should need any Difference at all of Food; of which the most simple has ever been esteem'd the best, and most wholesome; according to that of the Naturalist, *Hominis cibus utilissimus simplex*.* And that so it is in other Animals, we find by their being so seldom afflicted with Mens

Distempers, deriv'd from the Causes above-mentioned: And if the many Diseases of *Horses* seem to contradict it, I am apt to think it much imputable to the Rack and Manger, the dry and wither'd Stable Commons, which they must eat or starve, however qualified; being restrained from their Natural and Spontaneous Choice, which Nature and Instinct directs them to: To these add the Closeness of the Air, standing in an almost continu'd Posture; besides the fulsome Drenches, unseasonable Watrings, and other Practices of ignorant *Horse-Quacks* and surly Grooms: The Tyranny and cruel Usage of their Masters in tiring Journeys, hard, labouring and unmerciful Treatment, Heats, Colds, &c. which wear out and destroy so many of those useful and generous Creatures before the time: Such as have been better us'd, and some, whom their more gentle and good-natur'd Patrons have in recompence of their long and faithful service, dismiss'd, and sent to Pasture for the rest of their Lives (as the *Grand Seignior** does his *Meccha-Camel*......*) have been known to live *forty*, *fifty*, nay (says *Aristotle*,)* no fewer than *sixty five* Years. When once Old *Par** came to change his simple, homely Diet, to that of the *Court* and *Arundel-House*, he quickly sunk and dropt away: For, as we have shew'd, the Stomack easily concocts plain, and familiar Food; but finds it an hard and difficult Task, to vanquish and overcome Meats of different Substances: Whence we so often see temperate and abstemious Persons, of a Collegiate Diet, very healthy; Husbandsmen and laborious People, more robust, and longer liv'd than others of an uncertain extravagant Diet.

> ——*Nam variae res*
> *Ut noceant Homini, credas, memor illius escae,*
> *Quae simplex olim tibi sederit——*

> For different Meats do hurt;
> Remember how
> When to one Dish confin'd, thou
> healthier wast than now:

was *Ofellus's** *Memorandum* in the Poet.

Not that variety (which God has certainly ordain'd to delight and assist our Appetite) is unnecessary, nor any thing more grateful, refreshing and proper for those especially who lead sedentary and studious Lives; Men of deep Thought, and such as are otherwise disturb'd with Secular Cares and Businesses, which hinders the Function of the Stomach and other Organs: whilst those who have their Minds free, use much Exercise, and are more active, create themselves a natural Appetite, which needs little or no Variety to quicken and content it.

And here might we attest the *Patriarchal* World, nay, and many Persons since; who living very temperately came not much short of the *Post-Diluvians** themselves, counting from *Abraham* to this Day; and some exceeding them, who liv'd in pure Air, a constant, tho' course and simple Diet; wholsome and uncompounded Drink; that never tasted *Brandy* or *Exotic Spirits*; but us'd moderate Exercise, and observ'd good Hours: For such a one a curious Missionary tells us of in Persia; who had attain'd the Age of *four hundred* Years, (a full *Century* beyond the famous *Johannes de Temporibus**) and was living *Anno* 1636, and so may be still for ought we know. But, to our Sallet.

Certain it is, Almighty God ordaining *Herbs* and *Fruit* for the Food of Men, speaks not a Word concerning *Flesh* for two thousand Years. And when after, by the *Mosaic* Constitution,* there were Distinctions and Prohibitions about the legal Uncleanness of *Animals*; *Plants*, of what kind soever, were left free and indifferent for every one to choose what best he lik'd. And what if it was held undecent and unbecoming the Excellency of Man's Nature, before Sin entred, and grew enormously wicked, that any Creature should be put to Death and Pain for him who had such infinite store of the most delicious and nourishing Fruit to delight, and the Tree of Life to sustain him? Doubtless there was no need of it. Infants sought the Mother's Nipple as soon as born; and when grown, and able to feed themselves, run naturally to Fruit, and still will choose to eat it rather than Flesh and certainly might so persist to do, did not Custom prevail, even against the very Dictates of Nature: Nor, question I, but that what the Heathen *Poets* recount of the Happiness of the

Golden Age, sprung from some Tradition they had received of the *Paradisian* Fare, their innocent and healthful Lives in that delightful Garden. Let it suffice, that *Adam*, and his yet innocent Spouse, fed on Vegetables and other Hortulan Productions before the fatal Lapse; which, by the way, many Learned Men will hardly allow to have fallen out so soon as those imagine who scarcely grant them a single Day; nay, nor half a one, for their Continuance in the State of Original Perfection; whilst the sending him into the Garden; Instructions how he should keep and cultivate it; Edict, and Prohibition concerning the *Sacramental* Trees; the Imposition of Names, so apposite to the Nature of such an Infinity of Living Creatures (requiring deep Inspection) the Formation of *Eve*, a meet Companion to relieve his Solitude; the Solemnity of their Marriage; the Dialogues and Success of the crafty Tempter, whom we cannot reasonably think made but one Assault: And that they should so quickly forget the Injunction of their Maker and Benefactor; break their Faith and Fast, and all other their Obligations in so few Moments. I say, all these Particulars consider'd; Can it be supposed they were so soon transacted as those do fancy, who take their Measure from the Summary *Moses* gives us, who did not write to gratifie Mens Curiosity, but to transmit what was necessary and sufficient for us to know.

This then premis'd (as I see no Reason why it should not) and that during all this Space they liv'd on *Fruits* and *Sallets*; 'tis little probable, that after their Transgression, and that they had forfeited their Dominion over the Creature (and were sentenc'd and exil'd to a Life of Sweat and Labour on a cursed and ungrateful Soil) the offended God should regale them with Pampering *Flesh*, or so much as suffer them to slay the more innocent Animal: Or, that if at any time they had Permission, it was for any thing save Skins to cloath them, or in way of Adoration, or *Holocaust* for Expiation,* of which nothing of the *Flesh* was to be eaten. Nor did the Brutes themselves subsist by Prey (tho' pleas'd perhaps with Hunting, without destroying their Fellow Creatures) as may be presum'd from their long Seclusion of the most Carnivorous among them in the Ark.

Thus then for two thousand Years, the Universal Food was *Herbs* and *Plants*; which abundantly recompens'd the Want of *Flesh* and other luxurious Meats, which shortened their Lives so many hundred Years; the μακροβιότητα* of the Patriarchs, which was an Emblem of Eternity as it were (after the new Concession) beginning to dwindle to a little Span, a Nothing in Comparison.

On the other side, examine we the present Usages of several other Heathen Nations; particularly (bessides the *Ægyptian* Priests of old) the *Indian Bramins*, Relicts of the ancient *Gymnosophists** to this Day, observing the Institutions of their Founder. *Flesh*, we know was banish'd the *Platonic* Tables,* as well as from those of *Pythagoras*; (See *Porphyry** and their Disciples) tho' on different Accounts. Among others of the Philosophers, from *Xenocrates, Polemon,** &c. we hear of many. The like we find in *Clement Alexand.** *Eusebius** names more. *Zeno, Archinomus, Phraartes, Chiron*, and others, whom *Lærtius** reckons up. In short, so very many, especially of the Christian Profession, that some, even of the ancient Fathers themselves, have almost thought that the Permission of eating Flesh to *Noah* and his Sons, was granted them no otherwise than *Repudiation* of Wives was to the *Jews*, namely, for *the Hardness of their Hearts*, and to satisfie a murmuring Generation that a little after loathed *Manna* it self, and *Bread from Heaven*. So difficult a thing it is to subdue an unruly Appetite; which notwithstanding *Seneca* thinks not so hard a Task; where speaking of the Philosopher *Sextius*, and *Socion's** (abhorring Cruelty and Intemperance) he celebrates the Advantages of the *Herby* and *Sallet* Diet, as *Physical*, and *Natural* Advancers of Health and other Blessings; whilst Abstinence from Flesh deprives Men of nothing but what *Lions, Vultures*, Beasts and birds of Prey, blood and gorge themselves withal, The whole *Epistle* deserves the Reading, for the excellent Advice he gives on this and other Subjects; and how from many troublesome and slavish Impertinencies, grown into Habit and Custom (old as he was) he had Emancipated and freed himself: Be this apply'd to our present excessive Drinkers of Foreign and *Exotic* Liquors.

And now I am sufficiently sensible how far, and to how little purpose I am gone on this *Topic*: The Ply is long since taken, and our raw *Sallet* deckt in its best Trim, is never like to invite Men who once have tasted *Flesh* to quit and abdicate a Custom which has now so long obtain'd. Nor truly do I think Conscience at all concern'd in the Matter, upon any Account of Distinction of *Pure* and *Impure*; tho' seriously consider'd (as *Sextius* held) *rationi magis congrua,** as it regards the cruel Butcheries of so many harmless Creatures; some of which we put to merciless and needless Torment, to accommodat them for exquisite and uncommon *Epicurism*. There lies else no positive Prohibition; Discrimination of Meats being Condemn'd as the *Doctrine of Devils*:* Nor do Meats *commend us to God*. One eats *quid vult* (of every thing:) another *Olera*, and of *Sallets* only: But this is not my Business, further than to shew how possible it is by so many Instances and Examples, to live on wholsome Vegetables, both long and happily: For so

The Golden Age, *with this Provision blest,*
Such a Grand Sallet *made, and was a Feast.*
The Demi-Gods *with Bodies large and sound,*
Commended then the Product of the Ground.
Fraud then, nor Force were known, nor filthy Lust,
Which Over-heating and Intemp'rance nurst:
Be their vile Names in Execration held,
Who with foul Glutt'ny first the World defil'd:
Parent of Vice, and all Diseases since,
With ghastly Death sprung up alone from thence.
Ah, from such reeking, bloody Tables fly,
Which Death for our Destruction does supply.
In Health, *if* Sallet-Herbs *you can't endure;*
Sick, you'll desire them; or for Food, *or* Cure.

As to the other part of the Controversie, which concerns us, αἱματοφάγοι, and *Occidental Blood*-Eaters;* some Grave and Learn'd Men of late seem to scruple the present Usage, whilst they see the Prohibition appearing, and to carry such a Face of *Antiquity, Scripture, Councils, Canons, Fathers*; *Imperial Constitutions*, and *Universal Practice*, unless it be among us of these Tracts of *Europe*, whither, with other Barbarities, that of eating the *Blood* and *Animal* Life of

Creatures first was brought; and by our Mixtures with the *Goths*, *Vandals*, and other Spawn of Pagan *Scythians*;* grown a Custom, and since which I am persuaded more Blood has been shed between *Christians* than there ever was before the Water of the Flood covered this Corner of the World: Not that I impute it only to our eating *Blood*; but sometimes wonder how it hap'ned that so strict, so solemn and famous a *Sanction* not upon a *Ceremonial Account*; but (as some affirm) a *Moral* and *Perpetual* from *Noah*, to whom the Concession of eating *Flesh* was granted, and that of Blood forbidden (nor to this Day once revok'd) and whilst there also seems to lie fairer Proofs than for most other Controversies agitated among *Christians*, should be so generally forgotten, and give place to so many other impertinent Disputes and Cavels about other superstitious Fopperies, which frequently end in Blood and cutting of Throats.

As to the Reason of this Prohibition, its favouring of Cruelty excepted, (and that by *Galen*, and other experienc'd Physicians, the eating Blood is condemn'd as unwholsome, causing Indigestion and Obstructions) if a positive Command of *Almighty God* were not enough, it seems sufficiently intimated; because *Blood* was the *Vehicle* of the *Life* and *Animal Soul* of the Creature: For what other mysterious Cause, as haply its being always dedicated to *Expiatory Sacrifices*, &c. it is not for us to enquire. 'Tis said, that *Justin Martyr** being asked, why the *Christians* of his time were permitted the eating *Flesh* and not the *Blood*? readily answer'd, That God might distinguish them from Beasts, which eat them both together. 'Tis likewise urg'd, that by the *Apostolical Synod*......* (when the rest of the *Jewish* Ceremonies and Types were abolish'd) this Prohibition was mention'd as a thing *necessary*, and rank'd with *Idolatry*, which was not to be local or temporary; but universally injoyn'd to converted Strangers and *Proselytes*, as well as *Jews*: Nor could the Scandal of neglecting to observe it, concern them alone, after so many Ages as it was and still is in continual Use; and those who transgress'd, so severely punish'd, as by an *Imperial Law* to be scourg'd to *Blood* and Bone: Indeed, so terrible was the Interdiction, that *Idolatry* excepted (which was also Moral and perpetual) nothing in

Scripture seems to be more express. In the mean time, to relieve all other Scruples, it does not, they say, extend to that ἀκρίβεια* of those few diluted Drops of *Extravasated Blood*,* which might happen to tinge the Juice and Gravy of the Flesh (which were indeed *to strain at a Gnat*) but to those who devour the *Venal* and *Arterial Blood* separately, and in Quantity, as a choice Ingredient of their luxurious Preparations and *Apician* Tables.*

But this, and all the rest will, I fear, seem but *Oleribus verba facere*,* and (as the Proverb goes) be Labour-in-vain to think of preaching down *Hogs-Puddings*,* and usurp the Chair of *Rabby-Busy*:* And therefore what is advanc'd in Countenance of the *Antediluvian* Diet, we leave to be ventilated by the Learned, and such as *Curcellæus*,* who has borrow'd of all the Ancient Fathers, from *Tertullian, Hierom, S. Chrysostom*,* &c. to the later Doctors and Divines, *Lyra, Tostatus, Dionysius Carthusianus, Pererius*,* amongst the *Pontificians*; of *Peter Martyr, Zanchy, Aretius, Jac. Capellus, Hiddiger, Cocceius, Bochartus*,* &c. amongst the *Protestants*; and *instar omnium*,* by *Salmasius, Grotius, Vossius, Blundel*:* In a Word, by the Learn'd of both Persuasions, favourable enough to these Opinions, *Cajetan** and *Calvin** only excepted, who hold, that as to *Abstinence* from *Flesh*, there was no positive Command or Imposition concerning it; but that the Use of *Herbs* and *Fruit* was recommended rather for Temperance sake, and the Prolongation of Life: Upon which score I am inclin'd to believe that the ancient θεραπευταί,* and other devout and contemplative Sects, distinguish'd themselves; whose Course of Life we have at large describ'd in *Philo** (who liv'd and taught much in Gardens) with others of the Abstemious *Christians*; among whom, *Clemens* brings in St. *Mark* the *Evangelist* himself, *James* our Lord's Brother. St. *John*, &c. and with several of the devout Sex, the famous *Diaconesse Olympias*,* mention'd by *Palladius** (not to name the rest) who abstaining from Flesh, betook themselves to *Herbs* and *Sallets* upon the Account of Temperance, and the Vertues accompanying it; and concerning which the incomparable *Grotius* declares ingenuously his Opinion to be far from censuring, not only those who forbear the eating *Flesh* and Blood, *Experimenti Causa*, and for Discipline sake; but such as forbear *ex*

Opinione, and (because it has been the ancient Custom) provided they blam'd none who freely us'd their Liberty; and I think he's in the right.

But leaving this Controversie (*ne nimium extra oleas**) it has often been objected, that *Fruit*, and *Plants*, and all other things, may since the Beginning, and as the World grows older, have universally become *Effœte*, impair'd and diverted of those Nutritious and transcendent Vertues they were at first endow'd withal: But as this is begging the Question, and to which we have already spoken; so all are not agreed that there is any, the least *Decay in Nature*, where equal Industry and Skill's apply'd. 'Tis true indeed, that the *Ordo Foliatorum, Feuillantines** (a late Order of *Ascetic Nuns*) amongst other Mortifications, made Trial upon the *Leaves* of *Plants* alone, to which they would needs confine themselves; but were not able to go through that thin and meagre Diet: But then it would be enquir'd whether they had not first, and from their very Childhood, been fed and brought up with *Flesh*, and better Sustenance till they enter'd the *Cloyster*; and what the Vegetables and the Preparation of them were allow'd by their Institution? Wherefore this is nothing to our Modern Use of *Sallets*, or its Disparagement. In the mean time, that we still think it not only possible, but likely, and with no great Art or Charge (taking *Roots* and *Fruit* into the Basket) substantially to maintain Mens Lives in Health and Vigour: For to *this*, and less than this, we have the Suffrage of the great *Hippocrates* himself; who thinks, *ab'initio etiam hominum* (as well as other Animals) *tali victu usum esse*,* and needed no other Food. Nor is it an inconsiderable Speculation, That since *all Flesh is Grass* (not in a *Figurative*, but *Natural* and *Real* Sense) *Man* himself, who lives on *Flesh*, and I think upon no Earthly Animal whatsoever, but such as feed on Grass, is nourish'd with them still; and so becoming an *Incarnate Herb*, and Innocent *Canibal*, may truly be said to devour himself.

We have said nothing of the *Lotophagi*,* and such as (like St. *John* the *Baptist*, and other religious *Ascetics*) were Feeders on the *Summities* and Tops of Plants: But as divers of those, and others we have mention'd, were much in times of Streights, Persecutions, and

other Circumstances, which did not in the least make it a Pretence,
exempting them from Labour, and other Humane Offices, by en-
snaring Obligations and vows (never to be useful to the Publick, in
whatever Exigency) so I cannot but take Notice of what a Learned
Critic speaking of Mens neglecting plain and Essential Duties,
under Colour of exercising themselves in a more sublime Course
of Piety, and being Righteous above what is commanded (as those
who seclude themselves in Monasteries) that they manifestly discover excessive Pride, Hatred of their Neighbour, Impatience of In-
juries; to which *add, Melancholy Plots and Machinations*; and that he
must be either stupid, or infected with the same Vice himself, who
admires this ἐθελοπερισσοθρησκεία* or thinks they were for that
Cause the more pleasing to God. This being so, what may we then
think of such Armies of *Hermits*, *Monks* and *Friers*, who pretending
to justifie a mistaken Zeal and meritorious Abstinence; not only by
a peculiar Diet and Distinction of Meats (which God without Distinction has made the moderate Use of common and indifferent
amongst *Christians*) but by other sordid Usages, and unnecessary
Hardships, wilfully prejudice their Health and Constitution? and
through a singular manner of living, dark and *Saturnine*; whilst they
would seem to abdicate and forsake the World (in Imitation, as they
pretend, of the Ancient *Eremites*)* take care to settle, and build their
warm and stately Nests in the most Populous Cities, and Places of
Resort; ambitious doubtless of the Peoples Veneration and Opinion
of an extraordinary Sanclity; and therefore flying the *Desarts*, where
there is indeed no use of them; and flocking to the *Towns* and *Cities*
where there is less, indeed none at all; and therefore no Marvel that
the Emperour *Valentinian** banished them the Cities, and *Constantine Copronymus** finding them seditious, oblig'd them to marry, to
leave their Cells, and live as did others. For of these, some there are
who seldom speak, and therefore edifie none; sleep little, and lie
hard, are clad nastily, and eat meanly (and oftentimes that which is
unwholsom) and therefore benefit none; Not because they might
not, both for their own, and the Good of others, and the Publick;
but because they will not; Custom, and a prodigious Sloth accompanying it; which renders it so far from *Penance*, and the Mortifi-

cation pretended, that they know not how to live, or spend their Time otherwise. This, as I have often consider'd, so was I glad to find it justly perstring'd, and taken notice of by a Learned Person,* amongst others of his useful Remarks abroad.

'These', says he, 'willingly renouncing the innocent Comforts of Life, plainly shew it to proceed more from a chagrin and morose Humour, than from any true and serious Principle of sound Religion; which teaches Men to be useful in their Generations, sociable and communicative, unaffected, and by no means singular and fantastic in Garb and Habit, as are these (forsooth) Fathers (as they affect to be call'd) spending their Days in idle and fruitless Forms, and tedious Repetitions; and thereby thinking to merit the Reward of those Ancient, and truly pious *Solitaries*, who, God knows, were driven from their Countries and Repose, by the Incursions of barbarous Nations (whilst these have no such Cause) and compell'd to Austerities, not of their own chusing and making, but the publick Calamity; and to *labour* with their *Hands* for their own, and others necessary Support, as well as with their *Prayers* and holy Lives, Examples to all the World: And some of these indeed (bessides the *Solitaries* of the *Thebaid*,* who wrought for abundance of poor Christians, sick, and in Captivity) I might bring in, as such who deserv'd to have their Names preserv'd; not for their rigorous Fare, and uncouth Disguises; but for teaching that the Grace of Temperance and other Vertues, consisted in a cheerful, innocent, and profitable Conversation.'

And now to recapitulate what other Prerogatives the *Hortulan Provision* has been celebrated for, bessides its Antiquity, Health and *Longævity* of the *Antediluvians*; that Temperance, Frugality, Leisure, Ease, and innumerable other Vertues and Advantages, which accompany it, are no less attributable to it. Let us hear our excellent *Botanist* Mr. *Ray*.*

'The Use of Plants (says he) is all our Life long of that universal Importance and Concern, that we can neither live nor subsist in any Plenty with Decency, or Conveniency or be said to live indeed at all without them: whatsoever Food is necessary to sustain us, whatsoever contributes to delight and refresh us, are supply'd and brought forth out of that plentiful and abundant store: and ah, how much more innocent, sweet and healthful, is a Table cover'd with these, than with all the reeking Flesh of butcher'd and slaughter'd Animals: Certainly Man by Nature was never made to be a *Carnivorous* Creature; nor is he arm'd at all for Prey and Rapin,* with gag'd and pointed Teeth and crooked Claws, sharp'ned to rend and tear: But with gentle Hands to gather Fruit and Vegetables, and with Teeth to chew and eat them: Nor do we so much as read the Use of *Flesh* for Food, was at all permitted him, till after the Universal Deluge, *&c.*'

To this might we add that transporting Consideration, becoming both our Veneration and Admiration of the infinitely wise and glorious Author of Nature, who has given to *Plants* such astonishing Properties; such fiery Heat in some to warm and cherish, such Coolness in others to temper and refresh, such pinguid Juice to nourish and feed the Body, such quickening *Acids* to compel the Appetite, and grateful vehicles to court the Obedience of the Palate, such Vigour to renew and support our natural Strength, such ravishing Flavour and Perfumes to recreate and delight us: In short, such spirituous and active Force to animate and revive every Faculty and Part, to all the kinds of Human, and, I had almost said Heavenly Capacity too. What shall we add more? Our Gardens present us with them all; and whilst the *Shambles* are cover'd with Gore and Stench, our *Sallets* scape the Insults of the Summer *Fly*, purifies and warms the Blood against Winter Rage: Nor wants there Variety in more abundance, than any of the former Ages could shew.

Survey we their *Bills of Fare*, and Numbers of Courses serv'd up by *Athenæus*, drest with all the Garnish of *Nicander** and other *Grecian* Wits: What has the *Roman Grand Sallet* worth the naming? *Parat Convivium*,* The Guests are nam'd indeed, and we are told,

—— *Varias, quas habet hortus opes?*

How richly the Garden's stor'd:

*In quibus est Luctuca sedens, & tonsile porrum, Nec deest ructatrix Mentha, nec herba salax, &c.**

A Goodly Sallet!

Lettuce, *Leeks, Mint, Rocket, Colewort-Tops*, with *Oyl* and *Eggs*, and such an *Hotch-Pot** following (as the Cook in *Plautus** would deservedly laugh at). But how infinitely out-done in this Age of ours, by the Variety of so many rare *Edules* unknown to the Ancients, that there's no room for the Comparison. And, for Magnificence, let the *Sallet* drest by the Lady for an Entertainment made by *Jacobus Catsius* (describ'd by the Poet *Barlæus*)* shew; not at all yet out-doing what we every Day almost find at our *Lord Mayor's Table*, and other great Persons, Lovers of the Gardens; that sort of elegant Cookery being capable of such wonderful Variety, tho' not altogether wanting of old, if that be true which is related to us of *Nicomedes** a certain King of Bithynia, whose Cook made him a *Pilchard* (a Fish he exceedingly long'd for) of a well dissembl'd Turnip, carv'd in its Shape, and drest with *Oyl, Salt*, and *Pepper*, that so deceiv'd, and yet pleased the Prince, that he commended it for the best Fish he had ever eaten. Nor does all this exceed what every industrious *Gardiner* may innocently enjoy, as well as the greatest Potentate on Earth.

> *Vitellius** *his Table, to which every Day*
> *All Courtiers did a constant Tribute pay,*
> *Could nothing more delicious afford*
> *Than Nature's Liberality.*
> *Help'd with a little Art and Industry,*
> *Allows the meanest Gard'ners Board,*
> *The Wanton Taste no Fish or Fowl can chuse,*
> *For which the Grape or Melon she would lose.*
> *Tho' all th' Inhabitants of Sea and Air*
> *Be lifted in the Glutton's Bill of Fare;*
> *Yet still the* Sallet, *and the* Fruit *we see*
> *Plac'd the third Story high in all her Luxury.*

So the Sweet *Poet*,* whom I can never part with for his Love to this delicious Toil, and the Honour he has done me.

Verily, the infinite Plenty and Abundance, with which the benign and bountiful Author of Nature has stor'd the whole Terrestrial World, more with *Plants* and *Vegetables* than with any other Provision whatsoever; and the Variety not only equal, but by far exceeding the Pleasure and Delight of Taste (above all the Art of the *Kitchen*, than ever *Apicius** knew) seems loudly to call, and kindly invite all her living Inhabitants (none excepted) who are of gentle Nature, and most useful, to the same *Hospitable* and Common-Board, which first she furnish'd with *Plants* and *Fruit*, as to their natural and genuine Pasture; nay, and of the most wild, and savage too *ab origine*: As in *Paradise*, where, as the *Evangelical* Prophet adumbrating the future Glory of the *Catholick Church*, (of which that happy *Garden* was the *Antitype*) the *Wolf and the Lamb, the angry and furious Lion, should eat Grass and Herbs together with the Ox*. But after all, *latet anguis in herba*,* there's a *Snake* in the Grass; Luxury, and Excess in our most innocent Fruitions. There was a time indeed when the Garden furnish'd Entertainments for the most Renown'd Heroes, virtuous and excellent Persons; till the Blood-thirsty and Ambitious, over-running the Nations, and by Murders and Rapine rifl'd the World, to transplant its Luxury to its new Mistriss, *Rome*. Those whom heretofore two Acres of Land would have satisfied, and plentifully maintain'd; had afterwards their very Kitchens almost as large as their first Territories: Nor was that enough: Entire *Forests* and *Parks*, *Warrens* and *Fish-Ponds*, and ample Lakes to furnish their Tables, so as Men could not live by one another without Oppression: Nay, and to shew how the best, and most innocent things may be perverted; they chang'd those frugal and *inemptas Dapes** of their Ancestors, to that Height and Profusion; that we read of *Edicts* and *Sumptuary Laws*,* enacted to restrain even the Pride and Excess of *Sallets*. But so it was not when the *Pease-Field* spread a Table for the Conquerors of the World, and their Grounds were cultivated *Vomere laureato, & triumphali aratore*:* The greatest Princes took the *Spade* and the *Plough-Staff* in the same Hand they held the Sceptre; and the Noblest Families thought it no Dishonour, to derive their Names from *Plants* and *Sallet-Herbs*; They arriv'd, I say to that Pitch of ingrossing all that was but green, and could be vary'd by the Cook

(*Heu quam prodiga ventris!*) that, as *Pliny** tells us (*non sine pudore,* not without blushing) a poor Man could hardly find a *Thistle* to dress for his Supper; or what his hungry *Ass* would not touch, for fear of pricking his Lips.

Verily the Luxury of the East ruin'd the greatest Monarchies; first, the *Persian*, then the *Grecian*, and afterwards *Rome* her self: By what Steps, see elegantly describ'd in Old *Gratius* the *Faliscian*,* deploring his own Age compar'd with the former:

> *O quantum, & quoties decoris frustrata paterni!*
> *At qualis nostris, quam simplex mensa Camillis!*
> *Qui tibi cultus erat post tot, serrane, triumphos?*
> *Ergo illi ex habitu, virtutisq; indole priscæ,*
> *Imposuere orbi Romam caput:——*

> Neighb'ring Excesses being made thine own,
> How art thou fall'n from thine old Renown!
> But our *Camilli* did but plainly fare,
> No Port did oft triumphant *Serran* bear:
> Therefore such Hardship, and their Heart so great
> Gave *Rome* to be the World's Imperial Seat.

But as these were the Sensual and Voluptuous, who abus'd their Plenty, spent their Fortunes and shortned their Lives by their Debauches; so never did they taste the Delicaces, and true Satisfaction of a sober Repast, and the infinite Conveniences of what a well-stor'd *Garden* affords; so elegantly describ'd by the *Naturalist*,* as costing neither Fuel nor Fire to boil, Pains or time to gather and prepare, *Res expedita & parata semper.** All was so near at hand, readily drest, and of so easie Digestion; as neither to offend the Brain, or dull the Senses; and in the greatest Dearth of Corn, a little Bread suffic'd. In all Events,

> *Panis ematur, Olus, Vini Sextarius adde*
> *Queis humana sibi doleat natura negatis.**

> Bread, Wine and wholsome Sallets you may buy,
> What Nature adds besides is Luxury.

They could then make an honest Meal, and dine upon a *Sallet* without so much as a Grain, of *Exotic Spice*; And the *Potagere* was in such Reputation, that she who neglected her *Kitchen-Garden* (for that was still the Good-Woman's Province) was never reputed a tolerable Hus-wife: *Si vespertinus subitò te oppresserit hospes*,* she was never surpriz'd, had all (as we said) at hand, and could in a Trice set forth an handsome *Sallet*: And if this was Happiness, *Convictus facilis sine arte mensa** (as the *Poet* reckons) it was here in Perfection. In a Word, so universal was the *Sallet*, that the Un-bloody Shambles (as *Pliny* calls them) yielded the *Roman* State a more considerable Custom (when there was little more than honest *Cabbage* and *Worts*) than almost any thing besides brought to Market.

They spent not then so much precious time as afterwards they did, gorging themselves with *Flesh* and *Fish*, so as hardly able to rise, without reeking and reeling from Table.

> ——*Vides ut pallidus omnis*
> *Cœna desurgat dubia? quin corpus onustum*
> *Hesternis vitiis, animum quoque prægravat unà,*
> *Atque affigit humo divinæ particulam auræ.**

See but how pale they look, how wretchedly,
With Yesterday's Surcharge disturb'd they be!
Nor Body only suff......'ring, but the Mind,
That nobler Part, dull'd and depress'd we find.
Drowsie and unapt for Business, and other nobler Parts of Life.

Time was before Men in those golden Days: Their Spirits were brisk and lively.

> ——*Ubi dicto citius curata sopori*
> *Membra dedit, Vegetus præscripta ad munera surgit.**

With shorter, but much sweeter Sleep content,
Vigorous and fresh, about their Business went.

And Men had their Wits about them; their Appetites were natural, their Sleep *molli sub arbore*,* sound, sweet, and kindly: That excellent Emperour *Tacitus* being us'd to say of *Lettuce*, that he did *somnum se mercari** when he eat of them, and call'd it a sumptuous Feast, with a *Sallet* and a single *Pullet*, which was usually all the Flesh-Meat that sober Prince eat of; whilst *Maximinus** (a profess'd Enemy to *Sallet*) is reported to have scarce been satisfied, with sixty Pounds of Flesh, and Drink proportionable.

There was then also less expensive Grandure, but far more true State; when *Consuls*, great Statesmen (and such as atchiev'd the most renown'd Actions) sup'd in their *Gardens*; not under costly, gilded, and inlaid Roofs, but the spreading *Platan*; and drank of the Chrystal Brook, and by Temperance, and healthy Frugality, maintain'd the Glory of *Sallets*, *Ah, quanta innocentiore victu*! with what Content and Satisfaction! Nor, as we said, wanted there Variety; for so in the most blissful Place, and innocent State of Nature, See how the first *Empress* of the World *Regal's* her *Celestial* Guest:

> *With sav'ry Fruit of Taste to please*
> *True Appetite,——and brings*
> *Whatever Earth's all-bearing Mother yields*
> *——Fruit of all kinds, in Coat*
> *Rough, or smooth-Rind, or bearded Husk, or Shell.*
> *Heaps with unsparing Hand: For Drink the Grape*
> *She crushes, inoffensive Moust, and Meads*
> *From many a Berry, and from sweet Kernel prest,*
> *She temper'd dulcid Creams.——*

Then for the Board.

> *——Rais'd of a grassy Turf*
> *The Table was, and Mossy Seats had round;*
> *And on the ample Meaths from Side to Side,*
> *All Autumn pil'd: Ah Innocence,*
> *Deserving Paradise!**

Thus, the *Hortulan* Provision of the *Golden Age* fitted all *Places*, *Times* and *Persons*; and when Man is restor'd to that State again, it will be as it was in the Beginning.

But now after all (and for Close of all) Let none yet imagine, that whilst we justifie our present Subject through all the *Topics of*

Panegyric, we would in Favour of the *Sallet*, drest with all its Pomp and Advantage turn Mankind to *Grass* again; which were ungratefully to neglect the Bounty of Heaven, as well as his Health and Comfort: But by these Noble Instances and Examples, to reproach the *Luxury* of the present Age; and by shewing the infinite Blessing and Effects of Temperance, and the Vertues accompanying it; with how little Nature, and a Civil Appetite may be happy, contented with moderate things, and within a little Compass, reserving the rest, to the nobler Parts of Life. And thus of old,

*Hoc erat in votis, modus agri non ita magnus, &c.**

He that was possess'd of a little Spot of Ground, and well-cultivated *Garden*, with other moderate Circumstances, had *Hæredium.** All that a modest Man could well desire. Then,

Happy the Man, who from Ambition freed,
A little Garden, little Field does feed.
The Field gives frugal Nature what's requird;
The Garden what's luxuriously desir'd:
The specious Evils of an anxious Life,
*He leaves to Fools to be their endless Strife.**

O Fortunatos nimium bona si sua norint Horticulos!*

FINIS

APPENDIX

THO' it was far from our first Intention to charge this small Volume and Discourse concerning *Crude Sallets,* with any of the following Receipts: Yet having since received them from an *Experienc'd Housewife;* and that they may possibly be useful to correct, preserve and improve our *Acetaria,* we have allow'd them Place as an *Appendant* Variety upon Occasion: Nor account we it the least Dishonour to our former Treatise, that we kindly entertain'd them; since (besides divers Learned *Physicians,* and such as have *ex professo* written *de Re Cibaria*)* we have the Examples of many other *Noble* and *Illustrious* Persons both among the *Ancient* and *Modern.*

1. *Artichoak.* Clear it of the Leaves and cut the Bottoms in pretty thin Slices or Quarters; then fry them in fresh Butter with some Parsley, till it is crisp, and the Slices tender; and so dish them with other fresh melted Butter.

How a *Poiverade* is made, and the Bottoms preserv'd all the Winter, See *Acetaria.* pp. 144, 166.

Ashen-keys. See *Pickle.*
Asparagus. See *Pickle.*
Beets.
Broom.
Buds. } See *Pickle.*
Capers.
Carrot. See *Pudding.*
Champignon. See *Mushroom.*

2. *Chessnut.* Roasted under the Embers, or dry fryed, till they shell, and quit their Husks, may be slit; the Juice of Orange squeezed on a Lump of hard Sugar dissolv'd; to which add some Claret Wine.

Collyflower.
Cucumber.
Elder flowers. } See *Pickle.*
Flowers.
Gilly-flowers.

Herbs. See *Pudding* and *Tart*.
Limon. See *Pickle.*

3. *Mushroom.* Chuse the small, firm and white Buttons, *growing* upon sweet Pasture Grounds, neither under, or about any Trees: strip off the upper Skin, and pare away all the black spungy Bottom part; then slice them in quarters, and cast them in Water a while to cleanse: Then Boil them in fresh Water, and a little sweet Butter; (some boil them a quarter of an hour first) and then taking them out, dry them in a Cloth, pressing out the Water, and whilst hot, add the Butter; and then boiling a full Hour (to exhaust the Malignity) shift them in another clean Water, with Butter, as before till they become sufficiently tender. Then being taken out, pour upon them as much strong Mutton (or other) Broth as will cover them, with six Spoonfuls of White-Wine, twelve Cloves, as many Pepper-Corns, four small young Onions, half an Handful of Persly bound up with two or three Spriggs of Thyme, an *Anchovy,* Oysters raw, or pickl'd; a little Salt, sweet Butter; and so let them stew. See *Acetar.* p. 213. *Another.*

Prepared, and cleans'd as above, and cast into Fountain-Water,* to preserve them from growing black; Boil them in fresh Water and Salt; and whilst on the Fire, cast in the *Mushrooms,* letting them boil till they become tender: Then stew them leisurely between two Dishes (the Water being drained from them) in a third Part of White-Wine and Butter, a small Bundle of sweet Herbs at discretion. To these add Broth as before, with Cloves, Mace, Nutmeg, *Anchovies* (one is sufficient) Oysters, *&c.* a small Onion, with the green Stem chopt small; and lastly, some Mutton-Gravy, rubbing the Dish gently with a Clove of Garlick, or some *Rocombo* Seeds in its stead. Some beat the Yolk of a fresh Egg with Vinegar, and Butter, and a little Pepper.

In *France* some (more compendiously being peel'd and prepared) cast them into a Pipkin,* where, with the Sweet Herbs, Spices, and an Onion they stew them in their own Juice, without any other Water or Liquor at all; and then taking out the Herbs and Onion, thicken it with a little Butter, and so eat them.

In *Poiverade*.

The large Mushrooms well cleansed, *&c.* being cut into quarters and strewed with Pepper and Salt, are broil'd on the Grid-iron, and eaten with fresh Butter.

In *Powder*.

Being fresh gathered, cleans'd, *&c.* and cut in Pieces, stew them in Water and Salt; and being taken forth, dry them with a Cloth: Then putting them into an Earth-Glazed Pot, set them into the Oven after the Bread is drawn: Repeat this till they are perfectly dry; and reserve them in Papers to crumble into what Sauce you please. For the rest, see *Pickle*.

4. *Mustard.* Procure the best and weightiest Seed: cast it into Water two or three times, till no more of the Husk arise: Then taking out the sound (which will sink to the Bottom) rub it very dry in warm course Cloths, shewing it also a little to the Fire in a Dish or Pan. Then stamp it as small as to pass through a fine Tiffany Sieve:* Then slice some Horse-Radish and lay it to soak in strong Vinegar, with a small Lump of hard Sugar (which some leave out) to temper the Flower with, being drained from the Radish, and so pot it all in a Glaz'd Mug, with an Onion, and keep it well stop'd with a Cork upon a Bladder, which is the more cleanly: But this *Receit* is improv'd, if instead of Vinegar, Water only, or the Broth of powder'd Beef be made use of. And to some of this *Mustard* adding Verjuice, Sugar, Claret-Wine, and Juice of Limon, you have an excellent Sauce to any sort of Flesh or Fish.

Note, that a Pint of good Seed is enough to make at one time, and to keep fresh a competent while. What part of it does not pass the *Sarse,** may be beaten again; and you may reserve the Flower in a well closed Glass, and make fresh Mustard when you please. See *Acetaria*, pp. 155, 174.

Nasturtium. Vide *Pickle*.

Orange. See *Limon* in Pickle.

5. *Parsnip.* Take the large Roots, boil them, and strip the Skin: Then slit them long-ways into pretty thin Slices; Flower and fry

them in fresh Butter till they look brown. The sauce is other sweet Butter* melted. Some strow Sugar and Cinamon upon them. Thus you may accomodate other Roots.

There is made a Mash or Pomate of this Root, being boiled very tender with a little fresh Cream; and being heated again, put to it some Butter, a little Sugar and Juice of Limon; dish it upon Sippets;* sometimes a few *Corinths* are added.

Peny-royal. See *Pudding.*

Pickles.

⚜ 6. *Pickl'd*
Artichoaks. See *Acetaria*, p. 207.

⚜ 7. *Ashen-keys.* Gather them young, and boil them in three or four Waters to extract the Bitterness; and when they feel tender, prepare a Syrup of sharp White-Wine Vinegar, Sugar, and a little Water. Then boil them on a very quick Fire, and they will become of a green Colour, fit to be potted so soon as cold.

⚜ 8. *Asparagus.* Break off the hard Ends, and put them in White-Wine Vinegar and Salt, well covered with it; and so let them remain for six Weeks: Then taking them out, boil the Liquor or Pickle, and scum it carefully. If need be, renew the Vinegar and Salt; and when 'tis cold, pot them up again. Thus may one keep them the whole Year.

⚜ 9. *Beans.* Take such as are fresh, young, and approaching their full Growth. Put them into a strong Brine of White-Wine Vinegar and Salt able to bear an Egg. Cover them very close, and so will they be preserved twelve Months: But a Month before you use them, take out what Quantity you think sufficient for your spending a quarter of a Year (for so long the second Pickle will keep them sound) and boil them in a Skillet of fresh Water, till they begin to look green, as they soon will do. Then placing them one by one, (to drain upon a clean course Napkin) range them Row by Row in a *Jarr,* and cover them with Vinegar, and what Spice you please; some Weight being laid upon them to keep them under the Pickle. Thus you may preserve French-Beans, *Harico's,* &c. the whole Year about.

❧ 10. *Broom-Buds* and *Pods.* Make a strong Pickle, as above; stir it very well, till the Salt be quite dissolved, clearing off the Dregs and Scum. The next Day pour it from the Bottom; and having rubbed the Buds dry pot them up in a Pickle-Glass, which should be frequently shaken, till they sink under it, and keep it well stopt and covered.

Thus may you-pickle any other *Buds.* Or as follows:

❧ 11. Of *Elder.* Take the largest *Buds,* and boil them in a Skillet* with Salt and Water, sufficient only to scald them; and so (being taken off the Fire) let them remain covered till Green; and then pot them with Vinegar and Salt, which has had one Boil up to cleanse it.

❧ 12. *Collyflowers.* Boil them till they fall in Pieces: Then with some of the Stalk, and worst of the Flower, boil it in a part of the Liquor till pretty strong: Then being taken off, strain it; and when settled, clear it from the Bottom. Then with *Dill,* Gross Pepper,* a pretty Quantity of Salt, when cold, add as much Vinegar as will make it sharp, and pour all upon the *Collyflower;* and so as to keep them from touching one another; which is prevented by putting Paper close to them.

Cornelians are pickled like *Olives.*

❧ 13. *Cowslips.* Pick very clean; to each Pound of Flowers allow about one Pound of Loaf Sugar, and one Pint of White-Wine Vinegar, which boil to a Syrup, and cover it scalding-hot. Thus you may pickle *Clove-gillyflowers, Elder,* and other Flowers, which being eaten alone, make a very agreeable Salletine.

❧ 14. *Cucumbers.* Take the *Gorkems,* or smaller *Cucumbers;* put them into *Rape-Vinegar,*,* and boyl, and cover them so close, as none of the Vapour may issue forth; and also let them stand till the next day: Then boil them in fresh White-Wine Vinegar, with large Mace, Nutmeg, Ginger, white Pepper, and a little Salt, (according to discretion) straining the former Liquor from the *Cucumbers;* and so place them in a Jarr, or wide mouthed Glass, laying a litle Dill and Fennel between each Rank; and covering all with the fresh scalding-hot Pickle, keep all close, and repeat it daily, till you find them sufficiently green.

In the same sort *Cucumbers* of the largest size, being peel'd and cut into thin Slices, are very delicate.

Another.

Wiping them clean, put them in a very strong Brine of Water and Salt, to soak two or three Hours or longer, if you see Cause: Then range them in the *Jarr* or *Barrellet* with Herbs and Spice as usual; and cover them with hot Liquor made of two parts Beer-Vinegar, and one of White-Wine Vinegar: Let'all be very well closed. A Fortnight after scald the Pickle again, and repeat it, as above: Thus they will keep longer, and from being so soon sharp, eat crimp and well tasted, tho' not altogether so green. You may add a Walnut-Leaf, Hysop, Costmary, &c. and as some do, strow on them a little Powder of *Roch-Allom*,* which makes them firm and eatable within a Month or six Weeks after.

Mango of Cucumbers.*

Take the biggest *Cucumbers* (and most of the *Mango* size) that look green: Open them on the Top or Side; and scooping out the Seeds, supply their Place with a small Clove of Garlick, or some *Roccombo* Seeds. Then put them into an Earthen Glazed *Jarr,* or wide-mouth'd Glass, with as much White-Wine Vinegar as will cover them. Boil them in the Vinegar with Pepper, Cloves, Mace, &c. and when off the Fire, as much Salt as will make a gentle Brine; and so pour all boyling-hot on the *Cucumbers,* covering them close till the next Day. Then put them with a little Dill, and Pickle into a large Skillet; and giving them a Boyl or two, return them into the Vessel again: And when all is cold, add a good Spoonful of the best *Mustard,* keeping it from the Air, and so have you an excellent *Mango.* When you have occasion to take any out, make use of a Spoon, and not your Fingers.

Elder. See *Buds.*

Flowers. See *Cowslips,* and for other *Flowers.*

❧ 15. *Limon.* Take Slices of the thick Rind Limon, Boil and shift them in several Waters, till they are pretty tender: Then drain and wipe them dry with a clean Cloth; and make a Pickle with a little White-Wine Vinegar, one part to two of fair Water, and a little Sugar, carefully scum'd. When all is cold, pour it on the peel'd Rind, and cover it all close in a convenient Glass Jarr. Some make a Syrup of Vinegar, White-Wine and Sugar not too thick, and pour it on hot.

❧ 16. *Melon.* The abortive and after-Fruit of Melons being pickled as *Cucumber,* make an excellent Sallet.

❧ 17. *Mushrom.* Take a Quart of the best White-Wine Vinegar; as much of White-Wine, Cloves, Mace, Nutmeg a pretty Quantity, beaten together: Let the Spice boil therein to the Consumption of half; then taken off, and being cold, pour the Liquour on the *Mushroms;* but leave out the boiled Spice, and cast in of the same sort of Spice whole, the Nutmeg only slit in Quarters, with some Limon-Peel, white Pepper; and if you please a whole raw Onion, which take out again when it begins to perish.

Another.

The *Mushroms* peel'd, &c. throw them into Water, and then into a Sauce-Pan, with some long Pepper, Cloves, Mace, a quarter'd Nutmeg, with an Onion, Shallot, or Roccombo-Seed, and a little Salt. Let them all boil a quarter of an hour on a very quick Fire: Then take out and cold, with a pretty Quantity of the former Spice, boil them in some White-Wine; which (being cold) cast upon the *Mushroms,* and fill up the Pot with the best White-Wine, a Bay-Leaf or two, and an Handful of Salt: Then cover them with the Liquor; and if for long keeping, pour Sallet-Oil over all, tho' they will be preserved a Year without it.

They are sometimes boil'd in Salt and Water, with some Milk, and laying them in the Colender to drain, till cold, and wiped dry, cast them into the Pickle with the White-Wine, Vinegar and Salt, grated Nutmeg, Ginger bruised, Cloves, Mace, white Pepper and Limon-Peel; pour the Liquor on them cold without boiling.

❧ 18. *Nasturtium Indicum.* Gather the Buds before they open to flower; lay them in the Shade three or four Hours, and putting them into an Earthen Glazed Vessel, pour good Vinegar on them, and cover it with a Board. Thus letting it stand for eight or ten Days: Then being taken out, and gently press'd, cast them into fresh Vinegar, and let them so remain as long as before. Repeat this a third time, and Barrel them up with Vinegar and a little Salt.

Orange. See *Limon.*

❧ 20. *Potato** The small green Fruit (when about the size of the Wild Cherry) being pickled, is an agreeable Sallet. But the Root being roasted under the Embers, or otherwise, open'd with a Knife, the Pulp is butter'd in the Skin, of which it will take up a good Quantity, and is seasoned with a little Salt and Pepper. Some eat them with Sugar together in the Skin, which has a pleasant Crimpness.* They are also stew'd and bak'd in Pyes, &c.

❧ 21. *Purselan.* Lay the Stalks in an Earthen Pan; then cover them with Beer-Vinegar and Water, keeping them down with a competent Weight to imbibe, three Days: Being taken out, put them into a Pot with as much White-Wine Vinegar as will cover them again; and close the Lid with Paste to keep in the Steam: Then set them on the Fire for three or four Hours, often shaking and stirring them: Then open the Cover, and turn and remove those Stalks which lie at the Bottom, to the Top, and boil them as before, till they are all of a Colour. When all is cold, pot them with fresh White-Wine Vinegar, and so you may preserve them the whole Year round.

❧ 22. *Radish.* The Seed-Pods of this Root being pickl'd, are a pretty Sallet.

❧ 23. *Sampier.* Let it be gathered about *Michaelmas* (or the Spring) and put two or three hours into a Brine of Water and Salt; then into a clean Tin'd Brass Pot, with three parts of strong White-Wine Vinegar, and one part of Water and Salt, or as much as will cover the *Sampier,* keeping the Vapour from issuing out, by pasting down the Pot-lid, and so hang it over the Fire for half an Hour only. Being taken off, let it remain covered till it be cold; and then put it up into small Barrels or Jars, with the Liquor, and some fresh Vinegar, Water and Salt; and thus it will keep very green. If you be near the Sea, that Water will supply the place of Brine. This is the *Dover* Receit.

24. *Walnuts.* Gather the Nuts young, before they begin to harden, but not before the Kernel is pretty white: Steep them in as much Water as will more than cover them. Then set them on the Fire, and when the water boils, and grows black, pour it off, and supply it with fresh, boiling it as before, and continuing to shift it till it become clear, and the *Nuts* pretty tender: Then let them be put into clean Spring Water for two Days, changing it as before with fresh, two or three times within this space: Then lay them to drain, and dry on a clean course Cloth, and put them up in a Glass Jar, with a few Walnut Leaves, Dill, Cloves, Pepper, whole Mace and Salt; strowing them under every Layer of Nuts, till the Vessel be three quarters full; and lastly, replenishing it with the best Vinegar, keep it well covered; and so they will be fit to spend within three Months.

To make a Mango with them.

The green Nuts prepared as before, cover the Bottom of the Jar with some Dill, an Handful of Bay-Salt, *&c.* and then a Bed of Nuts; and so *stratum* upon *stratum,* as above, adding to the Spice some *Roccombo-Seeds;* and filling the rest of the Jar with the best White-Wine Vinegar, mingled with the best Mustard; and to let them remain close covered, during two or three Months time: And thus have you a more agreeable *Mango* than what is brought us from abroad; which you may use in any Sauce, and is of it self a rich Condiment.

Thus far *Pickles*.

25. *Potage Maigre.** Take four Quarts of Spring-Water, two or three Onions stuck with some Cloves, two or three Slices of Limon Peel, Salt, whole white Pepper, Mace, a Raze or two of Ginger,* tied up in a fine Cloth (Lawn or Tiffany) and make all boil for half an Hour; Then having Spinage, Sorrel, white Beet-Chard, a little Cabbage, a few small Tops of Cives, wash'd and pick'd clean, shred

them well, and cast them into the Liquor, with a Pint of blue Pease boil'd soft and strain'd, with a Bunch of sweet Herbs, the Top and Bottom of a *French Roll;** and so suffer it to boil during three Hours; and then dish it with another small *French Roll,* and Slices about the Dish: Some cut Bread in slices, and frying them brown (being dried) put them into the Pottage just as it is going to be eaten.

The same Herbs, clean wash'd, broken and pulled asunder only, being put in a close cover'd Pipkin, without any other Water or Liquor, will stew in their own Juice and Moisture. Some add an whole Onion, which after a while should be taken out, remembring to season it with Salt and Spice, and serve it up with Bread and a Piece of fresh Butter.

26. *Pudding* of *Carrot.* Pare off some of the Crust of Manchet-Bread,* and grate of half as much of the rest as there is of the Root, which must also be grated: Then take half a Pint of fresh Cream or New Milk, half a Pound of fresh Butter, six new laid Eggs (taking out three of the Whites) mash and mingle them well with the Cream and Butter: Then put in the grated Bread and Carrot, with near half a Pound of Sugar; and a little Salt; some grated Nutmeg and beaten Spice; and pour all into a convenient Dish or Pan, butter'd, to keep the Ingredients from sticking and burning; set it in a quick Oven for about an Hour, and so have you a Composition for any *Root-Pudding.*

27. *Penny-royal.* The Cream, Eggs, Spice, &c. as above, but not so much Sugar and Salt: Take a pretty Quantity of Peny-royal and Marigold flower, &c. very well shred, and mingle with the Cream, Eggs, &c. four spoonfuls of Sack; half a Pint more of Cream, and almost a Pound of Beef-Suet chopt very small, the Gratings of a Two-penny Loaf, and stirring all well together, put it into a Bag flower'd and tie it fast. It will be boil'd within an Hour: Or may be baked in the Pan like the *Carrot-Pudding.* The sauce is for both, a little Rose-water, less Vinegar, with Butter beaten together and poured on it sweetned with the Sugar Caster.

Of this Plant discreetly dried, is made a most wholsom and excellent Tea.

🌿 28. Of *Spinage*. Take a sufficient Quantity of *Spinach*, stamp and strain out the Juice; put to it grated Manchet, the Yolk of as many Eggs as in the former Composition of the *Carrot-Pudding;* some Marrow shred small, Nutmeg, Sugar, some Corinths, (if you please) a few Carroways, Rose, or Orange-flower Water (as you best like) to make it grateful. Mingle all with a little boiled Cream; and set the Dish or Pan in the Oven, with a Garnish of Puff-Paste.* It will require but very moderate Baking. Thus have you Receits for *Herb Puddings*.

🌿 29. *Skirret-Milk*. Is made by boiling the Roots tender, and the Pulp strained out, put into Cream or new Milk boiled, with three or four Yolks of Eggs, Sugar, large Mace and other Spice, &c. And thus is composed any other Root-Milk. See *Acetar*. p. 161 *Skirrets*.

🌿 30. *Tansie*. Take the Gratings or Slices of three Naples-Biscuits, put them into half a Pint of Cream; with twelve fresh Eggs, four of the Whites cast out, strain the rest, and break them with two Spoonfuls of Rose-water, a little Salt and Sugar, half a grated Nutmeg: And when ready for the Pan, put almost a Pint of the Juice of Spinach, Cleaver, Beets, Corn-Sallet, Green Corn, Violet, or Primrose tender Leaves, (for of any of these you may take your choice) with a very small Sprig of Tansie, and let it be fried so as to look green in the Dish, with a Strew of Sugar and store of the Juice of Orange: some affect to have it fryed a little brown and crisp.

🌿 31. *Tart* of *Herbs*. An *Herb-Tart* is made thus: Boil fresh Cream or Milk, with a little grated Bread or *Naples-Biscuit* (which is better) to thicken it; a pretty Quantity of Chervile, Spinach, Beete (or what other Herb you please) being first par-boil'd and chop'd. Then add *Macaron*, or Almonds beaten to a Paste, a little sweet Butter, the Yolk of five Eggs, three of the Whites rejected. To these some add Corinths plump'd in Milk, or boil'd therein, Sugar, Spice at Discretion, and stirring it all together over the Fire, bake it in the Tart-Pan.

🌿 32. *Thistle*. Take the long Stalks of the middle Leaf of the *Milky-Thistle*, about *May*, when they are young and tender: wash and scrape them, and boil them in Water, with a little Salt, till they are very soft, and so let them lie to drain. They are eaten with fresh Butter melted not too thin, and is a delicate and wholsome Dish. Other Stalks of the same kind may so be treated, as the *Bur,* being tender and disarmed of its Prickles, &c.

⚜ 33. *Trufles,* and other *Tubers,* and *Boleti,* are roasted whole in the *Embers;* then slic'd and stew'd in strong Broth with Spice, &c. as *Mushroms* are. Vide *Acetar.* p. 208 *Mushroom.*

⚜ 34. *Turnep.* Take their Stalks (when they begin to run up to seed) as far as they will easily break downwards: Peel and tie them in Bundles. Then boiling them as they do *Sparagus,* are to be eaten with melted Butter. Lastly,

⚜ 35. *Minc'd,* or *Sallet-all-sorts.* Take Almonds blanch'd in cold Water, cut them round and thin, and so leave them in the Water; Then have pickl'd Cucumbers, Olives, Cornelians, Capers, Berberries, Red-Beet, Buds of *Nasturtium,* Broom, &c. Purslan-stalk, Sampier, Ash-Keys, Walnuts, Mushrooms (and almost of all the pickl'd Furniture) with Raisins of the Sun ston'd, Citron and Orange-Peel, Corinths (well cleansed and dried) &c. mince them severally (except the Corinths) or all together; and strew them over with any Candy'd Flowers, and so dispose of them in the same Dish both mixt, and by themselves. To these add roasted *Maroons, Pistachios, Pine-Kernels,* and of Almonds four times as much as of the rest, with some Rose-water. Here also come in the Pickled Flowers and Vinegar in little *China* Dishes. And thus have you an Universal *Winter-Sallet,* or an *All sort* in Compendium, fitted for a City Feast, and distinguished from the *Grand-Sallet:* which shou'd consist of the Green blanch'd and unpickled, under a stately *Pennash* of *Sellery,** adorn'd with Buds and Flowers.

And thus have we presented you a Taste of our *English Garden Housewifry* in the matter of *Sallets:* And though some of them may be Vulgar, (as are most of the best things;) Yet she was willing to impart them, to shew the Plenty, Riches and Variety of the *Sallet-Garden:* And to justifie what has been asserted of the Possibility of living (not unhappily) on *Herbs* and *Plants,* according to *Original* and *Divine Institution,* improved by Time and long Experience. And if we have admitted *Mushroms* among the rest (contrary to our Intention, and for Reasons given, *Acet.* p. 208.) since many will by no means abandon them, we have endeavoured to preserve them from those pernicious Effects which are attributed to, and really in them: We cannot tell indeed whether they were so treated and ac- commodated for the most Luxurious of the *Cæsarean Tables,* when that Monarchy was in its highest Strain of *Epicurism,* and ingross'd this *Haugout* for their second Course; whilst this we know, that 'tis but what *Nature* affords all her Vagabonds under every Hedge.

And now, that our *Sallets* may not want a Glass of generous Wine of the same Growth with the rest of the Garden to recom- mend it, let us have your Opinion of the following.

Cowslip-Wine. To every Gallon of Water put two Pounds of *Sugar;* boil it an Hour, and set it to cool: Then spread a good brown *Toast* on both Sides with Yeast: But before you make use of it, beat some Syrup of *Citron* with it, an Ounce and half of Syrup to each Gallon of Liquor: Then put in the *Toast* whilst hot, to assist its *Fer- mentation,* which will cease in two Days; during which time cast in the *Cowslip-Flowers* (a little bruised, but not much stamp'd) to the Quantity of half a Bushel to ten Gallons (or rather three Pecks) four *Limons* slic'd, with the Rinds and all. Lastly, one Pottle* of *White* or *Rhenish Wine;* and then after two Days, tun it up in a sweet Cask. Some leave out all the Syrup.

And here, before we conclude, since there is nothing of more constant Use than good Vinegar; or that has so near an Affinity to all our *Acetaria,* we think it not amiss to add the following (much approved) Receit.

Vinegar. To every Gallon of Spring Water let there be allowed three Pounds of *Malaga-Raisins:** Put them in an Earthen Jarr, and place them where they may have the hottest Sun, from *May till Michaelmas:* Then pressing them well, Tun the Liquor up in a very strong Iron-Hooped Vessel to prevent its bursting. It will appear very thick and muddy when newly press'd, but will refine in the Vessel, and be as clear as Wine. Thus let it remain untouched for three Months, before it be drawn off, and it will prove Excellent *Vinegar*.

Butter. *Butter* being likewise so frequent and necessary an Ingredient to divers of the foregoing *Appendants:* It should be carefully melted, that it turn not to an Oil; which is prevented by melting it leisurely, with a little fair Water at the Bottom of the Dish or Pan; and by continual shaking and stirring, kept from boiling or over-heating, which makes it rank.

Other rare and exquisite *Liquors* and Teas* (Products of our *Gardens* only) we might super-add, which we leave to our *Lady Housewives*, whose Province indeed all this while it is.

THE END

EXPLANATORY NOTES

KALENDARIUM HORTENSE

3 *munera nondum intellecta Deum* (Lucan, *Bellum civile* 5. 528–9): gifts of the gods not yet appreciated (by mortals).

4 *intermedial spaces*: spaces in the middle, or in an intermediate position, in-between.

Columella Lucuys Junius Moderatus Columella (fl. *c.*AD 60), a Roman writer on agriculture, gardening, and arboriculture and author of the twelve-book *De Re Rustica*.

The Kid, the Dragon, and Arcturus…Hellespont: a reference to three stellar constellations: the Kid refers to Capricorn, the Dragon is the constellation Draco, in the northern sky, and Arcturus is the brightest star in the Boötes constellation.

5 *Georgic I*: the *Georgics* by Virgil (Publius Vergilius Maro, 70–19 BC) a poem in four books that deals with tillage, pasturage, the vine and olive, horses, cattle, and bees.

Periods: monthly happenings, particularly referring to astrological events. It was following the seventeenth century that the phrase came to be associated specifically with the female menstrual cycle.

hypercritical Puntillos: from the Spanish *puntillo* (diminutive of *punto*), meaning a small point, a detail; cf. modern English 'punctilio'.

in such and such an exact minute of the Moon: *Kalendarium* contains a number of references to the state of the moon and lunar months. In general terms it was (and still is) considered good practice to sow and plant when the moon is waxing (coming up to full moon) and during its waning to pick, harvest, and prune. See also *Cider-making*, note to p. 39.

In hac autem Ruris disciplina non desideratur ejusmodi scrupulositas (Columella, *De re rustica* II. I. 32): but in this country discipline [agriculture] such minute exactness is not required.

suspecta tempora (ibid.): uncertain weather.

Synoptical Tables: tables giving all requisite information in one view.

pretermit: to omit, to leave out.

M. Rose, Gard'ner to His Majesty…to Her Grace the Duchess of Somerset:

John Evelyn held John Rose (1629–77) in high regard, particularly enjoying the formality of his garden designs. Rose was sent by the Earl of Essex, Robert Devereux (1591–1646), to study under Le Nôtre at Versailles. On his return he was employed by the Duchess of Somerset, Lady Frances Devereux (d. 1660), sister of the Earl, to be Keeper of the Gardens, Essex House, Strand, London, a position he vacated when Charles II appointed him to a similar position at St James's Garden (Park) in 1666. With the help of Evelyn, John Rose published two books, *The English Vineyard Vindicated* (1666) and *A Treasure Upon Fruit Trees* (1688). He is represented in a painting by Danckerts, entitled 'Rose, the Royal Gardener Presenting the First Pine-Apple Raised in England to Charles II'.

5 *M Turner, formerly of Wimbleton in Surrey*: probably Robert Turner (fl. 1626–80s), who was known as the 'Astrological botanist' and wrote *Botanologia: the British Physician* (1664). Wimbledon House, Merton, London was built in 1588 by Thomas Cecil, 1st Earl of Exeter (1542–1622). The house was purchased by Charles I in 1639 for Queen Henrietta Maria who had the gardens redesigned by André Mollet (d. *c.*1665). By 1649 the house was owned by Henry Danvers, Earl of Danby (1573–1645) the horticultural patron of the newly formed Oxford Botanic Garden, whose Orangery in Surrey contained forty-two orange trees as well as a very large lemon tree. By 1662 Wimbledon House had been bought by George Digby, 2nd Earl of Bristol (1612–77), who invited John Evelyn to view the gardens on 17 February to '*help contrive the garden after the moderne*' (*Diary*, 1662).

6 *Parterre*: formal intricate flower beds and garden layout which originated in France and came to England during the lifetime of John Evelyn. A parterre consists of a level, usually rectangular, area divided into a series of ornamental flowerbeds often separated by an edging of dwarf box or similar low-growing shrubs, 1639.

torpent: sluggish, dull.

Enchiridion: a handbook or manual.

Palladius…Markham: Rutilius Taurus Aemilianus Palladius (4th cent. AD), Roman author who wrote *De Re Rustica* (*On Agriculture*) in fourteen books. See also *Acetaria* p. 196; *de Serres* (Olivier of the Greenhouses) (1529–1619), French soil scientist and author of *Théâtre d'Agriculture,* the most authoritative textbook on French agriculture in the 1600s; *Augustino Gallo* (fl. 1500s), Italian writer on agriculture, who in his book of 1569 wrote of the sweet orange as a plant whose cultivation dated from time immemorial; *Vincenzo Tanara* (d. 1667) renowned Italian gastronome and agronomist, and one of the first to establish the technique of asparagus farming; *Herrera*: Gabriel Alonso de Herrera (fl. 1513) was the Agricultura General of Spain; *Tusser*: (*c.*1524–80), Thomas Tusser, agricultural writer and poet and author of *One Hundred Pointes of Good Husbandrie* (1557), lived most of his life in East Anglia, but died a prisoner of debt in London; *Markham*: (*c.*1568–1637), Gervase Markham, writer on agriculture and horticulture and author of *English Husbandman* (1613) and *Farewell to Husbandry* (1620).

9   *Olitory-Garden*: kitchen or a pot-herb garden, 1658.

Ablaqueation: to loosen or remove the soil around roots, 1656. See also p. 43 and *Directions*, p. 64 *Ablaqueation*.

my French Gard'ner: this is a reference to *Le Jardinier François* (1651), writ-ten by Nicolas de Bonnefons (fl. 1650). In 1659 John Evelyn, probably with some assistance from his university friend Thomas Henshaw (1618–1700) translated it into *The French Gardiner: Instructing How to Cultivate All Sorts of Fruit-Trees and Herbs, for the Garden. Together with Directions to Dry and Conserve them in their Natural.*

Cyons for Graffs: an early spelling of scion, a detached shoot or bud, often known as a graft (graff) or slip, which is grafted onto a rootstock of a dif-ferent variety, as in the case of many fruit trees. Grafting was known to the earliest Mesopotamians and the Chinese, and later to the Greeks and Ro-mans. There are two advantages to grafting as opposed to growing from seed: the resulting plant reproduces the desired variety, and it reaches maturity quicker. See also notes to *Graff, Slip,* and *Graff by Approach* on pp. 13, 17, and 32, See also *Directions*, note to p. 101.

10 *Hot-bed*: it was during the late sixteenth century that the idea of making dung-beds reached Britain (the word 'hotbed' dates from 1626 and John Parkinson is credited with recording the name, by which it is still known). The idea of using fermenting manure to force seeds and plants to grow during the coldest part of the year had first been recorded in *c.* 961 in An-dalusia (modern Spain), when aubergine and gourd seeds were to be planted in December for transplantation four months later in April. While manure was used to enrich the soil it was Thomas Hill (fl. 1540s–70s) under the pen-name of Didymus Mountain who first described the method of making a dung-bed in his book *Gardener's Labyrinth* (1577). The idea spread rapidly, as it was a practical solution in helping to use up some of the continuous supply of manure that must have accumulated. The heat from a well-made dung bed extended the growing season, earlier sowing and germination could be achieved, and young or tender plants were shel-tered from frosts. It was particularly useful for the raising and growing of melons (see also p. 30 *the newly-invented Curcurbit-Glasse*). Its introduction

223

also fitted in neatly with the arrival of increasing numbers of foreign plants, many of which needed some warmth during the winter months.

Turn up your Bee-hives: there are several references to bees and bee-hives throughout the *Kalendarium*. They were important in the garden, not for the pollination of plants (which at the time was not understood) but as a supply of honey, and therefore sweetness. Sugar was expensive and not readily available. Beehives, or skeps as they were sometimes called, were usually made from thick straw and dome-shaped, although they could also be made from wood, which lasted longer. Discoveries regarding their behaviour interested Evelyn, and while visiting Dr Wilkins of Wadham College, Oxford he was shown the 'transparent apiaries which he had built like castles and palaces and so order'd them one upon another as to take the hony without destroying the bees. These were adorn'd with a variety of dials, little statues, vanes, &c. and he was so aboundantly civil as finding me pleas'd with them, to present me with one of the hives' (*Diary*, 1654). Extracting the honey and keeping bees through the winter was a difficult process, as earlier Thomas Tusser noted in his December husbandry:

> Go looke to thy bees, if the hive be too light
>
> Set water and honie, with rosemary dight. [prepared]
>
> Which set in a dish ful of sticks in the hive,
>
> From danger of famine to save them alive.

> *Five Hundred Points of Good Husbandry* (1573)

Until the nineteenth century bees were often ejected from the hive for the winter, or killed with sulphur to enable the honey to be harvested. New swarms would have been searched for each succeeding spring (they need a temperature of at least 12 °C (14 °F) to be enticed to remain in a hive). However, from the details given by Evelyn it appears that he kept his bees, or at least some of them, throughout the winter. See also *Acetaria*, note to p. 173 *Sugar*.

a little warm and sweet Wort: an infusion or decoction of malt or other grain, sometime known as brewer's wort. In Anglo-Saxon usage it is the name for a root, particularly a plant herb or vegetable used as food or medicine, often as the second element of the plant name. Later in the eighteenth century a wort came to mean any member of the cabbage family, e.g. colewort.

11 *light mould*: loose, or friable earth, the surface soil of which is easily broken up. See also Directions note to p. 70 *new mould*.

blowing: blossoming.

Recension: a survey or review, 1638.

12 *plash*: in hedging, to bend stems and branches down or across so that they can be interwoven; they can then be slashed on the slant to encourage new shoots, thus thickening the hedge.

Mural-fruit: fruit trees growing against and fixed to a wall.

Palisade Hedges: a row of trees or shrubs forming a close (or stockproof) hedge.

Circumposition: potting up a plant.

13 *Graff in the Cleft*: the stock tree is cut to about 1.2 m (4 ft) above ground, and a split is made in the centre of the trunk to receive the scion, taken from a different tree. In this type of graft the split frequently extends further than the scion, thus producing an insecure union. This method of grafting is rarely used today. See as before p. 9 *Cyon*, p. 17 *Slip*, p. 32 *Graff by Approach*, 17. See also *Directions*, p. 124, *Cleft*, p. 101, *Apples, peares, & cherries…by whipstock*.

the New-Moon: see note to p. 5, *in such and such…Moon*.

14 *Stercoration*: manuring with dung, 1605.

16 *perennial Greens*: Britain has very few native evergreens (yew, holly, ivy, gorse, etc., and one pine, *Pinus sylvestris*) so the introduction of such trees as the Silver fir, *Abies alba*, and the Holm oak, *Quercus ilex* (*c*.1580) were welcomed into the winter landscape. Evelyn was always keen to experiment with newly arrived plants, particularly evergreens, and even recommended using 'American Yucca' *Yucca filamentosa* (*c*.1656) to be grown as a hedge: '*it is a hardier plant than we take it for*', he states in '*Sylva*'.

fine willow earth: compost made of rotten willow branches.

17 *Slip*: a small shoot, cutting, or scion for grafting or planting. See as before p. 9 *Cyon's for Graffs*, p. 13 *Graff in the Cleft*, p. 32 *Graff by Approach*.

18 *Brumal Jacynths*: winter-flowering hyacinths. See Glossary of Plant Names: **Hyacinthus**.

21 *in Full Moon*: see note to p. 5, *in such and such…Moon*.

natural (not forc'd) Earth…to nourish the fibres: in other words, using dug soil from the ground, not enriched with manure etc., followed by earth which has been enriched, and then a further layer of dug soil.

22 *drouth*: drought.

Pennach'd: from the word 'Pennaceous', in botanical terms meaning markings resembling feathers. This may refer to feathered or parrot tulips. See also *Acetaria* see note to p. 218 *Pennash of Sellary*, see also Glossary of Plant Names: **Tulips**.

Matrasses supported on cradles of hoops: a mattress was a case of canvas or sacking stuffed with hair, flocks, straw, or leaves, anything light enough to protect plants, which could then be draped across the hoops.

Conservatory: Evelyn is credited with introducing the word *Conserve* to mean greenhouse, a shortened form of *Conservatory*, a place in which to preserve tender plants, in 1664. Heated sheds, cellars, or temporary structures were all used as winter protection for citrus fruit. Evelyn is also credited with the introduction of the word *Greene-house* in 1664. The two words gradually came to have different meanings. The greenhouse became the practical building for growing tender vegetables and storing plants safely through the winter whereas the conservatory developed as an area for the artistic display of exotic plants. See also p. 48 and note *Greenhouse*.

22 *tonsile*: a shaped and clipped hedge or shrub. 1664.

    Mow carpet-walks: see also p. 46 *Beat Roll and Mow Carpet Walks*.

23 *Ply the Laboratory*: the word 'laboratory' was first recorded in 1605 to mean a building set apart for experiments in natural science, especially chemistry. Evelyn uses the more modern (1652) 'Elaboratorie' when describing the building he had built in his garden at Sayes-Court (*The Legend of Sayes-Court*, nos. 57 and 58).

24 *fother'd on*: a 'fother' is a good cart-load, so probably means 'well manured'.

    screen'd: sifted through a sieve (1664).

    Neat: archaic word for cattle.

25 *Faggot-spray or the like...keep the earth loose for fear of rotting the fibres*: cases were pot-shaped but were either made from planks of wood (like orange tubs) or woven from willow, reeds, canes, or any other vegetative material that could be brought into use, hence the need to make sure the drainage was good. Faggot-sprays were the smallest twigs that could be placed in the bottom to support the weight of soil and plant. Pot gardening was begun by the Chinese at least two thousand years ago. Clay pots were eventually manufactured in different sizes, and the number that could be made from a certain amount of clay became known as 'the cast'. Innumerable sizes and shapes were developed, but in gardeners' jargon there was 'a small sixty' being sixty 3½-inch pots which could be made from the cast, 'forty-eights' of 5-inch pots, and the biggest clay-pot, a 10-inch known as the 'twelve'.

    the vertue: the goodness in the soil. Today we might perhaps use the term 'trace elements'.

26 *Inoculate*: set or insert the eye, bud, or scion in a plant for propagation.

27 *Hoofs*: gillyflowers were considered to be particularly prone to earwig attack, and sheep's hooves were pushed onto sticks placed as near as possible to the plants. Earwigs feed during the night, and the hooves provided a hiding-place in the morning from which they could easily be collected and killed. See also *Directions*, note to p. 111 *Kexas*.

29 *Emulsions of the cooler seeds*: bird-seed soaked in water to produce a mush to feed the aviary birds.

30 *Sow later Pease to be ripe six weeks after Michaelmas*: Michaelmas is 29 September, so the peas should be ready for harvesting by about the middle of October.

 umbrage: shade, especially the shade of trees (1540).

 the new-invented Cucurbit-Glasses: in 1629 John Parkinson recorded that 'Greate hollow glasses like unto bell-heads had newly arrived from Italy to help with the ripening of melons (*Paradisi in Sole Paradisus Terrestris*). A short time later smaller gourd-shaped or cucurbit glasses were developed. It was these that Evelyn found so useful to fill with beer and honey to trap wasps and other insects. Fifty melon glasses were listed as part of the inventory of the garden at Sayes Court in 1686. See also *Directions*, note to p. 70 *Bell glass*.

31 *lignous Plants*: 'ligneous', or woody, plants, a rare spelling (1664).

32 *spindles*: the stalks or stems upon which the flowers form (1601).

 Graff by Approach, Inarch: both words mean grafting by connecting a growing branch or twig to a growing parent plant, whereby the scion and stock both continue to grow on their own roots until the union is completed. This was also known as Ablactation. All three words came into use during Evelyn's lifetime. See also p. 9 *Cyon*, p. 13 *Graff*, p. 17 *Slip*, as before.

33 *Take up your Gladiolus now yearly...or else their Off-sets will poison the ground*: there appears to be no current evidence for this statement.

 Brine, Pot-ashes...Tobacco refuse: potash is an alkaline powder, at that time made of vegetable and wood ash crudely leached and evaporated in clay or iron pots. Today it is refined as potassium, and is a component of the compound fertilizer NPK: N = nitrogen for foliage development, P = phosphorus for root growth, K = potassium (originally known as kanite) for flower and fruit development. When tobacco was first introduced in 1573 it came not only in dried form for smoking, but also as a plant to grow in the garden. *Nicotiana tabacum* is in a genus of about forty-five species that come mainly from South America. It had two purposes: for pleasure, as pipe tobacco, but also as an insecticide to fumigate plants. To achieve this, the whole plant was infused in water and then boiled, the ensuing concoction being sprinkled onto paths, gravel walks, and so on in an effort to keep the weeds from growing and worms from making their casts. See also *Directions*, note to pp. III and *pot ashes*.

35 *vindemiate*: harvest the grapes. See also *Directions*, note to p. 105, *pot-soape*.

37 *Mucilage*: a viscous or sticky substance obtained from seeds, roots, or leaves.

Bartholomew-tide: the feast day of St Bartholomew, 24 August.

39 *Esculent, or Physical Plants*: edible and medicinal plants. See also *Directions*, note to p. 73.

Cider-making: cider is an ancient drink, and it is believed to be the Romans who first introduced the growing of the suitably sweet apples to Britain. By the seventeenth century so many cider-apple varieties were available that John Scudamore, 1st Viscount Scudamore (1601–71) of Holme Lacy, Herefordshire began classifying them. He was a close friend of Evelyn's, and was present at the dinner he gave on the eve of his departure for the Continent in 1649, and again in happier times when Evelyn had returned from his sojourn abroad and was settling into Sayes court with his bride. The second visit took place on 22 January 1653, just three days after the planting of Evelyn's orchard, when Evelyn recorded a '*new moone, wind W*'. During the 1660s The Royal Society commissioned a series of lectures on cider apples and cider-making. These seven lectures, including one by John Evelyn, were published as '*Pomona or an Appendix Concerning Fruit-Trees in Relation to Cider*' in the 1669 edition of *Sylva* along with *The Kalendarium Hortense*. See also note to p. 5, *in such and such…Moon*.

40 *Latifol*: 'broad-leaved', e.g. in *Anemone latifolia*.

41 *Capillaries*: thin hair-like tubes, part of the root system, that enable water and nutrients to be sucked from the earth into the plant.

Conserve: See note to p. 22, *Conservatory*.

43 *Orcharding*: cultivating fruit trees in an orchard (1664).

dry Trees: bare-rooted trees, grown in the nursery, dug up when ready, and planted in position in the garden or grounds.

46 *Beat, Roll, and Mow Carpet-walks*: Evelyn is following the recommendations of Francis Bacon (*Lord Verulam*, see note to p. 52) in his famous essay '*Of Gardens*' (1625), where he writes, 'nothing is more pleasant to the eye than green grass kept finely shorn'. Turf was taken from the wild

to make lawns and walks, and its unevenness was dealt with by a turf
beater or rammer; this was listed in *Directions* as one of the necessary
tools for a gardener. The grass was then rolled and mowed (scythed).
Grass plots were usually hemmed in with wooden planking. 'Carpet-
walk' is one of Evelyn's own phrases, and aptly describes what was
required. See also p. 22 *Mow carpet-walks*.

47 *spending*: using, or storing (1650).

    long-dung: manure which has been kept at least a month before using.

48 *qualified water*: water that includes some feed (dung water) for the plant.

    Greenhouse: see note to p. 22, *Conservatory*.

49 *Pent-house*: a building with a sloping roof, or an awning or canopy.

50 *Sow...Pomace of Cider-pressings*: mulch with crushed apple waste. See also
    p. 39 *Cider making*.

52 *Lord Verulam's design*: Francis Bacon, Baron Verulam, Viscount St Albans
    (1561–1626) was a philosopher, jurist, and English pioneer of the scientific
    form of investigation. His *Essays* were first published in 1597 and again in
    1625; *Essay XLVI* is '*Of Gardens*' and begins with the much-quoted phrase
    'God Almighty first planted a garden'. See also *Acetaria*, p. 185 *Lord Bacon*.

    Doctor Sharrock: Revd Robert Sharrock (1630–84), b. Drayton, Parslow,
    Bucks., Rector of Bishop Waltham, author of *History of Propagation and
    Improvement of Vegetables* (1660).

DIRECTIONS FOR THE GARDINER

57 *Venio nunc ad voluptates Agricolarum* (Cicero, *Cato maior* 51): Now I come
    to the delights of the Farmers.

    Quis non Epicurum Suspicit, exigui lætum plantaribus Horti? (cf. Juv: 13. 122–
    3): Who does not admire Epicurus, happy with the young saplings of his
    tiny garden?

70 *Beds of Sweete-herbs*: the sweet or aromatic herbs are used in cooking to
    impart flavour, and include the perennials: rosemary, sage, fennel, mint,
    bay, thyme, and winter savory. They and others, raised annually, are listed
    as being grown in the Kitchen Garden. See also pp. 71 and 72 *Plants for the
    Kitchen-Garden*.

    new moulded: the soil around a plant loosened and aerated. See also *Kalen-
    darium*, note to p. 11 *light mould*.

Bell glasses: developed for protecting melons, cucumbers, lettuce, and other tender seedlings, the glasses were about a foot (30 cm) wide, and a lipped-bell shape with a knob on the top to act as a handle. In use by 1629, they were manufactured from thick green glass that let in little light, and were heavy to move. Although in time the glass became both clearer and thinner, it was another two hundred years before the ventilation cap was developed. See also *Kalendarium* note to p. 30 *Cureurbit-glass*.

Haw: hoe.

plants hasten to run to seede…clap some mould about them: this is not a practice in use today, the idea would seem to have the opposite effect: if a plant feels threatened in any way, e.g. by having its roots disturbed, hastening to flower and set seed would be one of its reactions.

to pome & head: to make the heart or head of the cauliflower (1664). The word 'pome' is still in use and usually refers to a fruit formed with a large amount of flesh surrounding the core, with the carpels encasing the seeds, e.g. apples, pears.

73 *Physic-garden…Physical plants*: area set aside for the growing and cultivation of edible and medicinal plants. See also *Kalendarium*, note to p. 39 *Esculent*.

76 *Rarer Simples & Exotics*: the Doctrine of Signatures, although anciently developed, was laid down in documentary form in 1588, by Giambattista della Porta the famous inventor of the camera obscura and telescope. Nearly a hundred years later Robert Turner of Reading, an 'astrological botanist', confirmed the idea in *Botanologia: The British Physician*. About the same time William Coles of Oxford wrote his *Art of Simpling*, explaining that simples were medicines made from a single herb; using two or more the mixture was known as a compound. Plants were said to hold a particular sign or signature indicating how they were to be used; different coloured saps, the structure or shape of leaves or petals, the colouring and patterns of vegetation, or the availability of seeds all contributed to the choice of material to make the medicine. See also *Acetaria* p. 165 *Simples*.

77 *Coronary Garden*: originally used to mean 'crown-like', by 1682 the word had broadened its meaning to encompass the gathering of crown-making material and the making of garlands or wreaths. Evelyn is using the word to head a complex listing of flowering plants.

80 *will be variegated…but not by their seeds*: variegation in a plant occurs for three reasons, the first two are to do either with a lack of chlorophyll in the plant or infection by a virus. The third reason lies in propagation, and to maintain a truly variegated plant it must be propagated from cuttings,

not grown from seed (although there are a few exceptions); even then it may slowly revert and lose its variegation. Variegated plants are usually not quite as robust as their plainer counterparts.

84–5 *Vulgar/Not-Vulgar*: describing a plant as being vernacular and native or foreign and introduced.

87 *s^r W; Temple*: Sir William Temple (1628–99), statesman and for many years Ambassador to Holland. A keen gardener and experimental fruit-grower, he had a celebrated walled fruit-garden at West Sheen, Richmond, Surrey, which Evelyn visited in 1678. By 1660 Sir William had introduced several new fruit varieties into England, and had distributed them among his friends and local people, including John Evelyn who records that he was growing one of his Black Cherries at Sayes Court. In 1685 Sir William published *Upon the Gardens of Epicurus*. See also Glossary of Plants: **Peach, Plum**.

88 *Bish: of Lond:*: the Bishop of London, Hon. & Revd Henry Compton (1632–1713), introduced many exotic trees (particularly from America) to the garden at Fulham Palace (from 1675 when he became Bishop of London). Evelyn held him in high regard as a prelate, and he was a friend of both John Ray (1627–1705) and, when he was Bishop of Oxford (1674), Jacob Bobart (1641–1719), Professor of Botany and Horti Praefectus at Oxford Botanic Garden. See also Glossary of Plants: **Abricots**.

s^r: H: Capel, Sheens: Sir Henry Capel (d. 1696), Baron Capel of Tewkesbury, Lord Deputy of Ireland 1695, brother to the Earl of Essex. Owned a celebrated garden at Kew (close to Sheen) that later became part of Royal Botanic Gardens, with 'the choicest fruit of any plantation in England' (*Diary*, 1678).

92 *one p^t of Tanners' stuff...the Tan-pit*: crushed bark, usually of oak, as well as human urine had been used by tanners for generations to cure skins to make leather. By Evelyn's time the finished mixture was used to enrich the soil and help the growth of plants. It was known also to act as a preservative, and when spread on canvas, particularly sails, and fishing nets helped to prolong their life. About the same time it was realized that fermenting tan-bark generated an immense amount of heat, although the first record of its use to heat sail was not until 1720, when the honour fell to the gardener of Sir Matthew Decker (1679–1749), Henry Telende, who managed to grow a pineapple in his garden at Richmond Green, Surrey.

House y^r Oranges about Mich:...not out 'til mid Aprill: Michaelmas is 29 September, it would be considered inordinately early to house tender shrubs; however, by adding the eleven days in 1752, with the alteration of the calendar from the Julian to the Gregorian calendar, the date Evelyn suggests seems more likely. Conversely the emergence of the oranges during mid-April remains much the same.

insolated: water that has been warmed or exposed to the sun (1612).

All cold & noysomeness hurts them: noisesomeness refers to vexatious annoyances, or in this instance sudden squalls, draughts, and so on. The growing of citrus fruit in England was a relatively new idea, having first been experimented with in 1599, when Sir Francis Carew of Beddington in Surrey planted Seville oranges, *Citrus aurantium*. There are sixteen *Citrus* species, and they all require protection if they are to survive the winter in England. A number of species were introduced during the seventeenth century, including the lemon, *C. limon*, and the lime, *C. aurantifolia*, both of these, as well as the citron, *C. medica*, were being cultivated by 1648 at the Oxford Botanic Garden. The sweet orange, *C. sinensis*, arrived a little later, and became both a popular shrub to grow and a fruit to eat. Samuel Pepys made many references to them in his *Diary*, including an entry in December 1665, when during a busy day of meetings he found the time to purchase 'oysters and lemons (6d. per piece) and oranges, (3d.)', for a friendly supper he was giving at Greenwich. (Samuel Pepys, *Diary*, 1665).

98 *Bough-pots*: from 'Beau-pots', for holding ornamental boughs or flowers (1583).

99 *Trunchions*: truncheons, lengths cut from a plant, stout cuttings for grafting (1572).

100 *Apples for Dwarfs, on the paradise Kernell-stock*: the tiny shrubby crab apple, pomme de Paradis or the Paradise apple, was frequently used for dwarfing as was the Doucin, the Sweeting, and St John's apple. See also Glossary of Plants: Apples, Pears.

101 *Apples, peares, & Cherries, are best grafted in the Clef or by Whipstock*: this entails the cutting of the stock tree at about (4 ft) 1.2 m, with a cut made into the centre of the trunk for the insertion of the scion; a suitable branch could also be used. See also *Kalendarium*, p. 9 and note, and note to p. 13, *Graff in the Cleft*.

M. de la Quintine: Jean-Baptiste de La Quintinie (1628–88), French lawyer and later a gardener. In 1665 he was appointed jardinier du roi to King Louis XIV, and was responsible for the potager du roi at Versailles. La Quintinie rose to become the director of the royal kitchen gardens and then jardinier en chef (head gardener). He wrote *Instructions pour les jardins fruitier et potagers*, published posthumously in 1690. An English translation, *The Compleat Gard'ner*, was probably undertaken by George London with assistance from John Evelyn in 1693. See also *Acetaria*, note to p. 175, *Mr. London*.

102 *St. James' tide*: the feast day of the Apostle James the Greater, 25 July.

103 *pibbles*: pebbles.

105 *Thus may you feede Vines with blood*: dried blood is one of the best organic fertilizers. The nitrogen contained in it becomes more readily available when activated by lime either added or already present in the soil. See also *Kalendarium* note to p. 35, *Vindemiate*.

clowt: clout, a piece of cloth.

106 *the bearing buds from the leafe buds*: bearing buds are those that hold an embryonic flower. The bud at the tip of the growing shoot is usually referred to as the terminal bud.

The Pome-Granade delights to be often purged: the pomegranate, *Punica granatum*, requires good, loamy, well-drained soil and when in growth it is recommended that a liquid fertilizer is applied at monthly intervals. See also Glossary of Plants: Pome Granade.

108 *pilasters*: columns or pillars.

109 *buck-ashes:* the sweepings from the cart.

110 *a broad Rammer*: a tool used to tamp and level grass pathways and lawns. See also *Kalendarium*, note to p. 46 and note to p. 46, *Beat, Roll, and Mow*.

pot-ashes: potash is required for the healthy development of flowers and fruits. See also *Kalendarium*, note to p. 33, *Brine, Pot-ashes*.

lime newly from the Kiln: lime, or quicklime, is obtained by heating chalk or limestone with coal until it glows red. Combined with a small amount of water it swells up and crumbles into a soft dry powder, and applied to soil supplies calcium to reduce acidity. The amount of lime in the soil determines whether the ground is alkaline, neutral, or acid.

sweepings of refuse Tabacco: See also *Kalendarium*, note to p. 33 *Brine, Pot ashes*.

Kexes: the dry, usually hollow stem of a plant; such sticks were placed in the ground near fruit trees to attract earwigs, slugs, snails, etc., into their shade, from where they could be shaken out and disposed of. See also *Kalendarium* note to p. 27, *Hoofs*.

Sampsons-posts: a type of mouse-trap, the name of which is believed to allude to the Old Testament story of Samson pulling down two pillars and destroying the Philistine's temple in Gaza. (Judges 16: 29–31).

beaten coprus: from Gk. κόπρος , dung.

112 *A Tulip or other roote being cankered is cured…it become dry*. Canker is a disease of some root crops and also a fungus that particularly attacks fruit trees. Evelyn is using the word in a general sense of rot or decay; tulip bulbs do not thrive in poorly drained soil, so replanting them will rarely if ever cure the problem.

Unslack'd lime: dry (unslaked) lime. See above note to p. 111, *lime newly from the kiln*.

A plaster of Diachylon: originally composed of the juices of vegetables, but later the name given to lead-plaster made from boiling together lead oxide (litharge), olive oil, and water, which adhere together when heated.

113 *Mr. Berckley*: probably the nephew of John Evelyn's old friend Philip Packer of Groombridge in Kent.

Ch: Howard: probably a member of the prestigious Arundel family with whom Evelyn was on intimate terms.

Dr Merret: Christopher Merrett (1614–95), glass maker, Keeper of the Library and Museum of the College of Physicians (1654), author of *Pinax Rerum Naturalium Britannicarum, A Picture of Natural British Objects* (1666). Evelyn was invited to the college to meet Dr Merrett on 3 October 1662, twelve days before Evelyn gave his famous discourse '*concerning Forest Trees*' to the Royal Society (*Diary*, 1662).

114 *Wall-Fruite planted at Wotton in the Flower gardens, 1700*: this list appears beneath a sketch of Wotton House viewed from the south. 'The Green-Grove' is labelled to the west of the gardens, and 'The pottagere or Kitchin herb-Garden' to the east.

119 *secundum Artem*: according to the (rules of the) art.

Tewksberry mustard: Tewkesbury was the centre of the growing and making of mustard from earliest times to the middle of the eighteenth century, when it was overtaken by Durham. Shakespeare certainly knew of its fame, as he writes of Poins' wit being '*as thick as Tewkesbury mustard*' (*2 Henry IV*) See also *Acetaria*, p. 174, *the best Tewksberry*.

120 *Furnitures*: the adjuncts of a salad, the spices, condiments, or dressings.

123 *Magazines*: storehouses, or the contents in them.

Gardiners Almanac & Discourse of Earth: *Kalendarium Hortense*, first published in 1664, and *A Philosophical Discourse of Earth* (1676).

124 *Graff in the clet*: see also *Kalendarium*, p. 13 and note *Graff in the cleft*.

decrease of the Moone: Evelyn refers quite regularly to the phases of the moon and their influence on various garden practices. A waning moon is considered an efficacious time to cut, prune, and harvest. See also *Kalendarium*, p. 5 *in such and such an exact minute....*

ACETARIA

133 *John Lord Somers of Evesham*: John First Baron (1651–1716), Whig statesman, created Lord Chancellor in 1697, and one of William III's most trusted ministers. He served as President of the Royal Society from 1698 to 1703. In 1699 John Evelyn dedicated the newly published *Acetaria* to him, upon which he notes in his diary for 21 October '*the Lord Chancellor...return'd me thanks in an extraordinary civil letter*' (*Diary*, 1699).

a Great and Learned Chancellor: Edward Hyde, Earl of Clarendon (1609–74), Lord Chancellor, 1658–67.

a very Learned Lord: William 2nd Viscount Brounker of Castle Lyons (1620–84), Irish mathematician, educated at Oxford. He had been Chancellor to the widowed Queen Henrietta Maria and was the first President of the Royal Society, 1662–77.

a no less Honorable and Learned Chancellor: Charles Montague Earl of Halifax (1661–1715), Chancellor of the Exchequer, and President of the Royal Society immediately preceding Lord Somers.

134 *Great Chancellor* (*one of Your Lordship's Learned Predecessors*): Edward Hyde. See above.

135 *Geoponicks*: relating to the cultivation of the ground (1608).

Younger Pliny: Nephew and adopted son of Pliny the Elder (see below). Gaius Plinius Caecilius Secundus (61/2–112/13), Roman Senator and prominent legal orator.

the Naturalist: Gaius Plinius Secundus, known as Pliny the Elder (AD 23–79), Roman scholar, administrator, and author of *Naturalis Historia* in thirty-seven volumes.

136 *the Worthiest Emperor the Roman world ever had*: Trajan, emperor AD 98–117, whose self-description as *princeps optimus*, 'the best First Citizen', was accepted in later ages.

Ninth Day: every ninth day by the Roman count (every eighth day in ours) was a market day, but public business was by no means confined to such days.

qui nullos habuit hortos: 'who had no gardens' (cf. Cornelius Nepos, *Vita Attici* 14. 3).

Pomponius Atticus: Titus Pomponius Atticus (110–32 BC) businessman and man of letters, great friend of Cicero. See below.

Cicero: Marcus Tullius Cicero (106–43 BC), writer, statesman, and Rome's greatest orator. Several of his letters to Atticus concern the purchase of gardens: note especially 13. 1. 2: 'There is no other kind of possession I prefer.'

Rostra: platform from which a speaker addressed a meeting of the Roman people. A speaker in Cicero's dialogue *De oratore* (3. 63) speaks of being called away from the rostra by Epicurean philosophy, resting in its gardens.

Isthmian Games: athletic festival of ancient Greece, celebrated on the Isthmus of Corinth in 582 BC and every other year thereafter. The prizes consisted of crowns made from parsley.

Apician Art: fine and luxurious food and gourmet meals. The name comes from Apicius, a Roman epicurean. See also *Apicius*, note to p. 202 *Apicius*.

Supplicia Luxuriae (Seneca the Younger, *Epistulae morales* 95. 18): 'torments of luxury'.

Seneca: Lucius Annaeus Seneca the Younger (4 BC–AD 65).

137 *Lasciva pagina, vita proba*: '[my] page [i.e. writing] is wanton, my life is upright' (Martial 1. 4. 8).

Lemma: motto (*OED* s.v. lemma¹ 2.a).

In hac arte consenui: 'in this profession I have grown old'. (Cf. Epicurus, cited at Seneca, *Epistulae morales* 21. 10, *in hac voluptate consenui*, 'I have grown old in this pleasure', *sc.* that of gardens.)

the Plan annext to these Papers: this is a contents list for an ambitious volume to be called 'The Plan of a Royal Garden' in three books, covering everything from landscaping and ornaments to waterworks and flower painting, which was never finished.

Laureato Vomere (cf. Pliny the Elder, *Naturalis Historia* 18. 19): 'with a Laurelled Ploughshare', i.e. tilled by a man who had celebrated a triumph. Cf. p. 202, *Vomere laureato, & triumphali aratore* and note.

138 *Aristotle*: (384–322 BC), Greek philosopher and scholar and a pupil of Plato, he founded his own school in Athens. His works, of which many survive, include *Prior Analytics*, *De Interpretatione*, *Ethica Eudimia* (The Ethics of Well-being).

Theophrastus: (*c.*372–286 BC) Greek philosopher, a native of Lesbos. Studied first under Plato in his Academy, and and then undertook botanical studies with Aristotle, with whom he became firm friends. He established botany as a science and was the author of *Enquiries into Plants* in nine books and the earliest surviving European botanical work, as well as the six-book *Aetiology of Plants* (*On the Causes of Plants*).

Dioscorides: Dioscorides Pedanius (1st century AD), was a Greek physician in the Roman Army. He was the author of *Materia Medica*, a book that has had a lasting influence on the understanding of the plant world.

139   *Cuncta me dicturum...non poterit* [correctly *poterat*]*...consummata sit ingenio* (cf. Columella 5. 1. 1–2): '[I had given no assurance] that I would say everything which the immensity of that science comprehended, but very many things; for it could not fall within the wisdom of one man, and there is no other Discipline or Art, which has been perfected by an individual talent.'

140   *aliquam partem tradidisse*: 'to have handed on a certain part'. Cf. Columella 5. 1. 2, *maximam partem tradidisse*, 'to have handed down the greatest part'.

Inutilis olim Ne Videar vixisse: 'Lest at some time I seem to have lived uselessly' (cf. Pier Angelo Mazolli of La Stellata near Ferrara, in Latin Marcellus Paligenius Stellatus, *Zodiacus vitae* 1. 27–8).

141   Ὅλος: correctly ὅλος, 'whole'.

Παν πᾶν, 'everything', fancifully suggested at Isidore, *Etymologiae* 20. 2. 15 as an etymology of Latin *panis*, 'bread'.

ab Olendo, i.e. Crescendo: from a supposed verb *olere*, 'to grow', inferred from *adolescere*, 'to grow up'. See Joseph Justus Scaliger in his edition of *M. Terentii Varronis opera quae supersunt* ([Geneva], 1581), v [[7]]ʳ.

Younger Scaliger...his Father Julius: Joseph Justus Scaliger (1540–1609), Calvinist scholar, who was sometimes known as 'the learned antagonist', and his father Julius Caesar Scaliger (1484–1558) a French scholar. See also note to p. 152, *Jos. caliger and Casaubon* and p. 189, *Learned antagonist*.

Theophrastus: the passage cited (in Latin translation) is from *Historia plantarum* 7. 7. 1; for the comment see Julius Caesar Scaliger, *Annotationes in Historias Theophrasti* (Lyon, 1584), 285. See also p. 138 *Theophrastus*.

ab Alendo: 'from feeding', i.e. from *alere*, 'to feed'. See Isidore, *Etymologies* 17. 10. 2.

Cumini Sectores: cumin-cutters, translating a Greek term for κυμινοπρίσται, either misers or pedants, cf. 'hair-splitters'.

142   ψυχραὶτράπεζαι: (Plutarch, *Quaestiones convivales* 733 F), 'cold tables'.

Salmasius: Claude Saumaise, latinized to Claudius Salmasius (1588–1653), a French protestant and classical scholar. He held a professorship at Leiden University; his magnum opus was his *Plinianae Exercitationes* (1629).

λάχανα : garden herbs.

Pliny: see note to p. 135, *the Naturalist.*

Hermolaus: Hermolaus Barbarus, *Castigationes Plinianae* (Milan, 1495), I [[4]]ʳ.

Oxybaphon: from Gr. ξ βαφον, literally 'acid-dip'.

Sapidity: from 'sapid', having taste or flavour (1646).

Oluscula: plural diminutive of *olus*, garden herb.

143   *Dr Muffet:* Thomas Muffet/Moufet/Moffet (1553–1604), naturalist, physician, and entomologist. Studied the silkworm industry in Italy, edited and expanded *Theatrum Insectorum,* an unfinished work by the botanist and entomologist Thomas Penny (*c.*1530–89), and was the author of *Health's Improvement,* a work on nutrition, in 1595. Dr Muffet was fascinated by spiders, and his daughter Patience was the original 'little Miss Muffet' of the nursery rhyme. He is believed to have recommended eating mashed spiders to cure the common cold and supposedly when his daughter was ill, reputed to have had a tubful of spiders tipped over her.

Pliny: see note to p. 135, *Pliny the Younger.*

Sestertia [corrected by Hardouin to *Sestertium*] *Sena Millia:* Pliny, *Natural History* 19. 152, states that at Cartagena (not Carthage) and Córdoba 'thistles [i.e. cardoons, the ancestors of the modern artichoke] yield six thousand sesterces each [year] from small patches'. The sesterce (worth 4 denarii) was the normal Roman money of account; all conversions into modern values are fanciful, but 6,000 sesterces was not a large sum of money, and nowhere near £30,000 even in current values, let alone those of Evelyn's day. Evidently he has misunderstood the sum as 6 million sesterces.

144   *Innocentior quam Olus:* 'more innocent than a cabbage'. See Pliny the Elder, *Natural History* 19. 133 'medici nocentiorem quam olus esse iudicavere' (the doctors have judged it [the beet] to be more harmful than a cabbage), where most manuscripts read *innocentiorem*; contrary to Evelyn's assertion, Hardouin saw that the sense required *nocentiorem*.

Harduin: Jean Hardouin (1646–1729), French Jesuit and classical scholar, born in Quimper (Brittany), Librarian of the Collège de Louis le Grand in Paris. He produced an edition of Pliny's works and volumes on Numismatics.

Diphilus: Diphilus of Siphnos, a Greek writer on vegetables. Quoted by Athenaeus, *Deipnosophists* 9. 371A, as saying that 'the beet is juicier than the cabbage and moderately nourishing'. See also note to p. 189 *Diphilus.*

Martial: Marcus Valerius Martial (*c.* AD 40), a native of Bilbilis (now Calatayud) in Spain, he was a Latin poet, and famous for his epigrams.

Fabrorum prandia: 'craftsmen's lunches' (Martial, *Epigrams* 13. 13. 1).

Turiones: young shoots rising out of the ground, produced from a subterranean bud.

145 *Gaudia semper ago*: 'I always rejoice.'

Averroes: Ibn Rushd (1126–98), b. Córdoba in Spain, a Muslim peripatetic philosopher.

Euphrosynum: from εὐφροσύνη, 'cheerfulness'.

Nepenthes: 'ungrieving', a sorrow-dispelling drug dispensed by Helen.

Homer: (?8th century BC), Greek epic poet, believed to have lived in Ionia in Asia Minor. The presumed author of *The Iliad* and *The Odyssey*. See also p. 156, and p. 183 *Homer*.

Corrago: borage, in Spanish it is known as *corrago* and *borraja*. See also Glossary Borrage.

Pompey's: Gnaeus Pompeius (106–48 BC) was a Roman general and politician, a rival to and enemy of Julius Caesar, who defeated him at the Battle of Pharsalus, Greece in 48 BC.

Cato: Marcus Porcius Cato Censorius (234–149 BC), Roman statesman, historian, and orator; author of *De Agri Cultura c.*160 BC.

Pythagoras: (6th century BC), Greek philosopher, native of the island of Samos; he believed that 'all things are numbers' and although he is known for his 'Pythagoras theorem', the mathematically minded Babylonians had earlier discovered the same theory. See also p. 152 *Pythagorus* and p. 193 *Porphyry*.

Chrysippus the Physician: (281–c.207 BC), head of the philosophical school of the Stoa in Athens.

C. Celsus: Aulus Cornelius Celsus (fl. first half of 1st century AD), author of *Artes,* an encyclopedia on agriculture, medicine, and allied subjects. See note to p. 181 and p. 189 *Celsus*.

146 *Nitre*: potassium nitrate, saltpetre.

Halmyridia: Pliny, *Natural History* 19. 142, explains that they are so called [in Greek: 'salty things'] because they are found only by the sea.

Pliny: see note to p. 135, *the Naturalist*.

Athenæus: (fl. 2nd to 3rd century AD), born at Naucratis, a Greek trading centre in Egypt. Greek rhetorician and grammarian, the author of *Deipnosophistai* (*The Banquet of the Learned*) in fifteen volumes, which describes a symposium at which the participants discuss literature, philosophy, history, medicine, and other subjects, including that of courtesans. See also note to p. 144 *Diphilus*.

apiata marina & florida: see Athenaeus 9. 369 E, where three kinds of cabbage are distinguished—'parsley-like', 'salty', and 'smooth-leaved'—which Evelyn, citing a Latin translation, gives as 'parsley-like', 'marine', and 'flowery'.

Sea-keele: i.e. sea-kale.

Crambe: κράμβη was by Roman times the normal Greek word for cabbage, though Theophrastus had used the Athenian word ῥάφανοι.

Theophrastus: see note to p. 188. It is not clear what passage is intended; at *Historia Plantarum* 4. 16. 6 he asserts the efficacy of cabbage against drunkenness.

Pliny: see *Naturalis Historia* 20. 85.

Eructations: belches or burps.

Sir Anth. Ashley: Anthony Ashley 1st Baronet (d. 1628), of St Giles's House, Wimborne St Giles, Dorset. Secretary of War during Elizabeth's reign, he was the grandfather of the 1st Earl of Shaftsbury, an acquaintance of Evelyn, who is mentioned several times in the *Diary*. Evelyn called him 'the crafty and ambitious Earle' during the 'exclusion' crisis regarding James, Duke of York of 1683.

sweet Butter: unsalted butter.

147 *Calices*: chalices, flower-cups (1650).

148 *Tavernier*: Jean-Baptiste Tavernier (1605–89), French traveller to the Middle East, Persia, India, and the Far East. On his return to France he published *Les Voyages de J.'B. Tavernier*, Paris (1676).

Good-Wife Hecale: Hecale gave hospitality to Theseus on his way to fight the Marathonian bull.

149 *Theseus*: son of the god Poseidon who killed the Minotaur in Crete.

149 *Theas*: infusions or teas.

Country-man's Theriacle: an antidote to poison.

Uliginous: water logged, or swampy.

150 *Latona*: Latin name of the Greek goddess Leto, mother of Apollo and Artemis.

Mortuorum Cibi: 'food of the dead'.

Adonis and his sad Mistriss: Venus is said to have wrapped Adonis' corpse in lettuce-leaves.

151 *Galen*: Claudius Galenus (AD 129–99), native of Pergamum, NW Asia Minor. He was a well-known physician, medical writer, and anatomist, who studied in Greece and Alexandria. For his praise of the lettuce see especially *De alimentorum facultatibus* 2. 40.

Pinguid: rich and fertile (1635).

Subdulcid: sweetish.

Sana: probably from 'sanative', having the power to heal.

Augustus: born Gaius Octavius (63 BC–AD 14), the first Roman emperor. He defined the eastern frontier of the Roman empire along the line of the Danube and Rhine rivers, and conquered a further five provinces.

Tacitus: Roman emperor AD 275–6, of whom there is a largely fictitious biography in the *Historia Augusta*.

Somnum se mercari illa sumptus effusione: 'that he purchased sleep by that outlay of expense' (*Historia Augusta* 37. II. 2).

Aristoxenus: an otherwise unknown philosopher of the hedonistic school founded by Aristippus of Cyrene, not to be confused with Aristoxenus of Tarentum, the Greek musicologist and philosopher who was a pupil of Aristotle. For the anecdote see Athenaeus, *Deipnosophists* I. 7C.

152 *Pythagoras*: see note to p. 145 *Pythagorus* and note to p. 193 *Porphyry*. The story is in Aelian, *Varia Historia* 4. 17.

Epimenides: Cretan miracle worker and religious teacher (?7th–5th BC), who is alleged to have lived for either 157 years, or possibly 299 years, during which he was believed to have slept for 50 consecutive years. Plato in *Laws* 3. 677 D–E speaks of his putting into practice what Hesiod had taught, which was understood as a reference to *Works and Days* 41, 'what great benefit there is in mallow and asphodel'.

Plato: (*c*.428–347 BC), Greek philosopher, follower of Socrates, who in 387 founded the Academy in Athens. Works include *The Republic, The Symposium, Phaedo*. See also note to p. 193, *Platonic Tables*.

Galen: see note to p. 151 *Galen*; he discusses the virtues of the marrow in *On Simples* 6. 5. I.

Dioscorides: see note to p. 138 *Dioscorides*. At *De materia medica* 2. 118 he discusses the garden and wild varieties of mallow, but without discussing their medicinal virtues.

Nonius probably Nonmus (5th cent. AD) Greek poet of Panopolis (Egypt) who was the author of *Dionysiaca* a Bacchus epic poem.

Lentor: clamminess, viscidity.

Jos Scaliger and Casaubon: Isaac Casaubon (1559–1611), French humanist who was appointed a prebendary of Canterbury. See note to p. 141 *Younger Scaliger*.

153 *Tiberius*: Tiberius Caesar (42 BC–AD 37), Roman Emperor AD 14–37. See Pliny, *Natural History* 19. 64.

By the Orator call'd Terræ, by Porphyry Deorum filii: i.e. 'called sons of the earth by Cicero, sons of the gods by Porphyry'. Neither passage can be traced. Porphyry is the Greek name of Malchus of Tyre (AD *c*.233–*c*.305), scholar and philosopher.

154 Βρῶμα θεῶν: food of the gods; Nero's description of the mushroom for the reason stated (Cassius Dio, *Roman History* 60. 35. 4).

Emperor Claudius: Tiberius Claudius Nero Germanicus (10 BC–AD 54), Emperor of Rome AD 41–54.

Commander Annæus Serenus: (fl. 1st century AD), relative and intimate friend of the younger Seneca. He died of eating poisonous fungi (Pliny, *Natural History* 22. 97); for Seneca's grief see *Epistulae morales* 63. 14–15.

the Naturalist: see note to p. 135 *the Naturalist*.

Quæ voluptas tanta ancipitis cibi?: 'what is this great desire for dangerous food?' (Pliny, *Natural History* 22. 97).

Nil amplius edit: 'he [Claudius] ate nothing more' (Juvenal 5. 148).

Βάρη πνιγόεντα μυκήτων: Nicander, *Georgica*, fr. 78. 3, 'the choking weight of mushrooms'.

Athenæus: see note to p. 146 *Athenaeus*. The citation of Nicander comes from *Deipnosophists* 2. 60 F.

Euripides's: (480/5–407/6 BC), the youngest of the three great Athenian playwrights. Among his works are *Medea, Alcestis, The Trojan Women*, and *Electra*.

Nasute Swine: keen-scented pig (1653).

Lord Cotton's: Charles Cotton (1630–87), Master in Ancient and Modern Languages at Cambridge; a poet who was interested in horticulture and arboriculture. He had a notable garden at Beresford, Staffs., and was the author of a practical booklet on fruit trees entitled *Planter's Manual Being Instructions for the Raising Planting and Cultivation all sorts of Fruit Trees* (1675). A friend of Isaac Walton, he contributed to the *Compleat Angler*. John Evelyn was related by marriage to the family, his brother George being married to the widow of Sir John Cotton.

Voluptuaria Venena (cf. Seneca, *Epistulæ morales* 95. 25): 'delightful poisons'.

Dr. Lyster: Martin Lister (c.1638–1712), physician to Queen Anne, and zoologist. Friend of Revd John Ray. See also note to p. 168 *Learned Dr Lister*.

Pedicule: pedicel, a small stalk or stalk-like structure in a plant (1676).

Peiresky: Nicolas-Claude Fabri de Peiresc (1580–1637), French astronomer, antiquary, and savant.

mordicant: sharp, biting. See also note to p. 158, *mordicancy*.

Cephalick: relieving disorders of the head (1656).

Antiscorbutick: antiscorbutic, of use in preventing scurvy (1696).

Phlegmatick Humours: evolved from ancient physiology; regarded as one of the four bodily 'humours', Phlegmatic being described as cold & moist. The others are Choleric, Melancholic, and Sanguine. Diseases were ascribed to be of a hot or cold nature, and cures were made up from the plants thought to belong under various headings: fire (hot and dry), air (hot and moist), earth (cold and dry), or water (cold and moist). Nicholas Culpeper, the astrologer and physician, did much to elaborate the ideas in his *Complete Herbal* (1653). See also note to p. 158, *Pituit Humor*, and to p. 180, *Nicholas Culpeper*.

155 *Embamma*: ointment of aromatic oil.

156 *Edulcorated*: sweetened, freed from harsh and acrid properties (1641).

Hecamedes: a mistake for Hecamede, Nestor's serving-maid, who at *Iliad* 11. 630 serves onions to Nestor's guest Patroclus.

Patroclus: Greek companion to Achilles; in the Trojan war he was slain by Hector.

Homer. See note to p. 145 *Homer*.

Regalo: a gift, particularly of choice food or drink (1622).

Pituit Humor: derived from 'Pituita', the secretion of phlegm (1699). See also note to p. 155, *Phlegmatick Humours*.

157 ’Οξύβαφα: plural of ὀξύβαφον ('acid-bath').

succedaneum: a substitute (1643).

Cardialgium: cardialgy, heartburn (1655).

158 *Levain*: the French form of 'leaven', which is the naturally fermented grain used as a form of yeast.

Naples-Biscuit: Naples biscuits were twice cooked and in the shape of long thick fingers, they were very popular, particularly in the eighteenth and nineteenth centuries. Italy was renowned throughout Europe for the high standard of its confectionery.

Mordicancy: a biting irritation (1693). See note to p. 155 *mordicant*.

Edulcorated: see note to p. 156 *Edulcorated*.

Olitories: see *Kalendarium*, note to p. 9 *Olitory-Garden*.

L'Insalata non è buona, ne bella, Ove non è la Pimpinella: 'the salad is neither good nor fair, if the Pimpinella is not there.'

Dr. Muffet: see note to p. 142 *Dr Muffet*.

159 *Pliny*: see note to p. 135 *the Naturalist*.

Raphanus ex auro dicatus: 'a radish of gold, dedicated' (cf. Pliny, *Natural History* 19. 86).

Moschius: an error for Moschion, a Greek physician; see Pliny, *Natural History* 19. 87. Moschion prescribed radishes for women whose milk was too thick (Soranus, *Gynaecia* 2. 29. 1).

Hippocrates: (460–380/70 BC), Greek, born on the island of Cos; the most famous physician of the ancient world; founded a school of Medicine at the Temple of Asclepius, Cos.

Vitiosae, innatantes ac aegre concoctiles: 'corrupted, floating and scarcely digestible' (of the radish root) (Hippocrates, *De diaeta* 2. 54).

Cibus Illiberalis: 'ignoble food', as causing belches (Pliny, *Natural History* 19. 79).

Inimicous: hostile.

Dioscorides: at *Materia medica* 2. 112 radishes are commended both before and after the meal.

Galen: see note to p. 151 *Galen*. At *De alimentorum facultatibus* 2. 70 Galen disapproves of eating raw radishes after dinner.

160 *Summities*: heads, from 'summit'.

161 *Prætors Feasts*: mayoral or Judges' banquets.

162 *Omphacia*: 'omphacine', a dish made of unripe grapes or olives.

Galen: *On Simples* 8. 18. 33.

163 *edulcorated*: see note to p. 156 *Edulcorated*.

Cimata: from 'cyme', a head of unexpanded leaves, today it refers to a domed or flat flower-head where the growing point ends in a flower and there are further flowering side shoots.

Pliny: see note to p. 135, *the Naturalist*.

164 *Capreols*: tendrils; the capriole is also a variety of roebuck.

Hesiod: (fl. late 8th century BC), Greek poet whose works include

Theogony, which gives an account of the origins of the world. He wrote the earliest surviving didactic poem, *Erga kai Hemerai*, 'The Works and Days'.

Lobel: Mathias de l'Obel (1538–1616), French physician and plantsman, who settled in London and was acquainted with both John Parkinson and John Tradescant (sen.), and after whom the lobelia family is named.

165 *Galen*: De alimentorum facultatibus 2. 48.

Dodonæus: Rembert Dodoens (1517–85), Flemish physician and botanist. Author of *Cruydeboeck,* an influential herbal, translated into French as *Histoire des Plantes* by Carolus Clusius in 1557. The genus named in his honour, *Dodonaea*, is a member of the Sapindaceae family, and is a native of the Southern hemisphere, particularly Australia and South Africa.

Simples: see *Directions*, note to p. 76 *Rarer Simples and Exotics*.

Macaroons: macaroon biscuits seem to have been made first by the Greeks; the word itself equates to the Greek word for 'happy', and the ingredients, almonds and pine kernels, would have been familiar crops. There is also evidence that during the tenth century Greek traders introduced the biscuits to Naples, whence they slowly spread throughout Europe, arriving in Britain probably during the late sixteenth century. Evelyn is quite right in saying that pine nuts can be used as an ingredient in the making of macaroons. Pine nuts (usually the seed from Mediterranean native Umbrella pine, *Pinus pinea*) as an ingredient in savoury and sweet cooking are widely used around the Mediterranean, from the French *omelette landaise* to Turkish sweetmeats. Perhaps most sophisticated of all is the Genoese *pesto*, in which pounded pine nuts, garlic, cheese, and basil are made into the delicious summer pasta sauce.

Pliny: see note to p. 135, *the Naturalist*.

166 *Poiverade*: pepper sauce, 1699.

Silphium: see note below, *Cyrenaic Africa*; see also Glossary of Plants: Silphium.

Emperor Nero: Nero Claudius Cæsar (AD 37–68), Roman emperor AD 54–68. Totally committed to the arts, although he was both unstable and homicidal.

Julius Cæsar: Julius Caesar (100–44 BC) Roman general, invaded Britain in 55 BC and conquered Gaul.

Cyrenaic Africa: the coast of North Africa centred on the ancient Greek city of Cyrene. Famed for the production of *Silphium,* now extinct; this giant fennel was so critical to the economy of ancient Cyrene that its image appeared on its coins. The plant was the source of an aromatic gum used both medically and as flavouring. See also Glossary of Plants: Silphium.

Βάττου σίλφιον: 'Battus' silphium', proverbial for a precious commodity.

Battus: founder of the city of Cyrene in *c*.630 BC.

Botanosophists: a combination of two comparatively new words in the seventeenth century: 'botanist', 1682, combined with 'sophist'—meaning 'a learned man' (1614).

Laserpitium: Umbelliferae, see above, *Cyrenaic Africa.* See also Glossary of Plants: **Silphium**.

Benzoin: a resinous substance extracted from the tree *Styrax benzoin* of Sumatra, and used as one of the main ingredients in 'Friars Balsam'. 'Benzoin' is an Arabic word and has been used in English since 1558.

167 *Aristophanes:* (*c*.450–*c*.385 BC), Greek Athenian playwright. Works include *The Wasps, Lysistrata, The Frogs.*

Scholiast: one who writes explanatory notes upon a text, particularly an ancient or Byzantine commentary upon a classical writer.

Hautgouts: haut-goût, a strong relish or piquant flavour (1645). See p. 183 *Lectures of Hautgouts.*

Garcius: Garcia (Abraham) da Orta (*c*.1499–1568), Portuguese physician and naturalist who settled in Goa in 1534. His most famous work is *Colloquies on the Simples and Drugs of India.*

Bontius: Jacobus Bontius (1592–1631), native of the Low Countries. As physician to the Dutch East India Company he made an official tour of the Moluccas and Timor. In Java he was the first European to investigate the natural history of the area. His four books on the subject were all published following his death. Linnaeus commemorated his work in the genus *Bontia.*

Bramins: Brahmins, the priestly caste of Hindu religion.

168 *Mr. Ray:* (Revd) John Ray (1627–1705), a Dissenter who was deprived of his living in 1662. He pursued his interest in botany and in 1670 published a study of British flora entitled *Synopsis Methodica Stirpium Britannicarum,* which remained an authoritative account for over a century. Sixteen years later he began publishing his major work on botany, *Historia Plantarum Generalis.* He is often referred to as the 'Father of English natural history'. See p. 199 *Mr Ray.*

excellent Poet: Abraham Cowley (1618–67), a metaphysical poet and great friend of Evelyn. Cowley lived at Barn Elms, SW London, and during the Civil War served as secretary to Queen Henrietta Maria. The second edition of *Kalendarium Hortense* is dedicated to him, and Evelyn makes many Diary references to him. See note to p. 170 *Sweet Cowley* and p. 206 *Happy the Man*.

Columna: the Neapolitan naturalist Fabio Colonna (1567–1650).

Cimex: bed-bug.

Learned Dr. Lyster: See note to p. 154.

Grillus: one of Circe's enchanted pigs who features in a treatise in Plutarch's *Moralia* where a humorous dialogue takes place between the hero Odysseus and Gryllus the pig.

169 *Plutarch*: Lucius Mestrius Plutarchus (*c.* AD 46–120) Greek historian, biographer, essayist, and Middle Platonist. His principal works include *The Parallel Lives* and the *Moralia*. See above, *Grillus*.

Sarcophagists: flesh-eating animals or persons (1617).

πάνφαγα: 'omnivorous'.

Basilisk: the fabulous reptile whose very breath or look was believed could kill.

Analogically: by means of a proportion or part of something.

Pectorals: medicines, either food or drink, that cured the afflictions of the chest or lungs (1601). *Contra* Evelyn, they were not effective for the bowels.

170 *Endemial…Epidemical*: Evelyn is explaining that native salad plants and herbs are good for confounding '*scorbute*' (scurvy), or rotting gums.

sweet Cowley: author of the following extract from 'The Garden'. See note to p. 168, *excellent Poet*.

Sapor: taste, flavour.

Damoxenus: Greek comic poet of the 3rd century BC, cited by Athenaeus, *Deipnosophists* 3. 102A–103B.

πῶς ἐστιν αὐτοῖς συμφωνία: 'how can they have consonance?'

Diatessaron: the musical interval of the perfect fourth.

Diapente: in musical terms, the consonance of a perfect fifth.

Diapason: the consonance interval of an octave.

171 *Sapores minime consentientes*: 'tastes or odours that do not agree'. Latin translation from Damoxenus cited at Athenaeus, *Deipnosophistae* 3. 102E.

Democritus: (*c.*460–364 BC), from the Thracian city of Abdera, a philosopher and the author of several works on botany, medicine, and geography.

Macrobius: Macrobius Ambrosius Theodosius (early 5th century AD), possibly from Africa, a pagan writer, the author of *Commentarii in Somnium Scipionis* and *Saturnalia*.

Paradisian Bard: John Milton (1608–74) had composed *Paradise Lost* (1667) and *Paradise Regained* (1671).

Dr. Grew: Dr Nehemiah Grew (1641–1712) was named the '*Learned Doctor*' by Evelyn. Grew called himself a 'Plant anatomist', and studied first at Cambridge and later at Leiden University. He practised as a doctor, but in his twenties began the research into the structure of plants, roots, and seeds that culminated in the publication of *The Anatomy of Plants* (1682), where he accurately described for the first time the sexual relationship of plants.

σκευασία: 'preparation'.

172 *ex foliis pubescentibus*: 'out of ripening leaves' (Bacon, *Historia vitae et mortis* 5. 25).

Martial: Marcus Valerius Martial (*c.* AD 40) Latin poet, a native of Bilbilis, Spain, famous for composing epigrams.

Prototomi rudes: 'young vegetables cut early' (Martial 10. 48. 16).

Wood-Culver, *Stock-Dove*: a wood-culver is a wood pigeon; both species belong to the *Columbidae* family.

Intinctus: intinction, a dipping in, or an infusion.

Cibarium: literally 'relating to food', but often used of food fit only for slaves, as in the passage cited here, Columella 12. 52. 18.

Omphacine: oily liquid expressed from unripe olives.

Luca Olives: Lucca was a city state in Italy, which Evelyn visited on 22 May 1645. He records it being 'small but pretty…with noble and pleasant walkes of trees'.

humectate: moisten, wet (1659).

173 *aliorum Condimentorum Condimentum*: 'relish of other relishes', translated from Plutarch, *Quaestiones convivales* 4. 4. 3, 668 F.

detersive: cleansing.

Bay grey-Salt: imported from the Bay of Bourgneuf (south of Saint-Nazaire and the entrance to the River Loire) from the thirteenth century, the name later came to include sea salt from Spain and Portugal. From Neolithic times sea salt has been evaporated naturally in bays or enclosures; it was also known as *gros sel*.

utmost poinant and Relevèe: greatest sharpness.

Alcalizate: alkalizate, alkaline (1622).

Calcination of Baulm: the burning to ashes (1641) of balm, *Melissa officinalis*, a native perennial herb. See also Glossary of Plants: **Balme**.

Franciscus Redi: Francesco Redi (1626–97), b. Arezzo, Italy, physician to the Dukes of Tuscany and a poet.

Learned Doctor: see note to p. 171, *Dr Grew*.

Lixivial: lixivium is water impregnated with alkaline salts extracted from wood ash (1612).

Of Sugar (by some call'd Indian–Salt): Evelyn is commenting on the product of sugar cane *Saccharum officinarum*, the tall cane-stemmed grass, native of tropical and sub-tropical Asia. Known in India from a very early date, the word is derived from Sanskrit. In 510 BC the Persians had noted sugar in cultivation in the Indus valley, and the Greeks had also learned of its use during Alexander's great Asian invasion. By the sixteenth century sugar cane had been introduced throughout the Mediterranean to Spain and Portugal, and had become firmly established on the continent of America. European trade was centred on Venice, and it was during the sixteenth century that sugar began to be imported into England. See also *Kalendarium*, note to p. 10, *Bees*.

174 *the best Tewksberry…and weightiest Yorkshire Seed*: there are three species of mustard plant: all are crucifers related to the cabbage and indigenous to Europe. Black mustard, *Brassica nigra*, was traditionally grown to make the condiment, as it produced the best seed. It has an exceedingly pungent flavour. However, because of its height—anything up to 2 m (6 ft)—and its readiness to shed seeds in advance of harvesting, the plant has proved to be unsuitable for modern mechanical farming. The Yorkshire seed Evelyn refers to was probably from the large black mustard plant, as was the seed taken to America, probably during the late seventeenth century, where it now grows wild. The species now used is the brown or Indian mustard, *Brassica juncea*, and although this produces a milder flavour it is a stockier plant and is better suited to commercial use. Mustard was probably introduced into Britain by the Romans; later the seed was ground by millers and sold as dry powder or made into a paste and sold in parchment-covered earthenware pots. Tewkesbury was a well-known centre for mustard manufacture from Shakespeare's time. See also p. 184 and note *Half Crown*.

Gally-Pot: gallipot, a small glazed earthenware pot usually used by apothecaries.

Jamaica-Pepper: ground-up allspice berries from the tree *Pimenta dioica*, known also as myrtle pepper. The tree is a native of tropical America and the bulk of the berries used in England came from Jamaica. The tree is in the Myrtaceae family, hence its other name of myrtle pepper.

175 *Mr Boyle*: Hon. Robert Boyle (1627–91), natural philosopher, physicist, and chemist, known as the 'father of modern chemistry'. Evelyn greatly admired Boyle and there are many references to him in the *Diary*. They were both founder members of The Royal Society, with Boyle later becoming its President.

Mr. London: George London (d. 1714) English garden designer, connected with the development of many great gardens including Castle Howard, Longleat House, Chatsworth, Melbourne Hall, and Canons. John Evelyn was a great admirer of his work, as was Stephen Switzer (1682–1745). In 1681 George London with three others founded a nursery at Brompton Park on the site of what is now the South Kensington Museums. See also *Directions*, note to p. 101, *M. de la Quintine*.

176 *Pugil*: see *Directions*, note to p. 126 *Weights and their Notes*.

Fascicule: a handful (1609).

180 *Culpeper*: Nicholas Culpeper (1616–54), physician, herbalist, astrologer, and author of *The English Physician Enlarged, or the Herbal*, which first appeared in 1653 and has been in print ever since. See also note to p. 155, *Phlegmatick Humours*.

Figure-flingers: astrologers.

181 *Muriated*: pickled in brine.

Tansie: tansy, a pudding or omelette flavoured with the juice of tansy (*Tanacetum vulgare*). See also Glossary of Plants: Costmary. See also p. 217 *Tansie*.

Condites: pickles or preserves.

Horarii: lasting an hour.

Fugaces Fructus: fleeting, short-lived fruit.

Celsus: see *De medicina* 1. 2. 9. See note to p. 145 *C. Celus*.

Prima... & Porris fila refecta suis: 'First, lettuce will be served you, beneficial for moving the bowels, and green tops cut from the leeks to which they belonged' (Martial 11. 52. 5–6).

Domitian's: Titus Flavius Domitianus (AD 51–96), Roman emperor for fifteen years (81–96). His government became increasingly absolute and created a reign of terror, which precipitated his murder. Evelyn has inferred the date of the change from Martial 13. 14.

οἱ μέντοι ἀρχαῖοι (Athenaeus, *Deipnosophists* 3, 101 B): 'the ancients, however'.

Gratáque nobilium [*requies*] *Lactuca ciborum*: 'And the Lettuce, a welcome respite from noble foods', from the *Moretum* falsely ascribed to Virgil, line 74. The word *requies* has been accidentally omitted.

182   *Ante-cœnia*: hors-d'œuvres.

     Olio: hotch-potch of various meats, either stewed or boiled (1648).

183   *Mithacus*: Mithaecus of Syracuse (5th century BC). Author of works on food.

     Eruditæ Gulæ: erudite gluttons [lit. 'throats'].

     Hautgouts: see note to p. 167.

     Archestratus: Archestratus (*fl.* 330 BC), Greek poet, from Sicily, best known as the author of *The Life of Luxury*, a book on Mediterranean food which Athenæus praised it in his own book *The Banquet of the Learned*. See note to p. 146 *Athenaeus*.

     Shambles: a slaughter-house, a meat-market, or butcher's shop.

     Nidor: the strong smell or odour of cooking meat (1619).

     Guinny-pepper: Guinea pepper or Cayenne pepper, the seeds of two species of *Anomum* found on the west coast of Africa.

184   *Half-Crown Piece*: the first half-crowns, in silver, were minted in 1603 and 1604, during the first years of the reign of James I. See note to p. 174 *the best Tewksberry*.

     Οὐπαντὸς ἀνδρῴ ἐστιν ἀρτῦσαι καλῶς : 'It is not everyone who can season properly': Cratinus, Athenian comic poet of the fifth century BC, cited at Athenaeus, *Deipnosophists* 2, 68 A.

     Non est cujusvis rectè condire: Latin translation of the above.

     Flesh-Shambles: a butcher's shop. See note to p.183 *Shambles*.

     Antediluvians mention'd Gen. 1.29: 'Here are all the herbs, God told them, that seed on earth, and all the trees, that carry in them the seeds of their own life, to be your food.' Chapters 5 and 9 detail the great ages of Adam's progeny and descendants and 9: 3–4 give further details of the food they may or may not eat (Knox trans. of the Old Testament, 1949).

185   *Hundreds of Essex*: in England, a hundred was an Anglo-Saxon sub-division of a county or shire, having its own court. There were twenty hundreds in Essex.

     Pabulum: any nutrient taken in by animal or plant (1678).

Junior Gordian: Gordian II, son of Gordian I, emperor for a few days in January 238. See *Historia Augusta* 20. 21. 1–2.

Lord Bacon: see *Kalendarium*, note to p. 52 *Lord Verularn's design*.

186 *Cardan*: Geronimo Cardano, later Hieronymus Cardanus (1501–76), Italian mathematician, naturalist, physician, and philosopher. Author of over a hundred treatises on physics, ethics, and music. see p. 189 *Cardan*.

Pituit: see notes to pp. 156, *Pituit Humour*, and 155, *Phlegmatick Humours*.

187 *Learned Person*: Sir Thomas Browne (1605–82), English author and doctor, who studied medicine in Padua and at Leiden University. An erudite and thoughtful writer, he corresponded with Evelyn. They met in 1671, when Evelyn visited him at his home in Norwich, where he spoke of 'His whole house and garden being a paradise'; later Sir Thomas took him on a tour of Norwich to explore 'all the remarkable places of this ancient Citty' (*Diary*, 1671).

Præcoces: very early.

Roger Bacon's: Bacon (*c*.1214–92), was a Franciscan philosopher and polymath whose research took him into medicine and astronomy.

Perflatile: exposed to the wind, airy.

Marle, Chalk, Lime: marl (soil composed mainly of clay) mixed with carbonate of lime. Used as a fertilizer during the sixteenth century.

188 *super-seminating*: sowing seeds thickly.

Adepti: adepts, those skilled in all secrets (1685).

Honoratus Faber: seventeenth-century philosopher, author of *Dialogue de Lumine*.

189 *John Beverovicius…Peter Moxa*: both are pseudonyms of Johan van Beverwijcks (1594–1647), Dutch physician.

Diphilus: see note to p. 144 *Diphilus*.

Athenæus: see *Deipnosophists* 2. 70 A.

Cardan: see note to p. 186.

Learned Antagonist: Joseph Scaliger. See note to p. 141 *Younger Scaliger*.

Celsus: see note to p. 145 *C. Celsus*.

Eduntur facilius…pertinent: 'They are consumed more easily; but the kind of substance and the quantity have their effect on digestion' (Celsus 3. 5. 12).

Hominis cibus utilissimus simplex: 'Man's most beneficial food [is] plain.'

A better reading is *Homini*, 'Plain food is the most useful to man.' (Pliny, *Natural History* II. 282.)

190   *Grand Seignior*: the Sultan, the Grand Turk.

     his Meccha-Camel: the camel on which he makes his pilgrimage to Mecca.

     says Aristotle: the statement has not been traced.

     Old Parr: Thomas Parr (?1483–1635), a farm servant who eventually became a celebrity on account of his supposed great age. In his eighties he is thought to have married and sired two children, later, aged 100, he was believed to have had an affair, with a child born out of wedlock. He became a widower, but remarried in 1603 at the unbelievable age of 122. As news of 'Old Parr' spread he was made a spectacle, painted both by Reuben's and Van Dyke, and brought to London by a friend of Evelyn's Thomas Howard 2nd Earl of Arundel to be presented to the King. The excitement, and the rich diet, proved too much for the old man and he died in London. His celebrity continued after his demise when at the explicit instructions of Charles I he was buried in Westminster Abbey on 15 November 1635.

     Ofellus's: Ofellus is a speaker in Horace, *Sermones* 2. 2, from which Evelyn has just quoted lines 71–3.

191   *Post-Diluvians*: people who lived following Noah's Flood.

     Johannes de Temporibus: 'John of the Times', said to have been one of Charlemagne's warriors who lived to the age of 361 and died in the twelfth century.

     Mosaic Constitution: relating to Moses the Lawgiver (1662).

192   *Holocaust for Expiation*: a complete sacrifice or offering.

193   μακροβιότητα: longevity; it is not clear why Evelyn has used the accusative case.

     ancient Gymnosophists: a sect of ancient Hindu philosophers of ascetic habits, who wore little or no clothing, denied themselves meat, and gave themselves up to mystical contemplation. They were known to the Greeks through Alexandrian reports.

     the Platonic Tables: in the seventeenth century the philosophy of Plato received attention from a group of theologians and philosophers under the leadership of Benjamin Whichcote (1609–83). They became known as the 'Cambridge Platonists', and believed that religion and reason were in harmony. See also note to p. 152 *Plato*.

     Porphyry: he wrote *On Abstinence*, in four books. See note to p. 145 *Pythagoras* and p. 152 *Pythagorus*.

Xenocrates, Polemon: Xenocrates of Chalcedon (4th century BC). Pupil of Plato, and the third head of his Academy (339–314 BC). His works concerned practical, ethical, and theological questions. *Polemon*: Polemon, 1st King of Pontus (d. 8 BC). As a reward for military services to the Roman empire in 37 BC he was given the kingdom of Pontus, which bordered the Black Sea and Armenia, now part of NE Turkey.

Clement Alexand: Clement of Alexandria (Clemens Alexandrinus) (*c.*150–*c.*215), Church father and philosopher, head of the Catechetical School in Alexandria.

Eusebius: Eusebius of Caeserea (*c.*264–340), b. Palestine, known as the 'father of Church history', became Bishop of Caeserea in 313. His published works include *Chronicon*, *A History of the World*, and *Ecclesiastical History*. He was the author of the contemporary account of the life and work of the Emperor Constantine.

Zeno ...Lærtius: probably Zeno (335–263 BC) b. Citium in Cyprus, Greek philosopher, founder of the movement of Stoicism, and author of *Politics*. *Archinomus*: (6th–5th century BC), possibly the father of the Greek philosopher Empedocles who founded the doctrine that the world is made up of earth, air, fire, and water. *Phraartes*: Phraates IV, King of Persia (*c.*38 BC–2 BC), murdered his father and was later himself murdered. *Chiron*: in Greek mythology, king of the Centaurs. *Lærtius*: Diogenes Laërtius (fl. first half of 3rd century AD), Greek epicurian; a phrase attributed to him is often quoted: 'The foundation of every state is the education of its youth' he was the author of *Lives and Opinions of Eminent Philosophers*.

Seneca, Sextius, Socion's: the reference is to *Epistulae morales* 108. 17. *Sextius*: Quintus Sextius the Elder (*c.*50 BC) Roman philosopher and praised by Seneca. Sextius believed that man could find sufficient nourishment to sustain life without resorting to any form of meat and blood, and that a habit of cruelty is formed whenever butchery is practised for pleasure. *Socion's*: properly Sotion, a Peripatetic philosopher.

194 *rationi magis congrua*: 'more in accordance with reason'.

Doctrine of Devils: Evelyn quotes three instances from the Bible: 1 Cor. 8: 8; 1 Timothy 4: 1, 3, 4; Romans 14: 3.

αἱματοφάγοι *and Occidental Blood-Eaters*: blood-eaters and Western meat-eaters.

195 *Goths, Vandals...Pagan Scythians*: the Goths and Vandals were the Germanic tribes who invaded Western Europe in the fourth and fifth centuries. By 1663 the word 'vandal' had come to mean a wilful or ignorant destroyer of anything beautiful. The Scythians were a nomadic race originally from

Scythia, an ancient region extending over a large part of European and Asian Russia.

Justin Martyr: Justin the Martyr (*c.* AD 100–65), a Greek born in Nablus (anciently known as Shechem) in Palestine. He became a Christian in *c.*130 and is regarded as the first Christian philosopher. Justin was martyred in 165; the records of his trial survive in Rome.

Apostolical Synod: the meeting in Jerusalem described in Acts 15; see v. 29.

196 ἀκρίβεια: '(pedantic) exactness'.

Extravasated Blood: blood that has flowed or been ejected from a blood vessel (1669).

Apician Tables: See notes to p. 136, *Apician Arts*, and 202, *Apicius*.

Oleribus verba facere: 'to speak to vegetables', perhaps a garbling of the Greek proverb 'additions of vegetables' for useless activities.

Hogs-Puddings: entrails of a pig variously stuffed with oatmeal, suet, and tripe or flour, currants, and spices; the sausage-like mixture is available today, and can be cooked and eaten sliced either hot or cold (1614).

Chair of Rabby-Busy: Rabbi Busy is a character referred to in the comedy '*Bartholomew Fair*' of 1614 by Ben Johnson. 'Rabbi Busy, Sir, he is more than an Elder, he is a Prophet, sir.' Response 'O, I know him! A Baker, is he not?'

Curcellæus: Étienne de Courcelle (1586–1659), b. Geneva, a Protestant theologian who became Professor of Theology in Amsterdam.

Tertullian, Hierom, S. Chrysotom: Quintus Septimus Florens Tertullianus (*c.*160–235), an early Church leader and apologist, known as the 'Father of the Latin Church'; a prolific writer and author of *Apologeticus*. *Hierom*: St Jerome Eusebius Sophronius Hieronymus (*c.*342–420), aesthete, scholar, and monk who produced the Vulgate, the standard Latin text of the Bible. *S. Chrysostom*: St John Chrysostom (*c.*317–407) became Archbishop of Constantinople in 398.

Lyra…Pererius: Nicholas of Lyra (*c.*1270–1349: biblical commentator who concentrated on the literal sense of the text and made large use of Jewish scholarship. *Tostatus*: Alonso Tostado, known as Tostatus Abulensis (from Ávila) (*c.*1400–55), was the Spanish Bishop of Ávila and Grand Chancellor of Castile. *Dionysius Carthusianus*: Dionysius van Leeuwen (1402/3–71), from Limbourg Province (part of modern Belgium), Carthusian monk and Thomist philosopher. *Pererius*: Benedictus Pererius (1535–1610), Jesuit priest who taught philosophy in Rome. Author of *De principis*.

Peter Martyr…Bochartus: Peter of Verona (1205–52), a Dominican friar and

196   priest famous for his preaching, murdered in 1252. *Zanchy*: Hieronymus
Zanchy, early seventeenth-century theologian and author. *Aretius*:
Aretaeus (fl. AD 100), Greek physician. *Jac. Capellus*: Claude Capellus,
Professor of Hebrew at Samur, France. *Hiddiger*: Johann Heinrich Hei-
degger (1633–98), a Swiss theologian, first Professor of Moral Philosophy
and later of Theology at Zurich. *Cocceius*: Johannes Koch (1603–69), theologian; in 1650 he became Professor of Hebrew at Leiden University.
Bochartus: Samuel Bochart (1599–1667), French Protestant biblical scholar
and antiquarian.

instar omnium: 'the pattern for all'.

Grotius, Vossius, Blundel: Huig van Groot (Hugo Grotius) (1583–1645),
Dutch jurist and theologian. In 1625 he published his great work on In-
ternational Law, *De Jura Belli et Pacis*. From 1635 he was the Swedish Ambassador at the French court. While Evelyn was travelling in Italy during
1646, he was introduced to the son of Grotius in Venice. *Vossius*: Gerhard
Johann Eanie Vossius (Vos) (1577–1649), Dutch classical scholar and
Protestant theologian, appointed as Professor of Rhetoric to Leiden University, and a Prebend of Canterbury Cathedral. He later became Professor of History at the Athenaeum Illustre in Amsterdam. *Blundel*: David
Blondel (1591–1655), French Protestant historian and classical scholar; became Professor of History at Amsterdam.

Cajetan: Thomas de Vio (Cardinal Gaetano) (1469–1534), the General of
the Dominican Order; in 1520 at Augsburg, when Luther burnt the Bull
of Excommunication that had been drawn up against him, Cajetan
pleaded with him to recant.

Calvin: John Calvin (1509–64), French Protestant reformer.

θεραπευταί: literally 'carers'. The Therapeutai were a Jewish ascetic sect
described at length in Philo, *De vita contemplativa*.

Philo: Philo of Alexandria (20 BC–AD 50), also known as Philip Judaeus,
Yedidia, or Philo the Jew. He was a Hellenistic Jewish philosopher who
harmonized Greek philosophy with Judaism.

Diaconesse: deaconess. *Olympias*: holy woman whose life is recounted by
Palladius, *Historia Lausiaca* 56.

Palladius: See *Kalendarium* note to p. 6 *Palladius*.

197   *ne nimium extra oleas*: 'not to go too far outside the olive trees'.

Feuillantines: Cistercian nuns; the Order was founded in 1587, and their
Rule was simple and strict: their lives were spent in silence, with prayer
and manual labour; the nuns subsisted on a plain diet of bread, water, and

vegetables, seasoned only with salt. The Order ceased to exist at the time of the French Revolution.

ab'initio etiam hominum...tali victu usum esse: 'that from the beginning of the human race he ate such food'.

Lotophagi: lotus-eaters, a people in Greek legend who lived on the fruit of the lotus, which caused a dreamy forgetfulness, 1601.

198 ἐθελοπερισσοθρησκεία: 'deliberately over-precise worship'.

Eremites: recluses or anchorites.

Valentinian: there were three Roman emperors of this name; this is probably Valentinian Ist (d. AD 374), who fought many campaigns in the north of the Empire and restored its northernmost frontier, Hadrian's Wall.

Constantine Copronymus: Emperor Constantine V (718–75) of Byzantium, who was a successful general, a harpist, bisexual, and an iconoclast. His nickname 'Copronymus', (Dungname), refers to his disgracing himself in the baptismal font.

199 *Learned Person*: see note to p. 154, *Dr. Lyster*.

Thebaid: the Egyptian desert around Thebes.

Rapin: rapine, robbery, pillage, plunder.

Mr. Ray: See note to p. 18, *Mr. Ray*.

200 *Nicander*: (3rd–2nd century BC), Greek poet and native of Colophon City in Ionia. He was the author of *Georgica*, 'On Farming', and a book on poisonous reptiles entitled *Theriaca*.

Parat Convivium: 'prepares the banquet'.

In quibus est Luctuca sedens ...nec herba salax, &c.: 'In which is a Lettuce sitting, and a clipped leek, and Mint which produces belching, and herbs provoking lust are not missing.'

201 *Hotch-Pot*: hodge-podge, a simple mixture of ingredients, usually leftover meats mixed with gravy (1622).

Plautus: (d. 184 BC), Roman comic poet.

Jacobus Catsius (describ'd by the Poet Barlæus): Jacob Cats (1577–1660), a Dutch jurist, statesman, poet, and humorist, was knighted by Charles I and became a Grand Pensionary of Holland. Known in Holland as Father Cats. Caspar Barlaeus or Kaspar van Baarle (1584–1648), Dutch polymath, humanist theologian, poet, and historian, became Professor of Logic at the University of Leiden.

Nicomedes: the name of four kings of Bithynia from the third to the first centuries BC. Bithynia was an ancient region of Asia Minor, south of the Black Sea.

Vitellius: Aulus Vitellius (15–69), Roman emperor, was a favourite of Tiberius, Caligula, Claudius, and Nero. During his brief reign of less than a year, he gave himself up to debauchery and feasting. The extract is taken from 'The Garden', stanza 6, written by Abraham Cowley. See note to p. 168, *excellent Poet*.

Sweet Poet: See note to p. 168, *excellent Poet*.

202 *Apicius*: M. Gavius Apicius (*c*.40 BC–*c*. AD 40), Roman gourmet of the Augustan era and author of several culinary treatises. See also note to p. 136, *Apician Arts*.

latet anguis in herba: 'a snake is hidden in the grass' (Virgil, *Buscolics*).

inemptas Dapes: 'unpurchased Stately feasts', the quotation is from Virgil, *Georgics* 4. 133.

Edicts and Sumptuary Laws: from L. *sumptuarius* (expenditure); those laws that attempted to regulate habits of consumption, in particular to restrain luxury or extravagance in the matter of clothes or food, have always proved notoriously ineffectual. The earliest recorded sumptuary law comes from the West Locrian code of the seventh century BC, which stipulated that 'No free woman should be allowed any more than one maid to follow her, unless she was drunk' (Diodorus Siculus 12. 21. 1).

Vomere laureato, & triumphali aratore: 'by the laurelled ploughshare, and a ploughman who had celebrated a triumph' (Pliny, *Naturalis Historia* 18. 19). Cf. note to p. 137, *Laureato Vomere*.

203 *Pliny*: see note to p. 135, *the Naturalist*.

Gratius the Faliscian: Grattius, reportedly from Falerii (hence called *Faliscus*), who wrote a poem on hunting (*Cynegetica*) in the late first century BC or the earliest years AD. The quotation is from lines 320–4.

the Naturalist: see note to p. 135 THE *Naturlist*.

Res expedita & parata semper (cf. Pliny, *Naturalis Historia* 19. 58): 'a thing uncomplicated and always ready'.

Panis ematur…natura negatis: from Horace, *Sermones* 1. 1. 74–5.

204 *Si vespertinus subitò te oppresserit hospes*: 'if a guest should suddenly come upon you in the evening' (Horace, *Sermones* 2. 4. 17).

Convictus facilis sine arte mensa: 'easy fellowship, a simple meal'; among the things that make life happier (Martial 10. 47. 8).

Vides ut pallidus…particulam auræ: Horace, *Sermones* 2. 2. 76–9.

Ubi dicto citius...ad munera surgit: ibid. 80–1.

molli sub arbore: under a gentle tree. A garbled reminiscence of Virgil, *Georgics* 2. 470, 'mollesque sub arbore somni' (and gentle sleep beneath a tree) see note to p. 204 *somnum se mercari*.

205   *somnum se mercari*: 'that he purchased sleep'. See note to p. 204 *molli sub arbore*.

Maximinus: Maximinus Thrax, Roman emperor AD 235–8; see *Historia Augusta* 19. 4. 1–2.

With sav'ry Fruit...Deserving Paradise: Milton, *Paradise Lost*, Book V (1667).

206   *Hoc erat in votis, modus agri non ita magnus, &c.*: (Horace, *Sermones* 2. 6. 1): 'This was something I had wished for, a farm not too great in extent.'

Hæredium: from *heres* 'heir', meaning any type of property that may be inherited.

Happy the Man...their endless Strife: extract from verse by Abraham Cowley. See also note to *excellent Poet* and note to p. 170 *Sweet Cowley*.

O Fortunatos nimium bona si sua norint Horticulos!: 'O gardeners too happy, if only they knew their blessings!' Adapted from Virgil, *Georgics* 2. 458–9, where the final word is *agricolas*, 'farmers'.

207   *de Re Cibaria*: ('On Food', or 'On Diet'), the title of several Renaissance medical treatises, in particular twenty-two books by Jean-Baptiste Bruyerin or Joannes Baptista Bruyerinus Campegius) (Lyon, 1560), and four by Luis Núñez or Ludovicus Nonnius (Antwerp, 1627).

208   *Fountain-Water*: spring-water.

Pipkin: small earthenware pot used mainly in cooking.

209   *Tiffany Sieve*: tiffany was a thin transparent muslin or silk, and could be used to decorate dresses, or in this case used for sieving or straining (1606).

Sarse: possibly from sarsenet, a very soft, fine cloth.

210   *sweet Butter*: unsalted butter.

Sippets: small pieces of toast or fried bread, served in broth or with meat.

221   *Skillet*: cooking utensil made of brass or copper, used for boiling and stewing meat.

Gross Pepper: whole peppercorns.

Rape-Vinegar: rape (*Brassica napus*) was recommended for cultivation as a green manure in 1577 by Barnaby Googe in *The Four Bookes of Husbandry*.

212   *Roch-Allom*: rock alum, a mineral salt.

Mango of Cucumber: Evelyn was using the word 'Mango' as a 'pickle', made of cucumbers and/or melons, which resembled that made from green mangoes (1699). The fruit of *Mangifera indica* was known in England by 1582.

214 *Potato*: it is not clear whether Evelyn is describing the Sweet potato (*Ipomoea batatas*, or the potato (*Solanum tuberosum*), or has muddled them both up. Earlier references were confused too, as tubers brought back to Spain in 1553, and by Sir John Hawkins in 1573 probably refer to the Sweet potato, he called the tuber 'the most delicate root that may be eaten', while it was thirty-three years later that possibly Thomas Heriot, a botanist with Sir Francis Drake, returned to England with the potato. The confusion between them arises from the similarity of the names, the Sweet potato being known by the Andean Indians as 'batata', which the Spanish turned into 'batatas' and the potato was (and is) called the 'patatas'. Evelyn's recommendation to pickle 'small green fruit...an agreeable Sallet' cannot refer to the *Solanum* species, which belong to the Nightshade family and all green parts are poisonous.

Crimpness: friability, brittleness, or crispness.

215 *Potage Maigre*: a vegetarian soup made particularly for days during the Church calendar when meat was not to be eaten.

Raze or two of Ginger: small quantity, a scraping, as a graze.

216 *molli sub arbore*. *French Roll*: small loaf, usually one that has been rolled over or doubled over before baking.

Manchet-Bread: finest kind of wheaten bread; the flour was sieved several times, and the loaf weighed not more than 175 g (6 oz).

217 *Puff-Paste*: most of the countries bordering the Mediterranean seem to have had an early tradition of pastrymaking going back to the Ancient Egyptians. Different recipes and styles slowly developed, first in southern Europe and Asia Minor, only gradually spreading towards northern Europe (1611).

218 *Pennash of Sellery*: from pennaceous, 'feathery'. See *Kalendarium* note to p. 22 *Pennach'd*.

219 *Pottle*: a pot or vessel measuring half a gallon.

Malaga-Raisins: traditionally raisins were dried muscatel grapes from Málaga, dried first while still on the vine and then laid on mats in the sun.

220 *Teas*: The word 'tea' usually refers to a beverage made from the leaves of *Camellia sinensis* (1655). However, within ten years (1665) 'tea' became the word for infusions using any leaves or flowers, drunk mainly for medicinal purposes.

GLOSSARY OF PLANT NAMES

The Glossary lists every plant (over 800) named by Evelyn in the three manuscripts in this volume. Evelyn's name for the plant is followed by the modern common name(s), if any, and the botanical Latin name; the plant's origins, native or otherwise; and the date of introduction into Britain (unless of native origin). Where identification has not been possible, Evelyn's name only is listed.

A number of contemporary and modern sources have been consulted, listed below. Where BOBART, BERNWODE, GURLE, HANMER, LUCAS, PARKINSON, or TRADESCANT are cited in the Glossary, the plant is listed in these sources with the same spelling; where the name or spelling differs, this is noted.

ABBREVIATIONS

BERNWODE	Modern specialist fruit nursery, with an interest in conserving old varieties
BOBART	Jacob Bobart (1599–1680), head gardener of Oxford Botanic Garden. *Catalogus plantarum Horti Medici Oxoniensis*, 1648
GURLE	Leonard Gurle (*c.*1621–85), nurseryman of Whitchapel. Catalogue 1674
HANMER	Sir Thomas Hanmer (1612–78), *The Garden Book of Sir Thomas Hanmer*, 1659
LUCAS	William Lucas (d. 1679), seedsman of The Naked Boy, Strand, London. *A Catalogue of Seeds, Plants &c, c.*1677
PARKINSON	John Parkinson (1567–1650), *Paradisi in Sole, Paradisus Terrestris*, 1629
TRADESCANT	John Tradescant (d. 1638)/son John Tradescant (1608–62), of Lambeth, London, lists of plants growing in their garden for 1634 and/or 1656

Abele White Poplar *Populus alba*, C & S Europe to W Asia, long cultivated and naturalized in the British Isles; **Aspen** *Populus tremula* native/Europe/ N Africa/Asia Minor.

Abies Firrs/Firrs Norway/Silver firrs European Silver Fir *Abies alba*, mountainous regions of Europe, *c.*1603.

Abricots Apricots *Prunus armeniaca*, China, introduced into cultivation via E Mediterranean (supposedly by the gardener to Henry VIII), *c.*1500; **Bish: of Lond: Abricot Fullham** The horticulturally minded Bishop of London was Henry Compton (1632–1713) whose duties included sending missionaries to N America. He made the gardens of Fulham Palace famous for the exotic trees and shrubs he grew there, many of which had been sent to him by the same missionaries. He also grew the first magnolia in Europe (*Magnolia virginiana*), receiving the seed in 1688; **Brussels; Dutch Abricot** TRADESCANT: Small Holland Apricocke; **Hardy Abricot; Langdque Masculin** TRADESCANT: Masculine Apricocke, available GURLE, 1674; **Musque Abricot** TRADESCANT: Longe muske Apricock; **Ordinary great-bearer** HANMER: Great Apricocke, TRADESCANT: Ordinary Apricocke; **Orange Abricot** HANMER: Orenge Apricocke.

Abrotanum Lad's love/Old man/Southernwood *Artemisia abrotanum*, S Europe, 1000, reintroduced 1548; **Abrotonum mas. faem.** probably Southernwood *Artemisia abrotanum* S Europe, 1000, reintroduced 1548; **Abrotanum Ungoventarium** Small absinth *Artemisia pontica*, C Europe, 1570; **Absynithium Latifolium arborescens** Could be *Artemisia arborescens*, S Europe, 1640, or Common Wormwood *Artemisia absinthium*, possibly native/Europe; **Dragon/Dragons** Tarragon known as Dragon's herb *Artemisia dracunculus* C & E Europe, 1548. *See also* **Serpentaria** and **Dracontium**; **Mug-wort** Mugwort *Artemisia vulgaris*, native.

Acacia flo: albo Possibly Gum Arabic tree *Acacia arabica* (syn: *A vera*), N Africa, *c.*1656; **Acacia flo: Ægyptiaca** Possibly Opoponax *Acacia farnesiana*, Mediterranean, *c.*1656.

Acanthus sativus/Beares-breech Bear's breeches/Brank-ursine *Acanthus mollis*, S Europe, pre-1000; **Acanthus sylvestris** *Acanthus spinosus*, S Europe, pre-1000.

Aconite/Aconits/ Monks-hood: Monkshood *Aconitum napellus*, N Europe, long cultivated; **Winter Aconite** *Eranthis hyemalis*, S Europe, garden escapee, *c.*1576.

Adders tongue Common adder's tongue *Ophioglossum vulgatum*, native/ Europe/W Asia/N America.

Adiantum Verum Common maidenhair fern *Adiantum capillus-veneris*, native/cosmopolitan.

Ægrimonie/Agrimony/Hemp agrimony *Eupatorium cannabinum*, native/ Europe/Asia.

African Marygolds/African flo. *See* **Flos Africanus.**

Agnus Castus Chaste/Castis-spotted Tree *Vitex agnus castus*, S Europe, 1570.

Alaternus Buckthorn *Rhamnus alaternus* SW Europe, pre-1629; **Alaternus prima Clusii** possibly *Rhamnus myrtifolius*, Spain, *c.*16th cent.; **Alaternus variegatus-Albo** probably variety of *Rhamnus alaternus*; **Alaternus variegatus ex Fusco**; **Bay Alaternus**; **Rhamnus–Buck-horne** Buckthorn *Rhamnus alaternus*, SW Europe, pre-1629.

Alb. Lavendula Multif. *See* **Lavender.**

Alcanet/Anchusa sempervivens Alkanet/Green alkanet *Pentaglottis sempervirens* (syn: *A sempervirens*), SW Europe, *c.*1500.

Alder Common alder *Alnus glutinosa*, native/Europe/Asia Minor/N Africa.

Aleppo Narciss. *See* **Narcissus.**

Alexanders/Alesanders/Alisanders/Hipposelinum Alexanders/Horse-parsley *Smyrnium olusatrum*, now naturalized/ N Africa pre-1000.

Alexandrian laurel *See* **Laurel.**

Alkekengi/Alkikengi Winter/Bladder Cherry *Physalis alkekengi*, Caucasus/ Japan, 1548.

Allelujah Wood-sorrel *Oxalis acetosella*, native/Europe, often confused with Common sorrel *Rumex acetosa*, native/Europe. The earliest mention of the name 'Allelujah' has been found in a 13th-cent. Latin herbal by Rufinus of Genoa, an Italian monk, who stated that herb-gatherers supplied wood-sorrel under that name to the druggists of Bologna for making a cooling syrup; *see also* **Sorrel.**

Almond *Prunus dulcis* (syn: *P amygdalus P communis*), N Africa to W Asia, 16th cent., possibly earlier.

Aloes Possibly Bitter aloes/First aid plant *Aloe vera* (syn: *A arabica A barbadensis A indica*), origin unknown, ?1656; **Aloe American** *Agave americana* (syn: *A altissima*), Mexico, 1648.

Althæa Frutex Rose of Sharon *Hibiscus syriacus*, China to India, 1596.

Amaranths/Amaranthus Love lies bleeding *Amaranthus caudatus*, Tropics, 1596; **Amaranthus holosericus** Cockscomb *Celosia argenta* var. *cristata*, equatorial Asian tropics/Africa/N/C/S America, 1570; **Amaranthus tricolor** Joseph's coat/Chinese spinach/*Amaranthus tricolor*, Tropics, *c.*16th cent; **Ameranthus spersa Pannicula** Prince's feathers *Amaranthus cruentus*, tropical America, 1684.

Amomum plinii See **Night-shade.**

Anagallis of Portugal/Lusitanica Blue pimpernel *Anagallis monellii*, Mediterranean particularly Spain, *c.*1648.

Anapodophylon American mandrake, May apple *Podophyllum peltatum*, N America, 1664.

Anchusa sempervivens See **Alcanet**.

Androsænum maximum Hispanicum Possibly Tutsan/Great/St John's wort *Hypericum androsaemum*, native & C Europe/SW Asia/N Africa; **Toutsaine** Tutsan (*Fr.* Tout-saine 'all-heal') *Hypericum androsaemum*, native/ W & S Europe/SW Asia/N Africa.

Anemonies Probably *Anemone coronaria* S Europe to C Asia, 1596; **Anemonie tenuifolia** *Anemone coronaria*, S Europe to C Asia, 1596; **Double anemonies** *Hepatica noblis* 'Rubra Plena' (syn: *Anemone hepatica/Hepatica triloba*), Europe, 16th cent., see also **Hepatica; Persian anemonies** possibly *Anemone pavonina*, Balearic Is./Italy/Balkans, *c.*16th cent.; **Single anemonies** probably *Pulstilla alpina* (syn: *Anemone alpina*), S Europe/Balkans/Caucasus, 1658.

Angelica/Arch-Angel *Angelica archangelica* (syn: *Archangelica officinalis*), naturalized in Britain/N Europe, 1618.

Aniseed/Anniseeds/Annis/Anis Anise *Pimpinella anisum*, Greece/Middle East, pre-1000.

Anthyllis barba-jovis Jupiter's beard *Anthyllis barba jovis*, Spain, 1629.

Antirrhinum/Snapdragon Snapdragon *Antirrhinum majus*, SW Europe/ Mediterranean, *c.*1500.

Apocynum *Apocynum androsaemifolium*, Virginia to Canada, 1693; **Dog-bane** Dogbane *Apocynum venetum*, S Europe to Syria, thus named because believed to be poisonous to dogs, pre-1648.

Apples *Malus domestica*, native/Europe/Asia; Crab apple *Malus sylvestris*, native/Europe/Asia; **Æthiopic Apples/ Ethiopic Apples**, TRADESCANT; **Andrew-apples; Apis**, possibly Api Noir, BERNWODE: French Pomme D'Api; **The Belle-bonne/Belle-et-bonne** TRADESCANT: Winter Belliboorue? **Calvils omn: generum; Cardinal**, also known as Korbovka, a Russian apple, introduced under the name Peter the Great. (It is appropriate that Evelyn lists the tree, as in the 1680s he let Sayes Court to Peter the Great for three months, with disastrous results); **Catts-head** also known as Pig's Snout. The name comes from the unusual shape of the fruit, which is tall and angular. Named by PARKINSON 1629; **Chessnut; Cinnamon-apple; Codling**, 'Codlin' used to mean a hard type of apple not suitable to be eaten raw; HANMER: Coddling (Keswick), this gave rise to Grenadier apple; **Costard** TRADESCANT: Smelling Costard/Grey Costard, a cooking apple; **Courpendus** ?Court Pendu Plat, known as Court Pendu Rouge and the Wise Apple, possible Roman introduction, has been cultivated since 1613; **Cushion Apple;**

Deux-ans/Deuxans/or John apples HANMER: Applejohns or Deuxans, *see also* **John apple; French; Gilly-flower apples** HANMER: Gilliflowers, TRADESCANT: Gillefloure Apple, PARKINSON: Gilloflower, 1629; **Golden-doucet/ducket; Golden mundi apple** ?Gloria Mundi or the Ox Apple, recorded in the USA in 1804, but may have come from middle Europe (information BERNWODE); **Go-no-further or Cats head** *see* Catts head; **Great-belly; Harvey-apple** TRADESCANT: ?Harry apple, Golden Harvey, named for Dr Gabriel Harvey (*c.*1550–1630), Master of Trinity Hall, Cambridge. Described by PARKINSON (1629), as 'a faire great goodly apple, & very well relished'. Cultivated in Norfolk 2006 (information BERNWODE); **Honey-meal; John-apple** HANMER/ TRADESCANT, ?John Standish, tends to crop biennially; **Julyfloore; Juneting** Juneating is a corruption of the word 'Joan-nina', meaning apples ripening around St John the Baptist's Day, 24 June; HANMER: Janettings, TRADESCANT: Ginitings, BERNWODE: Joaneting and Geneting; known since at least 1600, mentioned by Sir Francis Bacon: (1) **Ju-niting Red** known as this from 1665 until 1752 when its name was altered to Margaret: after the change from the Julian to the Gregorian calendar the apple ripened closer to the feast day of St Margaret, 20 July, rather than the feast day of St John the Baptist; (2) **Juniting White.**

Kentish; Kerkham/Kirkham Apple; Kirton; Ladies Longing; Leather-coat/Leathern Coate ?Leathercoat Russet, a very old apple and so named on account of its heavily russeted skin; named by Shakespeare in his play IV Henry II. iii when the apples are presented to Lord Bardolph: 'There's a dish of leather-coats for you'; **Lording Apple; Maligar** ?Margil, also called Reinette Musquée/Small Ribston/Never Fail, possible introduction from France by George London, a friend of John Evelyn; **Margaret-apple** *see* Juneting; **Mary-gold/Mari-gold; May-flower; Parsley-apples; Passe-pome; Pear-apple** TRADESCANT: Russet Peare apples.

Pearmain/Pear-maine, an ancient name derived from the Latin 'of Parma', the name applies to both apple and pear varieties; known in England since the 13th cent.; (1) **Lones-pearmain;** (2) **Summer Permain**, also known as Autumn Pearmain, and one of the oldest recorded dessert apples, the name has been traced to the late 1500s. Mentioned PARKINSON (1629), and TRADESCANT (1656) (information BERNWODE); (3) **Winter-permain** One of the oldest of English apples, first recorded in 1204, and described by John Gerard in 1597, TRADESCANT.

Pepins (*Pepin* is French for a seedling): (1) **Bloody-Pepin;** (2) **French-pepin**, TRADESCANT; (3) **Golden-pepin** HANMER: Golden Pippens, PARKINSON: Golden Pippin, an autumn apple, flourished in the environs of

London; (4) **Holland-pepin**, HANMER; (5) **Juniting pepin**; (6) **Kentish-pepin**, HANMER: 'the best suppos'd in England', TRADESCANT; (7) **Kirton-pepin**; (8) **Russet-pepin**, HANMER: Russet pepin/Sommer Pepin, TRADESCANT: Russet pepin/Sommer Pepin Black Pipin/Mother Pipin), *see also* **Russet**.

Pomewater/Pome-water: (1) **Pome d'Apis/Pome-Apis**; (2) **Pome-roy** ?Pomeroy (Kings Apple) possibly a very early Norman variety.

Queene Apple ?**Quince-apple**, TRADESCANT: Quince apple/ Quince Crab; **Red Fennouil; Red greening ribb'd** ?Green Custard, described by BERNWODE as having a green ridged skin. Possibly from Sussex and maybe the 'Green Costard' named by PARKINSON; **Reinet/Reineting/ flat Reinet** derived from the French word *reinette* meaning tree-frog, the fruit being so named because of the spotted markings on some varieties; **Robillard**.

Russet/Russeting/Rousseting All varieties of russet apples have rough skin with muted autumnal colour and reddish or brownish markings. The name also applies to varieties of pear that exhibit similar characteristics; TRADESCANT; *see also* **Russet-pepin**: (1) **Golden-Rousset pepin**, ?TRADESCANT: Yellow Russeting/Great Russeting; (2) **Winter Russetting**, HANMER: Russetings, ?Royal Russet.

Seaming Apple; Sheeps Snout, TRADESCANT: Snouting; **Short-Start; Spicing**, TRADESCANT: Yellow Spising; **Violet-apple**, a cider-making apple, known in France from 1628 and later in the century as Black Apple or Black Prince; named Violette for its very dark colour and violet bloom (TRADESCANT); **West-berry apples; The William**, TRADESCANT: Master William/Red master Williams; **Winter Chess-nut; Winter-Queening; Winter Reed**.

Arbor Judæ Judas tree *Cercis siliquastrum*, SE Europe to SW Asia, 1596.

Arbor Thyrea /Lignum vitæ Tree of Life/ White Cedar/American Arbor-vitae *Thuja occidentalis*, E America, *c.*1534.

Arbutus Strawberry tree *Arbutus unedo*, SW Europe/SW Ireland/Asia Minor, long cultivated, 1648.

Arch-Angel *See* **Angelica**.

Aristolochia Probably Birthwort/European Snakeroot *Aristolochia clematitis*, native/Europe.

Armerius *See* **Pinks**; Sweet William/Deptford Pink *Dianthus armeria*, native/Europe/W Asia.

Ars-Smart Water-pepper *Polygonum hydropiper* (syn: ?*Persicaria hydropiper*), native.

Artichocks/Artichoak/Artichaux/Artichocks flatheaded/Cinara/Carduus

sativus Globe Artichoke *Cynara scolymus*, N Africa probably Roman introduction; Jerusalem Artichoke *Helianthus tuberosus*, N America, 1622.

Arum/Aureum Probably Lords & Ladies/Cuckoo-pint *Arum maculatum*,
native/Europe/N Africa; **Arum Theophrastii ?Dracontium** *Arisaema
dracontium*, E America, pre-1648.

Asara-bacca/Assara-bassa/Azarum Asarabacca Wild Ginger *Asarum eu-
ropaeum*, naturalized/W Europe, pre-1000.

Ash/Ash-keys/Ashen-keys Common Ash *Fraxinus excelsior*, native/Europe/
Asia Minor.

Aspalathus Cret. /Aspalathus Creticus All Aspalathus are evergreen thorny
shrubs native of S Africa (*aspalathos*, Greek word for thorny shrubs).

Asparagus/ Sparagus Probably *Asparagus officinalis*, native/Mediterranean /
E Europe; **Dutch Asparagus.**

Aspen *See* **Abele.**

Asphodill/Asphodel/Asphodils Asphodel *Asphodelus albus*, S Europe, 1596,
and/or *A fistulosus* (syn: *A tenuifolius*), SW Europe to SW Asia, 1596.

Aster atticus Probably *Aster amellus*, C & E Europe to W Russia & Turkey,
1596.

Augusti-sol Could be what was known as 'Phillyrea angusto folio', *see* **Philyrea
angustifolio.**

Aureum *See* **Arum.**

Auricula /Auricula ursi *See* **Prim-rose.**

Autumnal Crocus *See* **Crocus.**

Autumnal Cyclamen *See* **Cyclamen.**

Autumnal Hyacinth *See* **Hyacinth.**

Azarum *See* **Asara-bacca.**

Azedarack/Bead tree Bead-tree/Pride of India *Melia azedarach*, N India/
China, *c.*17th cent.

Balme Balm *Melissa officinalis*, native/C & S Europe.

Balsam-apple *Momordica balsamina*, tropical Asia/Africa/Australia, 1568.

Balsame/Balsamine/Balsamine foem./Balsamus/Balsamun mas Probably Balsam *Impatiens balsamina*, India/Malay/China, 1596; **Noli-me-tangere**
Touch-me-not Balsam *Impatiens noli-tangere*, native/Europe/.Siberia.

Balaustia *See* **Pome Granade.**

Barba Jovis/Barba Jovis frutex Silver bush/Jupiter's beard *Anthyllis barba-jov*,
Spain, 1640.

Barren-wort Barrenwort *Epimedium alpinum*, N hemisphere, 1597.

Basil/Basile Sweet basil *Ocimum basilicum*, tropical/sub-tropical Asia/Mediter-
ranean, 1625.

Baulm *See* **Balme.**

Bay berries Bog myrtle/Sweet gale *Myrica gale*, native/Europe/Asia/N America; possibly Wax myrtle *Myrica cerifera*, E America, 1669.

Bays Alaternus *See* **Alaternus.**

Bead Tree *See* **Azedarack.**

Beane/French-bean Probably Broad/Horse bean also known as the French bean *Vicia faba*, ancient cultivation native/European; *see also* **Harriocs** which are also known as French/Kidney beans *Phaseolus vulgaris*, C America, 1597; **Scarlet Beans/Scarlet-beane/ Indian Phaseolus** Runner bean *Phasaeolus coccineus*, America, *c.*1650.

Beares-breech *See* **Acanthus.**

Bee flowers Plants grown for their nectar (modern list in *RHS Dictionary*).

Beech Common Beech *Fagus sylvatica*, native/Europe.

Beet/Beta/Beetes/Beet-chard/Chard-Beet, White/Red/Roman Beet & Orache/Spinach/Good King Henry all varieties of *Beta vulgaris*, native/ Europe/Asia; all have edible leaves and stalks, some also edible roots.

Bell-flowers *See* **Campanulas.**

Bellis/Daisies Daisy *Bellis perennis*, native/Europe/Asia. TRADESCANT lists eight different varieties; **Bellis Hispan.** possibly Blue Daisy *Globularia vulgaris*, Europe, 1629.

Bellvedere/Bell-verdere *Kochia scoparia*, S France eastwards to Japan, 1597.

Berberries Barberry *Berberis vulgaris*, native/Europe.

Betonie Betony *Stachys betonica*, native/Europe.

Bistort Snakeweed *Persicaria bistorta* (syn: *Polygonum bistorta*), native/ Europe/N & W Asia.

Black Frontiniac *See* **Grape.**

Black Hellebor *See* **Hellebor.**

Black Radish/Black-Spanish Radish *See* **Radish.**

Black-thorne Sloe, Blackthorn *Prunus spinosa*, native/Europe/N Africa/ W Asia.

Blattaria Moth mullein *Verbascum blattaria*, native/Europe; **Mullein** *Verbascum lychnitis* native/Europe/W Asia, or Dark mullein *Verbascum nigrum*, native/Europe.

Blite/Blitum/English Mercury/All-good/Good King Henry *Chenopodium bonus-henricus*, native/Europe, or Strawberry blite *C. capitatum* (syn: *Blitum capitum*), possibly naturalized/Europe.

Blood-wort Possibly Red-veined/Wood Dock *Rumex sanguineus*, native (rare), or Herb Robert *Geranium robertianum*, native/Europe/Canary Is./NW Africa/SW China, or Centaury *Centaurium erythraea*, native/Europe/

W Asia/N Africa; introduced N America & Australia.

Blue Pease *See* **Peas.**

Borrage Common Borage *Borago officinalis*, native/Europe.

Box/Box-tree *See* **Buxus.**

Brook-Lime *See* **Veronica.**

Brionia White Bryony/Mandrake *Bryonia dioica*, native/Europe.

Broome/Broom-buds Broom *Cytisus scoparius*, native/Europe.

Brumal-Jacyinth *See* **Hyacinthus.**

Bugloss/Buglosse Bugloss *Lycopsis arvensis*, native/Europe/W Asia, introduced
   N America; possibly Vipers-bugloss *Echium vulgare*, native/Europe.

Bulbous iris *See* **Iris.**

Bulbous violet/Snow-drops/Snow flowers Snowdrop *Galanthus nivalis*,
   E Mediterranean, 1596; naturalized/France east to Caucasus *c.*1500; *see also*
   Leucoium.

Bullis *See* **Plum.**

Burdoch/Lapatha Personata Great Burdock *Arctium lappa*, native/Europe/
   naturalized America.

Burnet/Pimpernel/Minor Pimpinella/Burnet Saxifrage Probably Salad Burnet *Sanguisorba minor* (syn: *Poterium sanguisorba*), native/Europe.

Buxus Common box *Buxus sempervirens*, native/Europe, and/or Edging box
   B. sempervirens 'Suffruticosa', Europe/N Africa, early 17th cent. During Evelyn's lifetime there was a continuing debate regarding the suitability of using
   box, mainly due to its acrid smell. Evelyn also writes in the unpublished
   'Elysium Britannicum' that the smell could be controlled by keeping the
   box cut very short, but that the roots impoverish the ground.

Cabbage *Brassica oleracea*, Mediterranean to temperate Asia, pre-1000; *Brassica
   oleracea* species is a polymorphic plant, and occurs in many different forms:
   (1) **Caully-flower/Cauly-flowres/Collyflowers** Cauliflower *Brassica oleracea*,
   subspp. *oleracea*, native/Europe; (2) **Cymæ**, young cabbage sprout; (3) **Large-
   sided Cabages**, variety of *Brassica oleracea*, possibly *B. o.* var. *ramosa*,
   C Europe, probably pre-1000; (4) **Long sided cabbage**; (5) **Mustard**, probably Black mustard *Brassica nigra*, possibly native/Europe; (6) **Navets**, Long
   rooted turnip *Brassica napus*, native/Europe; (7) **Savoy**, LUCAS, *c.*1677; (8)
   Turneps Turnip *Brassica rapa*, Mediterranean region anciently grown; (8)
   Napus/Navets Long rooted turnip *Brassica napus*, native/Europe.

Cabbage lettuce *See* **Lettuce.**

Calamint Common calamint *Calamintha sylvatica*, native/Europe.

Calamus aromaticus Sweet flag *Acorus calamus*, S Asia/Africa, early introduction

Europe where it has naturalized; by 1668 the iris was already established as growing wild in Norfolk.

Calceolus Mariæ Lady's slipper orchid *Cypripedium calceolus*, native (rare)/ Europe/Asia/N America.

Caltha palustris Marsh Marigold *Caltha palustris*, native/Europe.

Camilea Tricoccos/Chamelæa Alpestris Widow waile/Spurge olive *Cneorum tricoccum*, Mediterranean; prior to Evelyn earliest date 1793.

Camomile/Cammomile Golden/Ox–eyed marguerite *Anthemis tinctoria*, naturalized/C Europe/Turkey/Iran, 1561, and/or Lawn/Roman chamomile *Chamaemelum nobile* (syn: *Anthemis nobilis*), native/W Europe; **Iron-wort** Stinking chamomile *Anthemis cotula*, native/Europe/N & W Asia; supposedly iron-wort was able to heal old sores caused by accidents with iron tools.

Campanula/white/blue Bell flower/Canterbury/Coventry bells *Campanula medium*, S Europe, 1597; Peach-leaved bell flower *Campanula persicifolia* S Europe to C & S Russia/N & W Asia, pre-1596; Chimney-bellflower *C pyramidalis*, N Italy/NW Balkans, 1596.

Camilea Tricoccas/Chamelaea Alpestris waile/Spurge olive *Cneorum tricoccum* Mediterreanean region. Prior to Evelyn earlist date 1793.

Campions *See* **Lychnis**.

Candy-Tufts/Thlaspi Creticum/Tufts Candytuft *Iberis umbellata*, S Europe, 1596; 'Tufts' is the name HANMER called it.

Canna Indica Indian shot *Canna indica* (syn: *C edulis*), tropical/subtropical S America 1570; **Canna piscatoria**.

Capers/Capparis/Cappuchin capers Capers *Capparis spinosa*, S Europe, pre-1650.

Caprifol: Honisuckle vulgar/Caprifolium see **Honeysuckles**.

Caprifolium Americanum Trumpet honeysuckle, E & S America, 1656.

Capsicum Indicum/Indian Capsicum/Ginny-pepper/Guinny-pepper Capsicum/Chilli pepper *Capsicum annuum*, tropical N & S America, *c*.1548.

Caraway/Carroways Caraway *Carum carvi*, naturalized (rare)/Europe to N India.

Carduus benedictus Blessed Thistle *Cnicus benedictus*, Mediterranean, *c*.1656.

Carnations Clove-pink/Gilly flower *Dianthus caryophyllus*, W & S France. 11th cent.

Carob Tree/Carrobs Carob/Locust tree *Ceratonia siliqua*, S Europe, 1570.

Carrots *See* **Daucus**.

Carroways *See* **Caraway**.

Caryophyllata emn. gen. Water avens *Geum rivale*, native/Europe.

Caterpillars Caterpillar plant *Scorpiurus vermiculata*, S Europe/N Africa/ W Asia, 1621.

Catmint/Nep Catnep tea *Nepeta cataria*, native/Europe.

Caully-flower/Cauly-flowres *See* **Cabbage.**

Cedrus Bermudas Probably *Juniperus bermudiana*, Bermuda, 1683; **Cedrus Goa** Mexican Cypress/Cedar of Goa *Cupressus lusitanica*, Mexico/ Guatemala, pre-1680; **Cedrus Libani** Cedar of Lebanon *Cedrus libani*, Mt. Lebanon/Syria/SE Turkey, *c.*1610–20; **Cedrus Virginia**, probably Pencil cedar *Juniperus virginiana*, Quebec to Texas, 1664.

Celedon/Chelidonium Possibly Greater celandine *Chelidonium majus*, Europe/N Asia, possibly Roman introduction, introduced N America, New Zealand. The Greek word *chelidon* means 'swallow', the flower opening about the same time as the arrival of the swallow; could also be Pilewort *Ranunculus ficaria*, native/Europe/naturalized N America.

Centaurie/Knapweed Knapweed *Centaurea* spp. may be *Centaurea nigra*, native/Europe; *see also* **Sultan; Cyanus major** probably Blue bottle/ Cornflower *Centaurea cyanus*, native/Europe; **Jacea** Brown Knapweed *Centaurea jacea*, naturalized (rare)/Europe.

Chaerophilum *See* **Chervil.**

Chalcedon *See* **Iris.**

Chama-iris/Chamæ-iris *See* **Iris.**

Chard-beet *See* **Beet.**

Chardon/Chardoon Cardoon *Cynara cardunculus*, S Europe, 1658, possibly Globe artichoke *Cynara scolymus*, not found in the wild, probably a derivative of *C cardunculus*, 1548.

Chelidonium *See* **Celedon.**

Cherries Sweet cherry *Prunus avium*, native/Europe/W Asia; Sour cherry *Prunus cerasus* SE Europe/W Asia; all cherries have a long history of cultivation; **Amber; Agriot/Egriot** TRADESCANT; **Birds-cherry** *Prunus padus*, northern temperate regions including Britain; **Bigarreaux** believed to be an old variety, BERNWODE grows Bigarreau Gaucher; there is also Bigarreau de Mezel/B. de Schreker; **Black Cherry** ?Black Jaboulay/B. Napoleon/B. Reverchon/Kent Black; **Black-Cher: st W; Temple** grown by Sir William Temple; *see also* **Directions** note to p. 87 *W. Temple*; **Black-heart: true; Black Orleans/Black-Orleans** available GURLE, 1674; **Carnations** HANMER: 'Carnation cherry doe well in England in standards'; **Common-Cherry; Cherry-Bay; Croone; Cuxnation.**

Duke available GURLE, 1674: (1) **Black** HANMER; (2) **Red** HANMER; (3) **White** HANMER.

 Flanders HANMER, and available GURLE, 1674: (1) **Black** HANMER; (2) **Early Flanders**; (3) **Red** HANMER; (4) **White** HANMER 'good as standard'.

Flemish; **Great-bearer/Greate-bearer** TRADESCANT: the great bearing Cherrie; **Hartlib**, possibly named for Samuel Hartlib (*c.*1600–*c.*1670), who came to England from Poland and encouraged the development of agriculture during the Commonwealth.

Heart TRADESCANT: great Hart Cherry: (1) **Black** HANMER: 'the Blacke is best'; (2) **Red** HANMER; (3) **White** HANMER, there are a number of varieties with this name; information BERNWODE.

Kentish; **Luke-ward** TRADESCANT; **May-Cherry/cherrie** HANMER: Mayes, TRADESCANT: May Chery; **Monmoraney**; **Morella/Morellos** Sour/Morello Cherry *Prunus cerasus*, HANMER: Morillons; the fruit is almost black in colour, and derives its name from 'morello', the Italian word for 'very dark', which was a new word in Evelyn's day; **Morocca/Morroco/ Morocco-Cherry**; **Naples**; **Petworth Amber**; **Prince Royal/Prince-Royall**; **Red-heart**; **Spanish-black** TRADESCANT.

Chervil/Chervile/Chervill-sweete/Chaerophilum Bulbous-rooted Chervil *Chaerophyllum bulbosum*, S Europe, prior to Evelyn the earliest date of introduction 1726.

Chery-bay *See* **Laurus**.

Chessnut/Spanish Nut Sweet/Spanish Chestnut *Castanea sativa*, S Europe/ Asia minor/N Africa. *c.* AD 50.

Chibbols *See* **Onion**.

Chick-weed *Stellaria media*, native/Europe.

Chives/Cives/Scives Chives *Allium schoenoprasum*, N hemisphere.

Chondrilla *Chondrilla juncea*, N Europe.

Chrysanthemum angustifol [meaning narrow leaved]; **Chrysanthemum frutiferum**, probably Paris Daisy/Marguerite; *Argyranthemum frutescens* (syn: *Chrysanthemum frutescens*), Canary Is., 1699 (recorded in France from *c.*1600).

Cibbols *See* **Onion**.

Cichory *See* **Succory**.

Cicuta Cowbane *Cicuta virosa*, native/Europe; a genus of poisonous umbellifers, Cicuta was formerly the name of the Common hemlock now *Conium maculatum* native/Europe.

Cineraria/Jacobœa Marina/Rag-wort Ragweed/Sea ragwort *Senecio cineraria*, naturalized SW England/S Europe, long cultivated; introduced N America Australasia; **Senetio Arborescens**, possibly *Senecio doria*, C & S Europe, 1570.

Cinq-foile Cinquefoil/Tormentil *Potentilla erecta*, native/Europe/W Asia/ N Africa.

Cistus of all kinds Sage/Holy rose *Cistus* spp. *Cistus salvifolius*, Mediterranean, pre-1548; *C albidus*, Mediterranean, 1597; Gum cistus *C ladanifer*, Mediterranean, 1604; *C. inflatus* (syn: *C ladanifer*), SW Europe, 1650; *C populifolius*, SW Europe; **Cistus Hortorum; Cistus Ledon Clus**, probably *Cistus×glaucus* (syn: *Cistus ledon)*, S Europe; no date of entry; **Cistus Ragusaeus flo. Alb./Clus. cistus Ragusaeus flo. alb.**, Ragusaeus refers to the city of Ragusa (now Dubrovnik), so could be *Cistus hirsutus*, SW Europe, 1650; **Cistus mas.** *Cistus albidus*, SW Europe, 1648, BOBART: *Cistus mas* Male holy rose/cistus.

Citron Vernal Cyclamen *See* **Cyclamen**.

Citrus Ledon Clusii Probable misprint of Citrus *see* **Cistus**.

Cives *See* **Chives**.

Clary *Salvia sclarea*, Europe, *see also* **Horminum Creticum**.

Clavers Cleavers/Goose grass *Galium aparine*, native/Europe.

Clematis Probably Travellers Joy *Clematis vitalba*, native/Europe to N Africa; **Clematis Pannonica**, possibly Hungarian clematis/Bush Bower *Clematis intergrifolia*, S Europe, 1573; Pannonia was a Roman province now part of Austria and Hungary; **Clematis virginiana** recorded TRADESCANT 1656, now *Clematis ligusticifolia*, W America, however it could be May pops *Passiflora incarnata*, SE America, 1629; **Virgin's bower** *Clematis viticella*, SE Europe, 1569.

Clove/Clove-gillyflower sops-in-wine *Dianthus caryophyllus*, native/Europe.

Cluster-grape *See* **Grape**.

Cneorum Matthioli *See* **Mezerion**.

Cochlearia/ Scurvy-grasse Scurvy-grass/Spoonwort *Cochlearia officinalis*, native/NE Europe/Asia; **Horse reddish** Horse-radish *Cochlearia armoracia*, naturalized in Britain/E temperate Europe; **Spanish Black Horse Radish**, possibly *Cochlearia aestuaria*, Atlantic coasts of France and N Spain; no date of entry.

Colchicum/Meadow Saffron Autumn crocus *Colchicum autumnale*, native/Europe.

Collyflowers *See* **Cabbage**.

Colombine/Columbines *Aquilegia vulgaris*, native/Europe.

Coltsfoot Cleats/Son-before-father/Coughwort *Tussilago farfara*, native/Europe.

Colutea Odorata Cretica Probably Bladder senna *Colutea arborescens*, S Europe/Mediterranean, 1548; **Senna** *Colutea arborescens*, S Europe/ Mediterranean, 1548; possibly Scorpion Senna *Coronilla emerus*, C & S Europe; listed by Evelyn in *Directions,* under 'Trees & Shrubs rare not evergreen', so it would not be *Cassia* sp.

Comfery Comfrey/Knitbone/Ass-ear *Symphytum officinale*, native/Europe/ Siberia and/or *S tuberosum*, native/Europe.

Common Pansies *See* **Pansies**.

Condrilla *See* **Dandelion**.

Consolidum regale Probably Forked larkspur *Consolida regalis* or Larkspur *Delphinium consolida*, both native/Europe.

Constaninople chestnut *See* **Horse Chessnut**.

Convolvulus Probably Morning glory *Ipomoea purpurea* (syn: *Convolvulus major*), probably Mexico 1629 or dwarf form *C tricolor*, Spain, 1629.

Coriander *Coriandrum sativum*, naturalized/E Mediterranean, Roman introduction.

Corinth grape *See* **Grape**, named for Corinth, the city situated on the isthmus between the Peloponnese and C Greece.

Corinths Currant, red & black *Ribes sativum/R. nigrum*, Europe, early introduction, probably post-Roman; **Corinth Red**, the 'Great Redcurrant' was recorded by PARKINSON, which had been bred in Holland and imported by Tradescant (sen.) from the Harlem nurseryman Cornellis Helin in 1611 for Robert Cecil at Hatfield House; **Corinth White**, 'Whit Currant plants' were bought by Tradescant in Delft in 1611, for Robert Cecil at Hatfield House.

Cork-tree/Suber Cork-tree *Quercus suber*, S Europe/N Africa; listed in LUCAS, 1677; **Ilix Scarlet Oake** could be either Kermes/Scarlet Oak *Quercus coccifera*, S Europe/Asia Minor/N Africa, 1683, or *Quercus coccinea* Scarlet Oak, NE America, 1691; **Spanish-Oake** *Quercus falcata* (syn: *Quercus cuneata*), E & SC America, prior to Evelyn, earliest date of introduction 1763.

Cornelians/white/red Cornelian cherry/Cornel tree *Cornus mas*, Europe/ W Asia, long cultivated; record of a planting at Hampton Court in 1551; **Dog-wood** Common dog-wood *Cornus sanguinea*, native/Europe.

Corn-flag *See* **Gladiolus**.

Cornflower *See* **Cyanus**.

Corn-sallet/Corne-sallad/Corn-salet Corn Salad/Lambs Lettuce *Valerianella locusta*, native/Europe/Middle East/N Africa.

Cosse lettuce *See* **Lettuce**.

Costmary Alecost *Tanacetum balsamita* (syn: *Balsamita major/Chrysanthemum balsamita*), Europe to C Asia, long cultivated; **Febrefeu/Fibrefeu/Matricaria double flo.** Feverfew/Tansy *Tanacetum parthenium*, naturalized/SE Europe, pre-1000; **Tansy/Tansie** Buttons/Tansy *Tanacetum vulgare*, native/Europe; *see also Acetaria* pp. 181 and 217 and note.

Cotyledon double Venus navelwort *Omphalodes linifolia*, SW Europe, pre-1648.

Cowslip *See* **Prim-rose**.

Cresses/Cressus/Cressue/Cresses broad & curl'd Garden Cress *Lepidium sativum*, Egypt/W Asia, naturalized Europe/N America, 1548.

Crithmum marinum Samphire *Crithmum maritimum*, native/coasts of W & S Europe.

Crocus; Autumnal crocus *Crocus nudiflorus*, SW France/NE Spain, 15th cent., when it was cultivated for the production of saffron in the Halifax area; **Vernal crocus** Dutch crocus *Crocus vernus*, W Russia/Poland through the Balkans to Austria/Hungary/Italy, 15th cent.

Crow-foot *See* **Ranunculus.**

Crown-Imperial/Croun-Imperial *See* **Fritillaria.**

Crumpen Belgand/Crupen Belgrade/Crupen Belgun Bearded creeper/Common Crupin *Crupina vulgaris* SE Europe, pre-1634.

Cucumber/Cucumers *Cucumis sativus* Asia/India, possible Roman introduction/early 17th cent.

Cummin Cumin *Cumium cyminum*, E Mediterranean, pre-AD 1000.

Cupressus Italian cypress *Cupressus sempervirens*, Mediterranean/W Asia, *c.*1375.

Cyanus Saffron thistle/Bastard thistle *Carthamus tinctorius*, Egypt, 1551; **Cyanus major** *see Centaurea montana*, Europe, 1596.

Cyclamen Sowbread; **Autumnal Cyclamen**, probably *Cyclamen hederifolium* (syn: *C neapolitanum*) E Mediterranean, 1597; **Citron Vernal Cyclamen** *Cyclamen coum*, Bulgaria/Caucasus/Turkey/Lebanon, 1656; **Cyclamen Vernum** *Cyclamen vernum*, Caucasus/Syria/N Iraq; no date of entry; **Early Cyclamen**, probably *Cyclamen coum*, Bulgaria/Caucasus/Turkey/Lebanon, 1656; **Spring Cyclamen** *Cyclamen coum*, Bulgaria/Caucasus/Turkey/Lebanon, 1656; **Summer Purple Cyclamen** *Cyclamen purpurascens*, SE France to W Carpathians 1596; **Vernal Cyclamen white and red**, possibly *Cyclamen persicum*, SE Mediterranean/N Africa, 1596; **Winter-Cyclamen/Common winter cyclamen**, probably *Cyclamen vernum*.

Cymæ *See* **Cabbage.**

Cypresse Possibly Italian/Mediterranean cypress *Cupressus sempervirens, c.*1375.

Cytisus; Cytisus Lunatus/Cytisus Maranthe, *see* **Medicago; Cytisus rubra.**

Dactyls Cocksfoot *Dactylis glomerata*, Europe/N Africa/Asia, possibly 17th cent.

Daffodils *See* **Narcissus**; *see also* **Asphodil.**

Daisies *See* **Bellis.**

Dames-Violet *See* Hesperis

Damson *See* **Plums.**

Dandelion/Dan-de Lion/Dan-delion/Dens Leonis/Condrilla Dandelion/ Piss-a-Bed *Taraxacum vulgaria*, native/Europe.

Dates Date palm *Phoenix dactylifera*, N Africa/Middle East, 1597.

Datura/Dature double/single; Datura Turica, possibly Angel's trumpets *Datura fastuosa*, India, 1629; **Stramonium** Thorn apple/Jimsonweed *Datura stramonium*, cosmopolitan.

Daucus/Dauci Carrot *Daucus carota*, native/Europe/Asia.

Day-Eies Probably Daisies, *see* **Bellis**.

Dead Nettle *Lamium* sp. native/Europe/temperate Asia.

Delphinium Probably *Delphinium elatum*, Pyrenees to Mongolia, 1578.

Dens-Caninus/Dens Caninus three-leav'd Dog's tooth violet *Erythronium dens-canis*, Europe/Asia, 1590.

Deptford Pinkes *See* **Pinks**.

Devils-bit Devil's-bit scabious *Succisa pratensis* (syn: *Scabiosa succisa*), native/Europe/W Siberia/N Africa.

Digitalis/Digitatis Foxglove *Digitalis purpurea*, native/W Europe, and/or *Digitalis grandiflora* (syn: *D ambigua D orientalis*), C & S Europe to Siberia/Turkey, 1596, and/or *D ferruginea*, SE Europe/Turkey/Lebanon, 1597; **Digitalis Hispan** *Digitalis obscura*, Spain, pre-1656; **Iron-colour'd Foxgloves** *Digitalis ferruginea*, Europe, 1597.

Dill *Anethum graveolens* (syn: *Peucedanum graveolens*), SW Asia/India, pre-AD 1000.

Dittander Pepper-wort *Lepidium latifolium*, native/Europe/SW Asia/N Africa, introduced into N America.

Dock/Sharp-pointed Dock Probably Clustered dock *Rumex conglomeratus*, native/Europe.

Dog-bane *See* **Apocynum**.

Dog-wood *See* **Cornelians**.

Dogs-Mercury *Mercurialis perennis*, native/Europe.

Dorichnium congener Clusii Perhaps Leopard's bane *Doronicum clusii*, Swiss/ Austrian Alps, prior to Evelyn earliest known date of introduction 1819.

Double Daisies *See* **Bellis**.

Double Jonquil *See* **Jonquil**.

Double poppies *See* **Papaver**.

Dracontium *See* **Arum**.

Dragon/Dragons *See* **Abrotanum**, probably Tarragon known as Dragon's herb/mugwort *Artemisia dracunculus*, C & E Europe, 1548; *see also* **Serpentaria**.

Dulcamara *See* **Night-shade**.

Dutch Asparagus *See* **Asparagus.**

Dutch mezereon *See* **Mezerion.**

Early Cyclamen *See* **Cyclamen.**

Earth-Nut/Pig-nut/Ground nut/Earth chestnut *Conopodium majus*, native/ Europe.

Elder/Sambucus Elderberry *Sambucus nigra*, native/Europe, Common elder *Sambucus nigra*, native/Europe/N Africa/W Asia.

Eli-Campane Elecampane/Horseheal *Inula helenium*, native (v. rare)/ Europe/N Asia.

Eliochryson Helichrysum spp., possibly *Helichrysum rupestre*, Mediterranean, 1629, or Curry Plant *H serotinum* SW Europe, 1629, or Goldilocks *H. stoechas*, SW Europe/Balkans, 1629.

Elme English elm *Ulmus procera*, native; **Whitchin elme** Wych or Scotch Elm *Ulmus glabra*, native/Europe/N & W Asia.

Endive *Cichorium endivia* S Europe/temperate Asia/Ethiopia; Roman introduction (Cichorium is its Ancient Egyptian name); **Curl'd Endive**, Evelyn remarks it is 'more delicate'; *see also **Acetaria**, p. 148 Endive.*

English double: Primrose *See* **Primrose.**

English Mercury *See* **Blite.**

English Saffron *See* **Saffron.**

Erica Fuzz Erica spp. possibly *Erica erigena* (syn: *E. mediterranea/E. hibernica*) SW Europe/Ireland (Galway)/Tangier, 1648.

Eringo *See* **Eryngium.**

Eryngium Amethystinum/Eringo Sea holly *Eryngium maritimum*, native/ Europe; **Eryngium planum** Smooth sea-holly *Eryngium planum*, C & SE Europe to C Asia, 1596; **Eryngium totum Cæruleum** could be *Eryngium amethystinum*, Italy/Sicily/Balkans, 1648.

Eschalots/Shalot/Scalions Shallot *Allium cepa* var. *ascalonium*, Middle East, probably middle/late 16th cent.; *see also* **Onion.**

Eupatorium Hemp Agrimony *Eupatorium cannabinum*, native/Europe.

Everlasting-pease Probably *Lathyrus latifolius*, S Europe, 1629.

Expatorium of Canada Probably *Eupatorium cannabinum, see* above.

Febrefeu *See* **Costmary.**

Fennel/Fennell/Sweet-Fennel/Fenell-Sweete Fennel *Foeniculum vulgare*, Mediterranean Europe, naturalized throughout Europe, including Britain, and California. Evelyn considered the sweetest fennel came from Bologna; *see also* **Rampion.**

Fern listed with other 'Physical' plants, possibly the Royal Fern/Bog onion *Osmunda regalis*, native/wide distribution used as a cure for sprains/dislocations and bruises.

Ficus-Indicus/Ficus Indica Indian fig/Prickly pear *Opuntia ficus-indica* (syn: *O engelmannii/O megacantha*), Mexico, 1648.

Figs *Ficus carica* W Asia/eastern Mediterranean, possible introduction by Romans, and reintroduced 1548; **The White Scio; Purple; Blew.**

Filberts/Filberd *Corylus maxima*, S Europe/W Asia, long cultivated. The nuts are oblong in shape and completely enclosed in the outer husk. They differ in shape from the native rounded hazel/cob nuts *C avellana*, with a smaller husk; *see also* **Haysel; Red** *Corylus* 'Red Filbert', recorded by the nurseryman John Rea in 1665; **White** known since the 17th cent.

Firr/Firr-seeds *See* **Abies Firr.**

Firr Norway *See* **Abies Firr.**

Flag Yellow Iris *Iris pseudacorus*, native/Europe; *see* also **Calamus aromaticus.**

Flea-bane Common Fleabane *Pulicaria dysenterica*, native/Europe.

Florence-Iris *See* **Iris.**

Flos Adonis Pheasant's eye *Adonis aestivalis*, S Europe/SW Asia, 1629.

Flos Africanus/African Marygolds/African flo African marigold *Tagetes erecta*, Mexico naturalized parts of N Africa, 1535; **French-Mary-gold** French marigold *Tagetes patula*, New Mexico/Argentina, *c.*1573.

Flos Cardinalis Cardinal Flower *Lobelia cardinalis*, E Canada to Texas, 1626.

Flos Passionis *See* **Marococ.**

Flos-Solis/Sun-flower Common sunflower *Helianthus annuus*, N & C America, 1596.

Fluellen Sharp-Leaved fluellen *Kickxia elatine*, native/Europe.

Foennugreeke/Fœnugreeke Fenugreek *Trigonella faenum-graecum*, S Europe, 1597.

Fox taile & Glove Foxtail grass *Alopecurus pratensis*, native/Europe (in Turkey lilac *Syringa vulgaris* was known as Fox's Tail *c.*16th cent.); **Fox Glove,** *see* **Digitalis.**

Fraxinella Dittany/Burning bush *Dictamnus albus* (syn: *D fraxinella*), C & S Europe to N China/Korea, *c.*1570.

French-beans *See* **Beane.**

French-Mary-gold *See* **Flos Africanus.**

Fritillaria Fritillary, possibly *Fritillaria latifolia*, Caucasus, *c.*1604; **Crown-Imperial/Croun-Imperial** *Fritillaria imperialis*, S Turkey to Kashmir, pre-1580; **Fritillaria mont.; Persian Lilly** *Fritillaria persica*, Iran/S Turkey, 1584.

Frontiniac *See* **Grape.**

Fumary Probably Fumitory *Fumaria* sp., native/Europe.

Galingale *Cyperus longus*, native/Europe/N Africa/SW & C Asia.

Garden-poppy *See* **Papaver**.

Garlic/Garlick/Moly Garlic *Allium sativum*, C Asia, pre-1000; **Moly** Garlic *Allium sativum* Asia/China, *c.*1653, although a possible Roman introduction; **Homers Moly**, probably Wild garlic *Allium moly*, Mediterranean, 1597 ('Moly' was a fabulous plant and said by Homer to have been given by the messenger of the gods Hermes to Odysseus the legendary king of Ithaca, as a charm against the sorcery of Circe); **Moly Monspeliens**, possibly *Allium roseum*, Mediterranean; prior to Evelyn date of introduction cited as 1752; **White of Dioscorides** Honey garlic *Allium siculum* var. *dioscoridis* (syn: *A dioscoridis*), Crimea/Asia/Cyprus, pre-1656; **Yellow-Moly** Golden garlic, *Allium moly* SW and S Europe, *c.*1604.

Garnsey-Lilly/Garnzy Lillie /Japon Lillie Guernsey lily *Nerine sarniensis*, S Africa (N/W Cape), 1634; HANMER announced this flowered for the first time 7 Oct. 1634 in the Paris garden of Pierre 'Morynes', which Evelyn visited in 1644 and 1651.

Genista Hispanica/Spartum hispan Spanish broom *Spartium junceum*, Mediterranean/Ukraine/Turkey/Syria/N Africa, 1548; **Genista Hispan. flo alb** (flora alba) *Spartium junceum* var. *ochroleucum*, Europe/Ukraine/ Turkey/Syria/N Africa; no date of entry.

Genoa Lettuce *See* **Lettuce**.

Gentiana/Gentianella Gentiana spp. could be *Gentiana acaulis*, Europe, *c.*1648, or Willow gentian *G asclepiadea*, mts. of C & S Europe/Turkey, 1629, or Bitterwort/Yellow gentian *G lutea* Pyrenees/Alps/Apennines/Carpathians, early 17th cent.; **Gentianella annual** *Gentiana campestris*, native/Europe.

Geranium Cranesbill spp. Dusky cranesbill *Geranium phaeum*, native/Europe; Meadow cranesbill *G pratense*, native/Europe; Bloody cranesbill *G sanguineum*, native/Europe; *G tuberosum*, Mediterranean, 1596; *G versicolor* (syn: *G striatum*), naturalized Italy/Sicily/Balkans, 1629; **Geranium Creticum** *Erodium gruinum*, Sicily, 1648; **Geranium Nocte olens** *Pelargonium triste*, *see* below; **Geranium triste** *Pelargonium triste*, S Africa (N/W Cape); introduced Tradescant, *c.*1634; *see also* **Introduction** *see* p. xviii.

Germander Germander Speedwell, probably *Veronica chamaedrys*, native/ Europe; *see also* **Veronica**; **Marum Mastic-thyme**, probably Shrubby germander *Teucrium fruticans*, S Europe, 1633; **Marum Syariacum/Syrac.** Assyrian masticke (the name used at the time), Cat thyme *Teucrium marum*, islands of W Mediterranean, pre-1600; the plant exudes an odour that is irresistible to cats; *see **Kalendarium*** p. 42; **Marums: Water Anemonies** Water Germander *Teucrium scordium*, native (rare) Europe, *see* below; **Polium Montanum** *Teucrium polium*, Mediterranean to W Asia, 1562; **Scordium** Water Germander *Teucrium scordium*, native (rare) Europe; *see* above; **Teuchrium mas**, possibly *Teucrium polium*, Europe/W Asia, 1562.

Gilly flower/Gilly-flo Wild/Clove carnation/Sops-in-wine *Dianthus caryophyllus*, Mediterranean 11th cent., *see also* **Stock-Gilly-flowres.**

Gilly-flower apple *See* **Apples.**

Giniper' *See* **Juniperus.**

Ginny-pepper' *See* **Capsicum Indicum.**

Gladiolus Gladiolus spp. *Gladiolus communis* subsp. *byzantinus* (syn: *G byzantinus*), Spain/N Africa/Sicily, 1596; *G italicus* (syn: *G segtum)*, S Europe, 1597; *G imbricatus* C & E Europe/Latvia/Estonia, 1604; **Corn-flag** *Gladiolus llyricus* native (rare)/Europe, in cultivation since at least 1578.

Globe-thistle *Echinops sphaerocephalus*, C & S Europe/Caucasus/Siberia, 1542.

Gnaphalium Americanum Pearl everlasting *Anaphalis margaritacea*, N America/NE Asia, 1648.

Goates-Rue *Galega officinalis*, naturalized/N Europe, 1548.

Goats-beard Jack-go-to-bed-at-noon/Shepherd's Clock *Tragopogon pratensis*, native/Europe, *see also* **Salsifax.**

Golden Purslain *See* **Porselan.**

Golden rod Solidago spp. probably *Solidago canadensis*, naturalized/E America, 1648.

Goose-berries *Ribes uva crispa/R grossularia*, naturalized/Europe/N Africa, mid-1382; **Black; Blew; Chrystal; Great Amber; Purple; Red; Transparent.**

Gorkems *See* **Gurkems.**

Gourds Cucurbita spp. possibly *Cucurbita pepo*, tropical America, 1570.

Gramen Amygdalosum Probably *Phalaris arundinacea*, temperate N hemisphere.

Granads/Granad-trees *See* **Pome Granade.**

Grape flower *See* **Muscari.**

Grape *Vitis vinifera*, Caucasus region; Roman introduction; **Arboyse; Blew-grape, great & little**, possibly Blue grape *Vitis bicolor*, E & Mid America; no date of introduction; **Chasselas** *'the best sort of ye white muscadin; tis cal'd here ye pearle-Grape' (Directions* p. 91); **Cluster-grape** HANMER: 'The Cluster Currans...the bunches close set with small blew grapes, very sweete & good & great bearers'; **Corinth grape** Currants *Vitis vinefera corinthiaca*, Caucasus region; Roman introduction; **Currand/Common black; Early-blew;**

Frontiniac/Black Frontiniac, Frontignac grape, it makes a Muscat wine; HANMER: 'The ordinary Frontiniacke, it ripens not well here... The Blew or Red Frontiniacke a round red grape, not very bigg, but very sweete and musky, requires a good hot sun'; **Blew Frontinaque,** *see* HANMER above; **Grizlin Frontiniac; White Frontiniac; Morillon; Muscadine-grape** Muscadine *Vitis rotundifolia*, S & C America Prior to Evelyn earliest date of introduction 1806; HANMER: common white/early white Muscadine; **White Muscadine; Muscat black; Muscat white; Parsley** *Vitis vinifera* var. *aplifolia*; HANMER: 'white grape it beares very much & ripens reasonable well; it is called the parsley grape because the leaves are more hagged and deeper cutt than those of other vines'; **Pearle-Grape; Shasellas; Verjuice-grape,** acid juice of green or unripe grapes, used in cooking; **Greater Verjuice.**

Great Blew-grape *See* **Grape.**

Great Chalic'd *See* **Narcissus.**

Great Indian Fig *See* **Ficus Indica.**

Greate haisell *See* **Haysel,** *see also* **Filbert.**

Greater Verjuice *See* **Grape.**

Green Poppy *See* **Papaver.**

Ground Ivy *Glechoma hederacea*, native/Europe.

Groundsell Groundsel (for use in the aviary), *see also* **Senecio.**

Guinny-Pepper'*See* **Capsicum Indicum.**

Gurkems/Gorkems Gherkins *Cucumis anguria*, probably tropical America, 1692.

Halimus Sea purslane *Atriplex portulacoides*, native/Europe; **Halimus Latifolius** Tree purslane *Atriplex halimus*, S Europe, 1632.

Harricos/Haricos usually Haricot or Kidney beans *Phaseolus vulgaris*, C America, 1597; the word 'haricot' is a corruption of *ayecotl*, the Aztec word for kidney bean; *see also* **Beane.**

Harts horn Hartshorn/Swine's Cress *Coronopus squamatus*, native/Europe.

Harts-tongue Hart's-tongue *Asplenium scolopendrium* (syn: *Phyllitis scolopendrium*), Europe/W Asia.

Hauk-Weede *See* **Hieracium.**

Haysel/Greate haisell Hazel/Cobnut *Corylus avellana*, native/Europe/W Asia, *see also* **Filbert.**

Hedera Ivy *Hedera helix*, native/Europe.

Hedg-hogs Medick *Medicago intertexta*, Mediterranean Portugal, pre-17th cent.; **Cytisus Lunatus /Cytisus Maranthe** Moon trefoil *Medicago arborea*,

Canary Is./S Europe/Mediterranean/SW Asia, 1596; **Medica** *Medicago scutellata*, S Europe, 1648.

Hedysarum possibly French honeysuckle *Hedysarum coronarium*, Europe, 1596; **Hedysarum Clypeatum** possibly *Hedysarum capitatum*, Sicily; no date of entry.

Helichryson Probably Goldilocks *Helichrysum stoechas*, S Europe, 1629.

Heliotrop/Heliotrope in Evelyn's time, this was the name given to any plant whose flower moved with the sun; later the name *Heliotropium* described species from S America.

Hellebor/Hellebore/Helleborus Hellebore, probably Christmas rose *Helleborus niger*, Germany/Austria/Switzerland/Italy/Slovenia, *c.*1300; **Black Hellebor/Hellebore**, possibly *Helleborus viridis* native/Europe; **Hellebor white/Hellebor alb.** False hellebore/White hellebore *Veratrum album*, Europe/N Africa/Siberia, 1548.

Helleborine *Epipactis helleborine* spp., native/Europe.

Hemerocallis Day Lily *Hemerocallis fulva*, origin uncertain, 1576; **Yellow Hemerocallis** *Hemerocallis lilioasphodelus* (syn: *H. flava*) ?China, 1570.

Hemloc Hemlock/Mother Die *Conium maculatum*, native/Europe, *see also* **Cicuta**.

Hemp Devil's flower/Cannabis *Cannabis sativa* subsp. *indica/C sativa* subsp. *sativa*, India, 14th cent.

Hemp Agrimony *See* **Eupatorium**.

Hen-bane/Hyoscyamus Henbane *Hyoscyamus niger*, native/Europe.

Hepatica/single/double Liverwort probably varieties of *Hepatica nobilis* (syn: *H triloba*) native/N temperate zone, *see also* **Anemones**.

Herbe-paris Herb-paris/Devil-in-a-bush *Paris quadrifolia*, native/Europe.

Hercules-All-heale Self-heal/Allheal/London bottles *Prunella vulgaris*, Europe/Asia/N America.

Hermodactyls Snake's head *Hermodactylus tuberosus*, Middle East, pre-1600.

Hesperis/Dame-violet/Viola Matronalis Dame's violet/Sweet rocket *Hesperis matronalis*, naturalized/S Europe/Siberia W & C Asia, *c.*1200.

Hieracium/Hauk weed/Philosella/Pilosella Possibly Creeping Hawkweed/Mouse-ear *Hieracium pilosella*, native/Europe/Asia; **Hieraciun minus Alpesire**, possibly Alpine hawkweed *Hieracium alpinum*, native/Europe.

Holly probably all varieties of *Ilex aquifolium*, native/Europe; **Holly gilded white; Holly gilded yellow; Holly Hirsustus.**

Holy gilded white *See* **Holly.**

Holy gilded yellow *See* **Holly.**

Holy Hirsustus *See* **Holly.**

Holy-hock/Holy-hocks Holly-hock *Alcea rosea* (syn: *Althaea rosea*), W Asia, *c*.1260; **Marsh-mallow** *Alcea officinalis* (syn: *Althaea officinalis*), native/ Europe; *see also* **Mallow.**

Homers Moly *See* **Garlic.**

Honey-suckles/Hony-suckles; Caprifol: Honisuckle vulgar Honeysuckle/ Woodbine *Lonicera periclymenum*, native/Europe/N Africa; **Trumpet Honeysuckle** *Caprifolium Americanum*, E & S America, 1656; **White-hony-suckle**, probably a variety of *Lonicera periclymenum*; **Yellow hony-suckle**, probably a variety of *Lonicera periclymenum*.

Hops *Humulus lupulus*, native/Europe; always twines clockwise.

Hore-hound/Marrubum Probably Common/White horehound *Marrubium vulgare*, native (rare)/Europe.

Horminum Creticum Possibly Annual clary *Salvia viridis* (syn: *S horminum*), Mediterranean, 1596, *see also* **Clary.**

Horn-beame Common Hornbeam *Carpinus betulus*, native/Europe/Asia Minor.

Horse-Chessnut *Aesculus hippocastanum* Albania/N Greece/Macedonia *c*.1616.

Horse-Mint *See* **Mint.**

Horse-Radish/Horse-reddish *See* **Cochlearia.**

Horse-taile Horsetail *Equisetum* spp., native/Europe.

Hounds Tongue/Hounds-tongue *Cynoglossum officinale*, native (rare)/Europe/ naturalized N America.

House-Leeke House-leek *Sempervivum tectorum*, Europe, *c*.1100.

Humble plant *Mimosa pudica*, tropical America, 1637; **Sensitive plant** *Mimosa sensitiva*, tropical America, 1648.

Hyacinth stellatus *See* **Hyacinthus.**

Hyacinth Tuberose *See* **Hyacinthus.**

Hyacinth Zeboin *See* **Hyacinthus.**

Hyacinthus/Jacinth/Jacynths; Autumnal Hyacinth Probably a form of *Hyacinthus orientalis*, SW Asia widely naturalized Mediterranean, 16th cent.; **Brumal-Hyacinth** Winter hyacinth, probably a form of *Hyacinthus orientalis*, *see* above; **Hyacinthus stellatus** *Scilla bifolia*, Mediterranean, 1629; **Hyacinth Tuberose/Indian Tuberous Jacynth**/possibly **Narcissus Tuberosus** Tuberose *Polianthes tuberosa*, Mexico, 1629; **Hyacinth Zeboin**, a possible corruption of *Zumbul*, the Turkish name for the Great Roman hyacinth *H. orientalis* var. *alba*, Mediterranean, 1629; **Jacynth starry**, probably Cuban lily *Scilla peruviana*, Mediterranean, 1607; **Oriental-Jacinth** Hyacinthus *orientalis*, Mediterranean, pre-17th cent.; **Strip'ed Jacynth.**

Hyoscyamus *See* **Henbane.**

Hypericon St John's-wort *Hypericum* spp., native/Europe; **Hypericum frutex** *Spiraea hypercifolia*, SE Europe/Siberia/N Asia, 1633.

Hypericum frutex *See* **Hypericon.**

Hyssop *Hyssopus officinalis*, S Europe; long cultivated; used as a strewing herb for the house.

Ilex Holm/Holly Oak *Quercus ilex*, Mediterranean, *c.*1500.

Ilix Scarlet Oake *See* **Cork tree.**

Indian Capsicum *See* **Capsicum Indicum.**

Indian fig *See* **Opuntia.**

Indian Lily/Indian Lily Narcissus Possibly *Amaryllis belladonna,*S Africa, prior to Evelyn earliest date of introduction 1712, or *Haemanthus coccineus*, S Africa, 1629; HANMER: *'the Sphaericall Indian Narcissus, called also the great Indian Moly, and the Indian Ornithogalum is of great beauty and is rare in England, though it hath beene in France and Italy these twenty yeares.'* The word 'narcissus' was frequently used as a name for an unknown lily until the early 18th cent.

Indian Phaseolus/Indian Phaseoli /Ind Phaseoli *See* **Beane.**

Indian Pinks *See* **Pinks.**

Indian Tuberose/Indian Tuberous Jacynth *See* **Hyacinthus.**

Intybs *See* **Succory.**

Iris: Chame-iris/Chame-iris of all colours *Iris lutescens* (syn: *I chamaeiris*), S Europe, *c.*1596; **Early Bulbous Iris** English iris *Iris latifolia* (syn: *I xiphioides*), N Spain/Pyrenees, 1570; **Florence-Iris** probably Orris Root/Fleur de lis *Iris germanica* 'Florentina', Mediterranean, pre-1000; **Iris-Chalcedon/chalcaedon** Mourning iris *Iris susiana*, probably Lebanon, 1573, **Suza-Iris**, Chalcedon was named for the ancient city in Asia Minor (now Turkey) where the iris is indigenous; **Iris Clusii**, possibly *Iris planifolia* (syn: *I alata*), N Spain, 1596; **Persian Iris** *Iris persica*, S & SE Turkey/NE Syria/NE Iraq, *c.*1629; **Suza-Iris** Mourning iris *Iris susiana*, probably Lebanon, 1573, *see* above.

Iris-Chalcedon: Tuberose Iris.

Iron-colour'd Fox-gloves *See* **Digitalis.**

Iron-wort *See* **Camomile.**

Jacea *See* **Centaurea.**

Jacinth *See* **Hyacinthus.**

Jack-by-the-Hedge Garlic mustard *Alliaria petiolata*, native/Europe.

Jacobœa Marina *See* **Cineraria.**

Jacynth starry *See* Hyacinthus.

Jacynths *See* Hyacinthus.

Japon Lillie *See* Garnzey Lillie.

Jasmine: Spanish/Span. Jasmine *Jasminium grandiflorum*, subtropical Himalayas, 1629; **Yellow Indian Jasmine** Yellow jasmine *Jasminum humile*, Afghanistan/Himalayas, 1634; **Yellow Virginian Jasmine**, could be False Jasmine *Gelsemium sempervirens, see* below. (*Gelsemium* is the Italian word for Jasmine.)

Jasminum Americanum flo: luteo possibly False Jasmine *Gelsemium sempervirens*, SE America, 1640, or Trumpet climber *Campsis radicans*, SE America, 1640.

Jonquil/Junquills /Double Jonquil/Junquills great Chalic'd *See* Narcissus.

Jucca *See* Yucca.

Juniperus/Giniper Common juniper *Juniperus communis*, native/N hemisphere; **Sabina /Sabine baccifera** Juniper/Savin *Juniperus sabina*, C & S Europe/ China/N America, *c.*1200.

Junquills/Junquilles *See* Narcissus.

Keri/Keris Wallflower *Erysimum cheiri* (syn: *Cheiranthus cheiri*), S Europe, 1000.

Knap-weede *See* Centaurea.

Laburnum majus Golden chain *Laburnum anagyroides*, S Europe, 1560; **Laburnum Minus** Scotch laburnum *Laburnum alpinum*, S Europe, pre-1596.

Ladies Slipper Lady's slipper orchid *Cyprepedium calceolus*, native/Europe/ N Asia.

Lady-Smock Lady's-smock/Cukooflower *Cardamine pratensis*, native/ Europe/N Asia/N America.

Lady Thistle Lady's/Milk Thistle *Silybum marianum*, S Europe/N Africa/ SW Asia; Evelyn described the juice as 'a proper diet for wetnurses'. *See also* Thistle.

Lambs lettuce *See* Lettuce.

Langue de Boeuf Ox-tongue/Bugloss *Anchusa arvensis*, native/Europe/W Asia, introduced into N America.

Lapatha Personata *See* Burdoch.

Larch *See* Larix.

Large-sided Cabages *See* Cabbage.

Larix/Larinx Common/European Larch *Larix decidua*, Alps/Carpathian Mts., introduced TRADESCANT, 1620.

Larks-heel/Larks-heels/Larks-heel early/Larks heels of all colours/Larks-spurr Larkspur *Consolida ajacis* (syn: *Delphinium consolida)*, Mediterranean, 1573.

Larks-spurr *See* **Larks-heel.**

Laserpitium *See* **Silphium.**

Laurel: Alexandrian laurel *See* **Oleander; Laurus cerasus/Cherry-bay/Chery-bay** Common/Cherry laurel *Prunus laurocerasus*, E Europe/Asia Minor, 1576.

Laurus: Laurus common bay tree Sweet bay tree *Laurus nobilis*, S Europe, 1562; **Laurus verus Græcorum** possibly *Laurus lusitanica*, S Europe, 1648.

Laurustinus the strip'd Laurell/Laurus-tinus *Viburnum tinus* spp., possibly 'Variegatum', Mediterranean region/SE Europe, late 16th cent.; **Guelder rose** *Viburnum opulus*, native/N Europe.

Lavender/Lavender *Lavandula angustifolia* (syn: *L. spica)*, Mediterranean, 13th cent., *L dentata*, W Mediterranean/Arabian peninsula/Atlantic islands, *c*.1597; **Lavender-Cotton** *Santolina chamæcyparissus*, S Europe, *c*.1373; **Lavendula Multif. Clus** probably *L. multifida*, W Mediterranean/S Portugal, *c*.16th cent.; **Alb. Lavendula Multif** probably a white form of *Lavandula multifida* W Mediterranean/S Portugal, *c*.16th cent.; **Stoecas/Stoechas** French Lavender *Lavandula stoechas*, SW Europe, 1550.

Leeks/Leekes *Allium porrum*, S Europe/W Asia, pre-1000.

Lemon/Lemmons/limons *Citrus limon*, tropical Asia, 1648.

Lentiscus/Lentises Mastic tree *Pistacia lentiscus*, Morocco/Canary Is./Portugal/S Europe to Greece, 1632; **Terebinthus/Turpentine-tree** *Pistacia terebinthus*, Mediterranean, 1656; the sap is a resinous liquid used in medicine.

Lettuce *Lactuca sativa*, Europe, 1562 but probably much earlier. All eating lettuces are derived from two types: the **Cabbage** varieties, with soft leaves and a globular shape, and the **Cos** varieties, which have crisper, more upright leaves. They are believed to have originated from the Greek archipelago. Botanically all salad lettuces derive from *Lactuca scariola*, a native of S Europe, which has spread throughout the north; **Agnine,** *see* **Lambs Lettuce; Alphange of Montpelier; Ambervelleres; Arabic lettuce,** named by LUCAS *c*.1677; **Belgrade Lettuce or Crumpen Lettuce; Cabbage Lettuce,** by LUCAS *c*.1677 and *see* above; **Capuchin** probably the Italian 'capucina', a solid, crunchy lettuce, which when seasoned and oiled could be grilled and eaten sprinkled with orange juice; **Coss/Cosse Lettuce** Cos lettuce, *see* above; **Curl'd-Lettuce** named by LUCAS *c*.1677; **French Minion; Genoa Lettuce,** possibly *Lactuca perennis*, S Europe, 1596; **Imperial Lettuce; Lambs Lettuce/Agnine** Lambs lettuce/Corn salad *Valerianella locusta*, native/

Europe; **Lobbs/Lop Lettuce,** *see* above; **Oak-leaf Lettuce; Passion Lettuce; Roman Lettuce,** *see* above; **Silesian Lettuce,** *see* above.

Leucoium/Lucoium/Leuconium bulbosum/Leucoium bulbosum serotinum the Greek name *Leuk n i n* means white violet, early botanists prior to Linnaeus used this name for what they called Snowflakes *Leucojum* spp., native (S England)/S Europe, 16th cent., as well as Stock gillyflowers now Stocks *Matthiola incana,* coast of S & W Europe/C & SW Asia, *c.*1250; *see also* **Bulbous violet.**

Leuconium bulbosum *See* **Leucoium.**

Levantine-Narcissus *See* **Narcissus.**

Levantine tufted Narcissus *See* **Narcissus.**

Licoris Licorice *Glycyrrhiza glabra,* Mediterranean to SW Asia, introduced into Europe including Britain, 1562.

Lignum vitæ *See* **Arbor Thyrea.**

Ligustrum privet Common Privet *Ligustrum vulgare,* native/Europe.

Lilac /Syringa Common lilac *Syringa vulgaris,* Eastern Europe/Balkans 16th cent.; **Lilac flo alb /Syringa flo white,** probably white Persian lilac *Syringa persica* var. *alba,* Iran to China, 16th cent.; **Persian Jasmine** Persian lilac *Syringa persica,* Iran to China, 1640; **Syringa flo: purple** *Syringa vulgaris,* Eastern Europe/Balkans, 16th cent.

Lilium Convallium *See* **Lilly-Convalle.**

Lillies: Indian lilly probably *Lilium canadense,* NE America, 1620; **Martagon** Turk's cap lily *L martagon* Europe/Asia, 1596: (1) **White** *L martagon* var. *album,* Europe/Asia, pre-17th cent.; (2) **Red,** probably Scarlet Turk's cap lily *L chalcedonicum,* Palestine, *c.*1600; (3) **Virginian Martagon,** possibly *L superbum,* E America, *c.*1665; **Mountain Lilly white; Red,** probably *L bulbiferum,* E & C Europe, *c.*1656, TRADESCANT; **White** Madonna lily *L candidum,* Turkey/Asia Minor, pre-1000; **Persian Lillies/Lilly,** *see* **Fritillaria; Yellow Lillies** *L pyrenaicum,* Pyrenees, 1596.

Lilly-Convalle/Lilium Convallium Lilly-of-the-valley *Convallaria majalis,* Europe/NE Asia, introduced into N America.

Lime Common lime *Tilia* × *europaea* (syn: *T vulgaris*) Europe, probably pre-17th cent., most commonly used in the planting of lime avenues; **Tilia** probably Small-leaved lime *Tilia cordata,* native/Europe or as above.

Lime-tree *Citrus aurantifolia,* tropical Asia, 1648.

Limonium Sea lavender, probably *Limonium bellidifolium* (syn: *L reticulata/Statice bellidifolium*) coastal native/Mediterranean to the Black Sea; **Limonium elegans,** possibly *Limonium sinuatum,* Mediterranean, 1629.

Limons *See* **Lemon.**

Linaria Cretica Probably *Linaria purpurea*, naturalized/S Europe, 1648; **Toadflax** Common toadflax *Linaria vulgaris*, native/Europe/W Asia, introduced into N America and Australasia.

Little Blew-grape *See* **Grape**.

Liverwort *See* **Hepatica**.

Lobels Catchfly Sweet William catchfly *Silene armeria*, long naturalized in Britain/Europe.

Long-sided cabbage *See* **Cabbage**.

Lop Lettuce *See* **Lettuce**.

Lotus—several sorts/Tre-foile probably Bird's-foot-trefoil *Lotus corniculatus*, native/Europe/Asia, but could be Clover *Trifolium* spp., native/Europe.

Lotus hersutus Creticus possibly Date plum, *Diospyros lotus* China/Japan/W Asia/Himalaya, 1597.

Lovage Lovage *Ligusticum scoticum*, native/N Europe/NE America.

Lucoium *See* **Leucomium**.

Lunaria Honesty *L annua*, Sweden/Norway, 1595; **Rub. Lunatus**, probably Honesty *Lunaria annua* 'Atrococcinea', Sweden/Norway, 1595.

Lupines Probably includes the annual *Lupinus hirsutus*, S Europe, pre-1648, and the herbaceous *L perennis*, NE America, 1658.

Lychnis: Campion/Rose-Campion *Lychnis coronaria* (syn: *Agrostemma coronaria*), S Europe, 1350; **Lychnis Constant single & double**, probably what was known as 'Campion of Constantinople' *Lychnis chalcedonica*, E & European Russia, 1593; **Lychnis double white/Lychnis white & double**, probably *Lychnis chalcedonica*, E & European Russia, 1593; **Lychnis var. generum** probably *Lychnis chalcedonica*, E & European Russia, 1593; **Lychnis Chalcedon** *Lychnis chalcedonica*, E & European Russia, 1593.

Lysimachia siliquosa glabra minor Probably Codlins & cream *Epilobium hirsutum*, native/Europe. Both BOBART 1648, and TRADESCANT 1656 give the vernacular name of 'smooth codle' or 'codded'.

Macadonian Persley *See* **Sellery**.

Madder Common Madder *Rubia tinctorum*, C Europe/SW Asia, pre-1656.

Majoran/Origanon Common or wild Marjoram/Oregano *Origanum vulgare*, native/Europe/C & N Asia; **Pot-Marjoran** Winter/Pot marjoram *Origanum onites*, S Europe, pre-1000, also noted as reintroduction from Sicily, 1759; **Sweet/Sweete Majoran/Summer Sweet Marjoran** Sweet/Knotted marjoram *Origanum majorana*, Mediterranean, *c*.1200.

Mallow Various members of the Malvacæ family including the Common mallow *Malva sylvestris*, native/Europe, Marsh mallow *Althaea officinalis*, native/N Europe, and the Hollyhock/Holly-hock *Alcea rosea* (syn: *Althaea rosea*), W Asia, *c*.1260; *see also* **Holly-hock.**

Malva arborescens Probably Tree mallow *Lavatera arborea*, W Europe/ Mediterranean, *c*.16th cent.

Mandrake Devil's apples/Mandrake *Mandragora officinarum* and/or *Mandragora autumnalis*, both S Europe, 1548.

Marococ/Maracoc/Marcoc or Passion flowre/Flos Passionis Passion flower *Passiflora cærulea* C & W S America, 1699, or May Pops *Passiflora incarnata*, S America, 1568; they gained the suitably exotic name of Marcoc or Maracocs in England, having been introduced via Spain into Europe.

Marrow The three references could all refer either to the marrowbone, or to *Cucurbita* genus. Courgette or zucchini (names interchangeable), is the immature Vegetable marrow, which arrived in Italy from America within fifty years of Columbus's first voyage. It seems the word 'marrow', meaning the vegetable, was not used until the 18th cent.

Marrubum *See* **Hore-hound.**

Marsh-Mallows *See* **Holy-hock.**

Martagon *See* **Lillies.**

Marum Mastic-thyme *See* **Germander; Marum Syriacum/Syrac,** *see* **Germander; Marums: Water Anemonies,** *see* **Germander.**

Master-wort Masterwort *Peucedanum ostruthium*, S Europe, pre-1648.

Marvell of Peru/Mirabile Peruian Marvel of Peru *Mirabilis jalapa*, tropical S America, 1568.

Marygold/Mary-gold Marigold/Pot marigold *Calendula officinalis*, S Europe/ N Africa/W Asia, pre-1000, reintroduced 1100 and 1573; **Double Marigolds** variety of *Calendula officinalis*, *see* above.

Matricaria double flo. *See* **Costmary.**

Maudlin Sweet Nancy *Achillea ageratum*, Greece, pre-1648.

Meadow saffron *See* **Saffron.**

Medica *See* **Hedg-hogs.**

Medlar *Mespilus germanica*, naturalized (rare)/Europe/Asia, pre-1000; **Medlars without stones** perhaps the Great Medlar Tree of Naples, several of which were purchased by John Tradescant (sen.) from the Delft Nursery in 1611.

Melilote Melilot, could be one of the five species of *Melilotus*, all native and/or European.

Melissa *See* **Balme.**

Melon/Mellon Probably Cantaloupe melon *Cucumis melo*, Asia, 1570.

Mercurie Dog's mercury *Mercurialis perennis*, native/Europe; the same name,

Mercury, was earlier applied to Good King Henry *Chenopodium bonus-henricus*, native/Europe.

Mercury *See* **Blite.**

Mezerion/Mezereon Daphne *Daphne mezereum*, doubtful native/Europe/Siberia; **Cneorum Matthioli** White rockrose *Daphne cneorum*, S Europe, 1629; **Dutch mezereon** *Daphne mezereum*, presumably either purchased or bred in Holland.

Milky-Thistle *See* **Thistle.**

Millefolium Yarrow *Achillea millefolium*, native/Europe; **Millefolium luteum/yellow/Yellow Millefol.** probably *Achillea tomentosa* Europe/N Asia, pre-1648; **Millefolium double,** possibly Sneezewort *Achillea ptarmica*, native/Europe, *see* below; **Millefolium red**; **Millefolium white,** possibly Sneezewort *Achillea ptarmica*, *see* above.

Minor Pimpinella *See* **Burnet.**

Mint/Minths Probably Spearmint *Mentha spicata* native/Europe; **Horse-Mint** *Mentha longifolia/M aquatica*, native/Europe; **Pene-royall/Peneroyal/Penyroyal** Pennyroyal *Mentha pulegium*, naturalized (now rare)/C & S Europe/N Africa; **Pulegium** Pennyroyal *Mentha pulegium*, naturalized (now rare)/C & S Europe/N Africa.

Mirabile Peruian *See* **Marvell of Peru.**

Moly *See* **Garlic.**

Moly Monspeliens *See* **Garlic.**

Monks-hood *See* **Aconite.**

Monthly Rose *See* **Rose.**

Motherwort *Leonurus cardiaca*, native/Europe.

Mountain Lillies white *See* **Lillies.**

Mug-wort *See* **Abrotanum.**

Mulberries Black mulberry *Morus nigra*, C Asia, *c.*1200, but possibly a Roman introduction; **White Mulberie** White mulberry *Morus alba*, China, 1596, the tree silkworms feed upon.

Mullein *See* **Blattaria.**

Muscandine-grape *See* **Grape.**

Muscaris sp. *Muscari*, possibly Grape hyacinth *M botryoides*, Europe, 1596, and/or *Muscari comosum*, Europe, 1596; **Grape flowers** Grape hyacinth *Muscari botryoides*, Europe, 1596; **Muscara revers'd/Muscaria**; **Musk-grape-flower** Musk hyacinth *Muscari moschatum*, Asia Minor, 1565.

Muscipula (Latin for mousetrap) Red catchfly *Viscaria vulgaris* (syn: *Lychnis viscaria*), native Europe/Siberia/Japan.

Musk Rose/Musk-rose *See* **Rose.**

Musk violet *See* Violets.

Musk-Grape-flower *See* Muscaris.

Mustard *See* Cabbage.

Myrrh/Myrrhis/Spanish Myrrh Sweet Cicely *Myrrhis odorata*, naturalized/ S Europe; **Myrrhis Sylvestris**, probably Cow parsley *Anthriscus sylvestris*, native/Europe.

Myrtle-berries *See* Myrtus.

Myrtus Common Myrtle *Myrtus communis*, S Europe/W Asia, 1597; these are all varieties of the Common Myrtle: **Myrtus angustifol: non florens, Myrtus angusti folius florens, Myrtus broad-leav'd of Portugal, Myrtus flo: amplo florens, Myrtus Orange-leav'd, Myrtus tip'd with white, Myrtus upright birds-nest.**

Narcissus/Jonquil/Junquills: Aleppo Narciss. possibly another name for **Levantine-Narcissus**, *see* below; **Asiatic double/singles Narcissus of Japan**, *see* **Garnsey Lilly** and below; **Jonquil/Junquills** Wild jonquil/Queen Anne's Jonquil *Narcissus jonquilla*, Iberian Peninsula, 1596; **Double Jonquil,** probably Queen Anne's Jonquil *N jonquilla*, *see* above; **Junquills great Chalic'd,** possibly *Narcissus incomparabilis*, Spain/SW France/Tyrol, *c.*1560 (PARKINSON 'doth very well resemble the chalice'); **Levantine-Narcissus....../...Levantine tufted Narcissus,** possibly a form of *Narcissus tazetta*, Mediterranean region, *c.*17th cent. but probably earlier; **Narcissus common; Narcissus double; Narciss. pomum aureum,** possibly *Narcissus aureus*, S France, pre-1600; **Narciss pomum amoris; Narciss pomum Spinosum Ind; Narcissus English double,** possibly a form of the native Lent lily *Narcissus pseudonarcisus*; **Narcissus of Constantinople** *Narcissus tazetta*, Mediterranean, 1656, but probably earlier. HANMER: 'in Latin usually Bizantinus the flowers are all White commonly, but some have the middle a little yellow or purple. They are very sweet.'

Narcissus of Japan/Garnsey-Lilly *See* **Garnsey Lilly**; **Narcissus single; Narcissus Tuberosus,** *see* **Hyacinthus**; **Narcissus tufted; Narcissus white,** possibly Poet's narcissus *Narcissus poeticus*, naturalized in Britain/ Mediterranean, pre-16th cent.; **Persian autumnal Narcissus,** possibly *Narcissus serotinus*, Mediterranean, 1629; **Sea-Narcissus,** *see* **Pancration**; **Spanish Trumpets,** probably 'Great Spanish daffodill' grown by Gerard, *Narcissus hispanicus*, S France/Spain, 1576; **Sphaerical Narciss.** HANMER: 'The Sphaericall Indian Narcissus called also the great Indian Moly, and the Indian Ornithogalum', probably *Brunsvigia gigantea*, S Africa, 1752, related to Amaryllis; *see also* **Asphodil** and **Introduction** *see* p. xviii.

Nasturtium/Nasturtia Watercress *Rorippa · nasturtium-aquticum*, native/ Europe/W Asia, introduced into N America.

Nasturtium Indicum/Nasturtum Ind/Nasturt. Ind. Millefolium *Tropaeolum minus*, Peru, 1585; this was the first nasturtium to be described and called *Nasturtium indicum* by Dodoens in 1574; there is a dried specimen (*c.*1585) in the herbarium of Genoa Botanic Garden. The two plants listed are probably crossings or variations of *Tropaeolum* spp. **Nastur. Hybernicum Nasturt. Persicum.**

Navets *See* **Cabbage.**

Nectarine: Cluster; Brigniole round; Brignon violet/Brignon violet-nect; El-ruge *Prunus persica* var. *necatrina* 'Elruge'; GURLE, prior to 1661, had pro-duced an improved hardy nectarine that he called by his own name spelt backwards, 'elrug', later spelt with an added 'e'; the nectarine was noted by HANMER as 'Elrug or Gurle's Nectoran (which comes from a stone and is rare yet)'; the architect and landscape gardener Batty Langley reported in 1727 that the fruit ripened on 20 July (Beeton: *Garden Management*, *c.*1860); **Little Green; Muroy/Murry** HANMER: Murrey Nectoran/Greene Nec-toran. **Murry French; longish; round; Red-Roman** HANMER: Red Roman Nectoran; TRADESCANT: Roman red Nectorine; **Tawny** HANMER: Tawney Nectoran, Hunt's Tawny (Beeton: *Garden Management c.*1860); **Violet hative** 'Violette Hative' (Beeton: *Garden Management c.*1860); **Yellow** TRADESCANT: Little yellow Nectorine.

Nep *See* **Catmint.**

Nettles *Urtica dioica*, native/Europe.

Nigella Love in the mist *Nigella damascena*, Mediterranean area, 1570; **Nigella Romana** Fennel flower *Nigella sativa*, N Africa/Asia Minor, 1548.

Night-shade Probably Deadly nightshade *Solanum nigrum*, native/Europe; **Amomum plinii** Winter/Jerusalem cherry *Solanum pseudocapsicum*, S America, 1596; **Dulcamara** Bittersweet/Woody nightshade *Solanum dulcamara*, native/Europe/N Africa/Asia; **Shrub Night-shade**, possibly Bittersweet/Felonwood/Woody nightshade *Solanum dulcamara*, native/ Europe/Asia/N Africa.

Noli-me-tangere *See* **Balsame.**

Occulus christi Wild clary, vernacular names include Christ's eye/Clear eye/Eyeseed *Salvia verbenaca*, native/Europe/W Asia.

Oenanthe aquatica Fine-leaved water dropwort *Oenanthe aquatica*, native/ Europe.

Oleander red/white/Alexandrian laurel Rose bay/Common oleander *Nerium oleander*, E Mediterranean (possibly to W China), 1596.

Oleaster Oleaster *Elaeagnus angustifolia*, S Europe/W Asia, 1632.

Olive Olive *Olea europaea*, Mediterranean, 1570.

Onion *Allium cepa*, Middle East probably Roman introduction; **Cibbol** Chibol/Welsh onion *Allium fistulosum*, naturalized/Siberia; no date of introduction; *see also* **Eschalot**.

Opuntia Prickly pear, probably *Opuntia vulgaris*, NE America, 1596; **Smaller Indian fig**, probably *Opuntia ficus-indica*, tropical America ?1629.

Orange Probably the Sweet orange *Citrus sinensis*, China/Asia, *c.*1658; **Orang-seedlings** Evelyn recommended that seedlings from the hotbed gave the most aromatic flavour and were 'grateful to the stomach', and that the young leaves could be used in a salad; **Sevial orange** Seville orange *Citrus aurantium*, tropical Asia, 1599.

Orchis/Satyrion Also known as Dog/Goat/Fool-stones *Platanthera bifolia*, native/N Africa/N Asia, or *Platanthera chlorantha*, native/N Asia.

Oriental-Jacinth *See* **Hyacinthus**.

Oriental Platanus *See* **Platanus Oriental**.

Origanon *See* **Majoran**.

Ornithogallum/Ornithogalons Probably Drooping Star of Bethlehem *Ornithogalum nutans*, S Europe, naturalized in Britain; Evelyn lists this plant in *Kalendarium* as flowering during March: *O nutans* flowers in April, and allowing for the alteration from the Julian to the Gregorian calendar this appears to be the most likely variety; **Ornithogalum max: alba:/ Ornithogal:max: alb** *Ornithogalum latifolium*, Taurus Mts., 1629; **Ornithogalon Arab.** *Ornithogalum arabicum*, Mediterranean, 1629.

Orpin *See* **Sedum**.

Orrach Common orache *Atriplex patula*, native/Europe.

Oxyacanthus Hawthorn *Crataegus oxyacantha*, native/Europe; **White thorn** Hawthorn/Hedge-row thorn *Crataegus monogyna*, native/Europe.

Oxylapathum possibly *Oxypetalum*, from Gr. *xys*, sharp, *petalum*, in botanical L. a petal; now *Tweedia*, a species from a genus of about fifty, all native to Brazil, Mexico, and the W Indies.

Paeonies/Peonie First species known *Paeonia mascula*, Europe, pre-1000, *Paeonia officinalis*, France to Albania, 1548, *Paeonia peregrina*, Balkans, 1629.

Paliurus Christ's/Jerusalem thorn *Paliurus spina-christi*, C Europe, 1597.

Palma-Christi Castor-oil plant *Ricinus communis*, tropical Africa, 1590.

Palustral Apium *See* **Sellery**.

Pancration/Sea-Narcissus Sea daffodil *Pancratium maritimum* (syn: *P il-lyricum*), coastal SW Europe, 1615; HANMER: 'the Sea Daffodill, one of which hath White Flowers and is sometimes called in Latine Hemerocallis Valentina Clusy, and the other hath Red Flowers and is called Pancratium Maius Hispanicum.'

Pansies/Common pansies/Garden Pansy Pansy/Heartsease *Viola* sp.

Papaver Spinociss. Possibly *Papaver spicatum*, Asia Minor, *c.*17th cent.; **Double poppies red**, probably Corn poppy *Papaver rhoeas*, wide distribution over temperate Old World, early introduction; **Green Poppy; Horn'd Poppy**, possibly Red Horned-poppy *Glaucium corniculatum*, naturalized (rare)/ S Europe/SW Asia; no date of entry; **Papaver Corniculatum Luteum**, probably Yellow horned-poppy *Glaucium flavum*, Europe/Canary Is./ N Africa/W Asia; no date of entry; **Popies**, probably the Opium poppy *Papaver somniferum*, origin unknown, possible Roman introduction, thought to be the oldest species in cultivation; **Poppy-white/White Popy** possibly the white-flowered form of *Papaver somniferum*, for the making of 'poppy tea' to alleviate ague, *see* above.

Parietaria Lutea Pellitory possibly *Parietaria officinalis*, native/N Europe; **Pellitarie** Pellitory-of-the-wall *Parietaria judaica*, native/W & S Europe/N Africa, introduced into N America.

Parsley/Parsly/Persley *Petroselinum crispum* (syn: *P sativum, Carum petroselinum*), C & S Europe, early introduction.

Parsley-apple *See* **Apple.**

Parsley grape *See* **Grape.**

Parsneps/Parsnips Parsnip *Pastinaca sativa*, naturalized/probably E Mediterranean.

Passion flowre *See* **Marcoc.**

Peach *Prunus persica*, Western China/Tibetan highlands, established by 4th cent. BC in southern Europe, grown in England probably from Roman times; its Anglo-Saxon name is Perseoc-treou; **Admirable/Admirable late** Available GURLE, 1674; Late Admirable & Walberton Admirable (Beeton: *Garden Management c.*1860); **Alberge, sr:** *H: Capel, Sheens* probably received from Sir William Temple's garden at Sheen, Surrey. See also *Directions*, note to p. 87 *W. Temple*; **Alberge, yr** *Small yellow*; **Almond Violet; Belle Chervreuse; Bignon; Bourdin; Brignon; Brignon Musquè; Brignon violet-nect,** *see* **Nectarine; Bourdeaux Peach; Chevreuse; Crown Peach; Faire Chevreuse or Goate peach; Grand Carnation** HANMER/TRADES-CANT: Carnation; **Isabella; Lavar La Belle-Chevrous/Chevreuse; Le Bonne Clerke; Le Chancelière; Magdalene/Magdalen white/red,** available GURLE,

1674; **Malacoton; Man; Maudlin white/red; Mignon; Montaban; Minion; Morello,** available GURLE, 1674; **Musk/Musque** HANMER: Muske; **Musque Violet; Narbonne; Newington,** known by John Rea (d. 1681), author of *Flora, Ceres and Pomona,* who wrote that 'the Newington an old peach, well known, the fruit is fair, of a greenish white colour, and red on the side next the sun'; it was still grown in Victorian times as 'Old Newington'; HANMER: Newingtons 2 sorts, TRADESCANT: Newington; **Nivelle de Velvet; Nutmeg white/brown** HANMER: White Nutmeg/Red Nutmegg, TRADESCANT: Nutmeg Peach; **Orleans** HANMER, available GURLE 1674; **Pavie Magdalene:** (1) **Pavies/hard Peaches** TRADESCANT: Peach Pavi Jaune; (2) **Newington,** *see* above; (3) **Nutmeg brown;** (4) **Nutmeg white;** (5) **Persian,** known by the Romans as the Persian apple, *see* below; (6) **Violet Musque.**

Peach Des pot/Peach de peau HANMER: Peach de Pau; **Persian,** known by the Romans as the Persian apple, *see* above; **Persique; Portugal** HANMER: Portugall; **Quince; Rambouillet/Rambboullet/Rambullion** HANMER: Rambouillon Peach; **Roman** TRADESCANT; **Royall** HANMER; **Savoy Malacotan/Savoy Malacoten** HANMER: Royall; **Sion/Syon-peach; Vergoleuse; Violet; Violet Musqe/Muscat.**

Pear *Pyrus communis,* Spain east to China, probably grown here since Roman times; **Amidot/Amadot; Ambret; Ambrosia; Arundel/Arundell pear** TRADESCANT: Arrundell Peare; **Balsam-pear; Bell-pear,** possibly Belle magnifique/Beurre Diel/Beurré Hardy.

Bergamot ordinary TRADESCANT: Summer Burgamot, HANMER: Somer Bergamot, Gansel's Bergamot—Bonne Rouge, Bergamotte d'Hiver or Poire d'Espéren: (1) **Bergamot de Busy** HANMER: Bergamot de Bugi; (2) **Gascogne-Bergamot;** (3) **Hamdens Bergamot** *Bergamotte d'Heimberg;* (4) **Long Beramot;** (5) **Orange Bergamot** TRADESCANT: Orenge Burgamott; (6) **Winter-Bergamot** HANMER: Wynter Bergomots, TRADESCANT: Winter Burgamot.

Beurie du Roy HANMER: Beurré de Roy; **Bezy d'Hery/Bezy-d'Herie,** Evelyn writes of this fruit in 'Pomona' the cider-making appendix to *Sylva* that this pear 'was brought into the best Orchards of France from a Forest in Bretainy' (Brittany was independent of France until 1532); **Bingspear/Bing-peare; Bishops-pear/Bishop peare** HANMER: Bishops Peare/ ?Bishops Fencer TRADESCANT; **Black Worcester** HANMER: Black peare of Worcester, possibly of Roman origins; also known as Parkinson's Warden/Pound Pear/Warden (information BERNWODE); **Black-pear of Worcester Surrein** HANMER; **Blanquet; Bluster pear.**

Bon Chrestien/Bonne Chrestienne sans pepin: (1) **Bon- Chrestien**

Summer/Summer Bon Chrestien/Bonne-Chrestienne Summer HANMER: Somer Bon Chrestien, TRADESCANT: Summer Boon Critian; (2) **Bonne-Chrestiene-Winter peare/Winter-Bon Cretienne/Bonn-Chrestien Winter/Bonne Chrestienne winter/Bon-chrestien of winter/Winter-Bon-crestien/Bonne-Chretienne Winter Peare/Later Bon-Chrestien** Williams Bon Chretien (syn: Bartlett) 1770.

Boudin Musque; Brute bonne/Brule (v. bonne); Brunswick-pear; Bucree/Bueree HANMER: Beurre pears; **Burnt-Cat; Calliot Rosat/Callio; Cassolet/Cassolett; Catherine red/Red Catherine; Caw-pear/Caw-peare; Chasseraque; Chesil peare; Chessom; Clove-pear; Codling; Cuisse Madame; Dauphin; Deadmans-pear/Dead-mans pear; Denny Pear; Diego** TRADESCANT: Dego Peare; **Double-Blosson-pear/Double Blossom Pear** TRADESCANT: Double floure Peare; **Dove-pear** HANMER: Dove Peare; **Doyoniere; Elias Rose; Emperoours/Emperour's pear; Espine d'Yver; Frangepan d'Autune; French-King; Frith pear; Golden de Xaintonge/ Golden peare of Xaintonge,** originated in the town of Saintoin, in *département* Charente-Maritime, France; **Great Kairville; Great surrein; Green-butter pear** TRADESCANT: Greene Peare; **Green Chesil-pear; Green-field/ Greenfield** HANMER: Greenfield, TRADESCANT: Greenfield Peare; **Green-Royal; Grosse Rousslet,** *see* **Roussel,** possibly 'Gross Rowslettes' available GURLE, 1674; **Ice-pear** TRADESCANT: Snow Peare? **Jargonel/Jargonell** TRADESCANT: Gergonell? **July-Flowre; Juniting,** *see* Apples, under **Juneting:** (1) **Juniting red** HANMER: Geniting peare; (2) **Juniting white.**

King Catherine; King-peare TRADESCANT; **Lady-pear; La Marquaise; Lambout-pear/Lombart; Lansac/Lansaque; Lewes pear/Lewes-peare/Lewes red warden** HANMER: Lewys Peare; in 1668 William Snatt the curate of South Malling church wrote to John Evelyn sending him grafts of the Warden, and Pear Royals from a relation of Evelyn's, Mr Newton of Southover Grange in Lewes (I am grateful to Dr Colin Brent and Lewes District Council for drawing my attention to this information); **Little Dagobert; Long-bergamot; Lord-pear/Lording-pear; Madera; Martinsec; Maudlin** possibly Madeleine/ Citron des Carmes, ripens in July; **Mel-sire/Messire/Messier Jean** HANMER: Monsieur/Mounsieur John; **Mouille bouch,** possibly 'Mulbe bush' available GURLE, 1674.

Musk/Musque HANMER: Sommer Muske: (1) **Blanquet Musque;** (2) Boudin Musque; (3) **Musq/Musque Robin;** (4) **Petit Muscat;** (5) **Winter Musque/Winter Musk** HANMER: Wynter Muske.

Norwich HANMER: Norwich peare/Norwich Warden: (1) **Winter Norwich.**

Oak-pear; **Orange** HANMER: Orenge peare.

Peare-plum black; (1) **White-peare-plum.**

Pearl; Peare-maine; Petit Blanquet; Petit Rousslet, *see* **Roussel; Petit Tupin; Petworth pear (Winter Windsor)** HANMER: Pettworth peare; **Poire** a double fleur; Poire sans pepin.

Poppering/Popering TRADESCANT: French Popering: (1) **Summer Poppering**; (2) **Winter Poppering.**

Prester; Primat; Prusia Pear; The Queen hedg-pear; Red Catherine HANMER: Katherine Peare?/Russet Katherine; **Robin,** an old Norfolk dualpurpose pear; **Rolling peare; Rosatis/Rosats.**

Roussel-pear/Rousslet: (1) **Petit Roussel;** (2) **Rousslet-champagne;** (3) **Rousslet de Rheyms.**

Rowling-pear; Russet-pear/Ruset; Saffron-pear; Sans-pepin/Poire sans pepin; Saygar; Scarlet-pear TRADESCANT; **Slipper Pear** TRADESCANT: Sliper peare; **Sovereign; Spindle-pear; Squib-pear; St Andrew; St Germain/St Germaines peare; St Laurence-pear; St Michael; Stopple-pear; Sugar pear** TRADESCANT; **Summer-pear; Swans-egg,** anciently cultivated, recorded BERNWODE 2006; **Thorn-pear** HANMER: Wynter thorne peare; **Vergolat/Vergoleuse; Vermillion; Verte longue/Vert longuer; Violet-pear; Virgin.**

Warden HANMER: Spanish/English/Norwich Warden; Wardens are cooking pears: (1) **French;** (2) **Red;** (3) **White.**

Windsor/Windsore-peare /Winter-Windsor, possibly the same as the Petworth pear, *see* above; HANMER: Wynter Wyndsor/Somer Wyndsor, TRADESCANT: Winter Winsor/Summer Winsor.

Winter Bergamot, *see* **Pears Bergamot;**

Winter-Musk, *see* **Pear Musk; Winter-Norwich,** *see* **Pear Norwich; Winter Poppering,** *see* **Pear Poppering; Winter-Windsor,** *see* **Pear Windsor.**

Pearle-Grape *See* **Grape.**

Peas/Pease/Blue Pease/Pyces Pea *Pisum sativum*, probably W Asia. Evelyn would have been growing 'garden' peas rather than 'field' peas (*Pisum minus*), of which there were by then about twenty different varieties. All garden peas derive from *P sativum hortense*. Until the 17th cent., peas were grown to be stored and used through the autumn and winter; eating green, immature peas came into fashion during Evelyn's lifetime: (1) **Rounsevals** Rounceval pea *Pisum majus*, *c*.16th cent., grown at Roncesvaulx Abbey, Navarre, France, and the Hospital of St Mary Ronceval. BOBART: 'garden Rounc'; (2) **Sugar-pease** Sugar pea *Pisum saccharatum*, first recorded about 1680, probably developed from *P sativum*.

Pellitarie *See* **Parietaria.**

Pene-royall/Peneroyal/Peny-royal/Pulegium *See* **Mint.**

Peny-wort Probably Marsh Pennywort *Hydrocotyle vulgaris*, Europe/N Africa.

Peonie *See* **Paeonia.**

Peper-wort Pepper-wort/Dittander *Lepidium latifolium*, native/Europe/ W Asia, introduced into N America.

Periploca Virgin Silk vine *Periploca graeca*, SE Europe/Asia Minor, 1597.

Persian Iris *See* **Iris.**

Persian Jasmine *See* **Lilac.**

Persian Jasmine Spanish *See* **Jasmine.**

Persian Jasmine Vulgar *See* **Jasmine.**

Persian Lilly *See* **Fritillaria.**

Persly/Persley *See* **Parsley.**

Phalangium Possibly St Bruno's lily *Paradisea liliastrum*, S Europe, 1629;

Phalangium Allobrogium St Bruno's lily *Paradisea liliastrum*, S Europe, 1629; **Phalangium Creticum**, possibly *Anthericum ramosum*, W & S Europe, 1570; **Phalangium Virginian/Virgin. Phalangium/ Virginian Phalangium** Common spider-wort *Tradescantia virginiana*, E America, 1629.

Philipendul/Philipendula Probably Meadowsweet *Filipendula ulmaria*, native/Europe/Asia, introduced into N America.

Phillyrea/Philyrea angustifolio/angusti folio Jasmine box *Phillyrea angustifolia*, S Europe/N Africa, pre-1597; **Philyrea folio serrato** *Phillyrea latifolia*, SE Europe/Asia Minor, 1597.

Philosella/Pilosella *See* **Hieracium.**

Picea probably Common/Norway spruce *Picea abies*, N & C Europe, *c.*1500.

Pig-nut *See* **Earth-nut.**

Pile-wort *See* **Ranunculus.**

Pilosella *See* **Hieracium.**

Pimpernel *See* **Burnet.**

Pinaster Maritime/Bournemouth pine *Pinus pinaster*, W Mediterranean, 16th cent.

Pine-apples /Pines/late Pine-apples Pineapple *Ananas comosus*, Brazil, 1668.

Pinks: Armerius/Deptford Pinkes Sweet William/Deptford Pink *Dianthus armeria*, native/Europe/W Asia; **Indian Pinks** Chinese/Indian Pink *Dianthus chinensis*, E Asia, prior to Evelyn earliest date of introduction 1716; **Span. Pinkes** *Dianthus plumarius*, S Europe, 1629.

Pinus probably Scots pine *Pinus sylvestris*, native/Europe/N Asia.

Pistacio *See* **Lentiscus.**

Plantanes Plantains various spp.; probably Buck's-thorn *Plantago coronopus*,

W & C Europe/W Asia/N Africa, introduced to N America/Australasia, 1586, Ribwort *Plantago lanceolata*, native/Europe, Greater plantain *Plantago major*, native/Europe/N & C Asia, several species used medicinally; **Rib-wort** *Plantago cynops*, C & S Europe, 1596.

Platanus Oriental/Zinar Oriental Plane *Platanus orientalis*, SE Europe/Asia minor, early 16th cent.; **Platanus Occidental** Buttonwood *Platanus occidentalis*, N America, 1638.

Plums *Prunus domestica*, Europe/W Asia, long domesticated; **Abricot plum** TRADESCANT: Apricocke plum; **Black-Pear-plum; Blew** Tradescant: Blew pear plum; **Bullas white & black/Bullis** Bullace plum *Prunus insititia*, native/Europe, cultivated from prehistoric times; **Catharine/Catharin; Cinnamon-plum; Cheson/Chesson/Cheston** HANMER: Wall fruit Cheston; **Damasc** HANMER: Wall fruit White Damas: (1) **Denny Damasc;** (2) **Damasque /Damasc Violet** TRADESCANT: Damaske Violet.

Damascene/Damazeene HANMER: Wall fruit Damazeene, TRADESCANT: Damascene; **Damson white & black; Date plum** TRADESCANT: (1) **White Dates.**

Great Anthony; Imperial TRADESCANT: Imperiall; **Jane Plum; June; Kings-plum** TRADESCANT; **Lady Eliz. plum; Mirabel** Mirabelle de Nancy has been known in France since the 17th cent. The plum is a variety of *Prunus insititia*, HANMER: Wall fruit Mirabelle; the small, sweet, yellow plums are still very popular during mid to late August in France; **Morocco-plum** HANMER: Wall fruit Morocco, TRADESCANT: Moroco Plum, available GURLE, 1674; **Myrobalan** TRADESCANT: Red/White Mirabolans, stones from the plum Myrobalan (and four other varieties) were discovered on the Henry VIII flag-ship the *Mary Rose* sunk in Portsmouth harbour in 1545.

Pear-plum white & black (1) **Late Pear-plum.**

Peascod/Peas-Cod/Pescod TRADESCANT: Red peascod Plum; **Per-drigon white & blew** HANMER: Wall fruit Perdigan, TRADESCANT: Perdigon plum/White Perdigon, available as 'White Pardrigone plum', GURLE, 1674; **Primordial; Prune de Lisle vert; ?Psunpl white & violet; Q. Mother** HANMER: Wall fruit Queen Mother alias Cherry Plum; **Reyne Claud** ?Reine Claude Violette, an old plum of uncertain history; **St Julian; Sheen-plum** probably bred from Sir William Temple's garden. See also *Directions*, note to p. 90 *Plums*; **Spanish** TRADESCANT; **Tawny; Turkey** HANMER: Wall fruit Turkey; **Violet perdmigon,** *see* **Perdrigon; Violet sumas.**

Violet, available GURLE, 1674: (1) **Amber;** (2) **Blew;** (3) **Red;** (4) **White.**

White Holland; White Nutmeg TRADESCANT: Nutmeg Plum; **Yellow-Pear-plum**.

Polium Montanum *See* **Germander**.

Polyanthies Polyanthus, a garden race of Primulas *Primula×variabilis* that originated as a cross between the Primrose (*Primula acaulis*) and the Cowslip (*P veris*) known as the Oxlip, and first described by John Rea in 1665; *see also* **Prim-roses**.

Polypode Polypody/Adder's fern *Polypodium vulgare*, native/N temperate regions.

Pome Granade/Pomegranads/Balaustia Pomegranate *Punica granatum*, SW Asia, *c.*1350; **Pomegranads double** form of *Punica granatum*, SW Asia, *c.*1350.

Pomum amoris/Pomum aethiop Tomato/Love apple *Lycopersicon esculentum*, Peru/Ecuador, 1597.

Popies/Poppy white/ Garden poppy *See* **Papaver**.

Porselan/Purslan/Purselan/Purslain Purslane *Portulaca oleracea*, S Europe, probably Roman introduction; **Golden Purslain**, possibly *Portulaca grandiflora* var. *aurea*, Brazil, introduction date 1827.

Portugal Ranunculus *See* **Ranunculus**.

Potatoes/Potatos *Solanum tuberosum*, Chile/Peru *c.*1586; during Evelyn's time both the potato and the Sweet potato *Ipomoea batatas* (syn: *Batatas edulis*), were known; *see also* **Night-shade**.

Pot-Majoran *See* **Majoran**.

Pracoce /Praecose Tulips *See* **Tulips**.

Pride of London London Pride *Saxifraga umbrosa*, native, widely distributed.

Prim-roses/Primroses Primrose *Primula vulgaris*, native/W & S Europe; *see also* **Polyanthies; Auricula /Auricula ursi** *Primula auricula*, alpine Europe, 1596; Auricula ursi (Bears ears) the name used during 16th and 17th cents., reflecting the shape of the leaves; **Cowslip** *Primula veris*, native/Europe to W Asia; **English double:Primrose** *Primula vulgaris*, variety.

Prime-rose Tree Evening primrose *Oenothera biennis*, NE America, *c.*1621.

Prunella Self-heal *Prunella* spp., native/Europe/N Africa.

Pulegium *See* **Mint**.

Pulsatella/Pulsatilla Pasque flower *Pulsatilla vulgaris*, native/W France to Ukraine.

Purple Volubilis *See* **Volubilis**.

Purslan/Purslain/Purselan/Purslane *See* **Porselan**.

Pyces *See* **Peas**.

Quick-beame/Whichen Mountain Ash *Sorbus aucuparia*, native/Europe/
W Asia; **Service** *Sorbus domestica* var. *pyrifera* (syn: *Pyrus sorbus*), Europe,
long cultivated.

Quince *Cydonia oblonga*, SW Asia *c.*1200, this fruit was used in making the
original 'mermelada'; **Portugal**, an old variety introduced into Britain by
John Tradescant (sen.) in 1611; **Peach**.

Raccombo *See* **Roccombo**.

Radish/Reddish *Raphanus sativus*, temperate regions of N hemisphere, long
cultivated, probably derived from the wild *R. raphanistrum*, native throughout Europe; **Black Radish/Spanish Black Horse Radish**, a variety of
Raphanus sativus.

Radix-Cava *Corydalis cava* (syn: *C bulbosa* of gardens), native/Europe; **Radix
Lunaria**, possibly Hollow-root/Bulbous corydalis *Corydalis solida*, native
(rare)/Europe; **Radix Personata**, perhaps *Corydalis glauca*, Canada, 1683.

Rag-wort *See* **Cineraria**.

Rampions *Campanula rapunculus*, native/Europe/N Africa, the roots can be
used in salad; they were grown in the area of Bologna, and thought of as
fennel *Foeniculum vulgare* var. *dulce*; *see also* **Fennel**; **Rampion Belgrade**.

Ranunculus *Ranunculus* sp., possibly White Batchelors Buttons *R aconitifolius*,
Europe, 1596; **Crow-foot** Common buttercup *Ranunculus acris*, native/
Europe/N Asia; **Pile-wort** Pile/wort/weed/Lesser celandine *Ranunculus
ficaria*, native/Europe/W Asia, introduced to N America; **Portugal
Ranunculus**, possibly *Ranunculus amplexicaulis* Pyrenees/N & C Spain,
1633; **Ranunculus of Tipoly/Tripoly**, probably Persian buttercup *Ranunculus
asiaticus*, E Mediterranean/NE Africa/SW Asia, 1596.

Rasberries/Raspris Raspberry *Rubus idaeus*, native/Europe; **Red** named by
Parkinson 1629; **White** named by Parkinson 1629.

Red: double Poppies *See* **Papaver**.

Reddish *See* **Radish**.

Rhamnus-Buck-horne *See* **Alaternus**.

Rhododendron/Red Possibly Alpine rose *Rhododendron hirsutum*, European Alps,
1629; **White**, possibly Alpine rose *R. hirsutum albiflorum*, European Alps, 1629.

Rhubarb Probably Butterbur/Thunder-dock/Wild rhubarb *Petasites hybridus*,
Europe/N & W Asia. Seeds of the 'garden' rhubarb *Rheum palmatum* arrived
in Britain in 1762.

Rhus, myrtil Possibly *Coriaria myrtifolia*, S Europe/N Africa, 1629; **Sumach**
Stag's horn sumach *Rhus typhina*, NE America, 1629; **Virginian** Stag's horn
sumach *Rhus typhina*, NE America, 1629.

Rib-wort *See* **Plantanes**.

Roccombo Rocambole/Sand Leek *Allium scorodoprasum*, Europe/Asia Minor; the word comes from the Danish *rocken bolle* meaning 'rock onion', which along with 'sand leek' gives an indication of its habitat.

Rocket Spanish/Rochett/Rochet Rocket *Eruca sativa*, S Europe/W Asia, introduced into N America. Both the seed and the leaves were used as flavourings by the Romans, and it was much used in Elizabethan England, *c.*1570.

Roman Lettuce *See* **Lettuce**.

Rose-Campion *See* **Lychnis**.

Rose: Centifol Cabbage/Provence rose *Rosa* ×*centifolia*, E Caucasus, 1580, *see also* **Province**; **Cinamon/Cinnamon** Cinnamon rose *Rosa cinamonmea*, Europe/N & W Asia, 1586; **Damasque** Damask rose *Rosa damascena*, Asia Minor, 1573; **Dog-rose** Dog rose *Rosa canina*, native/N Europe; **Eglantine** Sweetbrier *Rosa eglanteria*, native/Europe; **Elias Rosa**; **Guelder rose**, *see* **Laurustinus**; **Monthly/Monethly/Monethlie** Damask rose *Rosa*×*damascena* (syn: *R italica*), Asia Minor, *c.*1573; according to HANMER, its 'Indian' name was Fuyo, and it had been introduced into Italy *c.*1570. The use of the term 'Monthly rose' predates the rose we now know as the Monthly rose, *Rosa chinensis*, China, 1768; **Musk Rose/Musk-rose** *Rosa moschata*, Himalaya/ Iran, *c.*1515; **Mundi** *Rosa gallica versicolor*, origin unknown, 16th cent.; **Plush or Velvet-rose**, probably *Rosa* 'Tuscany', origin unknown, often referred to as 'Old Velvet' and written about by John Gerard in 1597; **Province** Cabbage/Provence rose *Rosa centifolia*, E Caucasus, 1596; this was the rose Pliny referred to as 'Rosa Campana'; *see also* **Centifol**; **Red**, probably Apothecary's rose/Red Rose of Lancaster *Rosa gallica* var. *officinalis*, oldest cultivated form of the Gallica rose; origin unknown; **Rosa common**, probably Dog rose *Rosa canina*, native/N Europe; **White double**, possibly Great double white/Cheshire/Jacobite rose *Rosa alba maxima*, origin unknown, 1597; **White single**, possibly the White Rose of York *Rosa alba semi-plena*, origin unknown, *c.*16th cent.; **Yello double** *Rosa hemisphaerica*, W Asia, 1586; **Yello single** Austrian brier *Rosa foetida*, Armenia/Kurdistan/N Iran, pre-1600.

Rosemary / Rosemarie / Rose-mary Rosemary *Rosmarinus officinalis*, S Europe/Asia minor, long cultivated.

Ros-solis/Rosa Solis Sundew *Drosera rotundifolia*, native (rare)/N hemisphere.

Rounsevals *See* **Pease**.

Rub. Lunatus *See* **Lunaria**.

Rubus odaratus Ornamental bramble *Rubus odoratus*, N America, *c.*1656.

Rue Herb of Grace *Ruta graveolens*, S Europe/W Asia, pre-1000, possible reintroduction, 1562; **Ruta Caprina**, possibly a form of *Ruta graveolens*, S Europe/W Asia, pre-1000, possible reintroduction, 1562.

Ruscus Butchers broome Butcher's broom *Ruscus aculeatus*, native/Mediterranean/Iran.

Ruta caprina *See* **Rue**.

Sabina/Sabine baccifera *See* **Juniperus** Juniper/Savin *Juniperus sabina*, C & S Europe/China/N America, *c*.1200.

Saffran /Saffron Saffron crocus *Crocus sativus*, W Asia to Kashmir, *c*.1340, or Spring crocus *C vernus*, W Asia to Kashmir, *c*.1340; **English Saffron**, possibly *Crocus nudiflorus* naturalized (rare)/SW Europe, or Spring crocus *Crocus albiflorus* naturalized (rare) NE Europe; **Meadow Saffron**, *see* **Colchicum** Autumn crocus *Colchicum autumnale*, native/Europe.

Sage *Salvia officinalis*, S Europe, 1597; **Red-Sage Topps/Sage Tops**, probably *Salvia officinalis* var. *purpurascens*, S Europe, 1597.

Salletings Herbs, young vegetables, leaves, and young seedlings to be eaten usually with a dressing of oil and vinegar.

Salsifax/Salsifex possibly Salsify/Vegetable Oyster *Tragopogon porrifolius*, naturalized/N Europe; *see also* **Goat's-beard**.

Sambucus *See* **Elder**.

Sampier Rock Samphire *Crithmum maritimum*, naturalized/Mediterranean/N Africa.

Sancianella/Sanicle Sanicle *Sanicula europaea*, native/Europe/S, C, & E Asia/Africa.

Saponaria Soapwort/Bouncing Bet *Saponaria officinalis*, naturalized/N C Europe, *c*.1200; vigorously stirred in water it produces a soapy froth, and is sometimes used in the conservation of tapestries.

Sarsaparilla *See* **Smilax aspera**.

Satureia *See* **Savory**.

Satyrion *See* **Orchis**.

Savory/Savory Sommer/somer Summer savory (annual) *Satureja hortensis*, Mediterranean region, pre-1000, possibly reintroduced 1562; **Savory winter/Winter-Savoury** Winter savory (perennial) *Satureja montana*, naturalized (rare)/Mediterranean, pre-1000, possibly reintroduced 1562.

Savoy *See* **Cabbage**.

Scabious/Scabiosa Probably Sweet scabious *Knautia arvensis* (syn: *Scabiosa arvensis*), SW Europe, 1629.

Scalions *See* **Eschalots**, *see* also **Onion**.

Scarlet Beans/Scarlet-beane *See* **Beane**.

Scives *See* **Chives.**

Scordium *See* **Germander.**

Scorpion grass/Scorpoides. Medica Could be *Coronilla scorpioides*, S Europe, pre-1650, *Myosotis scorpioides* Forget-me-not, native/Europe, or *Scorpiurus vermiculata* Caterpillar plant, S Europe/N Africa, 1621.

Scorzonera Black Salsify *Scorzonera hispanica*, S Europe, 1576.

Scurvy-grasse *See* **Cochlearia.**

Sea-Narcissus *See* **Narcissus.**

Sedum/Trickmadam/Trip Madam Stonecrop/Wallpepper *Sedum acre*, native/Europe/Iran/ Norway to Morocco; **Orpin** Orpine/Live-long *Sedum telephium*, native/Europe; **Sedum arborescens** *Aeonium arboreum*, Morocco, but widely naturalized, 1633; **Sedum of all Sorts**, could include the House-leek *Sempervivum tectorum*, S Europe, 1100, Stone Orpine/Prickmadam *Sedum reflexum*, C & W Europe, pre-1630.

Sellery/Sellerie/Smalladge/Macedonian Persley/Palustral Apium Celery/Smallage *Apium graveolens*, native/temperate Europe/S Asia.

Senetio Arborescens *See* **Cineraria.**

Senna *See* **Colutea.**

Sensitive plant *See* **Humble Plant** *Mimosa sensitiva*, tropical America, 1648; *see also* **Humble Plant.**

Serpentaria trifol There is a certain amount of confusion about this plant, HANMER knew it as 'Of Dragons, or the Great Serpentaria', TRADESCANT called it 'grasse plantane' (*Plantago maritima* var. *serpentina*); there are older names associated with the word 'dragon', Dragon arum *Dracunculus vulgaris* Dragonwort Arum/Wake-robin *Arum maculatum*, native; *see also* **Dragons.**

Serpillium/Serpillum Citratum *See* **Thyme.**

Service *See* **Quick-beame Sesele Æthiopicum** Hare's ear *Bupleurum fruticosum*, S Europe, 1596.

Sevial orange *See* **Orange.**

Shalots/Shalott *See* **Eschalots**, *see also* **Onion.**

Shepherds-purse *Capsella bursa-pastoris*, cosmopolitan.

Shrub Night-shade *See* **Night-shade.**

Shrub Spirae *Spiraea salicifolia*, naturalized/SE Europe to NE Asia, pre-1640.

Silesian Lettuce *See* **Lettuce.**

Silphium/Laserpitium Extinct giant fennel, the source of an aromatic gum used both medically and as condiment; probably a member of the *Umbelliferae* family called *Cachrys ferulacea*, native from the Mediterranean to Iraq, 1753. There is also confusion with another member of the *Umbelliferae* family, *Laserpitium latifolium*, native to the mountains of S Europe and recorded as growing in Britain by 1568. Modern *Silphium* is Rosinweed, a perennial American herb. *See also **Acetaria*** and note to p. 174 *Cyrenaic Africa*.

Silver firr *See* **Abies Firrs**.

Sisymbrium double & simple/Sisynrichium Satin Flower *Sisyrinchium bermudiana*, Bermuda, TRADESCANT (jun.) introduction, 1629–33.

Skirrets *Sium sisarum*, Russia/Siberia/China, pre-1656.

Smalladge/Smallage *See* **Sellery**.

Smalledye Possible misspelling of above.

Smilax aspera /Sarsaparilla *Smilax aspera*, S Europe eastwards, 1648; Sarsaparilla is a common European name for the roots of *Smilax* species, most of which come from the tropical jungle of C America; when dried the roots are used in making root beer and flavouring soft drinks.

Snap-dragon *See* **Antirrhinum**.

Sneeeze-wort *Achillea ptarmica*, native/Europe/SW Asia/Siberia, introduced into N America.

Snow-drops/Snow flowers *See* **Bulbous violet**.

Solomons-Seales Solomon's-seal *Polygonatum multiflorum*, native/Europe/temperate Asia to Japan, introduced into N America.

Sorrel/Sorell Probably Common sorrel/Sour-dock *Rumex acetosa*, native/Europe; *see also* **Allelujah; Broad German; French Acetocella; Roman Oxalis; Sorell-French; Sorrell-Greene-land**.

Sowthistle Probably Smooth Sowthistle *Sonchus oleraceus*, native; records show it was cultivated as a pot-herb.

Span. Pinkes *See* **Pinks**.

Spanish bells Spanish bluebells *Hyacinthoides hispanica* (syn: *Endymion hispanicus/Scilla campanulata/S. hispanica*), Portugal/Spain/N Africa, 1683.

Spanish Black Horse Radish *See* **Cochlearia**.

Spanish Cardon *See* **Artichocks**.

Spanish/Span. Jasmine *See* **Jasmine**.

Spanish Myrrh *See* **Myrrh**.

Spanish Nut *See* **Chessnut**.

Spanish-Oake *See* **Cork tree**.

Spanish Trumpets *See* **Narcissus**.

Sparagus *See* **Asparagus**.

Spartum hispan *See* **Genista**.

Sphaerical Narciss. *See* **Narcissus**.

Spinach/Spinach, curled/Spinage Spinach *Spinacia oleracea*, E Mediterranean, 1568.

Spindle tree Common Spindle Tree *Euonymus europeaus*, native/Europe.

Spinosum/Spinosum Ind? (*Spinosus* Latin: spiny), possibly from India.

Spixia Theophrasti Possibly a species of Corn lily *Ixia* from S Africa; the Greek name was first used by Theophrastus.

Spring Cyclamen *See* **Cyclamen**.

Spurge/Tithmyal/Tithymal Tithymalus *Euphorbia* spp., native/Europe/SW Asia; twelve species are native to Britain, as well as Spurge laurel *Daphne laureola*, native/W & S Europe/Asia Minor.

Star-flower Possibly Greater Stitchwort *Stellaria holostea*, native/Europe, or Starwort Mouse-ear *Cerastium cerastoides*, native/Norway/ Sweden/Iceland; **Star wort** Stitchwort *Stellaria graminea*, native/ Siberia/W Asia to N India, *see* above; **Stitch-wort** Greater stitchwort *Stellarlia holostea*, native/ Europe/SW Asia, introduced into N America and New Zealand.

Stitch-wort *See* **Star-flower**.

Stock-Gilly-flowres/Yellow Stocks Stock/Gillyflower *Matthiola incana*, S & W Europe/Arabian peninsula/Egypt, *c.*1250; *see also* **Gilly flower**.

Stoecas/Stoechas/Stoccas *See* **Lavender**.

Stramonium *See* **Datura**.

Strawberries/Straw-berries Wild strawberry *Fragaria vesca*, native/Europe; **Greate-white**, possibly a variety of *Fragaria viridis*, Europe/N Asia; no date of entry; **Wood-strawberries** as above: Wild strawberry *Fragaria vesca*, native/Europe; **Verginan** Scarlet Strawberry *Fragaria virginiana*, N America, 1629.

Strip'ed Jacynth *See* **Hyacinthus**.

Styrax arbour Storax *Styrax officinalis*, S Europe/SW Asia Minor, 1597.

Suber Cork-tree *See* **Cork-tree**.

Succory/Cichory/Intybs Chicory/Succory *Cichorium intybus*, native/S Europe.

Sugar-Pease *See* **Pease**.

Sultan/Sultana Sweet Sultan *Amberboa moschata* (syn: *Centaurea moschata*), Turkey/Caucasus, 1629, named to honour the Sultan of Zanzibar.

Summer Sweet Majoran *See* **Majoran**.

Sun-flower *See* **Flos Solis** Common sunflower *Helianthus annuus*, N to C America, 1596.

Suza Iris *See* **Iris**.

Sweet-Fennel *See* **Fennel**.

Sweete-Majoram *See* **Majoran**.

Sweet-williams/Sweete-Williams Sweet William *Dianthus barbatus*, garden escapee/S Europe, 1573.

Sycomore Sycamore (in Scotland often known as the Plane tree) *Acer pseudo-platanus*, naturalized/Europe.

Syringas/Syringa flo: purple/Syringa flo: white *See* Lilac.

Tabacco *See* Tobacco.

Tamariscus English Tamarisk *Tamarix anglica*, SW coast England/France.

Tansy/Tansie *See* Costmary.

Tarragon *Artemesia dracunculus*, S Europe, 1548.

Taxus yew *Taxus baccata*, native/Europe/Asia/Himalayas.

Teasel *Dipsacus fullonum*, cosmopolitan.

Terebinthus *See* Lentiscus Turpentine-tree.

Teuchrium mas *See* Germander.

Thalictrum (purple) Possibly *Thalictrum calabricum*, S Italy; no date of introduction.

Thapsia Probably *Thapsia garganica*, Mediterranean, 1683.

Thistle/Our Lady's Milk/Milky-thistle Milk thistle *Silybum marianum*, garden
escapee/N Europe; no date of introduction. *See also* Lady Thistle.

Thlaspi Creticum *See* Candy-Tufts.

Thoro-wax *Bupleurum fruticosum*, S Europe, 1596.

Thyme/Time Serpillium Wild Thyme *Thymus serpyllum*, native/Europe; **Serpillum Citratum** Lemon-scented thyme *Thymus × citriodrus*, probably of
garden origin, pre-1630; **Thymus Capitatus** *Thymus capitatus* (syn: *Cori-
dothymus capitatus*), Portugal to Palestine, pre-1656.

Tilia *See* Lime.

Time *See* Thyme.

Tithmyal/Tithymal (Tithymalus) *See* Spurge.

Toad-flax *See* Linaria.

Tobacco/Tabacco *Nicotiana tabacum*, tropical America, 1565; not only used as
pipe tobacco, but as a decoction or powder to sprinkle onto gravel walks to
kill weeds as well as worms, to prevent casts, made by boiling and then
straining the plants in water; by the end of the eighteenth century, tobacco
smoke was being used as an insecticide.

Tout-saine *See* Androsænum maximum Hispanicum.

Trachelium Blue throatwort *Trachelium caeruleum*, W & C Mediterranean,
1640.

Tragacantha Goats thorn/Gum tragacanth *Astragalus tragacantha*, S Europe,
1640.

Tre-foile *See* Lotus.

Trick-Madame/Trip-madame *See* Sedum.

Tuberose *See* Hyacinthus.

Tuberose Iris *See* Iris.

Tufts *See* **Candy tufts.**

Tulips Probably all the tulips noted by Evelyn are grouped under the name Linnaeus gave all the old species, *Tulipa gesneriana*; **Tulips medias**, tulips that flower following the early flowering tulips; **Tulips Pennach'd**, perhaps feathered or parrot tulips, taken from the word 'Pennaceous', in botanical terms meaning markings resembling feathers; **Tulips Praecose/praecoce**, early flowering tulips, probably *Tulipa praecox*, Middle East naturalized in S Europe; **Tulips Serotin**, late-flowering tulips.

Tulip-tree *Liriodendron tulipifera*, Nova Scotia to Florida, 1638; Evelyn records its arrival in Britain in *Sylva*.

Turneps *See* **Cabbage.**

Turpentine-tree *See* **Lentiscus.**

Valerian *Valeriana officinalis*, native/Europe.

Venus looking-glasse *Legousia speculum–veneris* (syn: *Specularia speculum–veneris*) C & S Europe/N Africa/Cyprus/W Syria/N Iraq, 1596.

Verbena nodi flo. Cretica Probably Vervain/Pigeon's grass *Verbena officinalis*, native/Europe.

Verjuice-grape *See* **Grape.**

Vermicularis (wormlike) *Suaeda vera*, native/N Europe, grows on rocky sea shores above high-tide.

Vernal Crocus *See* **Crocus.**

Vernal Cyclamen white & red *See* **Cyclamen.**

Veronica double/single/Veronica purple odoriferous Speedwell *Veronica spicata* (syn: *V kellereri*), native (rare)/Europe; *see also* **Germander; Brook-Lime** Brooklime *Veronica beccabunga*, native/Europe; **Veronica mag.; Veronica parva.**

Vetonica doub. flo ?**Veronica.**

Vine *See* **Grape.**

Vine-parsley *See* **Grape.**

Viola Matronalis *See* **Hesperis.**

Viola pentaphyl. (five-leaved) Probably a form of Sweet violet *Viola odorata*, native/Europe/N Africa/Asia; **Violets**, probably most of the violets listed come from the Sweet violet *Viola odorata* or the Dog-violet *Viola canina*, native/Europe/Asia: **Bulbous violets**, *see* **Bulbous violets; Double violets** Sweet violet *Viola odorata*, native/Europe/N Africa/Asia; **Musk violets; Single violets; White violets; Yellow Dutch violets; Yellow moutain Hearts-ease**, possibly *Viola biflora*, Europe to N Asia/N America; prior to Evelyn earliest date of introduction 1752; **Yellow violets**, perhaps Heartsease

Viola tricolor, native/Europe/Asia; **Yellow violets with large leaves**, possibly *Viola pubescens*, E America; no date of entry.

Viper-grass Common Viper's-grass *Scorzonera hispanica*, S Europe, 1576.

Virgin bower *See* **Clematis**.

Virgin Maple Red/Scarlet/Virginian Maple *Acer rubrum*, TRADESCANT (jun.) seed introduction, E America, *c.*1656.

Virginian martagon *See* **Lillies**.

Virginian Phalangium *See* **Phalangium**.

Virginian Wallnutt *See* **Wall-nuts**.

Volubilis/Voubilis/Purple Volubilis Bindweed, possibly Dwarf convolvulus *Convolvulus tricolor*, Sicily/Spain/Portugal, 1629.

Wall-nuts the greate Whinnsheld Common walnut, E Europe/S Asia, 995; **Virginian Wallnutt** Black walnut *Juglans nigra*, E America, 1656.

Water-Cress/Water-cresse Watercress *Rorippa nasturtium-aquaticum*, W & C Europe/W Asia, introduced into N America.

Water-Lilly White water lily *Nymphæ alba,* and/or Yellow water lily *Nuphar lutea*, both native/Europe.

Whichen *See* **Quick-beame**.

Whitchin elme *See* **Elme**.

White-hony-suckle *See* **Honey-suckles**.

White of Dioscorides *See* **Garlic**.

White-Mulberie *See* **Mulberry**.

White Popy *See* **Papaver**.

White Thorn *See* **Oxyacanthus**.

White violets *See* **Violets**.

Willow Withy Crack willow *Salix fragilis*, native/Europe; **Ozier** Common osier *Salix viminalis*, native/Europe, used for basket-making; **Salow** Goat/Sallow willow *Salix caprea*, native/Europe/NE Asia.

Willow-Weede Probably Yellow Loosestrife *Lysimachia vulgaris*, native/Europe/Asia.

Winter-Aconite *See* **Aconite**.

Winter-Savoury *See* **Savory**.

Woad *Isatis tinctoria*, native/Europe/Asia.

Wolfe-bane *See* **Aconite**.

Wood-sorrell *See* **Allelujah**.

Worme-wood/Wormwood Wormwood *Artemisia absinthium*, temperate Eurasia.

Yallow hony-suckle *See* **Honey-suckles.**

Yarrow *Achillea millefolium*, native/Europe/W Asia, introduced into N America.

Yellow Dutch Violets *See* **Violets.**

Yellow Hemerocallis *See* **Hemerocallis.**

Yellow Indian Jasmine *See* **Jasmine.**

Yellow Lillies *See* **Lillies.**

Yellow Millofol. *See* **Millofolium.**

Yellow-Moly *See* **Garlic.**

Yellow mountain heartsease *See* **Violets.**

Yellow Stocks *See* **Stock-Gilly-flowres.**

Yellow violets with large leaves *See* **Violets.**

Yellow Virginian Jasmine *See* **Jasmine.**

Yucca/Yuca/Jucca Spanish dagger *Yucca gloriosa*, America (N Carolina to Florida), 1550.

Zinar *See* **Platanus Oriental.**